POWER AND SOCIETY
An Introduction to the Social Sciences

NINTH EDITION

THOMAS R. DYE
Florida State University

Harcourt College Publishers

Fort Worth   Philadelphia   San Diego   New York   Orlando   Austin   San Antonio
Toronto   Montreal   London   Sydney   Tokyo

Publisher	**Earl McPeek**
Acquisitions Editor	**David Tatom**
Marketing Strategist	**Laura Brennan**
Developmental Editor	**Peggy Boone Howell**
Project Editor	**Jim Patterson**
Art Director	**Sherry J. Ahlstrom**
Production Manager	**Suzie Wurzer**

Cover Image Credit: D. E. Cox/Tony Stone Worldwide

ISBN: 0-15-506642-0

Library of Congress Catalog Card Number: 2001086104

Portions of this work were published in previous editions.

Address for Editorial Correspondence: Harcourt College Publishers, 301 Commerce Street, Suite 3700, Fort Worth, TX 76102

Address for Orders: Harcourt, Inc., 6277 Sea Harbor Drive, Orlando, FL 32887-6777
1-800-782-4479

Web site: http://www.harcourtcollege.com

Printed in the United States of America

1 2 3 4 5 7 8 9 0 016 9 8 7 6 5 4 3 2 1

Preface

Power and Society: An Introduction to the Social Sciences is designed as a basic text for an introductory, interdisciplinary social science course. It is written specifically for first- and second-year students at community colleges and at four-year colleges and universities that offer a basic studies program.

Power and Society introduces students to central concepts in

anthropology	psychology
sociology	political science
economics	history

But more importantly, the text focuses these disciplinary perspectives on a central integrative theme—the nature and uses of power in society. In this way, students are made aware of the interdependence of the social sciences. Compartmentalization is avoided, and students are shown how each social science discipline contributes to an understanding of power.

Power and Society also introduces students to some of the central challenges facing American society:

ideological conflict	crime and violence
racism and sexism	community problems
poverty and powerlessness	international relations

Each of these challenges is approached from an interdisciplinary viewpoint, with *power* as the integrating concept.

Power has been defined as the capacity to modify the conduct of individuals through the real or threatened use of rewards and punishments. Doubtless there are other central concepts or ideas in the social sciences that might be employed to develop an integrated framework for an introduction to social science. But certainly *power* is a universal phenomenon that is reflected in virtually all forms of human interaction. Power is intimately related to many other key concepts and ideas in the social sciences—personality, behavior, aggression, role, class, mobility, wealth, income distribution, markets, culture, ideology, change, authority, oligarchy, the elite. Power is also a universal instrument in approaching the various crises that afflict human beings and their societies—racism, sexism, poverty, violence, crime, urban decay, and ideological and international conflict.

Several special features are designed to arouse student interest in the social sciences as well as to help students understand the meaning of various concepts. The first such feature is the identification of specific *masters of social thought* and the clear, concise presentation of their central contributions to social science. Specific attention is given to the contributions of:

Bertrand Russell	Sigmund Freud	John Locke
Ruth Benedict	B. F. Skinner	Martin Luther King, Jr.
Karl Marx	Adam Smith	C. Wright Mills
John M. Keynes		

The second special feature is the presentation of timely, relevant *case studies* in each chapter to illustrate important concepts. Topics include:

An Experiment in Crime Fighting
Using the *Statistical Abstract*
Authority and Obedience: The "Shocking" Experiments
Diagnosing Mental Illness
Achieving Economic Stability
The Performance of the American Economy
Watergate and the Limits of Presidential Power
Vietnam: A Political History
The Rise and Fall of Communism in Russia
Senior Power
The Death Penalty and the Constitution
The Insanity Defense
American Military Power: "Desert Storm"

In addition, illustrative *focuses* throughout the text help maintain student interest. Topics include:

The Vocabulary of Social Science
Abortion: A Hot Button Issue
Changing College Student Opinions
Social Science Looks at Sex in America
Power and the Aztec Empire
How Men and Women View Their Relations Today
Telltale Behavior of Twins
Evolutionary Psychology: The Mating Game
Drug Therapies
Concentrated Corporate Power
Rating the Presidents
Explaining Presidential Approval Ratings
Media Power—The Presidential Debates
Reconstruction and African-American History
How to Tell If You're Liberal or Conservative
A Declaration of Women's Rights, 1848
Who Are the Poor?
Getting High
Urban Stress
It's a Real Crime!

A fourth special feature is the *cross-national perspective* provided on important aspects of life in the United States. As this book introduces students to the social sciences with principal reference to the American experience, discussions in each chapter endeavor to place this experience in a global context. Thus *cross-national perspective* sections include:

Women in the Workforce
Beliefs About Equality and Opportunity
Global Inequalities

Suicide
The Self in Individualist and Collectivist Cultures
GNP and Standards of Living
The Multinationals' Worldwide Economic Power
The Role of Government
Capitalism and Socialism in the World
The Earnings Gap
Income of the Poor in Advanced Democracies
Worldwide Urbanization
Murder and Homicide
Patriotism

as well as anthropological observation on power among Polar Eskimos, power among Crow Indians, and power in the Aztec Empire.

A fifth special feature is *controversies in social science,* designed to stimulate student interest in social science, inspire classroom discussion, and warn students that the social sciences deal with many controversial topics that remain largely unresolved:

Can the Social Sciences Be Scientific?
Cultural Relativity and Female Circumcision
The Bell Curve
What Should We Do with the Budget Surplus?
Direct versus Representative Democracy
Should We Limit the Terms of Congress Members?
Charles Beard and the Economic Interests of the Founders
Affirmative Action and the Constitution
Is Welfare Reform Working?
Should Drugs Be Legalized?
Does Prison Building Reduce Crime?
Who Really Runs This Town?
When Should the United States Use Military Force?

Another important special feature is the *running study guide* provided in the wide page margins throughout the text. The study guide defines key vocabulary items and outlines central arguments, keeping pace with the student's progress through the text.

Finally, the special feature, *On the Web,* provides students with initial directions for further exploration on the Internet of the topics in each chapter. Web addresses are provided, together with brief descriptions of the information available at various sites.

Power and Society strives to be a "teachable" text by including a number of stimulative and provocative *focuses* and *case studies,* together with its *masters of social thought* and *cross-national perspectives,* as well as the feature *controversies in social science*—all of which provide timeliness, relevance, interest, and perspective to each chapter topic. Rather than evade or dilute "hot topics"—for example, genetics versus environmental influences on behavior, power and gender, sexual harassment, mental illness, the neglect of African-American and Native American history, affirmative action, violence in American history, abortion, drug legalization—it focuses on controversy as a means of developing student interest and appreciation for the social sciences. The ninth edition continues to resist the lamentable tendency in introductory texts to "dummy" material for undergraduate students and shows that social science research and scholarship is relevant to our current societal problems.

This edition continues the book's traditional focus on the condition of women and minorities in American society, with specific discussions of "Power and Gender," "Women in the Workforce," "Racism in American History," "The Civil Rights Movement," "Reconstruction and African-American History," "Martin Luther King, Jr., and the Power of Protest," "Hispanic Power," "Gender Inequality: Culture or Biology?," and "Sexual Harassment and the Law."

An instructor's manual filled with lecture ideas and test questions is available.

Students may purchase the study guide that provides multiple choice, true-false, completion, and essay questions to lead them through independent study of the text.

Many thanks to those who provided guidance on this and past editions: Hugh M. Arnold, Clayton College and State University; Michael S. Cummings, University of Colorado–Denver; William E. Kelly, Auburn University; William H. Taylor, Terra Community College; Charles Cotter, Florida State University; Paul George, Miami Dade Community College; Francis Moran, Jersey City College; Alex Velez, St. Mary's University; Brett Benson, Lewis-Clark State University; Howard Lucky, Prairie State College; and Fred Dauser, Talladega College.

Contents

PART TWO

POWER AND THE SOCIAL SCIENCES   34

Chapter 5

POWER AND PERSONALITY   91

Chapter 6

POWER AND THE ECONOMIC ORDER   127

Chapter 7

POWER AND GOVERNMENT   161

Chapter 10

POWER, RACE, AND GENDER   254

Chapter 11

POVERTY AND POWERLESSNESS   282

Chapter 12

POWER, CRIME, AND VIOLENCE   298

Chapter 13

POWER AND COMMUNITY   328

Chapter 14

POWER AMONG NATIONS   352

IN MEMORY OF
JAMES C. "JEFF" DYE

The Nature
and Study
of Power

PART ONE

The purpose of this book is to introduce you to the social sciences. Because power in society is a theme that pervades each of the social sciences, as well as the problems they study, we have chosen this theme as the focal point for our presentation. Part One is designed to familiarize you with the notion of power, with the nature of each of the social sciences, and with the scientific methods they employ. You will find that Chapter 1 reflects the structure of the entire text. Like the book as a whole, its first part focuses on the nature of power, its second part on the individual social sciences and the particular ways in which they contribute to our understanding of power, and its third and final part on the problems with which the social sciences are concerned. Chapter 2 is devoted to a discussion of the methods used in social science research—how social scientists gather data, how they endeavor to employ scientific and experimental methods of research, and the special problems they encounter in doing so.

Chapter 1

Power, Society, and Social Science

THE NATURE OF POWER

Ordinary men and women are driven by forces in society that they neither understand nor control. These forces are embodied in governmental authorities, economic organizations and markets, social values and ideologies, accepted ways of life, and learned patterns of behavior. However diverse the nature of these forces, they have in common the ability to modify the conduct of individuals, to control their behavior, and to shape their lives. **Power** *is the capacity to affect the conduct of individuals through the real or threatened use of rewards and punishments.* Power is exercised over individuals and groups by offering them things they value or by threatening to deprive them of those things. These values are the power base, and they can include physical safety, health, and well-being; wealth and material possessions; jobs and means to a livelihood; knowledge and skills; social recognition, status, and prestige; love, affection, and acceptance by others; and a satisfactory self-image and self-respect. To exercise power, then, control must be exercised over the things that are valued in society.

Power is a special form of influence. Broadly speaking, influence is the production of intended effects. People who can produce intended effects by any means are said to be influential. People who can produce intended effects by the real or threatened use of rewards and punishments are said to be powerful.

power
the capacity to affect the conduct of others through the real or threatened use of rewards and punishments

power
based on control of valued resources

unequally distributed

exercised in interpersonal relations

exercised through large institutions

Power can rest on various resources. The exercise of power assumes many different forms—the giving or withholding of many different values. Yet power bases are usually *interdependent*—individuals who control certain valued resources and are likely to control other resources as well. Wealth, economic power, prestige, recognition, political influence, education, respect, and so on, all tend to "go together" in society.

Power is never equally distributed. "There is no power where power is equal." For power to be exercised, the "powerholder" must control some base values. By *control* we mean that the powerholder is in a position to offer these values as rewards to others or to threaten to deprive others of these values.

Power is a relationship among individuals, groups, and institutions in society. Power is not really a "thing" that someone possesses. Instead, power is a relationship in which some individuals or groups have control over resources valued by others.

ELITES AND MASSES

The **elite** are the few who have power; the **masses** are the many who do not. The elite are the few who control what is valued in society and use that control to shape the lives of all of us. The masses are the many whose lives are shaped by institutions, events, and leaders over which they have little control. Political scientist Harold Lasswell wrote, "The division of society into elites and masses is universal," and even in a democracy, "a few exercise a relatively great weight of power, and the many exercise comparatively little."[1]

elite and masses
the few who have power and the many who do not

INSTITUTIONAL POWER

Power is exercised in large institutions—governments, corporations, schools, the military, churches, newspapers, television networks, law firms, and so on. Power that stems from high positions in the social structures of society is stable and far-reaching. Sociologist C. Wright Mills once observed: "No one can be truly powerful unless he has access to the command of major institutions, for it is over these institutional means of power that the truly powerful are, in the first instance, powerful."[2] Not all power, it is true, is anchored in or exercised through institutions. But institutional positions in society provide a continuous and important base of power. As Mills explained:

> If we took the one hundred most powerful men in America, the one hundred wealthiest, and the one hundred most celebrated away from the institutional positions they now occupy, away from their resources of men and women and money, away from the media of mass communication that are now focused upon them—then they would be powerless and poor and uncelebrated. For power is not of a man. Wealth does not center in the person of the wealthy. . . . To have power requires access to major institutions, for the institutional positions men occupy determine in large part their chances to have and to hold these valued experiences.[3]

POWER AND THE SOCIAL SCIENCES

social science
the study of human behavior

Social science is the study of human behavior. Actually, there are several social sciences, each specializing in a particular aspect of human behavior and each using different concepts, methods, and data in its studies. Anthropology, sociology, economics, psychology, political science, and history have developed into separate "disciplines," but all share an interest in human behavior.

Power is *not* the central concern of the social sciences, yet all the social sciences deal with power in one form or another (see Masters of Social Thought, "Bertrand Russell: Power Is to the Social Sciences What Energy Is to Physics"). Each of the social sciences contributes to an understanding of the forces that modify the conduct of individuals, control their behavior, and shape their lives. Thus, to fully understand power in society, we must approach this topic in an **interdisciplinary** fashion—using ideas, methods, data, and findings from all the social sciences.

interdisciplinary
the study of a topic using ideas, methods, and data from all of the social sciences.

ANTHROPOLOGY

anthropology
the study of people and their ways of life

Anthropology is the study of people and their ways of life. It is the most holistic of the social sciences in that it studies all aspects of a society. Some anthropologists are concerned primarily with the development of human biological and physical characteristics; this field is called **physical anthropology.** Other anthropologists are interested primarily in the ways of life of both ancient and modern peoples; this field is called **cultural anthropology.**

physical anthropology
the study of the development of human biological and physical characteristics

Archaeology uses the study of both the physical and cultural characteristics of peoples and societies that existed in the distant past. It is similar to history but reaches further back in time, into **prehistory,** the time before written records. It endeavors to reconstruct the history of a society from the remains of its culture. Some of these remains are as impressive as the Pyramids of Egypt and the Mayan temples of Mexico; some are as mundane as bits of broken pottery, stone tools, and garbage.

cultural anthropology
the study of the ways of life of both ancient and modern peoples

archaeology
the study of the physical and cultural characteristics of peoples and societies that existed prior to recorded history

Culture is all the common patterns and ways of living that characterize a society. A **society** is a group of people who are dependent on one another for their well-being and who share in a common culture. Cultural anthropologists describe and compare societies and cultures. They describe and explain a great many things: child rearing and education, family arrangements, language and communication, technology, ways of making a living, the distribution of work, religious beliefs and values, social life, leadership patterns, and power structures.

prehistory
the time before written records

Power is part of the culture or the way of life of a people. Power is exercised in all societies, because all societies have systems of rewards and sanctions designed to control the behavior of their members. Perhaps the most enduring structure of power in society is the family: Power is exercised within the family when patterns of dominance and submission are established between male and female and between parents and children. Societies also de-

culture
all the common patterns and ways of living that characterize society

society
a group of people who are dependent on one another and share a common culture

MASTERS OF SOCIAL THOUGHT

Bertrand Russell: Power Is to the Social Sciences What Energy Is to Physics

Bertrand Russell (1872–1970), English philosopher and mathematician, is regarded as one of the twentieth century's greatest thinkers, mainly because of his contributions to mathematics and symbolic logic. However, Russell possessed a great breadth of interest that included history, economics, and political science, as well as education, morals, and social problems. He received the Nobel Prize in literature "in recognition of his many-sided and significant authorship, in which he has constantly figured as a defender of humanity and freedom of thought." He summarized his views about the importance of power in society in a book significantly entitled *Power: A New Social Analysis*.

First of all, power is fundamental to the social sciences:

> The fundamental concept in the social sciences is power, in the same sense in which energy is the fundamental concept in physics.

Second, the desire for power as well as wealth motivates people:

> When a moderate degree of comfort is assured, both individuals and communities will pursue power rather than wealth: they may seek wealth as a means to power, or they may forgo an increase of wealth in order to secure an increase of power, but in the former case as in the latter, their fundamental motive is not economic. . . .

Third, power takes many forms:

> Like energy, power has many forms, such as wealth, armaments, civil authority, and influence on opinion. No one of these can be regarded as subordinate to any other, and there is no one form from which the others are derivative. The attempt to treat one form of power, say wealth, in isolation can only be partially successful. . . . To revert to

the analogy of physics, power, like energy, must be regarded as continually passing from any one of its forms into any other, and it should be the business of social science to seek the laws of such transformations.

Finally, power produces social change:

> Those whose love of power is not strong are unlikely to have much influence on the course of events. The people who cause social changes are, as a rule, people who strongly desire to do so. Love of power, therefore, is a characteristic of the people who are causally important. We should, of course, be mistaken if we regarded it as the sole human motive, but this mistake would not lead us so much astray as might be expected in the search for causal laws in social science, since love of power is the chief motive producing the changes that social science has to study.

SOURCE: Selection is reprinted from *Power: A New Social Analysis*, by Bertrand Russell, with the permission of W. W. Norton & Company, Inc., p. 11. Copyright © 1938 by Bertrand Russell. Copyright renewed 1966 by Bertrand Russell.

velop structures of power outside the family to maintain peace and order among their members, to organize individuals to accomplish large-scale tasks, to defend themselves against attack, and even to wage war and exploit other peoples.

In our study of power and culture, we shall examine how cultural patterns determine power relationships. We shall also examine patterns of authority in traditional and modern families and the changing power role of women in society. We will focus special attention in Chapter 3 on how social science looks at sex in America. We will also take up a long-standing controversy regarding value judgments about cultural practices in a feature called "Cultural Relativity and Female Circumcision." We shall examine the origins and development of power relationships, illustrating them with an example of an earlier society in which power was organized into a complex state (the Aztec Empire).

SOCIOLOGY

sociology
the study of relationships among individuals and groups

Sociology is the study of relationships among individuals and groups. Sociologists describe the structure of formal and informal groups, their functions and purposes, and how they change over time. They study social institutions (such as families, schools, and churches), social processes (for example, conflict, competition, assimilation, and change), and social problems (crime, race relations, poverty, and so forth). Sociologists also study social classes.

social stratification
the classification and ranking of members of a society

All societies have some system of classifying and ranking their members— a system of **stratification.** In modern industrial societies, social status is associated with the various roles that individuals play in the economic system. Individuals are ranked according to how they make their living and the power they exercise over others. Stratification into social classes is determined largely on the basis of occupation and control of economic resources.

Power derives from social status, prestige, and respect, as well as from control of economic resources. Thus, the stratification system involves the unequal distribution of power.

In our study of power and social class, we shall describe the stratification system and the extent of inequality in America. We shall discuss the differing lifestyles of upper, middle, and lower classes in America and the extent of class conflict. We will take up a heated controversy over general intelligence—its measurement, distribution, and meaning in peoples' lives in a feature, "The Bell Curve." We shall examine the ideas of Karl Marx about the struggle for power among social classes. We shall describe the differential in political power among social classes in America. Finally, we shall explore the ideas of sociologist C. Wright Mills about a "power elite" in America that occupies powerful positions in the governmental, corporate, and military bureaucracies of the nation.

PSYCHOLOGY

psychology
the study of the behavior of people and animals

Psychology may be defined as the study of the behavior of people and animals. Behavior, we know, is the product of both "nature and nurture"—that is, a product of both our biological makeup and our environmental conditioning. We shall examine the continuing controversy over *how much* of our behavior is a product of our genes versus our environment. There is great richness and diversity in psychological inquiry. **Behavioral psychologists**

behavioral psychology
the study of human and animal responses to stimuli

study the learning process—the way in which people and animals learn to respond to stimuli. Behavioral psychologists frequently study in experimental laboratory situations, with the hope that the knowledge gained can be useful in understanding more complex human behavior outside the laboratory. **Social psychologists,** on the other hand, study interpersonal behavior— the ways in which social interactions shape an individual's beliefs, perceptions, motivations, attitudes, and behavior. Social psychologists generally study the whole person in relation to the total environment. **Psychoanalytic (Freudian) psychologists** study the impact of subconscious feelings and emotions and of early childhood experiences on the behavior of adults. **Humanistic psychologists** are concerned with the human being's innate potential for growth and development. Many other psychologists combine theories and methods in different ways in their attempts to achieve a better understanding of behavior.

Personality is all the enduring, organized ways of behavior that characterize an individual. Psychologists differ over how personality characteristics are determined—whether they are learned habits acquired through the process of reinforcement and conditioning (behavioral psychology), products of the individual's interaction with the significant people and groups in his or her life (social psychology), manifestations of the continuous process of positive growth toward "self-actualization" (humanistic psychology), the results of subconscious drives and long-repressed emotions stemming from early childhood experiences (Freudian psychology), or some combination of all these.

In our study of power and personality, we will examine various theories of personality determination in an effort to understand the forces shaping an individual's reaction to power. We will explore the recurring question of "nature versus nurture," biology versus environment, in determining the human condition. Using a Freudian perspective, we shall study the "authoritarian personality"—the individual who is habitually dominant and aggressive toward others over whom he or she exercises power but is submissive and weak toward others who have more power; the individual who is extremely prejudiced, rigid, intolerant, cynical, and power-oriented. We shall explore the power implications of B. F. Skinner's ideas of behavioral conditioning for the control of human behavior. To gain an understanding of humanistic psychology's approach to power relationships, we shall examine Abraham Maslow's theory of a "hierarchy of needs." We will also describe the treatment of mental illness from these various psychological perspectives. Finally, in our case study, we shall describe the startling results of an experiment designed to test the relationship between authority and obedience.

ECONOMICS

Economics is the study of the production and distribution of scarce goods and services. There are never enough goods and services to satisfy everyone's demands, and because of this, choices must be made. Economists study how individuals, firms, and nations make these choices about goods and services.

social psychology
the study of interpersonal behavior

psychoanalytic (Freudian) psychology
the study of the effects of subconscious feelings and early childhood experiences on behavior

humanistic psychology
the study of the growth and development of the human personality

personality
all the enduring, organized ways of behavior that characterize an individual

economics
the study of the production and distribution of scarce goods and services

Economic power is the power to decide what will be produced, how much it will cost, how many people will be employed to produce it, what their wages will be, what the price of the good or service will be, what profits will be made, how these profits will be distributed, and how fast the economy will grow.

Capitalist societies rely heavily on the market mechanism to make these decisions. In our study of economic power, we shall explore both the strengths and weaknesses of this market system, as well as the ideas of economic philosophers Adam Smith and John Maynard Keynes. We shall examine America's great wealth—how it is measured, where it comes from, and where it goes. In addition, we shall consider the role of government in the economy, where it gets its money and how it spends it. And we will examine the current controversy over how to use surplus federal government revenues. We shall also examine the concentration of corporate power in America and whether the corporate elite use that power to benefit the stockholders or themselves. Finally, we shall describe the globalization of economic power and the emergence of giant multinational corporations.

POLITICAL SCIENCE

political science
the study of government and politics

authority
the legitimate use of physical force

Political science is the study of government and politics. Governments possess **authority,** a particular form of power; that is, the legitimate use of physical force. By *legitimate,* we mean that people generally consent to the government's use of this power. Of course, other individuals and organizations in society—for example, muggers, street gangs, the Mafia, violent revolutionaries—use force. But only government can legitimately threaten people with the loss of freedom and well-being to modify their behavior. Moreover, governments exercise power over all individuals and institutions in society—corporations, families, schools, and so forth. Obviously the power of government in modern society is very great, extending to nearly every aspect of modern life—"from womb to tomb."

Political scientists from Aristotle to the present have been concerned with the dangers of unlimited and unchecked governmental power. We shall examine the American experience with limited, constitutional government and the meaning of democracy in modern society. We shall observe how the U.S. Constitution divides power, first between states and the national government, and second among the legislative, executive, and judicial branches of government. We will review the continuing controversy over whether the people themselves should decide important issues by voting directly on them or whether elected representatives should do so. We shall examine the growth of power in Washington, D.C., and the struggle for power among the different branches. We will observe that the president of the United States enjoys more power than the writers of the Constitution envisioned. We will explore what factors appear to strengthen and weaken presidents, and how scholars rate the performances of past presidents. Finally, in our look at "Media Power: The Presidential Debates" on pages 198–199, we shall examine the growing power of television in American politics.

HISTORY

History is the recording, narrating, and interpreting of human experience. The historian recreates the past by collecting recorded facts, organizing them into a narrative, and interpreting their meaning. History is concerned with change over time. It provides a perspective on the present by informing us of the way people lived in the past. History helps us understand how society developed into what it is today.

The foundations of power vary from age to age. As power bases shift, new groups and individuals acquire control. Thus, power relationships are continuously developing and changing. An understanding of power in society requires an understanding of the historical development of power relationships.

In our consideration of the historical development of power relationships, we shall look at the changing sources of power in American history and the characteristics of the individuals and groups who have acquired power. We shall describe the people of power in the early days of the republic and their shaping of the Constitution and the government it established. We shall discuss Charles Beard's controversial interpretation of the Constitution as a document designed to protect the economic interests of those early powerholders. We shall also discuss how westward expansion and settlement created new powerholders and new bases of power. We shall explore the power struggle between northern commercial and industrial interests and southern planters and slave owners for control of western land, and the Civil War, which resulted from that struggle. In addition, we shall explore the development of an industrial elite in America after the Civil War, the impact of the depression on that elite, and the resulting growth of New Deal liberal reform. In a special feature, "Reconstruction and African-American History," we shall examine how history occasionally overlooks the experiences of powerless minorities and later reinterprets their contributions to society. Finally, we shall undertake a brief historical study, "Vietnam: A Political History," which argues that despite military victory, this war was "lost" through failures of America's political leadership.

history
the recording, narrating, and interpreting of human experience

SOCIAL SCIENCES AND SOCIAL PROBLEMS

Social problems—the major challenges confronting society—include ideological conflict, racism, sexism, poverty, crime, violence, urban decay, and international conflict. These problems do not confine themselves to one or another of the disciplines of social science. They spill over the boundaries of anthropology, economics, sociology, political science, psychology, and history—they are **interdisciplinary** in character. Each of these problems has its *historical* antecedents, its *social* and *psychological* roots, its *cultural* manifestations, its *economic* consequences, and its impact on *government* and public policy. The origins of these social problems, as well as the various solutions proposed, involve complex power relationships.

interdisciplinary study
the use of theory, methods, and findings from more than one social science

IDEOLOGICAL CONFLICT

ideology
an integrated system of ideas that rationalizes and justifies the exercise of power in society

Ideas have power. Indeed, whole societies are shaped by systems of ideas that we call **ideologies.** The study of ideologies—liberalism, conservatism, socialism, communism, fascism, radicalism—is not a separate social science. Rather, the study of ideologies spans all the social sciences, and it is closely related to philosophy. Ideologies are integrated systems of ideas that rationalize a way of life, establish standards of "rightness" and "wrongness," and provide emotional impulses to action. Ideologies usually include economic, political, social, psychological, and cultural ideas, as well as interpretations of history.

Ideologies rationalize and justify power in society. By providing a justification for the exercise of power, the ideology itself becomes a base of power in society. Ideology "legitimizes" power, making the exercise of power acceptable to the masses and thereby adding to the power of the elite. However, ideologies also affect the behavior of the elite, because once an ideology is deeply rooted in society, powerholders themselves are bound by it.

In our study of power and ideology, we shall first explore the ideology of *classical liberalism*—an ideology that attacked the established power of a hereditary aristocracy and asserted the dignity, worth, and freedom of the individual. Classical liberalism and capitalism justify the power of private enterprise and the market system. Whereas classical liberalism limits the powers of government, *modern liberalism* accepts governmental power as a positive force in freeing people from poverty, ignorance, discrimination, and sickness. It justifies the exercise of governmental power over private enterprise and the establishment of the welfare state. In contrast, *modern conservatism* doubts the ability of the governmental planners to solve society's problems; conservatism urges greater reliance on family, church, and individual initiative and effort.

We shall then look at ideologies that have influenced other societies. *Fascism* is a power-oriented ideology that asserts the supremacy of a nation or race over the interests of individuals, groups, and other social institutions. *Marxism* attacks the market system, free enterprise, and individualism; it justifies revolutionary power in overthrowing liberal capitalist systems and the establishment of a "dictatorship of the proletariat." *Socialism* calls for the evolutionary democratic replacement of the private enterprise system with government ownership of industry.

We shall describe the collapse of communism and the reasons for its failure in eastern Europe and the former Soviet Union, as well as its unpopularity among the Chinese people.

RACIAL AND GENDER INEQUALITY

Historically, no social problem has challenged the United States more than racial inequality. It is the only issue over which Americans ever fought a civil war. We shall describe the American experience with racism and the civil rights movement, which brought about significant changes in American life. We want to understand the philosophy of that movement, particularly the "nonviolent direct action" philosophy of Nobel Peace Prize winner Dr. Martin Luther King,

Jr. However, we shall also examine continuing inequalities between blacks and whites in income, employment, and other conditions of life in the United States. We shall also explore the problems confronting Hispanic Americans in our society and describe the tragic history of Native Americans. In addition, we look at sexism in American life, particularly in the economy. We shall describe the successes and failures of the women's movement over the years and examine the issue of sexual harassment and the constitutional status of abortion as a privacy right. We shall explore the controversy over "affirmative action" and "racial preferences" and its implication for how America is to achieve real equality.

POVERTY AND POWERLESSNESS

The American economy has produced the highest standard of living in the world, yet a significant number of Americans live in poverty. Poverty can be defined as **powerlessness**—a sociopsychological condition of hopelessness, indifference, distrust, and cynicism. We shall discuss whether or not there is a "culture of poverty"—a way of life of the poor that is passed on to future generations—and, if so, what are the implications for government policy. We shall describe government efforts to cope with poverty and discuss the controversial question regarding the effect of welfare reform policies on the poor. We shall focus special attention on homelessness in America. Finally, we shall examine the future of the Social Security program in a look at "Senior Power."

powerlessness
a sociopsychological condition of hopelessness, indifference, distrust, and cynicism

CRIME AND VIOLENCE

Governmental power must be balanced against *individual freedom*. A democratic society must exercise police powers to protect its citizens, yet it must not unduly restrict individual liberty. We shall explore the problem of crime in society and how crime is defined and measured. We shall also describe the constitutional rights of defendants and the role of the courts in protecting these rights. We will describe the economics of crime and explore a controversial question of whether or not more prisons mean less crime. An even more controversial question that will be addressed is the relationship between drugs and crime and whether or not drug use should be legalized. We shall summarize economic, psychological, and social explanations of crime and violence. Finally, we will describe briefly the history of violence in American society and the role that violence has played in American struggles for power.

a problem of democratic government
to protect its citizens without violating individual liberty

COMMUNITY LIFE

A variety of social problems affect the quality of life in the United States and around the world. The solution to these problems, if there is any solution, depends in great part on how governments choose to exercise their powers. We shall examine world population growth and worldwide urbanization. And we shall explore the growth of urban and suburban populations in the

Poverty can also be defined as powerlessness: Two homeless women shown outside a high-fashion New York City department store.

United States. We will try to describe the social and psychological patterns of urban life—the characteristic forms of social interaction and organization that typically emerge in a large metropolis—and the socioeconomic conflicts between cities and suburbs. We shall observe how our nation's communities are governed. We shall focus special attention on the social and economic problems of the inner city and how the concentration of social problems can make them worse. Finally, we shall present a social-science controversy, "Who Really Runs This Town?"

INTERNATIONAL CONFLICT

sovereignty
authority over internal affairs, freedom from outside intervention, and recognition by other nations

The struggle for power is global, involving all the nations and peoples of the world, whatever their goals or ideals. Nearly two hundred nations in the world claim **sovereignty:** authority over their internal affairs, freedom from outside intervention, and political and legal recognition by other nations. But sover-

Nations struggle for power through wars and diplomacy. The Patriot Missile Battery was used in the U.S. effort to liberate Kuwait from Iraqi occupation in the Gulf War.

eignty is a legal fiction; it requires power to make sovereignty a reality. Over the years, nations have struggled for power through wars and diplomacy. The struggle has led to attempts to maintain a fragile balance of power among large and small nations, as well as to attempts to achieve collective security through the United Nations and other alliances. We shall provide a brief history of the long Cold War between the nuclear "superpowers"—the United States and the former Soviet Union. We will describe the especially dangerous issue of nuclear arms and efforts to bring them under control. The United States continues to face challenges around the world; we shall describe various regional minibalances of power, notably in the Middle East. We will take up the highly controversial question, "When should the United States use military force?" Finally, we shall observe the continuing need for U.S. military power in our case study, "American Military Power: 'Desert Storm.' "

ON THE WEB

EXPLORING POWER AND SOCIETY

The World Wide Web (www), or more simply referred to as "the Web," is a system for exploring the Internet using hypertext links. The Internet is the world's largest computer network, spanning the entire globe and used by an estimated 100 million people in the United States alone.

The Web offers an abundance, indeed an *overabundance,* of information on society. It is doubtful that there is any topic in the social sciences for which the Web does *not* offer thousands of sites. Vast treasures of information are available on the Web on population, race, gender, government, politics, economics, anthropology, history, sociology, psychology, health and welfare, religion, public opinion, crime, drugs, income and poverty, education, international affairs, the military, and virtually every other topic that arises in the social sciences. One real problem, however, regarding the Web is that of sorting through all of the information offered to find relevant and reliable sources.

There are tools for searching (or "browsing") the Web. A variety of free search services ("browsers" or "search engines") allow users to enter keywords that are supposed to generate relevant Web-site links. For example, perhaps the best-known search engine is Yahoo (www.yahoo.com). The problem, however, is that search engines often produce thousands of sites in response to one keyword. These search engines may try to list these sites in the order of their believed relevance to the keyword entered by the user; but there is no assurance that the sites listed first are indeed what the user is searching for. These search services are most useful when the user simply wishes to "browse" the topic, rather than find answers to specific questions.

Web users must also be aware that virtually anyone, whether knowledgeable and responsible or not, can create a Web site and offer information. The reliability of information on the Web varies a great deal. Users should always be aware of the sponsorship of the Web site from which they are taking information.

The Internet allows unrestricted free expression, from scientific discourses on particle physics and information on the latest developments in medical science to invitations to join paramilitary "militia" and offers to exchange pornographic photos and messages. (Indeed, commercial sex sites outnumber any other category on the Web.) But the U.S. Supreme Court has given the Internet full First Amendment free-speech protection. In 1997, in the case of *Reno v. American Civil Liberties Union,* the Supreme Court struck down an attempt by Congress to outlaw "indecent" material on the Internet. The Supreme Court referred to the Internet as the freest form of public expression.

In order to provide students with some initial directions for further Internet exploration of the topics in *Power and Society,* special features, "On the Web," are offered at the end of each chapter. Web addresses are given in these features, but students should be aware that Internet addresses sometimes change or disappear without notice.

ABOUT THIS CHAPTER

Power in society is not just an abstract concept or a convenient focus for academic exercise. Nor is power something that is located exclusively in the nation's capitals. Power is very much a real factor that affects the lives of each of us. We experience it in some form in our families, in school, and at work; we feel its effects in the grocery store and on the highway. And we each react to it in characteristic ways. Our aim in this chapter was to understand just what power *is.* We also saw why it provides us with a useful perspective from which to gain a unified view of the social sciences and the social problems that concern us all.

Now that you have read this chapter, you should be able to

- define power in society and describe its characteristics
- define the area of study of each of the social sciences, as well as their common focus, and discuss how each relates to power in society
- identify the major social problems that the social sciences study and explain why they are interdisciplinary in nature and how they relate to power

DISCUSSION QUESTIONS

1. How would you define power? What characteristics of power deserve to be discussed in any definition of power?
2. Consider the power relationships that directly and indirectly affect your life. On the basis of your experiences and observations, assess the validity of these statements by Bertrand Russell: "The fundamental concept in the social sciences is power, in the same sense in which energy is the fundamental concept in physics. . . . When a moderate degree of comfort is assured, both individuals and communities will pursue power rather than wealth. . . . Love of power is the chief motive producing the changes which social science has to study."
3. Identify and briefly define the area of study of each of the social sciences. Discuss how you would study power from the perspective of each of these disciplines.
4. What is meant by the *interdisciplinary* study of social problems?

Chapter 2

Social Sciences and the Scientific Method

SCIENCE AND THE SCIENTIFIC METHOD

A *science* may be broadly defined as any organized *body of knowledge,* or it may be more narrowly defined as a discipline that employs the **scientific method.** If we use the broad definition, we can safely say that all the social sciences are indeed sciences. However, if we narrow our definition to only those disciplines that employ the scientific method, then some questions arise about whether the social sciences are really scientific. In other words, if science is defined as a *method of study,* rather than a *body of knowledge,* then not all studies in the social sciences are truly scientific.

The *scientific method* is a method of explanation that develops and tests theories about how observable facts or events are related. What does this definition really mean? How is this method of study actually applied in the social sciences? To answer these questions, let us examine each aspect of the scientific method separately.

scientific method
a method of explanation that develops and tests theories about how observable facts or events are related

EXPLAINING RELATIONSHIPS

The goal of the scientific method is explanation. When using this method, we seek to answer *why.* Any scientific inquiry must begin by observing and classifying things. Just as biology begins with the careful observation, description, and classification of thousands upon thousands of different forms of life, the social sciences also must begin with the careful observation, description, and classification of various forms of human behavior. But the goal is explanation, not just description. Just as biology seeks to develop theories of evolution and genetics to explain the various forms of life upon the earth, the social sciences seek to develop theories to explain why human beings behave as they do.

To answer the question of *why,* the scientific method searches for *relationships.* All scientific **hypotheses** assert some relationship between observable facts or events. The social sciences seek to find relationships that explain human behavior. The first question is whether two or more events or behaviors are related in any way—that is, do they occur together consistently? The second question is whether either event or behavior *causes* the other. Social scientists first try to learn whether human events have occurred together merely by chance or accident, or whether they occur together so consistently that their relationship cannot be a mere coincidence. A relationship that is not likely to have occurred by chance is said to be **significant.** After observing a significant relationship, social scientists next ask whether there is a *causal relationship* between the phenomena (that is, whether the facts or events occurred together because one is the cause of the other) or whether both phenomena are being caused by some third factor. The Focus, "The Vocabulary of Social Science," explains some of the terms used in scientific studies.

hypothesis

a tentative statement about a relationship between observable facts or events

significant

not likely to have occurred by chance

DEVELOPING AND TESTING HYPOTHESES

The scientific method seeks to develop statements (hypotheses) about how events or behaviors might be related and then determines the validity of these statements by careful, systematic, and logical tests. Scientific tests are really exercises in logic. For example, if we wanted to find out something about the relationship between race and party voting, we might collect and record data from a national sample of African-American and white voters chosen at random.* If our data showed that *all* blacks voted Democratic and *all* whites Republican, it would be obvious that there was a perfect relationship between race and voting. In contrast, if both blacks and whites voted Republican and Democratic in the *same* proportions, then it would be obvious that there was *no* relationship. But in the social sciences, we rarely have such obvious, clear-cut results. Generally our data will show a mixed pattern. For example, in the 2000 presidential election between Democrat Al Gore and Republican George W. Bush, polls indicated that 90 percent of African Americans voted Democratic and only 8 percent voted Republican. In that same election, 54 percent of whites voted Republican and only 42 percent voted Democratic. If

* Throughout this book we use the term *African American* when referring to specific individuals or the racial group, but in text and tables that compare African Americans and whites, we use parallel terms, *black* and *white.*

FOCUS

The Vocabulary of Social Science

Social science researchers use many special terms in their work, some of which have already been defined. It helps in reading social science research reports to understand the specific meanings given to the following terms:

Theory: A causal explanation of relationship between observable facts or events. A good theory fits the facts, explains why they occur, and allows us to predict future events.

Hypothesis: A tentative statement about a relationship between facts or events. The hypothesis should be derived from the theory and should be testable.

Variable: A characteristic that varies among different individuals or groups.

Independent variable: Whatever is hypothesized to be the cause of something else.

Dependent variable: Whatever is hypothesized to be the effect of something else.

Significant: Not likely to have occurred by chance.

Correlation: Significant relationships found in the data.

Spurious: Describing a relationship among facts or events that is *not* causal, but is a product of the fact that both the independent and dependent variables are being caused by a third factor.

Case study: An in-depth investigation of a particular event. A good case study should suggest theories and hypotheses that can then be used to study other cases.

---

there had been *no* relationship between race and voting, then blacks and whites would have voted Democratic and Republican in roughly the *same* proportions. But as we have just noted, blacks voted Democratic in far heavier proportions (90 percent) than whites (42 percent). This difference is not likely to have occurred by chance—thus we consider it "significant." The same pattern of heavy Democratic voting among African Americans can be observed in other elections (see Table 2-1). So we can make the **inference** that race is related to voting.

However, the existence of a statistically significant relationship does not prove cause and effect. We must employ additional logic to find out which fact or event caused the other, or whether both were caused by a third fact or event. We can eliminate as illogical the possibility that voting Democratic causes one to become an African American. That leaves us with two possibilities: Being African American may cause Democratic voting, or being an African American and voting Democratic may both be caused by some third condition shared by many African Americans. For example, the real causal relationship may be between low incomes and Democratic voting: Low-income groups, which would include a disproportionate number of African Americans, tend to identify with the Democratic Party. We can test this new hypothesis by looking at the voting behavior of both black and white low-income groups. It turns out that low-income blacks vote more

inference
a causal statement based on data showing a significant relationship

TABLE 2-1

Voting by Race in Presidential Elections
Testing the hypothesis: African Americans Tend to Vote Democratic

Election year	Candidates	All	Whites	Blacks
2000	Republican Bush	48*	54	8
	Democrat Gore	48	42	90
1996	Republican Dole	41	46	12
	Democrat Clinton	49	43	84
	Independent Perot	8	9	4
1992	Republican Bush	38	41	11
	Democrat Clinton	43	39	82
	Independent Perot	19	20	7
1988	Republican Bush	54	60	11
	Democrat Dukakis	46	40	89
1984	Republican Reagan	59	66	9
	Democrat Mondale	41	34	90
1980	Republican Reagan	51	56	10
	Democrat Carter	41	36	86
	Independent Anderson	7	7	2
1976	Republican Ford	48	52	15
	Democrat Carter	50	46	85
1972	Republican Nixon	62	68	13
	Democrat McGovern	38	32	87

* Figures are percentages of the vote won by each candidate. Percentages in each election may not add up to 100 because of voting for minor-party candidates.

SOURCE: Data from the *Gallup Opinion Poll* surveys.

heavily Democratic than low-income whites, so we can reject the low-income explanation. We may therefore infer that race is *independently* related to voting behavior. But there may be other possible alternatives to our explanation of the relationship between race and voting behavior. Social scientists must test as many alternative explanations as possible before asserting a causal relationship.

Every time we can reject an alternative explanation for the relationship we have observed, we increase our confidence that the relationship (as between race and voting behavior) is a causal one. Of course, in the areas of interest to social scientists, someone can always think of new alternative explanations, so it is generally impossible to establish for certain that a causal relationship exists. Some social scientists react to the difficulties of proving "cause" by refusing to say that the relationships they find are anything more than **correlations,** or simply statistical relationships. The decision whether or not to call a relationship "causal" is difficult. Statistical techniques cannot guarantee that a relationship is causal; social scientists must be prepared to deal with probabilities rather than absolutes.

correlations
significant relationships that may or may not be causal

DEALING WITH OBSERVABLE PHENOMENA

*The scientific method deals only with observable—**empirical**—facts and events.* In other words, the scientific method deals with what *is,* rather than what *should be.* It cannot test the validity of values, norms, or feelings, except insofar as it can test for their existence in a society, group, or individual. For example, the scientific method can be employed to determine whether voting behavior is related to race, but it cannot determine whether voting behavior *should be* related to race. The latter question is a *normative* one (dealing with "ought" and "should"), rather than an empirical one (dealing with "is"). The scientific method is *descriptive* and *explanatory,* but not **normative.** The social sciences can explain many aspects of human behavior but cannot tell human beings how they ought to behave. For guidance in values and norms—for prescriptions about how people should live—we must turn to ethics, religion, or philosophy.

empirical
referring to observable facts and events; what is

normative
referring to values or norms; what should be

DEVELOPING THEORY

The scientific method strives to develop a systematic body of theory. Science is more than crude empiricism—the listing of facts without any statement of relationships among them. Of course, especially in the early stages of a science, research may consist largely of collecting data; but the ultimate goal of the scientific method is to develop verifiable statements about relationships among facts and events. It is the task of social scientists to find patterns and regularities in human behavior, just as it is the task of physicists and chemists to find patterns and regularities in the behavior of matter and energy. The social scientist's use of the scientific method, then, assumes that human behavior is not random, but rather that it is regular and predictable.

Theories are developed at different *levels of generality*. Theories with low levels of generality explain only a small or narrow range of behaviors. For example, the statement that African Americans tend to vote Democratic is a fairly low-level generality about political behavior. Theories with higher levels of generality explain a greater or wider range of behavior. For example, the statement that racial differences cause political conflict has a higher level of generality. Strictly speaking, *a theory is a set of interrelated concepts at a fairly high level of generality.* Some social scientists concentrate on theory building rather than on empirical research; they try to develop sweeping social theories to explain all, or a large part, of human behavior. Still other social theorists provide insights, hunches, or vague notions that suggest possible explanations of human behavior, thus developing new hypotheses for empirical research.

theories
explanations of facts or events

MAINTAINING A SCIENTIFIC ATTITUDE

Perhaps more than anything else, *the scientific method is an attitude of doubt or skepticism.* It is an insistence on careful collection of data and systematic testing of ideas; a commitment to keep bias out of one's work, to collect and

CONTROVERSIES IN SOCIAL SCIENCE
Can Social Science Be Scientific?

The scientific method was devised in the physical and biological sciences. There are many difficulties in applying this method to the study of individuals, groups, economies, classes, governments, nations, or whole societies. Let us examine some of the obstacles to the development of truly *scientific* social sciences.

Personal Bias

Social science deals with subjective topics and must rely on interpretation of results. Social scientists are part of what they investigate—they belong to a family, class, race, gender, political party, interest group, profession, and nation. If the topic is an emotional one, the social scientist may find it much harder to suppress personal bias than does the investigator in the physical sciences: It is easier to conduct an unbiased study of migratory birds than of migrant workers.

Even the selection of a topic reveals the values of the researcher. Researchers study what they think is important in society, and what they think is important is affected by their personal values. Moreover, researchers' values are also frequently reflected in their perceptions of the data, in their statement of the hypotheses, in their design of the test for the hypotheses, and in their interpretations of the findings. An extreme version of this criticism of the social sciences (sometimes referred

to as "post-structuralism") argues that no knowledge is free of the race, gender, and class bias of the researcher. Indeed, it is even argued that the scientific method itself is a "white male way of thinking."

Public Attitudes

Another problem in the scientific study of human behavior centers on public attitudes toward social science. Few people would consider arguing with atomic physicists or biochemists about their respective fields, but most people believe they know something about social problems. Many people think they know exactly what should be done about juvenile delinquency, welfare dependency, and race relations. Very often their information is limited, and their view of the problem is simplistic. When a social scientist suggests that a problem is very complex, that it has many causes, and that information on the problem is incomplete, people may believe that the social scientist is simply obscuring matters that seem obvious.

Social science sometimes develops explanations of human behavior that contradict established ideas. Of course, the physical and biological sciences have long faced this same problem: Galileo faced the opposition of the established church when he argued that the earth revolved around the sun, and Darwin's theory of evolution continues

to be a public issue. But social science generates even more intense feelings when it deals with poverty, crime, sexual behavior, race relations, and other sensitive topics.

Limitations and Design of Social Science Research

Another set of problems in social science centers on the limitations and design of social science research. It is not really possible to conduct some forms of controlled experiments on human beings. For example, we cannot deliberately subject people to poverty and deprivation just to see if it makes them violent. Instead, social researchers must find situations of poverty and deprivation in order to make the necessary observations about causes of violence. In a laboratory, we can control all or most of the factors that go into the experimental situation. But in real-world observations, we cannot control many factors; this makes it difficult to pinpoint what it is that causes the behavior we are studying. Moreover, even where some experimentation is permitted, human beings frequently modify their behavior simply because they know they are being observed in a social science experiment. This phenomenon, known as the "Hawthorne effect," makes it difficult to determine whether the observed behavior is a product of the stimulus being introduced or merely a product of the experimental situation itself.

record all relevant facts, and to interpret them rationally regardless of one's feelings. Admittedly, it is difficult to maintain a truly **scientific attitude** when examining social behavior. (See Controversies in Social Science, "Can Social Science Be Scientific?") For the social scientist, it is the determination to test explanations of human behavior by careful observations of real-world experiences. It is a recognition that any explanation is tentative and may be modified or disproved by careful investigation. Even the scientific theories that constitute the core knowledge in any discipline are not regarded as absolutes by the true social scientist; rather, they are regarded as probabilities or generalizations developed from what is known so far.

scientific attitude
doubt or skepticism about theories until they have been scientifically tested

WHAT IS A "FACT"?

In the social sciences, very few statements can be made that apply to *every* circumstance. We cannot say, for example, that "all African Americans vote Democratic." This is a **universal statement** covering every African American, and universal statements are seldom true in the social sciences. Moreover, it would be difficult to examine the voting behavior of every African American in the past and in the future to prove that the statement is true.

universal statement
a statement that applies to every circumstance

A more accurate statement might be: "Most African Americans vote Democratic." This is a **probabilistic statement;** it does not exclude the possibility that some African Americans vote Republican. An even more accurate statement would be that "90 percent of African Americans cast their ballots for Democratic candidate Al Gore in the 2000 presidential election." This means there was a 90 percent *probability* of an African-American voter casting his or her ballot for Democrat Al Gore.

probabilistic statement
a statement that applies to some proportion of circumstances

A probabilistic statement is a fact, just like a universal statement. Students in the physical sciences deal with many universal statements—for example, "Water boils at 100°C." Water always does this. But social science students must learn to think in probabilities rather than in absolute terms.

Social scientists must also beware of substituting individual cases for statements of probability. They must be careful about reasoning from one or two observed cases. A statement such as "I know an African-American family that always votes Republican" may be true, but it would be very dangerous to generalize about the voting habits of all African Americans on the basis of this one case. We always build tentative generalizations from our own world of experiences. However, as social scientists, we must ensure that our own experiences are typical. We should keep in mind that the "facts" of the social sciences are seldom absolute—they rarely cover the complexity of any aspect of human behavior. So we must be prepared to study probabilities.

THE CLASSIC SCIENTIFIC RESEARCH DESIGN

An **experiment** is a scientific test that is controlled by the researcher and designed to observe the effect of a specific program or treatment. The *classic*

experiment
a scientific test controlled by the researcher to observe effects of a specific program or treatment

scientific research design involves the comparison of specific changes in two or more carefully selected groups, both of which are identical in every way, except that one has been given the program or treatment under study while the other has not.[1]

This design involves the following:

experimental group
the group that will participate in the program or undergo the treatment under study

control group
a group, identical to the experimental group, that does not undergo treatment; used for comparison

- Identification of the goals of the study and the selection of specific hypotheses to be tested.
- Selection of the groups to be compared—the **experimental group,** which will participate in the program or undergo the treatment being studied, and the **control group,** which is similar to the experimental group in every way, except that it will *not* participate in the program or undergo the treatment being studied.
- Measurement of the characteristics of both the experimental and control groups *before* participation in the experiment.
- Application of the program or treatment to the experimental group, but not to the control group. (Members of the control group may be given a *placebo*—some activity or program known to have no effect—to make them believe they are participating in the experiment. Indeed, the scientific staff administering the experiment may not know which group is the real experimental group and which group is the control group. When neither the staff nor the group members themselves know who is really receiving the treatment, the experiment is called a *double-blind experiment.*)

null hypothesis
a statement that the program or treatment has no effect

- Measurement of the condition of both the experimental and control groups *after* the program or treatment. If there are measurable differences between the experimental and control groups, the scientist can begin to infer that the program or treatment has a specific effect. If there are *no* measurable differences, then the scientist must accept the **null hypothesis**—the statement that the program or treatment has no effect.
- Comparison of the preprogram/pretreatment status versus the postprogram/posttreatment status in both groups. This is a check to see if the difference between the experimental and control groups occurred during the experiment (see Case Study: An Experiment in Crime Fighting). If there is no control group and only the experimental group is studied, this method is often called a "before-after" study.
- A search for plausible explanations for differences after treatment between the control and experimental groups that might be due to factors other than the treatment itself.

The classic research design is not without its problems. Social scientists must be aware of the more difficult problems in applying this research de-

An Experiment in Crime Fighting

Let us consider an example of applying the classic scientific research design to a specific social problem—neighborhood crime. A local government is considering the installation of street lighting in residential neighborhoods to combat crime. The hypothesis is that increased lighting will reduce crime rates. Before spending large sums of money to light up the entire city without knowing whether the plan will work, the city council decides to put the program to a scientific test. The council selects several neighborhoods that have identical characteristics (crime rate, land use, population density, unemployment, population age, income, racial balance, and so forth). Some of the areas are randomly selected for the installation of new street lighting. Crime rates are carefully measured before the installation of streetlights in those neighborhoods that received new lighting and in those neighborhoods that did not receive streetlights (see figure). After several months of new lighting, crime rates are again carefully measured in the experimental neighborhoods (which received lights) and the control neighborhoods (which did not). The results are compared. If a significant reduction in crime occurred in the neighborhoods with new lights but did not occur in the neighborhoods without lights and no other changes can be identified in the neighborhoods that might account for the differences, then the city can have some confidence that lighting reduces crime. An expansion of lighting to the rest of the city would then seem appropriate.

A Scientific Research Design for Crime Fighting

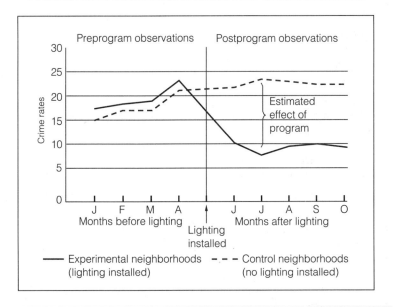

Most survey research is now undertaken by means of computer assisted telephone interviewing. Professional polling organizations serve the news media, political parties and candidates, and social scientists.

sign to social science research and must be prepared on occasion to change their procedures accordingly. These problems include the following:

- Members of the experimental group may respond differently to a program if they know it is an experiment. Members of a control group are often told they are participating in an experiment, even though nothing is really being done to the control group.
- If the experimental group is only one part of a larger city, state, or nation, the response to the experiment may be different from what it would have been had all parts of the city, state, or nation been receiving the program. For example, if only one part of a city receives streetlights, criminals may simply operate as usual (even with the lights), and total crime rates will be unaffected.
- If persons are allowed to *volunteer* for the experiment, then experimental and control groups may not be representative of the population as a whole.
- In some situations, political pressures may make it possible to provide one neighborhood or group with certain services while denying these same services to the rest of the city, state, or nation. If everyone *thinks* the program is beneficial before the experiment begins, no one will want to be in the control group.
- It may be considered morally wrong to provide some groups or persons with services, benefits, or treatment while denying the same to other groups or persons (control groups) who are identical in their needs or problems.

■ Careful research is costly and time-consuming. Public officials often need to make immediate decisions. They cannot spend time or money on research even if they understand the long-term benefits of careful investigation. Too often, politicians must operate on "short-run" rather than "long-run" considerations.

GATHERING DATA: SURVEY RESEARCH

How do social scientists go about observing the behaviors of individuals, groups, and societies? There are a variety of methods for gathering data; some fields rely more heavily on one particular method than on another. The *controlled experiment,* described earlier, is often used in psychology; the *survey* is frequently employed in political science and sociology; *field research,* or participant observation, is a major source of data in anthropology; and *secondary data analysis* is employed in all social sciences.[2]

SURVEY RESEARCH

Most surveys ask questions of a representative sample of the population rather than question the entire population. A selected number of people, the **sample,** is chosen in a way that ensures that this group is representative of the **universe,** the whole group of people about which information is desired. To ensure that the sample is representative of the universe, most surveys rely on random selection. **Random sampling** means that each person in the universe has an equal chance of being selected for interviewing. Random sampling improves the likelihood that the responses obtained from the sample would be the same as those obtained from the universe if everyone were questioned. Hypothetically, we must obtain a random sample of American voters by throwing every voter's name in a giant box and blindly picking out one thousand names to be interviewed. A more common method is to randomly select telephone area codes and then numbers from across the nation.

There is always the chance that the sample selected will *not* be representative of the universe. But survey researchers can estimate this **sampling error** through the mathematics of probability. The sampling error is usually expressed as a range above and below the sample response, within which there is a 95-percent likelihood that the universe response would be found if the entire universe was questioned. For example, if 63 percent of the people questioned (the sample) say they "approve" of the way the president is handling his job, and the sampling error is calculated at plus or minus 3 percent, then we can say that there is a 95-percent likelihood that the president's approval rating among the whole population (the universe) stands somewhere between 60 and 66 percent.

Large samples are not really necessary to narrow the sampling error. Large samples are not much more accurate than small samples. A sample of a few thousand—maybe even one thousand—is capable of reflecting the opinions of 1 million or 100 million voters fairly accurately. For example, a random

sample
in survey research, people are chosen to represent the opinions of a larger group

universe
the whole group about which information is desired

random sample
each person in the universe has an equal chance of being selected in the sample for interviewing

sampling error
the range of responses in which a 95-percent chance exists that the sample reflects the universe

sample of one thousand voters across the United States can produce a sampling error (plus or minus) of only 3 percent.

PROBLEMS IN SURVEY RESEARCH

survey research problems
unformed opinions

weakly held opinions

changing opinions

When polls go wrong, it is usually because public opinion is unformed, weakly held, or changing rapidly. If public opinion is really unformed on a topic, as may be the case in early presidential preference polls, people may choose a familiar name or a celebrity who is frequently mentioned in the news. Their thoughts about the presidential race are still largely unformed; as the campaign progresses, candidates who were once unknown and rated only a few percentage points in early polls can emerge as front-runners. Weakly held opinions are more likely to change than strongly held opinions. Political commentators sometimes say a particular candidate's support is "soft," meaning that his or her supporters are not very intense in their commitment, and, therefore, the polls could swing quickly away from the candidate. Finally, widely reported news events may change public opinion very rapidly. A survey can measure opinions only at the time it is taken. A few days later, public opinion may change, especially if major events are receiving heavy television coverage. Some political pollsters conduct continuous surveys until election night in order to catch last-minute opinion changes.

ASSESSING PUBLIC OPINION

public opinion
the aggregate of opinions of individuals on topics in survey research

Public opinion in democracies is given a great deal of attention. Indeed, survey research on public opinion is a thriving industry. Survey results command the attention of politicians and the news media, as well as social scientists.

But many opinion surveys ask questions that people had not considered before being interviewed. Few people are willing to admit that they know nothing about the topic or that they really have "no opinion." People believe they should provide an answer even if they have little interest in the topic itself. The result is that polls often seem to "create" public opinion.

salient issues
issues in which most people have thoughts about and hold strong and stable opinions

However, there are some "hot button" issues in which virtually everyone has an opinion and in which many people feel very intensely about. **Salient issues** are those that people think about most and hold strong and stable opinions (see Focus, "Abortion: A Hot Button Issue").

The wording or phrasing of public opinion questions can often determine the outcome of a poll. Indeed, "loaded" or "leading" questions are often asked by unprofessional pollsters simply to produce results favorable to their side of an argument. Ideally, questions should be clear and precise, easily understood by the respondents, and as neutral and unbiased as possible. But because all questions have a potential bias, it is usually better to examine changes over time in responses to identically worded questions. (Focus compares "College Student Opinions" responses to some of the same questions asked in 1970 and 1999.)

FOCUS

Abortion: A Hot Button Issue

Abortion is a salient issue—nearly everyone has an opinion on this topic, and many people feel very intensely about it. Survey research indicates that opinion on abortion has been quite stable over the years.

In response to the question, "Do you think abortions should be legal under any circumstances, legal only under certain circumstances, or illegal in all circumstances?" national opinion pools have reported very consistent results over the past twenty-five years.*

	1975	1980	1990	2000
Legal under any circumstances	21	25	31	27
Legal only under certain circumstances	54	53	53	55
Illegal in all circumstances	22	18	12	16

But survey research cannot resolve a public policy issue. Indeed, *interpretation* of poll results on a "hot button" issue often becomes a topic of conflict itself. For example, *pro-choice* proponents of legalized abortion interpret the results in the preceding table as overwhelming support for legalized abortion. In contrast,

pro-life opponents of abortion view the same results in the table as the majority support restricting abortion.

Most Americans appear to want to keep some abortions legal but, at the same time, believe government should place certain restrictions on abortion:†

Question: Do you favor or oppose . . .

Requiring parental consent before a girl under 18 years of age could have an abortion?
Favor: 78%   Oppose: 16%

Requiring a twenty-four-hour waiting period for women seeking an abortion before an abortion could take place?
Favor: 79%   Oppose: 16%

A law that would make it illegal to perform a specific abortion procedure often referred to as late term or "partial-birth," except when necessary to save the life of the mother.
Favor: 59%   Oppose: 37%

Allowing government Medicaid benefits to help pay for abortions for low-income women?
Favor: 43%   Oppose: 55%

Interestingly, the Supreme Court itself appears to be seeking a middle ground on abortion, not unlike public opinion on the topic. In 1973 in *Roe v. Wade,* the Supreme Court held that abortion was a privacy right guaranteed by the U.S. Constitution. Over the years, the Supreme Court has reaffirmed that right but, at the same time, has upheld modest restrictions. In 1980 in *Harris v. McRae,* the Supreme Court held that governments were not required to pay for abortions. In 1992 in *Planned Parenthood v. Casey,* the Supreme Court upheld a Pennsylvania law that requires minors to have consent of parents or a judge and that women be required to wait twenty-four hours after requesting an abortion before having one. But the Court warned that it would not permit restrictions on abortions that imposed an "undue burden" on women. In 2000, the Supreme Court struck down a state law prohibiting "partial birth" abortions.

* Gallup Opinions Survey, various years.   † CBS/The New York Times poll, 1998.

Even the most scientific surveys are not error-free, however. We have already noted that weakly held opinions can change rapidly. Some surveys ask questions about topics that most people had never considered before being interviewed. Then the pollsters report responses as "public opinion," when, in fact, very few people really had any opinion on the topic at all. Many

FOCUS

Changing College Student Opinions

The opinions of college students today appear to be somewhat more conservative than they were a generation ago. Each year the American Council on Education sponsors a survey of the opinions of entering college freshmen. An examination of responses to identically worded questions over the years reveals some interesting differences between the opinions of freshmen students in the early 1970s and the opinions of freshmen students today.

Students today are more concerned with their financial future than students were a generation ago and are less interested in "developing a meaningful philosophy of life." They are more likely to view the chief benefit of college as increasing their earning power. Students today also take a tougher line toward crime and drugs.

College students today are somewhat less likely to describe themselves as "liberals" than a generation ago. They prefer to describe themselves as "middle-of-the-road."

	1972	1999
Goals		
Being well off financially	41%	73%
Developing meaningful philosophy of life	71%	40%

	1972	1999
Chief benefit of college		
Increase one's earning power	60%	74%
Crime and drugs		
Death penalty should be abolished	33%	25%
Courts are too concerned with the rights of criminals	50%	72%
Marijuana should be legalized	47%	34%
Political ideology		
Far left	2%	3%
Liberal	33%	22%
Middle-of-the-road	48%	56%
Conservative	16%	18%
Far right	1%	2%

SOURCE: American Council on Education and University of California Los Angeles, *The American Freshmen,* 1972 and 1999.

---

halo effect

the tendency of respondents to give "good citizen" responses to pollsters

respondents do not like to admit they do not know anything about the topic, so they give a meaningless response. Another problem is the **halo effect**—the tendency of respondents to give "good citizen" responses, whether the responses are truthful or not. For example, people do not like to admit that they do not vote or that they do not care about politics. Surveys regularly report higher percentages of people *saying* they voted in an election than the *actual* number of ballots cast would indicate. Many people give socially respectable answers, even to an anonymous interviewer, rather than answers that suggest prejudice, hatred, or ignorance.

FIELD RESEARCH

field research

directly observing social behavior

Fieldwork is the cornerstone of modern anthropology. Many sociologists and political scientists also obtain their information through fieldwork. These social scientists study by direct, personal observation of people, events, and societies. **Field research** is essentially going where the action is, watching closely, and taking notes.[3]

Fieldwork is usually less structured than either experimental or survey research. The scientist is not able to control many variables, as in experimental research. Nor is the scientist able to know whether the peoples or societies being studied are truly representative of all other peoples or societies, as in survey research. However, careful field reports can provide qualitative information that is often missing from experimental and survey research. Researchers can report on emotions, feelings, and beliefs that underlie people's behavioral responses. Researchers can also report on attitudes, myths, symbols, and interpersonal relationships that could not be detected by other research methods. Most important, they can observe individuals, groups, and societies as they live in their subjects' environment.

Field research often involves **participant-observation,** where the researcher both observes and participates in the society being studied. Direct participation (moving to Appalachia and getting a job as a coal miner, for example) can provide insights that would otherwise escape a researcher. However, personal participation can also interfere with the detachment required for scientific inquiry. There is also the question of whether the scientist should identify himself or herself as a researcher, which could change the behavior of the people being studied, or conceal his or her identity, which could encourage people to act naturally but raises ethical questions. Some behavior simply cannot be observed if social scientists are identified as researchers. Consider the dilemma of the sociologist who wanted to study homosexual behavior in public toilets. It was not really feasible for him to go on field trips to public toilets identifying himself as a sociologist, asking people if they were homosexuals seeking contacts, and, if so, could he watch. So instead he began visiting public toilets where he suspected homosexual activity was taking place and volunteered to act as a "lookout" for those engaging in the action. He discovered that a lookout was an acceptable, even important, position, and he took advantage of it to study homosexual behavior. Later, after the publication of his study, he came under attack by homosexuals and others for deceiving his subjects.[4]

participant-observation
researchers both observe and participate in the behavior being studied

Anthropology relies heavily on field research. To describe cultures accurately, many anthropologists choose to live among the people they are studying, directly observing and participating in their lives. Many early anthropological studies were intuitive: They produced in-depth, firsthand observations of societies, but these observations were not very systematic. Some would focus on child rearing, religion, art, language, or particularly strange or bizarre practices. Later, anthropological fieldwork became more disciplined, and anthropologists began systematic comparisons of cultures.

Ethnography is the systematic description of a society's customary behaviors, beliefs, and attitudes. Ethnographic studies are usually produced by anthropologists who have spent some time living with, interviewing, and observing the people. Anthropologists in the field can test hypotheses by directly asking and observing the people and learning about the context of their behavior and beliefs. For example, an anthropologist in the field may think that the society he or she is studying practices polygamy (one man marries more than one woman simultaneously) because it has more women than men. But as ethnographic studies are gradually acquired for a larger number of different cultures, anthropologists can begin to test hypotheses by cross-cultural comparisons. They may find reports of some societies that practice polygamy even though the number of men and women is equal.

ethnography
systematic description of a society's customary behaviors, beliefs, and attitudes

TABLE 2-2

Using the *Statistical Abstract*

The *Statistical Abstract of the United States* is published annually by the U.S. Census Bureau. Statistics in each edition are for the most recent year or period available by October of the preceding year. Each new edition contains nearly nine hundred tables. The original source of the data is provided in footnotes to each table.

For example, Table 2-2 is a reproduction of *Table* 342 in the *Statistical Abstract of the United States 1999,* which summarizes U.S. crime rates from 1987 to 1997. The headings along the top of the table are *column* headings, and the headings at the left are *row* headings. In this table, the column headings indicate the total and type of crime, while the row headings indicate the number of crimes, the percentage of change, and the rate (number of crimes per 100,000 inhabitants) for the years 1987 through 1997. So, for example, we can see there were 24,700 murders in the United States in 1991 (note that the number of offenses is given in thousands), and we can see that there were 18,200 murders in 1977. We can also observe that the murder rate per 100,000 inhabitants fell from 9.8 in 1991 to 6.8 in 1997.

In Chapter 12, "Power, Crime, and Violence," we discuss social science explanations for changes in crime rates.

No. 342. Crimes and Crime Rates, by Type of Offense: 1987 to 1997

[Data refer to offenses known to the police. Rates are based on the U.S. Census Bureau estimated resident population as of **July 1, 1990, enumerated as of April 1.** See source for details. Minus sign (−) indicates decrease. For definitions of crimes, see text, this section.]

Item and year	Total	Violent crime Total	Murder[1]	Forcible Rape	Rob-bery	Aggra-vated assault	Property crime Total	Burglary	Lar-ceny— theft	Motor vehicle theft
Number of offenses (1,000):										
1987	13,509	1,484	20.1	91.1	518	855	12,025	3,236	7,500	1,289
1988	13,923	1,566	20.7	92.5	543	910	12,357	3,218	7,706	1,433
1989	14,251	1,646	21.5	94.5	578	952	12,605	3,168	7,872	1,565
1990	14,476	1,820	23.4	102.6	639	1,055	12,656	3,074	7,946	1,636
1991	14,873	1,912	24.7	106.6	688	1,093	12,961	3,157	8,142	1,662
1992	14,438	1,932	23.8	109.1	672	1,127	12,506	2,980	7,915	1,611
1993	14,145	1,926	24.5	106.0	660	1,136	12,219	2,835	7,821	1,563
1994	13,990	1,858	23.3	102.2	619	1,113	12,132	2,713	7,880	1,539
1995	13,863	1,799	21.6	97.5	581	1,099	12,064	2,594	7,998	1,472
1996	13,494	1,689	19.7	96.3	536	1,037	11,805	2,506	7,905	1,394
1997	13,175	1,635	18.2	96.1	498	1,022	11,540	2,461	7,726	1,354
Percent change, number of offenses:										
1987 to 1997	−2.5	10.2	−9.4	5.5	−3.8	19.6	−4.0	−24.0	3.0	5.0
1994 to 1995	−0.9	−3.2	−7.3	−4.6	−6.1	−1.3	−0.6	−4.4	1.5	−4.4
1995 to 1996	−2.7	−6.1	−8.8	−1.3	−7.8	−5.6	−2.1	−3.4	−1.2	−5.3
1996 to 1997	−2.4	−3.2	−7.6	−0.1	−7.0	−1.4	−2.2	−1.8	−2.3	−2.9
Rate per 100,000 population:										
1987	5,550.0	609.7	8.3	37.4	212.7	351.3	4,940.3	1,329.6	3,081.3	529.4
1988	5,664.2	637.2	8.4	37.6	220.9	370.2	5,027.1	1,309.2	3,134.9	582.9
1989	5,741.0	663.1	8.7	38.1	233.0	383.4	5,077.9	1,276.3	3,171.3	630.4
1990	5,820.3	731.8	9.4	41.2	257.0	424.1	5,088.5	1,235.9	3,194.8	657.8
1991	5,897.8	758.1	9.8	42.3	272.7	433.3	5,139.7	1,252.0	3,228.8	659.0
1992	5,660.2	757.5	9.3	42.8	263.6	441.8	4,902.7	1,168.2	3,103.0	631.5
1993	5,484.4	746.8	9.5	41.1	255.9	440.3	4,737.6	1,099.2	3,032.4	606.1
1994	5,373.5	713.6	9.0	39.3	237.7	427.6	4,660.0	1,042.0	3,026.7	591.3
1995	5,275.9	684.6	8.2	37.1	220.9	418.3	4,591.3	987.1	3,043.8	560.4
1996	5,086.6	636.5	7.4	36.3	201.9	390.9	4,450.1	944.8	2,979.7	525.6
1997	4,922.7	610.8	6.8	35.9	186.1	382.0	4,311.9	919.6	2886.5	505.8

TABLE 2-2 (CONTINUED)

USING THE *STATISTICAL ABSTRACT*

Item and year	Violent crime						Property crime			
	Total	Total	Murder[1]	Forcible Rape	Rob-bery	Aggra-vated assault	Total	Burglary	Lar-ceny—theft	Motor vehicle theft
Percent change, rate per 100,000 population:										
1987 to 1997	−7.2	3.0	−14.0	−4.2	−10.3	12.9	−8.5	−29.7	−1.0	−3.5
1984 to 1995	−1.8	−4.1	−8.9	−5.6	−7.1	−2.2	1.5	−5.3	−0.6	−5.2
1995 to 1996	−3.6	−7.0	−9.8	−2.2	−8.6	−6.6	−3.1	−4.3	−2.1	−6.2
1996 to 1997	−3.2	−4.0	−8.1	−1.1	−7.8	−2.3	−3.1	−2.7	−3.1	−3.8

[1] Includes nonnegligent manslaughter.

SOURCE: U.S. Federal Bureau of Investigation, *Crime in the United States,* annual.

This finding would cast doubt on the hypothesis that polygamy is caused by gender-ratio imbalances.

A **case study** is an in-depth investigation of a particular event in order to understand it as fully as possible. A case study may involve an examination of a single governmental decision, a single business firm, a single town, or a single society. A hypothesis may be tested in a case study, but researchers know that a single case is not sufficient to make generalizations about other cases. A single case study is more useful for generating hypotheses to be explored later in comparative studies involving larger numbers of cases. However, some case studies involve limited comparisons, as when two, three, or four cases are studied simultaneously.

case study
in-depth investigation of a particular event in order to understand it as fully as possible

SECONDARY SOURCE DATA

Social scientists do not always collect their own data, that is, primary source data. Often, social scientists rely on data collected by government agencies, other organizations, or other researchers; these data are known as secondary source data. One of the most important sources of data for social scientists is the U.S. Census Bureau, which not only provides the decennial census data on the population of the United States, but also regularly collects and publishes data on governments, housing, manufacturing, and so on. Each year, the Census Bureau also publishes the *Statistical Abstract of the United States,* which summarizes facts about birthrates and death rates, education, income, health, welfare, housing, election outcomes, government taxing and spending, crime, national defense, employment, prices, business, transportation, agriculture, trade, and manufacturing. Footnotes to the data summarized in the *Statistical Abstract* tell where additional data can be found on each topic (see Table 2-2).

secondary source data
data used by social scientists that have been collected by other organizations or governments or researchers

ON THE WEB

EXPLORING THE SOCIAL SCIENCES

The United States government, while not unerring, is the most reliable single source of information on American society. Virtually every U.S. government department and agency maintains a Web site with access to extensive information relevant to a particular sector of American society, for example, agriculture; commerce; defense; education; energy; environment; health and human services; housing and urban development; interior; crime and justice; labor, state and international affairs; trans-

portation; treasury; taxing and spending by all governments; and veterans affairs.

White House. A good place to start browsing is the White House Web site (www.whitehouse.gov). It not only provides information on the presidency, but also allows visitors to click through to all other federal departments and agencies.

U.S. Census Bureau. Perhaps the most extensive U.S. government database is that maintained by the U.S. Census Bureau (www.census.gov). This site directs visitors to information, from A to Z, on the United States. It even keeps a population clock, providing daily estimates of the U.S. and world populations. And the Census Bureau also maintains the

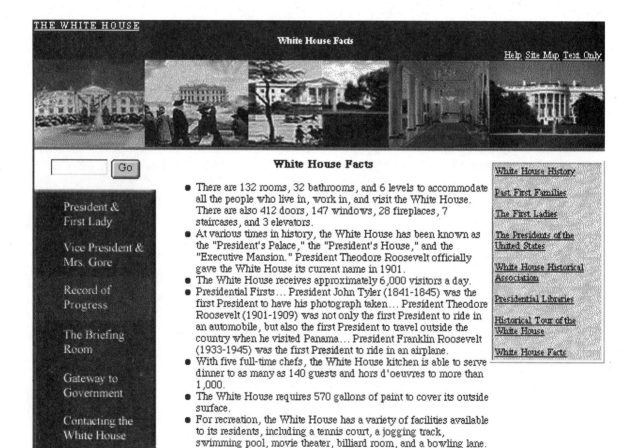

The White House Web site.

on-line version of the most recently published Statistical Abstract of the United States (www.census.gov/prod/www/statistical-abstract-US).

News Organizations. Finally, the nation's major news organizations, both print and broadcast, all maintain Web sites that post up-to-date stories on most of the topics of current interest in the social sciences. Among the most commonly accessed news sites are the following:

> ABC (www.abc.com)
> CBS (www.cbs.com)
> NBC (www.msnbc.com)
> CNN (www.cnn.com)
> *USA Today* (www.usatoday.com)

ABOUT THIS CHAPTER

What is a science, and what is the scientific method? How can the subject matter of the social sciences be studied scientifically? What are the obstacles to the scientific study of human behavior and social relations? How can theories and hypotheses be tested in social science research? How can data be collected? Social scientists are often accused of not being truly scientific. Are they guilty as charged, and if so, why? What are the problems, the promise, and the sometimes paradoxical effects of social science research?

These are the questions that Chapter 2 addressed. Now that you have read it, you should be able to

- define science and describe the scientific method
- illustrate how social scientists develop and test hypotheses
- describe the classic research design and discuss some of the problems that social scientists have in applying this design and the scientific method to their research

DISCUSSION QUESTIONS

1. You are about to begin a social science research project, and you want it to be scientific rather than normative. Describe the method you would choose, explaining how it works and what its goals are. Using this method, will you be able to prove cause and effect? Why or why not?
2. Discuss some of the difficulties the social scientist has in applying the scientific method to the study of social problems.
3. Suppose you are a school psychologist who wishes to determine if students learn more when television is used in the classroom than when only conventional teaching methods are used. Construct a classic research design for this purpose. Describe some of the problems you might encounter in applying the design.

Power and the Social Sciences

PART TWO

I n Part Two we shall take a close look at the ways in which each of the social sciences contributes to our understanding of power in society. In so doing, we hope to gain some feel not only for the different topics, theories, methods, and data of each of the social sciences but also for the goal they share—that is, an improved understanding of human behavior.

In Chapter 3 we shall focus on what *anthropology*, with its concern for culture, has to tell us about the growth of power relationships in societies. In Chapter 4 we shall examine the *sociology* of relationships between power and social class, particularly as evidenced by stratification in American society. In Chapter 5 we shall attempt to determine how and why individuals react in characteristic and different ways to power and authority. Here we shall turn to the theories of personality determination offered by various schools of *psychology*. Control of economic resources is an important base of power in any society, and in Chapter 6 we shall turn our attention to *economics*. In Chapter 7 we shall examine government and power from the point of view of *political science*. Finally, in Chapter 8 we shall look at how the perspective of *history* can increase our understanding of how power in society changes over time.

Chapter 3

Power and Culture

THE ORIGINS OF POWER

Power is exercised in all societies. Every society has a system of sanctions, whether formal or informal, designed to control the behavior of its members. Informal sanctions may include expressions of disapproval, ridicule, or fear of supernatural punishments. Formal sanctions involve recognized ways of censuring behavior—for example, ostracism or exile from the group, loss of freedom, physical punishment, mutilation or death, or retribution visited upon the offender by a member of the family or group that has been wronged.

functions of power in society
maintain internal peace

organize and direct community enterprises

conduct warfare

rule and exploit

Power in society is exercised for four broad purposes:

- to maintain peace within the society
- to organize and direct community enterprises
- to conduct warfare, both defensive and aggressive, against other societies
- to rule and exploit subject peoples

Even in the most primitive societies, power relationships emerge for the purposes of maintaining order, organizing economic enterprise, conducting offensive and defensive warfare, and ruling over subject peoples.

At the base of power relationships in society is the family or kinship group. Power is exercised, first of all, within the family, when work is divided between male and female and parents and children, and when patterns of dominance and submission are established between male and female parents and children. In the simplest societies, power relationships are found partially or wholly *within* family and kinship groups. True political (power) organizations begin with the *development* of power relationships *among* family and kinship groups. As long as kinship units are relatively self-sufficient economically and require no aid in defending themselves against hostile outsiders, political organization has little reason to develop. But the habitual association of human beings in communities or local groups generally leads to the introduction of some form of political (power) organization. The basic power structures are voluntary alliances of families and clans who acknowledge the same leaders, habitually work together in economic enterprises, agree to certain ways of conduct for the maintenance of peace among themselves, and cooperate in the conduct of offensive and defensive warfare. Thus, power structures begin with the development of cooperation among families and kinship groups.

Warfare frequently leads to another purpose for power structures: ruling and exploiting peoples who have been conquered in war. Frequently, primitive societies that have been successful in war learn that they can do more than simply kill or drive off enemy groups. Well-organized and militarily successful tribes learn to subjugate other peoples, retaining them as subjects, for purposes of political and economic exploitation. The power structure of the conquering tribe takes on another function—that of maintaining control over and exploiting conquered peoples.[1]

CULTURE: WAYS OF LIFE

The ways of life that are common to a society make up its **culture.** The culture of any society represents generalizations about the behavior of many members of that society; culture does not describe the personal habits of any one individual. Common ways of behaving in different societies vary enormously. For example, some societies view dog meat as a delicacy, whereas others find the idea of eating dog meat nauseating. Some people paint their entire bodies with intricate designs, while others paint only the faces of the females.

culture
all of the ways of life common to a society

The concept of culture is basic to what anthropology is all about. Anthropologist Clyde Kluckhohn once defined culture as all the "historically created designs for living, explicit and implicit, rational, irrational, and nonrational which may exist at any given time as potential guides for the behavior of man."[2] In contrast with psychologists, who are interested primarily in describing and explaining individual behavior, anthropologists tend to make **cultural generalizations.**

cultural generalizations
descriptions of commonly shared values, beliefs, pictures, and behaviors in a society

SUBCULTURES

subcultures
variations in ways of life within a society

Generalizations about a whole society do not apply to every individual, or even to every group within a society. In virtually every society, there are distinct variations in ways of life among groups of people. These variations are often referred to as **subcultures.** They are frequently observed in such things as distinctive language, music, dress, and dance. Subcultures may center on race or ethnicity, or they may center on age (the "youth culture") or class (see Is There a Culture of Poverty? in Chapter 11). Subcultures may also evolve out of opposition to the beliefs, values, or norms of the dominant culture of society—for example, a "drug culture" or the "counterculture."

MULTICULTURALISM

multiculturalism
acknowledging, protecting, and promoting multiple cultures and subcultures

Multiculturalism is currently very fashionable in American colleges and universities. Multiculturalism generally refers to acknowledging and promoting multiple cultures and subcultures. It seeks to protect and celebrate cultural variety—for example, Spanish language usage, African-American history, Native-American heritage. Multiculturalism tends to resist cultural unification—for example, English-only education, an emphasis on the study of Western Civilization, and the designation of "classic" books, music, and art.

At its best, multiculturalism invites students to explore the ways of life of societies other than their own—for example, non-Western cultures of Asia or Africa or pre-Western cultures of the Mayas or Aztecs. It also invites students to better understand subcultures in their own society—for example, Hispanic, African-American, Native-American, or Asian heritages. But at its worst, multiculturalism denigrates the unifying symbols, values, and beliefs of American society. It condones ignorance of Western European culture, including the foundations of individual freedom and democracy.

CULTURE IS LEARNED

Anthropologists believe culture is learned. They believe that culture is transferred from one generation to another, but it is *not* genetically transmitted. Culture is passed down through the generations because people in different societies are brought up differently. Individuals learn from other people how to speak, how to think, and how to act in certain ways.

THE COMPONENTS OF CULTURE

Anthropologists often subdivide a culture into various components in order to simplify thinking about it. These components of culture—symbols, beliefs, values, norms, sanctions, and artifacts—are closely related in any society.[3]

SYMBOLS

Symbols play a key role in culture. A heavy reliance on symbols— including words, pictures, and writing—distinguish human beings from other animals. A symbol is anything that has meaning bestowed on it by those who use it. Words are symbols, and language is symbolic communication. Objects or artifacts can also be used as symbols: A cross may be a symbol of Christianity. The color red may stand for danger, or it may be a symbol of revolution. The creation and use of such symbols enable human beings to transmit their learned ways of behaving to each new generation. Children are not limited to knowledge acquired through their own experiences and observations; they can learn about the ways of behaving in society through symbolic communication, receiving, in a relatively short time, the result of centuries of experience and observation. Human beings, therefore, can learn more rapidly than other animals, and they can employ symbols to solve increasingly complex problems. Because of symbolic communication, human beings can transmit a body of learned ways of life accumulated by many people over many generations.

symbols
anything that communicates meaning, including language, art, and music

BELIEFS

Beliefs are generally shared ideas about what is true. Every culture includes a system of beliefs that are widely shared, even though there may be some disagreement with these beliefs. Culture includes beliefs about marriage and family, religion and the purpose of life, and economic and political organization. (In Chapter 9, "Power and Ideology," we shall discuss the importance of belief systems in organizing the economic and political systems of societies.)

beliefs
shared ideas about what is true

RELIGION

Religion is evident in all known cultures. Although there are differences between societies in the nature of their religious beliefs, all cultures include some beliefs about supernatural powers (powers not human and not subject to the laws of nature) and about the origins and meaning of life and the universe. Anthropologists, in their professional roles, do not speculate about the truth or falsehood of religious beliefs. Rather, anthropologists are concerned with why religion is found in all societies and how and why religion varies from one society to another.

religion
a set of beliefs and practices pertaining to supernatural powers and the origins and meaning of life

Various theories have arisen about why religious beliefs are universal. Some theories contend that religious beliefs arise out of human anxieties about death and the unknown or out of human curiosity about the meaning, origins, and purpose of life. Other theories stress the social functions of religion, providing goals, purposes, rituals, and norms of behavior for people.

MASTERS OF SOCIAL THOUGHT
Ruth Benedict and Patterns of Culture

The concept of culture helps us to understand ourselves by allowing us to see ourselves in relation to individuals in other societies and other cultures. Through the study of diverse cultures, we realize that there are many different ways of living—many different ways in which people can satisfy their social and psychological needs as well as their biological requirements; that our own culture is not the only possible way of life.

Perhaps this perception of the diversity of human existence was the most important contribution of cultural anthropologist Ruth Benedict in her widely read *Patterns of Culture*. As professor of anthropology at Columbia University, Ruth Benedict (1887–1947) popularized the notion that different cultures can be organized around characteristic purposes or themes. According to Benedict, each culture has its own patterns of thought, action, and expression dominated by a certain theme that is expressed in social relations, art, and religion.

For example, Benedict identified the characteristic themes of life among Zuñi Pueblo Indians as modera-

tion, sobriety, and cooperation. There was little competition, contention, or violence among tribal members. In contrast, the Kwakiutls of the northwestern United States engaged in fierce and violent competition for prestige and self-glorification. Kwakiutls were distrustful of one another, emotionally volatile, and paranoid. Members of the Dobu tribe of New Guinea, too, were suspicious, aggressive, and paranoid:

Life in Dobu fosters extreme forms of animosity and malignancy which most societies have minimized by their institutions. Dobuan institutions, on the other hand, exalt them to the highest degree. The Dobuan lives out without repression man's worst nightmares of the ill-will of the universe, and according to his view of life virtue consists in selecting a victim upon whom he can vent the malignancy he attributes alike to human society and to the powers of nature. All existence appears to him as a cut-throat struggle in which deadly antagonists are pitted against one another in a contest for each

one of the goods of life. Suspicion and cruelty are his trusted weapons in the strife and he gives no mercy, as he asks for none.[a]

Yet Benedict was convinced that *abnormality* and *normality* were relative terms. What is "normal" in Dobuan society would be regarded as "abnormal" in Zuñi society, and vice versa. She believed that there is hardly a form of abnormal behavior in any society that would not be regarded as normal in some other society. Hence, Benedict helped social scientists realize the great variability in the patterns of human existence. People can live in competitive as well as cooperative societies, in peaceful as well as aggressive societies, in trusting as well as suspicious societies.

Today, many anthropologists have reservations about Benedict's idea that the culture of a society reflects a single dominant theme. There is probably a multiplicity of themes in any society, and some societies may be poorly integrated. Moreover, even within a single culture wide variations of individual behavior exist.

[a]Ruth Benedict, *Patterns of Culture* (Boston: Houghton Mifflin, 1934), 172.

Over 80 percent of the world's population identify themselves with a set of religious beliefs. About one-third of the world's population are Christian (see Figure 3-1). Islamic (Muslims), Hindu, and Buddist religions combined account for about 40 percent of the world's population. (Judaism accounts for about 0.2 percent of the world's population and is included in Figure 3-1 under "Other.")

FIGURE 3-1

Religious Populations of the World

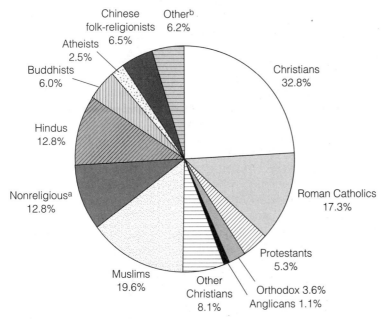

a. Persons professing no religion, agnostics, and secularists indifferent to all religions
b. Ethnic religions, Jains, Bahais, Jews, Mandaeans, Shintos, Sikhs, Spiritualists, Zoroastrians, and New Religionists
SOURCE: U. S. Bureau of the Census, *Statistical Abstract of the United States* 1999 (Washington, D.C.: U.S. Government Printing Office, 1999), 831.

VALUES

Values are shared ideas about what is good and desirable. Values tell us that some things are better than others; values provide us with standards for judging ways of life. Values may be related to beliefs. For example, if we believe that human beings were endowed by God with rights of life, liberty, and property, then we will value the protection of these rights. Thus, belief can justify our values. However, values can conflict with each other (that is, the value of individual freedom conflicts with the need to prevent crime), and not everyone in society shares the same values. Yet most anthropologists believe that every society has some widely shared values.

values
shared ideas about what is good and desirable

NORMS

Norms are shared rules and expectations about behavior. Norms are related to values in that values justify norms. If, for example, we value freedom of speech, we allow people to speak their minds even if we do not agree with

norms
shared rules and expectations about behavior

them. The norm of tolerance derives from the value we place on individual freedom. Fairly trivial norms, like lining up at ticket windows instead of pushing to the front, are called *folkways*. Folkways may determine our style of clothing, our diet, or our manners. *Mores* (pronounced "morays") are more important norms. These are rules of conduct that carry moral authority; violating these rules directly challenges society's values. Yet, like values and beliefs, some norms within a given culture conflict with each other, and not everyone shares a belief in all of society's norms.

SANCTIONS

sanctions
rewards and punishments for conforming to or violating norms

Sanctions are the rewards and punishments for conforming to or violating cultural norms. Rewards—praise, affection, status, wealth, reputation—reinforce cultural norms. Punishments—criticism, ridicule, ostracism, penalties, fines, jail, executions—discourage violations of cultural norms. But conformity to cultural norms does not depend exclusively on sanctions. Most of us conform to our society's norms of behavior even when no sanctions are pending and even when we are alone. We do so because we have been taught to do so, because we do not envision any alternatives, because we share the values on which the norms are based, and because we view ourselves as part of society.

ARTIFACT

artifact
physical product of a culture

An **artifact** is a physical product of a culture. An artifact can be anything from a piece of pottery or a religious object from an ancient culture to a musical composition, a high-rise condominium, or a beer can from a modern culture. But usually we think of an artifact as a physical trace of an earlier culture about which we have little written record. Anthropologists and archaeologists try to understand what these early cultures were like from the study of the artifacts they left behind.

POWER, AUTHORITY, AND LEGITIMACY

legitimacy
the belief that the exercise of power is right and proper

Legitimacy is the belief that the exercise of power is "right" or "proper," that people are morally obligated to submit to it. Legitimacy depends on people believing that the exercise of power is necessary and valuable to society. As long as people believe in the legitimacy of the institutions in which power is lodged and believe that power is being used rightfully and properly, force will seldom be required. People feel obliged to obey laws, follow rules, and abide by decisions that they believe to be legitimate. But if people begin to question the legitimacy of institutions (that is, governments, corporations, churches, the military, and so on), and if people come to believe that laws, rules, and decisions are no longer rightful or proper, then they will no longer feel morally obligated to abide by them. Institutional power will then rest on sheer force alone, as, for example, when unpopular, "illegitimate" governments rely on repression by police or military forces to exercise power over their populations.

AUTHORITY

Authority refers to power that is exercised legitimately. Not all power is legitimate: A thief who forces us to turn over money at gunpoint is exercising power, not authority. A tax collector from the Internal Revenue Service who forces us to turn over money under threat of a fine or jail sentence is exercising authority—power that is perceived as legitimate. Authority, then, is a special type of power that is believed to be rightful and proper.

authority
power that is exercised legitimately

Political leaders in all societies surround themselves with elaborate symbols of office in order to help legitimize their authority.

Authority and legitimacy depend on beliefs, attitudes, and values of the masses. Authority, like beauty, is in the eye of the beholder. The elite know this, so they try to influence mass beliefs and values in order to maintain the legitimacy of institutions they control and to reinforce their own authority. The elite do not like to rely on force alone.

SOURCES OF LEGITIMACY

sources of legitimacy
tradition

charisma

legality

What are the **sources of legitimacy**? Years ago a German sociologist, Max Weber (pronounced "Vayber"), suggested three general sources of legitimacy:

1. *Tradition:* Legitimacy rests on established beliefs in the sanctity of authority and the moral need to obey leaders.
2. *Charisma:* Legitimacy rests on the personal heroic qualities of a particular leader.
3. *Legality:* Legitimacy is based on a commitment to rules that bind both leaders and the people.

Historically, most leaders have depended on tradition for their authority. The rule of tribal chieftains, pharaohs and kings, and feudal lords and ladies has been accepted as right because "it has always been that way." Some have relied on charismatic leadership—from Napoleon to Hitler to Gandhi to Mao Zedong. The authority of these leaders was based on the faith of their followers. Still other elites depend on legitimacy conferred by rules agreed on by both leaders and followers. Weber referred to this as rational-legal authority. Leaders exercise their authority not because of tradition or personal charisma but because of the office or position they occupy.

THE FUNCTIONS OF CULTURE

Culture assists people in adapting to the conditions in which they live. Even ways of life that at first glance appear quaint or curious may play an important role in helping individuals or societies cope with problems. Many anthropologists approach the study of culture by asking what function a particular institution or practice performs for a society. How does the institution or practice serve individual or societal needs? Does it work? How does it work? Why does it work? This approach is known as **functionalism.**[4]

functionalism
the assumption that cultural institutions and practices serve individual or societal needs

FUNCTIONALISM

Functionalism assumes that there are certain minimum *biological needs,* as well as *social and psychological needs,* that must be satisfied if individuals and society are to survive. The biological needs are fairly well-defined: food, shelter, bodily comfort, reproduction, health maintenance, physical movement, and defense. Despite great variety in the way these needs are met in different cultures, we can still ask how a culture goes about fulfilling them and how well it does so. Social and psychological needs are less well defined, but they probably include affection, communication, education in the ways of the culture, material satisfaction, leadership, social control, security, and a sense of unity and belonging. Functionalists tend to examine every custom, material object, idea, belief, and institution in terms of the task or function it performs.

To understand a culture functionally, we have to find out how a particular institution or practice relates to biological, social, or psychological needs and how it relates to other cultural institutions and practices. For example, a society that fulfills its biological needs by hunting may fulfill its psychological needs by worshiping animals. Similarly, we find an agricultural society worshiping a sun-god or a rain-god. The function of magic is to give human beings courage to face the unknown; myth preserves social traditions; religion fosters individual security and social solidarity; and so forth.

Anthropology helps us appreciate other cultures. It requires impartial observation and testing of explanations of customs, practices, and institutions. Anthropologists cannot judge other cultures by the same standards that we use to judge our own. **Ethnocentrism,** or judging other cultures solely in terms of one's own culture, is an obstacle to good anthropological work.

ethnocentrism
judging other cultures solely in terms of one's own culture

CULTURAL RELATIVITY

But **cultural relativity**—uncritical acceptance of customs, practices, and institutions of other cultures—leads to moral dilemmas for scholars and students. While it is important to assess the elements of a culture in terms of how well they work for their own people in their own environment,[5] an uncritical or romantic view of other cultures is demoralizing. Consider, for example, the practice of female infanticide, a common practice in many cultures, including India (before infanticide was declared illegal by British rulers in 1870). Anthropologists might explain the preference for sons in terms of economic production based on hard manual labor in the fields. But understanding the functional relationship between female infanticide and economic conditions must not be viewed as a moral justification of the practice (see Controversies in Social Sciences, "Cultural Relativity and Female Circumcision").

Some elements of a culture not only differ from those of another culture, but are *better*. The fact that all peoples—Asians, Europeans, Africans, Native Americans, and others—have often abandoned features of their own culture in order to replace them with elements from other cultures implies that the replacements served peoples' purposes more effectively.[6] Arabic numerals are not simply different from Roman numerals, they are *better*. This is why the European nations, whose own culture derived from Rome, replaced Roman numerals with numerals derived from Arab culture (which had learned them from the Hindus of India). It is inconceivable today that we would express

cultural relativity
uncritical acceptance of customs, practices, and institutions of other cultures

CONTROVERSIES IN SOCIAL SCIENCE
Cultural Relativity and Female Circumcision

Anthropologists frequently battle against ethnocentrism and the tendency of western Europeans and Americans to view some cultures as "savage." They argue that as anthropologists they must suspend judgment on other peoples' cultural practices, asking only how a people's culture satisfies their particular needs and expectations. But this cultural relativism often conflicts with the idea of universal human rights.

Female circumcision is common in parts of Africa, Malaysia, and Indonesia. Worldwide, between 100 million and 200 million females have been circumcised. In some cultures, only the girl's clitoris is cut off, in others the clitoris and both the labia majora and the labia minora are excised. The surgery takes place between the ages of four and eight. It is often done without anesthesia; the pain is so excruciating that adults must hold the young girl down. Some of the risks are shock, extensive bleeding, infection, infertility, and death. Ongoing results include vaginal spasms, painful intercourse, and lack of orgasms.

What is the cultural explanation for this custom? Cultures that practice female circumcision believe that it reduces female sexual desire, thus making it more likely that a woman will be a virgin until marriage, and, afterward, remain faithful to her husband. Female circumcision is also a form of ritual torture to control female sexuality; the societies that practice it are male dominated. Mothers cooperate with the circumcision because in these societies an unmarried woman has virtually no rights, and an uncircumcised woman is considered impure and is not allowed to marry.

Some immigrants have brought the custom with them to the United States. Although the practice is specifically banned only in a few states, U.S. physicians will not perform it because they could be charged with child abuse. Some immigrant families take their daughters to their homeland for the operation. Should Western nations try to make other nations stop this custom? Or would this be ethnocentric, the imposition of Western values on other cultures?

large numbers in Roman numerals; for example, the year of American independence—MDCCLXXVI—requires more than twice as many Roman numerals as Arabic numerals and requires subtracting as well as adding numbers, depending on their place in the sequence. So it is important for scholars and students to avoid the assumption of cultural relativity—that all cultures serve their people equally well.[7]

AUTHORITY IN THE FAMILY

The family is the principal agent of socialization into society. It is the most intimate and important of all social groups. Of course, the family can assume different shapes in different cultures, and it can perform a variety of functions and meet a variety of needs. But in *all* societies, the family relationship centers on sexual and child-rearing functions. A cross-cultural comparison reveals that in all societies the family possesses these common characteristics:[8]

characteristics of the family

- sexual mating
- childbearing and child rearing
- a system of names and a method of determining kinship
- a common habitation
- socialization and education of the young
- a system of roles and expectations based on family membership

These common characteristics indicate why the family is so important in human societies. It replenishes the population and rears each new generation. Within the family, the individual personality is formed. The family transmits and carries forward the culture of the society. It establishes the primary system of roles with differential rights, duties, and behaviors. And it is within the family that the child first encounters *authority*.

MARRIAGE

To an anthropologist, marriage does not necessarily connote a wedding ceremony and legal certificate. Rather, **marriage** means a socially approved sexual and economic union between a man and a woman, intended to be more or less permanent and implying social roles between the spouses and their children. Marriage is found in all cultures, and anthropologists have offered a variety of explanations for its universality. One theory explaining marriage focuses on the prolonged infant dependency of humans. In most cultures infants are breast-fed for up to two years. This results in a division of roles between the female nurturer and the male protector that requires some lasting agreement between the partners. Another theory focuses on sexual competition among males. Marriage minimizes males' rivalry for female sexuality and thus reduces destructive conflict (see Focus, "Social Science Looks at Sex in America"). Still another theory focuses on the economic division of labor between the sexes. Males and females in every culture perform somewhat different economic activities; marriage is a means of sharing the products of their divided labor.

marriage
a socially approved sexual and economic union between a man and a woman, intended to be lasting, and implying social roles between the spouses and their children

ROMANTIC LOVE

While most Americans believe that romantic love should be the basis of a marriage, this ideal does not characterize marriages in many other societies. On the contrary, in many societies romantic love is believed to be a poor basis for marriage and is strongly discouraged. (Nonetheless, in most of the world societies, romantic love is depicted in love songs and stories.) Marriages based on romance are far less common in less developed societies where economic and kinship factors are important considerations in marriage.[9]

FOCUS

Social Science Looks at Sex in America

The popular media—advertising, films, television, magazines, novels—portrays sex in American culture as pervasive and relentless. The highly publicized "sexual revolution" of the 1960s, presumably fostered by birth control pills and women's renewed quest for equality, was widely believed to have inspired more, better, and livelier sex. Indeed, television talk shows, *Cosmopolitan* and *Playboy* magazine polls, music videos, and a host of movies depict America as a nation preoccupied with sex.

But the best social science evidence indicates that most Americans enjoy faithful, monogamous, conventional sex lives. The most comprehensive national survey of sex practices, conducted by the National Opinion Research Center of the University of Chicago, interviewed 3,432 Americans aged eighteen to fifty-nine. Unlike earlier magazine-reader polls, respondents were randomly selected to constitute a cross section of Americans. (The study was originally planned by the U.S. National Institutes of Health, but opposition in Congress to government-funded "sex research" obliged social sci-

entists to seek financial support from private foundations.) Trained interviewers were sent to households throughout the nation; respondents were interviewed in person and were also given a confidential form to fill out and return. The results destroy many popular myths about sex in America. Among the key findings:

- The vast majority of Americans (83%) have only one (or zero) sex partner in a year. Over a lifetime, 31% of women have had only one partner and an additional 36% have had only two partners; the median number of partners for women is two, for men, six.
- The vast majority of married Americans (75% of men and 85% of women) have never been unfaithful to their spouses.
- Only one-third of Americans have sex twice a week or more; an additional one-third have sex a few times a month, and one-third only a few times a year or not at all.
- Married people have more sex, and experience orgasm more often, than single people.

- Over 75% of men, but just 29% of women, almost always have an orgasm during sex.
- Among sexual practices, vaginal sex is the most popular practice (90% men, 86% women), followed by masturbation (63% men, 42% women), with oral sex a distant third (27% men, 19% women).
- Homosexuality is rare. Only 2.7% of men and 1.3% of women report having had a homosexual experience in the past year. Only 9% of men and 4% of women have ever had a homosexual experience in their lifetime.
- Fifty-four percent of men and 19% of women report that they think about sex daily.

The sociologists who conducted the study argue that our sex lives, in large part, follow social "scripts," that is, cultural norms that influence sexual behavior. They note that most Americans choose sexual partners who are close in age and educational and ethnic background. The result is greater sexual compatibility and more stable relationships.

SOURCE: Edward Laumann, Robert Michael, Stuart Michaels, and John Gaynon, *The Social Organization of Sexuality* (Chicago: University of Chicago Press, 1994). The popular bookstore version is *Sex in America: A Definitive Study* (New York: Little, Brown, 1994).

MONOGAMY

Family arrangements vary. First of all, the marriage relationship may take on such institutional forms as monogamy, polygyny, and polyandry. **Monogamy** is the union of one husband and one wife; *polygyny,* the union of one husband and two or more wives; *polyandry,* the union of one wife and two or more husbands. Throughout the world, monogamy is the most widespread marriage form, probably because the *gender ratio* (number of males per one hundred females) is near one hundred in all societies, meaning there is about an equal number of men and women.

monogamy
marriage union of one husband and one wife

THE FAMILY IN AGRICULTURAL SOCIETIES

In most agricultural societies the family is **patriarchal** and *patrilineal:* The male is the dominant authority, and kinship is determined through the male line. The family is an economic institution, as well as a sexual and child-rearing one; it owns land, produces many artifacts, and cares for its old as well as its young. Male family heads exercise power in the wider community; patriarchs may govern the village or tribe. Male authority frequently means the subjugation of both women and children. This family arrangement is buttressed by traditional moral values and religious teachings that emphasize discipline, self-sacrifice, and the sanctity of the family unit.

the patriarchal family
the male is the dominant authority and kinship is determined through the male line

Women face a lifetime of childbearing, child rearing, and household work. Families of ten or fifteen children are not uncommon. The property rights of a woman are vested in her husband. Women are taught to serve and obey their husbands and are not considered as mentally competent as men. The husband owns and manages the family's economic enterprise. Tasks are divided: Men raise crops, tend animals, and perform heavy work; women make clothes, prepare food, tend the sick, and perform endless household services.

THE FAMILY IN INDUSTRIALIZED SOCIETIES

Industrialization alters the economic functions of the family and brings about changes in the traditional patterns of authority. In industrialized societies, the household is no longer an important unit of production, even though it retains an economic role as a consumer unit. Work is to be found outside the home, and industrial technology provides gainful employment for women as well as for men. This means an increase in opportunities for women outside the family unit and the possibility of economic independence. The number of women in the labor force increases; today in the United States, about 65 percent of adult women are employed outside the home.

effects of industrialization on the family

The patriarchal authority structure that typifies the family in an agricultural economy is altered by the new opportunities for women in advanced industrial nations (see Cross-National Perspective, "Women in the Workforce").

role of women

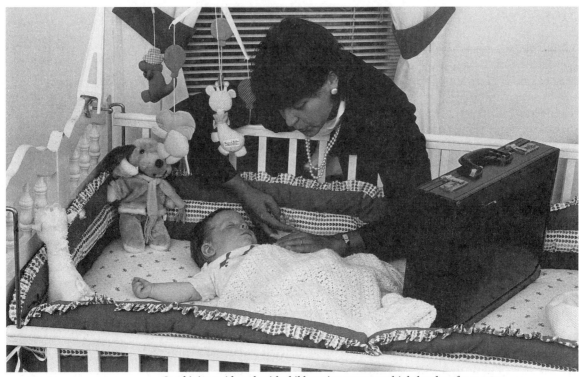

Combining paid work with child rearing creates multiple burdens for women.

Not only do women acquire employment alternatives, but their opportunities for education also expand. Independence allows them to modify many of the more oppressive features of patriarchy. Women in an advanced industrialized society have fewer children. Divorce becomes a realistic alternative to an unhappy marriage.

role of government

At the same time, governments in industrialized societies assume many of the traditional functions of the family, further increasing opportunities for women. The government steps into the field of formal education—not just in the instruction of reading, writing, and arithmetic, but in support of home economics, driver training, health care, and perhaps even sex education, all areas that were once the province of the family. Governmental welfare programs provide assistance to dependent children when a family breadwinner is absent, unemployed, or unable to provide for the children. The government undertakes to care for the aged, the sick, and others incapable of supporting themselves, thus relieving families of still another traditional function.

family as fundamental social unit

Despite these characteristics of industrial society, however, *the family remains the fundamental social unit.* The family is not disappearing; marriage and family life are as popular as ever. But the father-dominated authority structure, with its traditional duties and rigid gender roles, is changing. The family is becoming an institution in which both husband and wife seek indi-

Women in the Workforce

Over time, more and more women have joined the workforce throughout the world. Even in the last twenty years, international statistics indicate that the world's female labor force has increased rapidly.

In the United States, the percentage of women working outside the home rose from 31 percent in 1950 (not shown below) to nearly 60 percent in 1980 and over 70 percent today. Virtually all other nations have experienced similar increases in the percentage of women in the workforce. Nonetheless, fewer than half of women in some nations (Italy, Mexico, Spain, Turkey) are included in the workforce. In contrast, women in Scandinavian nations (Finland, Iceland, Norway, Sweden) have long had higher workforce-participation rates than American women.

[**In percent.** Female labor force of all ages divided by female population 15–64 years old]

Country	1980	1990	1995	1997	Country	1980	1990	1995	1997
Australia	52.7	62.9	64.8	64.7	Korea, South	(NA)	51.3	53.2	54.8
Austria	48.7	55.4	62.3	61.9	Luxembourg	39.9	50.7	58.0	60.9
Belgium	47.0	52.4	56.1	(NA)	Mexico	33.7	23.6	40.1	42.8
Canada	57.8	67.8	67.6	67.8	Netherlands	35.5	53.1	59.0	62.2
Czech Republic	(NA)	69.1	65.4	64.4	New Zealand	44.6	62.9	63.3	64.9
Denmark	(NA)	78.5	73.6	75.1	Norway	62.3	71.2	72.4	75.8
Finland	70.1	72.9	70.3	71.3	Poland	(NA)	(NA)	61.1	60.0
France	54.4	57.6	59.4	59.8	Portugal	54.3	62.9	62.4	65.1
Germany	52.8	57.4	61.7	61.8	Spain	32.2	41.2	45.1	47.1
Greece	33.0	43.6	45.9	(NA)	Sweden	74.1	80.1	76.1	74.5
Hungary	(NA)	(NA)	50.5	49.4	Switzerland	54.1	59.6	67.8	69.4
Iceland	(NA)	(NA)	82.4	(NA)	Turkey	(NA)	36.7	34.2	30.2
Ireland	36.3	38.9	47.8	50.4	United Kingdom	58.3	65.5	66.0	67.5
Italy	39.6	45.9	43.3	44.1	United States	59.7	68.9	70.7	71.3
Japan	54.8	60.3	62.1	63.7					

SOURCE: U.S. Bureau of the Census, *Statistical Abstract of the United States 1999* (Washington, D.C.: U.S. Government Printing Office, 1999), 849.

vidual happiness rather than the perpetuation of the species and economic efficiency. Many women still choose to seek fulfillment in marriage and child rearing rather than in outside employment. The important point is that now this is a *choice* and not a cultural requirement.

THE AMERICAN FAMILY

The American family endures. Its nature may change, but the family unit nonetheless continues to be the fundamental unit of society.

Today, there are more than 70 million families in America, and 238 million of the nation's 281 million people live in these family units.[10] Only about 15 percent of the population lives outside family units.

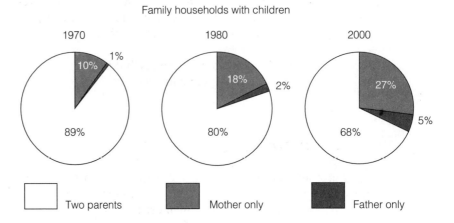

FIGURE 3-2

THE CHANGING AMERICAN FAMILY

Family households with children

1970   1980   2000

1%   10%   89%

18%   2%   80%

27%   5%   68%

☐ Two parents   ▨ Mother only   ■ Father only

However, the nature of the family unit has indeed been changing. Husband-wife families compose 68 percent of all families with children, whereas 32 percent of all families consist of a single adult and children. Female-headed families with no spouse present have risen from 10 percent of all families in 1970 to 27 percent of all families in 2000. (See Figure 3-2.) The birthrate has declined from 3.7 births per woman of childbearing age in the 1950s to 2.4 in the 1970s and to only 1.8 in 2000. This last figure is *below* the projected zero population growth rate (2.1 children per female of childbearing age). In addition, there are about four abortions for every ten live births in the United States.

It is not really clear what factors are contributing to these changes in the American family. Certainly new opportunities for women in the occupational world have increased the number of women in the workforce and altered the "traditional" patterns of family life. Economic concerns may be an even more important factor: Families must increasingly depend on the incomes of both husband and wife to maintain a middle-class lifestyle.

DIVORCE

Almost all societies allow for the separation of husband and wife. Many primitive societies have much higher divorce rates than the United States and other advanced industrialized societies. In 1998 in the United States, there were 4.3 divorces per 1,000 population, compared with 8.9 marriages.[11] At this rate, we would expect nearly half of all marriages to end in divorce. The U.S. divorce rate has moderated somewhat in recent years; it was higher at 5.2 divorces per 1,000 population in 1970. The median duration of marriages that end in divorce is seven years.

Women are more burdened by divorce than men. Most mothers retain custody of children. Although both spouses confront reduced family income from the separation, the burden falls more heavily on the mother who must both support herself and rear the children. Divorced fathers are generally required by courts to provide child-support payments; however, these payments rarely amount to full household support, and significant numbers of absent fathers fail to make full payments.

Most divorced persons eventually find new spouses, but these remarriages are even more likely to end in divorce than first marriages.

POWER AND GENDER

Although some societies have reduced sexual inequalities, no society has entirely eliminated male dominance.[12] **Gender** role differentiation in work differs among cultures (see Table 3–1), but the most common pattern is for women to work close to home (see Focus, "How Men and Women View Their Relations Today"). Moreover, comparisons of numbers of different cultures studied by anthropologists reveal that men rather than women are usually dominant in *political leadership and warfare.* A cross-cultural survey reports that in 85 percent of the societies studied, *only* men were political leaders.[13] In the other 15 percent of societies studied, female leaders were either outnumbered by male leaders or were less powerful than the males. In 88 percent of the world's societies women never participate in war. Even today, women on the average make up only about 10 percent of the representatives in national legislative bodies (congresses and parliaments) around the world.[14]

gender
in anthropology, a reference to the cultural characteristics linked to male and female that define people as masculine and feminine

sex
in anthropology, the reference to the biological characteristics distinguishing male from female

TABLE 3-1

DIVISION OF LABOR BY GENDER: A CROSS-CULTURAL COMPARISON

Numbers of cultures dominated by

	Men always	Men usually	Either gender equally	Women usually	Women always
Hunting	166	13	0	0	0
Herding	38	4	4	0	5
Fishing	98	34	19	3	4
Planting	31	23	33	20	37
Harvesting	10	15	35	39	44
Cooking	5	1	9	28	158
Carrying water	7	0	5	7	119

SOURCE: Adapted from George P. Murdock, "Comparative Data on the Division of Labor by Sex," *Social Forces* 15 (May 1985): 551–553.

FOCUS

How Men and Women View Their Relations Today

When a majority of women entered the workforce in the 1970s, expectations were high that soon equality of the sexes in both home and the workplace would become an accepted norm in our culture. But we have already observed continued gender differentiation in the workforce—the persistence of predominantly male and female occupations—as well as a continuing earnings gap. Moreover, the expectation that men would undertake to shoulder an equal burden in household and child-rearing duties has also failed to materialize. Survey evidence suggests that American women continue to perceive male advantages in the marketplace and male reluctance to undertake household chores.

A majority of women believe that men "still run almost everything," and a substantial number of women believe that "there are more advantages to being a man" in American so-

ciety today (see the table). Marriage is still very popular, with nine out of ten saying they would marry the same person again. But women are

still burdened with most of the household chores, whether they work outside of the home or not.

MARRIAGE ROLES FOR MEN AND WOMEN

	Responses by	
	Men	Women
Men still run almost everything and usually do not include women when important decisions are made.	41%	57%
In our society today, there are more advantages to being a man.	30%	43%
there are more advantages to being a woman.	16%	8%
Would marry the same person again.	93%	88%
Do you or your husband/wife share household chores equally?		
woman does more	35%	58%
share equally	46%	34%
man does more	15%	5%
Percent saying they		
never cook meals	12%	2%
never put out garbage	17%	22%
never clean bathroom	60%	10%
never iron clothes	82%	47%
never do laundering	51%	5%
never vacuum	51%	16%
never do household repairs	31%	64%
never wash dishes	40%	9%

SOURCES: Various national polls reported in *The American Enterprise* (September/October 1993): 88–95; and *Public Perspective* (July/August, 2000): 27.

---

theories to explain male dominance

physical strength

hunting

child care

aggression

Why have men dominated in politics and war in most cultures? There are many theories on this topic.

A theory of *physical strength* suggests that men prevail in warfare, particularly in primitive warfare, which relies mainly on physical strength of the combatants. Because men did the fighting, they also had to make the decisions about whether or not to engage in war. Decisions about whether to fight or not were vital to the survival of the culture; therefore, decisions about war were the most important political decisions in a society. Dominance in those decisions assisted men in other aspects of societal decision making and led to their general political dominance.

A related *hunting* theory suggests that in most societies men do the hunting, wandering far from home and using great strength and endurance. The skills of hunting are closely related to the skills of war; people can be hunted and killed in the same fashion as animals. Because men dominated in hunting, they also dominated in war.

A *child-care* theory argues that women's biological function of bearing and nursing children prevents women from going far from home. Infants cannot be taken into potential danger. (As we stated earlier in this chapter, in most cultures women breast-feed their children for up to two years.) This circumstance explains why women in most cultures perform functions that allow them to remain at home—for example, cooking, harvesting, and planting—and why men in most cultures undertake tasks that require them to leave home—hunting, herding, fishing. Warfare, of course, requires long stays away from home.

Still another theory, an *aggression* theory, proposes that males on the average possess more aggressive personalities than females. Some anthropologists contend that male aggression is biologically determined and occurs in all societies. Even at very young ages, boys try to hurt others and establish dominance more frequently than girls; these behaviors seem to occur without being taught and even when efforts are made to teach boys just the opposite.[15]

All these theories are arguable, of course. Some theories may be thinly disguised attempts to justify an inferior status for women—for keeping women at home and allowing them less power than men. Moreover, these theories do not go very far in explaining why the status of women varies so much from one society to another.

Although these theories help explain male dominance, we still need to explain the following: *Why do women participate in politics in some societies more than in others?* Generally, women exercise more political power in societies where they make substantial contributions to economic subsistence. Thus, women have less power in societies that depend on hunting or herding and appear to have less power in societies that frequently engage in warfare. Finally, some evidence exists that women have more power in societies that rear children with greater affection and nurturance.[16]

POWER AND POLITICAL SYSTEMS

The **political system** is the way that power is organized and distributed in a society, whether it is organizing a hunt and designating its leader or raising and commanding an army of millions. Some form of political system exists in all societies.[17]

political system
the organization and distribution of power in society

Anthropologists have identified various types of political systems. These systems can be arranged according to the extent to which power is organized and centralized, from family and kinship group to band, tribe, chiefdom, state, and nation.

FAMILY AND KINSHIP GROUPS

In some societies, no separate power organization exists outside the *family or kinship group*. In these societies, there is no continuous or well-defined system of leaders over or above those who head the individual families. These societies do not have any clear-cut division of labor or economic organization outside the family, and there is no structured method for resolving differences and maintaining peace among members of the group. Further, these societies do not usually engage in organized offensive or defensive warfare. They tend to be small and widely dispersed, have economies that yield only a bare subsistence, and lack any form of organized fighting force. Power relationships are present, but they are closely tied to family and kinship.

BANDS

band
a small group of related families who occupy the same territory and interact with each other

Bands are small groups of related families who occupy a common territory and come together periodically to hunt, trade, and make marriage arrangements. Bands are often found among nomadic societies, where groups of families move about the land in search of food, water, game, and subsistence.

While American men have begun to take a more active role in child-care and household duties, surveys indicate that American women continue to perceive male reluctance to undertake household chores.

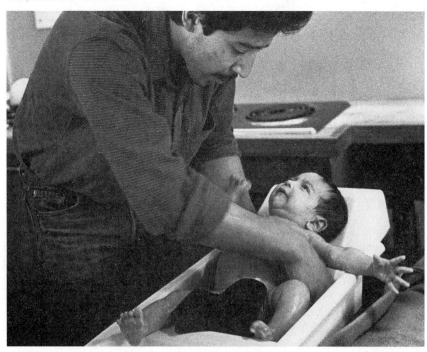

Anthropologists believe that bands were the oldest form of political organization outside of the family, and that all humans were once food foragers who moved about the land in small bands numbering at most a hundred people.

Authority in the band is usually exercised by a few senior heads of families; their authority most often derives from achievements in hunting or fighting. The senior headmen must decide when and where to move and choose a site for a new settlement. People follow the headmen's leadership primarily because they consider it in their own best interest to do so. Sanctions may range from scorn and ridicule, to ostracism or exile from the band.

TRIBES

Anthropologists describe **tribes** as groups of bands or villages that share a common language and culture who unite for greater security against enemies or starvation. (*Tribe* also has a distinct legal definition in the United States, referring to recognized political organizations of Native Americans. See "Native Americans: An Historical Overview" in Chapter 10.) Typically tribes are engaged in hunting, herding, or farming, and they live in areas of greater population density than bands. Tribal authorities must settle differences between bands, villages, and kinship groups. They must organize defenses as well as plan and carry out raids on other tribes. They must pool resources when needed as well as decide upon the distribution of common resources—the product of an organized hunt, for example. Authority may rest in the hands of one or more leaders respected for age, integrity, wisdom, or skills in hunting and warfare.

tribe
a group of separate bands or villages sharing a common language and culture who come together for greater security

CHIEFDOMS

Anthropologists also identify **chiefdoms**—highly centralized, regional societies in which power is concentrated in a single chief who is at the head of a ranked hierarchy of people. The position of chief is usually hereditary. People's status in the chiefdom is decided by their kinship to the chief; those closest to him are ranked socially superior and receive deferential treatment from those in lower ranks. The chief's responsibilities extend to the distribution of land and resources, the recruitment and command of warriors, and control over the goods and labor of the community. The chief may amass considerable personal wealth and other evidence of his high status.

chiefdom
a centralized society in which power is concentrated in a single chief who heads a ranked hierarchy of people

STATES

The most fully developed system of power relationships is the state. A **state** is a permanent, centralized organization with a well-defined territory and the recognized authority to make and enforce rules of conduct. The power of the state is legitimate, that is, considered rightful by its members. In state societies, populations are large and highly concentrated; the economy produces a

state
a permanent centralized organization with a defined territory and recognized authority to make and enforce rules

FOCUS

Power and the Aztec Empire

The Aztec Empire, which was conquered by the Spaniards under Hernando Cortés in 1521, is an excellent example of an early state. The rich agricultural economy developed by the Aztecs produced far in excess of their immediate needs. With the exchangeable surplus, there soon evolved a complex specialization of labor and an extensive trade that brought the Aztecs into frequent and profitable contact with neighboring groups.

Early in the fifteenth century, the Aztecs embarked on a series of military conquests that led ultimately to their economic and political control over most of central and southern Mexico. The Aztecs did not destroy the cities and states they had conquered. On the contrary, the commercially minded Aztecs permitted those cities and states to retain local autonomy, demanding only political allegiance and a yearly tribute in goods and services to the Aztec emperor. It was this

economic empire, politically a loose aggregate of city-states controlled from the Aztec capital city of Tenochtitlán, that Cortés took over in 1521.

The early Aztec power structure, although more complicated than that of primitive tribes, still retained a measure of democratic procedure. The core of the Aztec Empire was ruled by its citizens, the members of the *calpulli,* small groups composed of nuclear families that farmed their own land. Although the positions of chief and king were in part hereditary (they were customarily chosen from particular families), the choice of a leader also depended on reputation and ability. The king had great power as a military leader in a state more or less continuously at war, but his power was modified by councils of family heads.

As the Aztecs grew wealthier from their numerous conquests and ever-widening control of trade, the power structure underwent a gradual

change. Most important, a class division developed in Aztec society along socioeconomic lines. An upper class appeared, composed of honorary lords known as *tecutin.* These were men, *calpulli* members, who were given titles for outstanding services to the state as warriors, merchants, public officials, or priests. They were universally esteemed; had many privileges, including certain exemptions from taxation; were preferred for high governmental and military positions; and were given large estates and shares of tribute by the king, to be held as private property during their lifetime. These rewards clearly made the *tecutin* economically independent of their *calpulli* and, moreover, allied them with the king, who, while he gave the *tecutin* their honors, also had the power to withdraw them.

A middle class also emerged, made up of *calpulli* members who were not *tecutin.*

surplus; and there are recognized rules of conduct for the members of the society, with positive and negative sanctions. These societies have an organized military establishment for offensive and defensive wars. In war, conquered people are not usually destroyed but instead are held as tributaries or incorporated as inferior classes into the state. In the vast majority of these societies, power is centered in a small, hereditary elite (see Focus: "Power and the Aztec Empire").

Power in the state is employed to maintain order among peoples and to carry on large-scale community enterprises, just as in the band or tribe. But power in the state is also closely linked to defense, aggression, and the exploitation of conquered peoples. Frequently states emerge in response to attacks by others. Where there is a fairly high density of population, frequent

The Great Temple of Mexico, Tenochtitlán, as reconstructed by the twentieth-century pre-Conquest architectural historian Ignacio Marquina, according to the plans of Bernardino de Sahagún and Diego Durán.

for various crimes and who thus had no way of making a living except by hiring themselves out as agricultural laborers or as porters in the caravans of the merchants. Slaves were similarly dependent for a living on their own labor. Neither slaves nor propertyless freemen had a voice in the government. Though initially small, the lower class grew as conquests increased.

As class lines became more sharply drawn, Aztec government moved inevitably in the direction of an absolute *hereditary monarchy. Tecutin* clearly supported this tendency to their advantage and increasingly, by various devices, managed to pass on their titles and private property to their heirs. Slowly a *hereditary nobility* arose. At the time of the conquest, the Aztec Empire was essentially an emerging feudal order, with political power centered increasingly in the king and his *tecutin* rather than in the elected representatives of the *calpulli.*

These formed the bulk of the population of the capital city. They were self-supporting through their membership in the *calpulli* and had a voice in the government through their representatives in the state and great councils. Often they rented their *calpulli* lands, and some acquired great wealth.

Finally, a lower class was divided into propertyless freemen and slaves. Slaves were attached to the lands of the nobility. The propertyless were men exiled from the *calpulli*

and continuing contact among bands, and some commonality of language and culture, there is the potential for "national" unity in the form of a state. But a state may not emerge if there is no compelling motivation for large-scale cooperation. Motivation is very often provided initially by the need for defense against outside invasion.

NATIONS

A nation differs from a state in important ways. A **nation** is a society that sees itself as "one people" with a common culture, history, institutions, ideology, language, territory, and (often) religion. By this definition, there are probably

nation
a society that sees itself as one people with a common culture, history, institutions, ideology, language, and territory

five thousand or more nations in the world today. (The United Nations has only 188 member states; see Chapter 14.) Only rarely do nation and state coincide, as in Japan. Many states are multinational; that is, they include within their territorial boundaries more than one nation. When a state and nation do coincide, it is usually referred to as a nation-state.

The United States declares itself to be "one nation, indivisible, under God." Yet it encompasses multiple nationalities, languages, and cultures. The claim to nationhood by the United States rests primarily on a common allegiance to the institutions of democracy. Most other nation-states base their claim to nationhood on common ethnicity and ancestry as well as language and territory.

TYPES OF POLITICAL SYSTEMS

These types of power relationships in societies—bands, tribes, chiefdoms, states—certainly do not exhaust the variety of current and past power arrangements. They represent only broad divisions, each of which can be subdivided. (For example, a state can be classified in Aristotelian fashion as a *monarchy, aristocracy,* or *democracy*—rule by the one, the few, or the many.) Sharp lines cannot be drawn among these three states; each stage shades into the next, and there are many transitional forms.

POWER AND SOCIETY: SOME ANTHROPOLOGICAL OBSERVATIONS

power and the physical environment

Let us summarize the contributions that anthropological studies can make to our understanding of the growth of power relationships in societies. First, it is clear that the *physical environment* plays an important role in the development of power systems. Where the physical environment is harsh and the human population must of necessity be spread thinly, power relationships are restricted to the family and kinship groupings. Larger political groupings are essentially impossible. The elite emerge only after there is some concentration of population, where food resources permit groupings of people larger than one or two families.

power and the economy

Second, power relationships are linked to the *economic patterns* of a culture. In subsistence economies, power relationships are limited to the band or tribal level. Only in surplus-producing economies do we find states or statelike power systems. Developed power systems are associated with *patterns of settled life,* a certain degree of *technological advance,* and *economic surplus.*

power and warfare

Third, *patterns of warfare* are linked to the development of power relationships. Warfare is rare or lacking among people such as the Eskimos who have no real power system outside the family. Where power relationships emerge at the band or tribal level, as in the culture of the Crow, warfare appears to be continuous, in the form of periodic raiding for small economic gains or the achievement of personal glory and status; victory assumes the form of killing or driving off enemy groups. Only at the state level is warfare well organized and pursued for the purpose of conquest and economic exploitation. This does not mean necessarily that statelike power systems *cause* war, but rather, that some common factor underlies both the rise of state power systems and organized warfare. Warfare and conquest are not essential to the maintenance of the state; in fact, in the modern world, warfare between major states may slowly give way to other forms of competition, if only because of the increasing threat of total destruction.

power in advanced societies

Fourth, anthropological research makes it clear that power relationships exist in simple forms in primitive societies and that *no society is void of a power structure.* Power structures become more complex and hierarchical, and more impersonal and based on physical force, as societies move from the subsistence level with simple technology to a surplus-producing level with advanced technology and large cooperative enterprises. The simpler power systems are frequently headed by chiefs and councils selected for their age, wisdom, or demonstrated capacity as hunters or warriors. These leaders tend to rule more by example and persuasion than by formal decree or force. As more complex state systems emerge, leaders are endowed with the exclusive right to coerce. Characteristically, political and economic power in the state is concentrated in a small hereditary elite. Modern representative government, in the form of European and American democracies, is relatively rare in the history of human societies.

On the Web

EXPLORING ANTHROPOLOGY

Anthrotech. A good place to begin to browse the Web for information about anthropology is the Anthropology Resources and Services site (www.anthrotech.com), especially its general orientation link "What is Anthropology." This site directs visitors to databases, publications, conferences, directories, job opportunities, and discussion forums in anthropology.

Human Relations Area Files. A more advanced site is the Human Relations Area Files at Yale University (www.yale.edu/hraf). It is designed to "facilitate the cross-cultural study of human behavior, society, and culture." It includes links to the *Encyclopedia of Cultural Anthropology, Encyclopedia of World Cultures,* and other reference works and publications. This site is maintained by a consortium of universities; its data files are open only to students and faculty at member universities.

About this Chapter

Anthropologists, in their study of human culture, have been able to document that the exercise of power and the division of labor within the family constitute the most basic power relationship, the one from which true political power structures develop. What causes these structures to develop? Why should we need to control each other's behavior, and how do we manage to do it? How do anthropologists document the growth of power relationships? How, in fact, do they approach the study of something as diverse as human culture?

These questions were the focus of Chapter 3. Now that you have read it, you should be able to

- describe how power in society is exercised and for what purposes
- discuss how and why the family is the fundamental social unit in which power relationships originate
- discuss the changing roles of women in American society

- discuss the stages of development of power relationships and the factors that influence this development
- discuss anthropological approaches to the study of culture

DISCUSSION QUESTIONS

1. Describe how societies attempt to control the behavior of their members. Discuss the four broad purposes for which societies exercise power.
2. Describe how power and relationships begin within the family and how they develop into political organizations. What effect can warfare have on the power structure?
3. Choose a "subculture" that is familiar to you. If you were asked to explain in anthropological terms what sets this subculture apart from the society at large, what cultural categories would you examine? Identify the variations in lifestyle that make this a subculture.
4. Describe how an anthropologist of the functionalist school would approach the study of culture.
5. Discuss Ruth Benedict's contributions to anthropology.
6. Identify the characteristics of marriage that are found in all societies. Explain why the family is the most important social group.
7. Discuss changes in the American family. Comment on the continuing strength of family life, the number of families with a single adult, and the declining birthrate.
8. Discuss the changing roles of women in American society, particularly their changing role in the workforce.
9. Describe the broad stages of development of power relationships and the power groups associated with them. Compare these groups in terms of leadership, economic systems, patterns of warfare, population density, and patterns of settlement. How have anthropological studies contributed to our understanding of these power relationships?
10. "Culture is learned. . . . Culture is transferred from one generation to another, but . . . it is *not* genetically transmitted." What arguments do sociobiologists advance against this contention? Why does sociobiology arouse so much controversy? Identify the areas of human social behavior that sociobiologists believe may be genetically directed. Discuss your opinions about the relative effects on human behavior of genetics and culture.

Chapter 4

Power and Social Class

POWER PYRAMIDS AND PECKING ORDERS

All known societies have some system of ranking their members along a superiority-inferiority scale. Although many societies claim to grant "equality" to their members, in no society have people in fact been considered equal. The **stratification** of society involves the *classification* of individuals and the *ranking* of classifications on a superiority-inferiority scale. This system of classification and ranking is itself a source of prestige, wealth, income, authority, and power.

Individuals can be classified on a wide variety of characteristics—physical strength, fighting prowess, family lineage, ethnicity or race, age, gender, religion, birth order, and so on. But *the most important bases of stratification in a modern industrial society are the various roles that individuals play in the economic system.*

Individuals are ranked according to how they make their living and how much control they exercise over the livelihood of others. Ranking by occupation and control of economic resources occurs not only in the United States but in most other modern nations as well.[1]

The evaluation of individuals along a superiority-inferiority scale means, of course, a differential distribution of prestige. Thus, the top strata will receive

stratification
classifying people and ranking the classifications on a superiority-inferiority scale

stratification results in inequality
deference

styles of life

wealth and income

power

the *deference* of individuals who are ranked below them. Deference may take many forms: acquiescence in the material advantages or privileges of the elite (the use of titles and symbols of rank, distinctive clothing, housing, and automobiles); accordance of influence and respect; acceptance of leadership in decision making; and so on. The stratification system also involves *different styles of life:* foods eaten, magazines and books read, places of residence, favorite sports, schools attended, pronunciation and accent, recreational activities, and so forth. In addition, of course, the stratification system is associated with the *uneven distribution of wealth and income:* In every society, higher-ranking persons enjoy better housing, clothing, food, automobiles, and other material goods and services than persons ranked lower on the scale.

Finally, the stratification system involves the *unequal distribution of power*—the ability to control the acts of others. Sociologists agree that power and stratification are closely related, but they disagree on the specific value of this relationship. Some theorize that power is a *product* of economic well-being, prestige, or status. Others believe that power *determines* the distribution of wealth, prestige, and status.[2]

social class
a category and ranking in the stratification system

The stratification system creates social classes. The term **social class** simply refers to all individuals who occupy a broadly similar category and ranking in the stratification system. Members of the same social class may or may not interact or even realize that they have much in common. Because all societies have stratification systems, all societies have social classes.

STRATIFICATION IN AMERICAN SOCIETY

Social classes are of interest to sociologists, with their concern for the relationships among individuals and groups. Sociologists have devised several methods of identifying and measuring social stratification. These include: (1) the *subjective method,* in which individuals are asked how they see themselves in the class system; (2) the *reputational method,* in which individuals are asked to rank positions in the class system; and (3) the *objective method,* in which social scientists observe characteristics that discriminate among patterns of life they associate with social class.

methods of identifying and measuring stratification

⌐ Subjective Self-Classification

subjective identification
individuals identify their own social class

The American ideology encompasses the notion that status should be based on personal qualities and achievements. Individuals in a free society should have the opportunity to achieve the social rankings they can earn by ability, effort, and moral worth. These individuals are supposed to rise or fall according to their merits. In view of this ideology, it is not surprising that most Americans think of themselves as middle class. Nearly nine out of ten will describe themselves as middle class when they are forced to choose between this term and either upper or lower class. It is apparent that to characterize oneself as upper class is regarded as "snobbish," and to view oneself as lower class

TABLE 4-1

CLASS-IFYING OURSELVES

Question: If you were asked to use one of these four names for your social class, which would you say you belong to?

	1949	1975–1988	1996–1998
Upper class	2	3	3
Middle class	32	45	49
Working class	60	48	44
Lower class	6	4	4

SOURCE: Data derived from various surveys by the National Opinion Research Center. Early years reported in *The American Enterprise* (May/June 1993): 82–83.

is to admit that one is a loser in the great game of life. Even people who admit to being poor consider it an insult to be called "lower class."[3]

However, the fact that most Americans label themselves as middle class does not mean that American society is one big middle-class society. In fact, when *working class* is added to the list of choices, and individuals are asked for subjective evaluations of their own class membership, a different picture emerges. When given the option, about 44 percent of Americans identify themselves as "working class," and only slightly more identify themselves as "middle class." About 4 percent say they are "lower class," and even fewer, 2 to 3 percent, say they are "upper class." Over time "middle class" appears to be gaining in popularity as a label people apply to themselves.[4] (See Table 4-1.)

REPUTATIONAL PRESTIGE

Occupations differ in their reputational prestige. The prestige rankings of occupations is often used as a measure of the stratification system of modern societies. It is not polite to ask people how much money they make or how much money they have accumulated, but it is socially acceptable to ask what they do for a living. Often people ask others this question in order to identify social ranking.

Occupational prestige scores obtained from national surveys are fairly consistent (see Table 4-2). Note that prestige is not exactly the equivalent of income, although occupations near the top generally pay more than those at the bottom. ("College professor" is a notable exception.) Prestigious occupations, in addition to paying well, also tend to involve substantial authority; in contrast, close supervision and taking orders lower the prestige of occupations. Moreover, most highly ranked occupations require extensive education; indeed, some sociologists believe that education is the most important single factor influencing occupational prestige rankings.[5] Finally, it is interesting to note that most prestigious jobs are

reputational identification
individuals ranking the prestige of occupations

TABLE 4-2

OCCUPATIONAL PRESTIGE RANKINGS

Separate national surveys indicate that Americans are quite consistent in their ranking of various occupations.

Occupation	Ranking[a]	Occupation	Ranking[b]
Physician	82	Physician	95.8
College/university professor	78	Lawyer	90.1
Lawyer	76	College professor	90.1
Bank officer	72	Architect	88.8
Architect	71	Stockbroker	81.7
Airplane pilot	70	Electrical engineer	79.5
Clergy	69	Registered nurse	75.0
Secondary school teacher	63	Accountant	71.2
Registered nurse	62	High school teacher	70.2
Pharmacist	61	Grade school teacher	65.4
Elementary school teacher	60	Social worker	63.2
Electrician	49	Electrician	62.5
Machinist	48	Insurance agent	62.5
Police officer	48	Private secretary	60.9
Bookkeeper	48	Plumber	58.7
Insurance agent	47	Police officer	58.3
Secretary	46	Carpenter	53.5
Firefighter	44	Office secretary	51.3
Mail carrier	42	Auto mechanic	44.9
Farmer	41	Postal clerk	42.3
Welder	40	Beautician	42.1
Auto body repairperson	37	Truck driver	40.1
TV repairperson	35	Hairdresser	39.4
Hairdresser	33	Cashier	35.6
Bulldozer operator	33	Hospital aide	29.5
Truck driver	32	Assembly-line worker	28.3
Cashier	31	Delivery truck driver	26.9
File clerk	30	Housekeeper	25.3
Taxi driver	22	Coal miner	24.0
Bartender	20	Server in a restaurant	22.1
Waiter/waitress	20	Short-order cook	21.5
Farm laborer	18	Baby-sitter	18.3
Car washer	17	Garbage collector	16.3
		Janitor	12.5

SOURCES: (a)Adapted from *General Social Surveys, 1972–1996: Cumulative Codebook* (Chicago: National Opinion Research Center, 1999); (b)Adapted from C. E. Bose and Peter H. Rossi, "Gender and Jobs," *American Sociological Review* 48 (1983): 316–330.

"white-collar" occupations that involve mental activity rather than "blue-collar" occupations that require physical labor. These rankings have remained stable for several decades.

OBJECTIVE CLASSIFICATIONS

The principal **objective criteria** of social class are income, occupation, and education. If sociologists are correct in the assumption that occupation and control of economic resources are the source of stratification in society, then these indexes are the best available measures of class. Certainly income, jobs, and education are unequally distributed in American society, as they are in all other societies.

College graduates comprise about one quarter of the adults in the United States (see Figure 4-1). Over 82 percent are high school graduates, about 18 percent having dropped out of formal education without a high school diploma. This is a dramatic increase in formal education over previous generations.

Income is closely related to education. Generally individuals who have acquired higher educations tend to enjoy higher annual incomes. However, Table 4-3 also shows that there are separate scales by which income is distributed—one by gender and one by race. Women and blacks with equivalent educations tend to earn less than men and whites.

objective identification
ranking by occupation, income, or education

FIGURE 4-1

EDUCATIONAL ATTAINMENT

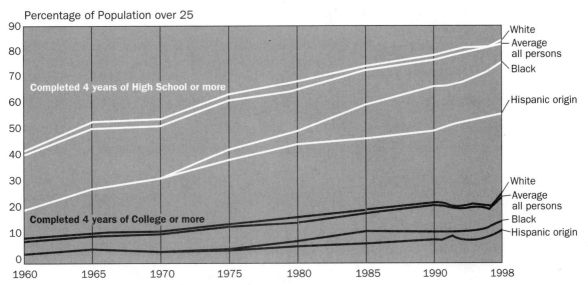

SOURCE: U.S. Bureau of the Census, *Statistical Abstract of the United States 1999,* 169.

TABLE 4-3

EDUCATION AND EARNINGS

	Mean Earnings				
	All persons	Men	Women	Whites	Blacks
Not a high school graduate	$16,124	$19,575	$10,725	$16,598	$13,185
High school graduate only	22,895	28,307	16,906	23,618	18,980
College Associate Degree	29,872	36,392	24,009	30,509	25,527
College Bachelor's Degree	40,478	50,056	30,119	41,439	32,062
Master's Degree	51,183	63,220	38,337	52,475	40,610
Professional Degree	95,148	109,206	62,113	97,487	51,004

SOURCE: U.S. Bureau of the Census, *Statistical Abstract of the United States 1999* (Washington D.C.: U.S. Government Printing Office, 1999), 170.

RACE AND ETHNICITY

Ethnic and racial stratification is visible on virtually all measures of social class—income, education, occupation. For example, in Figure 4-1, showing adult educational attainment levels since 1960, while all groups have gained in education, African-American and especially Hispanic high school and college completion percentages remain below those of whites. The educational gap between blacks and whites has narrowed somewhat over the years, but not the gap between Hispanics and whites. We will examine "Power, Race, and Gender" in greater detail in Chapter 10.

WHY DO WE HAVE SOCIAL CLASSES?

Sociologists disagree on why societies distribute wealth, power, and prestige unequally. On one side are the *functional theorists,* who argue that stratification is necessary and perhaps inevitable for maintaining society. On the other side are the *conflict theorists,* who argue that stratification results from the selfish interests of groups trying to preserve their advantages over others.[6]

FUNCTIONAL THEORY

functional theory
inequality is necessary to get people to work harder in more demanding jobs that require longer training and greater skills

The functional argument might be summarized as follows:

- Certain positions are more important to a society's survival than other positions and require special skills. For example, in most societies, occupations such as governor, physician, teacher, and priest are considered vital.
- Only a few persons in society have the ability (intelligence, energy, personality) to perform well in these positions.

- These positions require persons who do have ability to undergo extensive training and education before they occupy these positions.
- In order to motivate able people to endure the training and to sacrifice their time and energy for education, society must provide them with additional rewards.
- The result is social inequality, with some classes of people receiving more rewards than others. Inequality is inevitable and essential in order to ensure "that the most important positions are conscientiously filled by the most qualified persons."[7]

In other words, an expectation of inequality is essential in getting people to work harder in more difficult jobs that require longer training and greater skill.

CONFLICT THEORY

In contrast, **conflict theory** focuses on the struggle among competing groups in society over scarce resources. Conflict theorists have argued as follows:

conflict theory
inequality is imposed on society by those who want to retain their wealth and power

- People who possess property, income, power, or prestige—the upper classes—simply wish to protect their position in society. Thus, the stratification system is perpetuated.
- There are many "functionally important" positions in society that are not highly rewarded. It might be argued that an electrician, an auto mechanic, or a plumber is just as important to the survival of society as is a doctor or a lawyer.
- Many persons in the lower classes have the ability to perform in high-status occupations, but because of unequal educational opportunities, they never get the chance to do so.
- Wealth is not the only way of motivating people. Conceivably, societies might reward people merely by recognizing their services. Cooperation could then replace competition as a motivating force.
- Stratification negatively affects the thinking of members of the lower class. Stratification may even be "dysfunctional" to society if it fosters feelings of suspicion, hostility, and disloyalty to society among those in the lower classes.

In short, the stratification system is imposed on society by those at the top. It allows them to use their power and prestige to keep what they have. Later in this chapter we will examine the ideas of Karl Marx, who argued that the struggle between classes was the driving force in history and politics.

INEQUALITY IN AMERICA

Income is a key component of stratification, and income is unequally distributed in all societies. As long as societies reward skills, talents, knowledge, hard work, innovation, initiative, and risk taking, there will be inequalities of income. But the question remains: How much inequality is required to provide adequate rewards and incentives for education, training, work, enterprise, and risk?

INCOME DISTRIBUTIONS

measuring inequality
percentage of total national income received by each fifth of income earners

Let us try to systematically examine income inequality in America. Table 4-4 divides all American families into five groups—from the lowest one-fifth in personal income to the highest one-fifth—and shows the percentage of total family personal income received by each group over the years. (If perfect income equality existed, each fifth would receive 20 percent of all family personal income, and it would not even be possible to rank fifths from highest to lowest.) The poorest one-fifth received 3.5 percent of all family personal income in 1929; by 1970, this group had increased its share of all family personal income to 5.4 percent. (Most of the increase occurred during World War II.) The highest one-fifth received 54.4 percent of all family personal income in 1929; by 1970, this percentage has declined to 40.9. And the income share received by the top 5 percent of families declined from 30 percent in 1929 to 15.6 percent in 1970.

RISING INCOME INEQUALITY

increased inequality since 1970

Note, however, an *increase* in inequality in the United States since 1970. The income share of the lowest group of families has declined from 5.4 to 4.2 percent, while the income share of the highest group has risen from 40.9 to 47.3. And the income share of the top 5 percent of American families has risen from 15.6 to 20.7 percent.

TABLE 4-4

INCOME INEQUALITY

Percentage Distribution of Family Personal Income,
by Quintiles, and Top 5 Percent

Quintiles	1929	1970	1980	1990	1998
Lowest	3.5	5.4	5.2	4.5	4.2
Second	9.0	12.2	11.6	10.7	9.9
Third	13.8	17.6	17.5	16.6	15.7
Fourth	19.3	23.9	24.1	24.1	23.0
Highest	54.4	40.9	41.5	44.2	47.3
Top 5 percent	30.0	15.6	15.6	17.1	20.7

SOURCE: U.S. Bureau of the Census.

Social scientists and policy makers have voiced concern over this reversal of the historical trend toward greater income equality. This recent increase in inequality appears to be a product of several social and economic trends: (1) the relative decline of the manufacturing sector of the economy, with its middle-income blue-collar jobs, and the ascendancy of the information and service sectors, with a combination of high-paying and low-paying jobs; (2) an increase in the number of two-wage families, making single-wage households relatively less affluent; (3) demographic trends that include larger proportions of aged and larger proportions of female-headed families; and (4) global competition, which lowers wages in unskilled and semiskilled jobs while rewarding people in high-technology, high-productivity occupations.

INEQUALITY OF WEALTH

Inequalities of wealth in the United States are even greater than inequalities of income.[8] *Wealth* is the total value of a family's assets—bank accounts, stocks, bonds, mutual funds, business equity, houses, cars, and major appliances—minus outstanding debts, such as credit card balances, mortgages, and other loans.

The top 1 percent of families in the United States own almost 40 percent of all family wealth (see Figure 4-2). Inequality of wealth appeared to be diminishing until the mid-1970s, but in recent years it has surged sharply. Not surprisingly, age is the key determinant of family wealth; persons fifty to sixty-five are by far the wealthiest, with persons over sixty-five close behind; young families generally have less than one-third of the assets of older retirees.

FIGURE 4-2

DISTRIBUTION OF FAMILY WEALTH

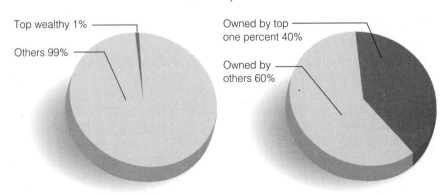

Total family wealth

Top wealthy 1%

Others 99%

Owned by top one percent 40%

Owned by others 60%

SOURCE: U.S. Bureau of the Census, *Statistical Abstract of the United States 1999*, 488.

EQUALITY OF OPPORTUNITY

equality of opportunity
equal chances for success based on ability, work, initiative, and luck

But most Americans are concerned more with equality of opportunity than with equality of results. (See Cross-National Perspective, "Beliefs about Equality and Opportunity.") **Equality of opportunity** refers to the ability to make of oneself what one can, to develop talents and abilities, and to be rewarded for work, initiative, and achievement. Equality of opportunity means that everyone comes to the same starting line in life with the same chance of success and that whatever differences develop over time do so as a result of abilities, talents, initiative, hard work, and perhaps good luck. Americans do not generally resent the fact that physicians, engineers, airline pilots, or others who have spent time and energy acquiring particular skills make more money than those whose jobs require fewer skills and less training. Nor do most Americans resent the fact that people who risk their own time and money to build a business, bring new or better products to market, and create jobs for others make more money than their employees. Nor do many Americans begrudge multi-million-dollar incomes to sports figures, rock singers, or movie stars, whose talents entertain the public. Indeed, few Americans object when someone wins a million-dollar lottery, as long as everyone had an equal chance at winning.

EQUALITY OF RESULTS

equality of results
equal incomes regardless of ability, work, or initiative

Equality of results refers to the equal sharing of income and material rewards regardless of one's condition in life. Equality of results means that everyone starts *and finishes* the race together, regardless of ability, talent, initiative, or work. Most Americans support a "floor" on income and material well-being—a level below which no one, regardless of their condition, should

TABLE 4-5

AMERICAN OPINION ON WEALTH ACCUMULATION

"People should be allowed to accumulate as much wealth as they can even if some make millions while others live in poverty."

	Strongly Agree or Agree (%)	Neither Agree nor Disagree (%)	Strongly Disagree or Disagree (%)
Total	56%	11%	30%
Income level			
Under $15,000	51%	12%	33%
$15,000 to $19,999	59%	7%	33%
$20,000 to $29,999	54%	11%	34%
$30,000 to $49,999	60%	11%	27%
$50,000 to $74,999	60%	10%	27%
$75,000 and up	65%	12%	22%

SOURCE: Everett Carl Ladd and Karlyn H. Bowman, *Attitudes Toward Economic Inequality* (Washington, D.C.: AEI Press, 1998).

CROSS-NATIONAL PERSPECTIVE
Beliefs about Equality and Opportunity

American social culture emphasizes equality of opportunity over equality of results. The Western European democracies also foster a belief in equality of opportunity but are much more inclined toward *equality of results*—reducing income differences between people—than Americans. Americans generally believe that government should provide a *floor*, or safety net, to protect people against true hardship; but they are generally unwilling to place a *ceiling* on incomes, or to give government the power to equalize income differences among people. Europeans are more likely than Americans to perceive obstacles to equality of opportunity in their countries. Thus, for example, Europeans are more likely than Americans to think that "coming from a wealthy family" or "having political connections" is very important for getting ahead in life. The following three tables demonstrate the various cross-national beliefs about equality and opportunity:

1. "It is the government's responsibility to reduce income differences between people."

	Percent agree
Italy	81
Hungary	77
Netherlands	64
Great Britain	62
Germany	56
Australia	42
United States	29

2. "Differences in income in my country are too large."

	Percent strongly agree
Austria	47
Italy	44
Hungary	41
Great Britain	27
Germany	25
Netherlands	19
Switzerland	19
Australia	14
United States	12

3. "For getting ahead in life, how important is . . . "

	"coming from a wealthy family?" Percent very important	"having political connections?" Percent very important
Italy	40	55
Hungary	34	30
Austria	30	43
Germany	25	23
Great Britain	22	7
Australia	18	15
Switzerland	15	25
United States	14	9
Netherlands	11	7

SOURCES: Table 1: Gallup International Research Institute as reported in *U.S. News & World Report,* August 7, 1989, 25. Tables 2 and 3: International Social Survey Program, 1987, as reported in Rodney Stark, *Sociology,* 5th ed. (Belmont, Calif.: Wadsworth, 1994), 273.

be permitted to fall. But very few Americans want to place a "ceiling" on income or wealth. This unwillingness to limit top income extends to nearly all groups in America, the poor as well as the rich (see Table 4-5). Generally Americans want people who cannot provide for themselves to be well cared for, especially children, the elderly, the ill, and the disabled. However, most Americans believe that a "fair" economic system rewards people for ability and hard work.

SOCIAL MOBILITY: THE UPS AND DOWNS

social mobility
the movement of people upward or downward in social class

Although all societies are stratified, societies differ greatly in social mobility—that is, in the opportunity people have to move from one class to another. The **social mobility** of individuals may be *upward*, when they achieve a status higher than that of their parents, or *downward*, when their status is lower. In the United States, there is a great deal of social mobility, both upward and downward.

The United States describes itself as the land of opportunity. The really important political question may be how much real opportunity exists for individual Americans to improve their conditions in life relative to others. The impression given earlier by Table 4-4 is one of a static distribution system, with families permanently placed in upper or lower fifths of income earners. But there is considerable evidence of both upward and downward movement by people among income groups. Children do not always end up in the same income category as their parents.

TRADITIONAL UPWARD MOBILITY

Throughout most of the twentieth century, Americans experienced more upward mobility than downward mobility. As the economy grew and changed, most Americans were able to improve their conditions in life or, at least, see their children do better than themselves. Early in the century, higher paid factory jobs replaced farm work. Later, the ranks of professional, managerial, sales, and other "white collar" workers grew. By 1970, white-collar workers outnumbered "blue-collar" workers—machine operators, mechanics, trade and craft workers, and laborers. Many sons and daughters of working-class parents were able to go to college and prepare themselves for careers in white-collar occupations.

THE SHRINKING MIDDLE CLASS

But in recent years, this general movement of upward social mobility has been replaced by a pattern of both upward and downward mobility. Today's young people can no longer assume that they will be better off than their parents. America may be experiencing a "shrinking middle class."

deindustrialization
a decline in the manufacturing sector of the economy

The American economy is undergoing **deindustrialation**—a decline in its manufacturing sector accompanied by increases in its financial, technical, information, and service sectors. Deindustrialation had resulted in the loss of millions of well-paying, mostly unionized, blue-collar jobs in manufacturing, including the once-dominant American steel and auto industries. In the 1950s and 1960s, these jobs allowed noncollege-educated workers to own their own homes in the suburbs and send their children to college. But the new information age economy replaced many of these jobs with two very different categories of jobs. The first category consists of highly skilled, highly paid technical jobs, such as computer engineer, systems analyst, information specialist, financial and investment adviser, accountant, and science technician. The second category consists of unskilled and semiskilled, low-paying service jobs, such as data processor, health-care aide, food server, and packager. This division of the occupational structure into high-paying and low-paying jobs adds to both inequality in society and to a pattern of upward and downward mobility.

Deindustrialization has been accompanied by economic **globalization**—increasing exchanges of goods and services by firms in different countries. Today, about one-quarter of the world's total economic output is sold in a country other than the one in which it was produced. Global competition heavily impacts the American economy and social structure. The opening of world markets benefits America's most productive workers—its highly skilled, well-educated, high-tech workers who are capable of competing and winning in the global marketplace. But at the same time, America's unskilled and semiskilled workers are placed at a serious disadvantage in competition with workers in less-developed countries. It is difficult to maintain the wage levels of American manufacturing jobs in the face of competition from huge numbers of extremely low-paid workers in economies such as Mexico, China, and India. Thus, the benefits of globalization flow unequally: Upper middle-class Americans benefit, while lower middle-class Americans suffer.

globalization
increasing exchanges of goods and services by firms in different countries

MOBILITY AND EDUCATION

Education is the most common path to social mobility. As indicated earlier, education is closely related to earnings (see Table 4-3). It is not surprising, then, that leaders in business and government in the United States argue that the "solution" to worsening inequality in downward social mobility is for American workers to improve their productivity through better education and increased training. According to the *Economic Report of the President,* "Ultimately, the only lasting solution to the increase in wage inequality . . . is better education and increased training, to allow low-income workers to take advantage of the technological changes that raise productivity." (However, for an argument, inequality is largely a result of inherited intelligence. See Controversies in Social Science, "The Bell Curve.")

CLASS AS A DETERMINANT OF LIFESTYLE

Life in each social class is different. Differences in ways of life mean differences in culture, or rather (because the style of life in each class is really a variant of one common culture in American society) a division of the culture into *subcultures.* Class subcultures have been described by many sociologists. Class differences exist in almost every aspect of life: health,

CONTROVERSIES IN SOCIAL SCIENCE

The Bell Curve

Two social scientists generated intense controversy following publication of their book *The Bell Curve: Intelligence and Class Structure in American Life* in 1994. Richard Herrnstein and Charles Murray set forth the argument that general intelligence largely determines success in life. General intelligence, they contend, is distributed among the population in a bell-shaped curve, with most people clustered around the median, a smaller "cognitive elite" with higher intelligence occupying one end, and an unfortunate few trailing behind (see Figure 4–3). Over time intelligence is becoming even more necessary for the performance of key jobs in the "information society." The result will be the continuing enhancement of the power and wealth of the cognitive elite and the further erosion of the lifestyle of the less intelligent.

Even more controversial is Herrnstein and Murray's contention that general intelligence is mostly (60 percent) genetic. And since intelligence is mostly inherited, they argue that programs to assist the underprivileged have few practical effects.

The cognitive elite, they predict, will continue to distance themselves from the masses in knowledge, skills, technical competence, income, and power, while social problems will be concentrated among the "dullest." Indeed, the authors

Cognitive Class	High School Dropout %	Women on Welfare Assistance %	Mean Age at First Childbearing	Criminal Convictions % (Young white males)
I Very Bright	0	0	27.2	3
II Bright	0	2	25.5	7
III Normal	6	8	23.4	15
IV Dull	35	17	21.0	21
V Very Dull	55	31	19.8	14

SOURCE: Adapted from various chapters in Herrnstein and Murray, *The Bell Curve: Intelligence and Class Structure in American Life* (New York: Free Press, 1994).

hygiene, vocabulary, table manners, standards of right and wrong, recreation and entertainment, religion, sexual activity, family and child-rearing practices, political beliefs and attitudes, club memberships, dress, birthrates, attitudes toward education, toilet training, reading habits, and so on (see Table 4-6). It is impossible to provide a complete description of all the class differences that have been reported by sociologists. Moreover, class lifestyles overlap, and in America there are no rigid boundaries between classes. Class subcultures should be thought of as being on a *continuous scale* with styles of life that blend; thus there are many "in-between" positions. And finally, it should be remembered that any generalizations about broad classes in the United States do not necessarily describe the lifestyle of any particular individuals; the following paragraphs are merely a general summary of the subcultures.

amass statistics showing that educational deficiencies, emotional problems, welfare reliance, early childbirth, and even criminal behavior are disproportionately concentrated in low-intelligence groups.

But critics of *The Bell Curve* point out that there is no consensus on the role of genetics in intelligence. Indeed, recent research on infant development indicates that brain activity and the interconnections among brain cells are greatly impacted by early human interaction. Infants who are frequently coddled, spoken to, sung to, etc., exhibit more brain activity on PET scans than those with little environmental stimuli (see Chapter 5). Moreover, the implication of *The Bell Curve* thesis is that social classes and elitism are both natural and evitable, and that most efforts to ensure equality of opportunity are useless. This thesis might be seen as a justification for widening inequality in society. Finally, *The Bell Curve's* authors add a racial dimension to their discussion that is unnecessary to their thesis. They contend that African Americans on average score fifteen IQ points below whites and that Asians on average score three points above. While they claim that these average racial scores should not matter if every individual were judged separately on IQ, clearly their argument reinforces racial stereotypes.

FIGURE 4-3

Population Distribution of IQ Scores

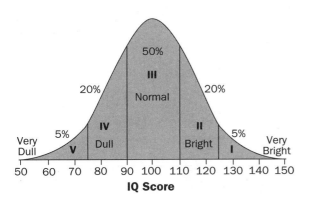

The Upper Class

The typical upper-class individual is future-oriented and cosmopolitan. Persons of this class expect a long life, look forward to their future and the future of their children and grandchildren, and are concerned about what lies ahead for the community, the nation, and humanity. They are self-confident, believing that within limits they can shape their own destiny and that of the community. They are willing to invest in the future—that is, to sacrifice some present satisfaction in the expectation of enjoying greater satisfaction in time to come. They are self-respecting; they place great value on independence and creativity and on developing their potential to the fullest. The goals of life include individuality, self-expression, and personal happiness. Wealth permits a wide variety of entertainment

TABLE 4-6

SOCIAL CLASS LIFESTYLES

	Approximate Percentage of Population	Representative Occupations	Likely Education	Leisure Activities	News Sources
Upper Class	7	Banker Corporate executive Physician Architect	Advanced degree (M.B.A., M.D.) Elite schools	Theater, travel, tennis, yachting, sailing, charity celebrity events	*The Wall Street Journal, The New York Times, New Yorker Magazine,* PBS, Internet
Middle Class	38	Small business owner Lawyer Professor Teacher Accountant Corporation middle manager	B.A. degree and some professional degrees (M.A., Ph.D., L.L.B.) State universities	Golfing, travel, parties, watching TV, sports, church events	*Time, Newsweek, U.S. News & World Report,* Local paper, TV, Internet
Working Class	40	Electrician Machinist Police officer Secretary Cashier Bartender	High school, some college, including A.A. degree Community college, vo-tech schools	Bowling, movies, visiting friends, watching TV, sports, church	*National Enquirer,* Local paper, TV
Lower Class	15	Unskilled, minimum-wage workers, or unemployed and welfare	High school dropout	Watching television	TV or none

and recreation: theater, concerts, art, yachting, tennis, skiing, travel abroad, and so on.

Upper-class individuals take a tolerant attitude toward unconventional behavior in sex, the arts, fashions, lifestyles, and so forth. They feel they have a responsibility to "serve" the community and to "do good." They are active in "public service" and contribute time, money, and effort to worthy causes. This "public-regardingness" inclines them toward "liberal" politics; the upper classes provide the leadership for the liberal wings of both the Republican and Democratic parties.

THE MIDDLE CLASS

Middle-class individuals are also future-oriented; they plan ahead for themselves and their children. But they are not likely to be as cosmopolitan as the upper-class person, because they are more concerned with their immediate families than with "humanity" in the abstract. They are confident about their

Entertainment for the upper class might include a polo match.

ability to influence their own futures and those of their children, but they do not really expect to have an effect on community, state, or national events.

Investing time, energy, and effort in self-improvement and getting ahead are principal themes of life. Middle-class people strongly want their children to go to college and acquire the kind of formal training that will help them get ahead. Recreation and entertainment include golf, swimming, movies, sports events, and travel usually within the United States. Middle-class individuals tend to be middle-of-the-road or conservative in politics and generally vote Republican. Though they join voluntary organizations, many of which are formally committed to community service, they give less of their money and effort to public causes.

THE WORKING CLASS

Working-class people are obliged to concern themselves more with the present then the future. They expect their children to make their own way in life. They are self-respecting and self-confident, but these feelings extend over a narrower range of matters than they do in middle-class individuals. The horizon of the working class is limited by job, family, immediate friends, and neighborhood.

Working-class individuals work to maintain themselves and their families; they do not look at their jobs as a means of getting ahead or as a means of self-expression. Their deepest attachment is to family; most visiting is done with relatives rather than friends. Working-class persons usually do

CROSS-NATIONAL PERSPECTIVE

Global Inequalities

Three of every four persons in the world today live in less-developed countries (LDCs)[a]. Traditionally, these countries encompassed most of the globe: South and Central America; Africa; the Middle East, with the exception of Israel; and Asia, with the exception of Japan and the rapidly developing "Four Dragons"—Hong Kong, South Korea, Taiwan, and Singapore.

While this broad category of less-developed countries is commonly used by social scientists and others, it is important to remember that it encompasses societies with different languages, diverse people, and distinct cultures. Nonetheless, there are common characteristics of less developed countries that can be observed by visitors as well as by social scientists. Americans can better appreciate their own society by knowing how the majority of the world's population lives.

Poverty

Poverty in LDCs is widespread and severe. The vast majority of the world's population lives well below the standard of living of America's poorest families. Hunger and ill health are common. It is estimated that one out of every five persons in the world today does not eat enough to enable him or her to work; one child in four dies before reaching the age of five. Life expectancy is short (see table).

Inequality

The limited resources of most LDCs are unequally distributed, with small elites controlling large proportions of land and wealth. In some societies, a caste system determines one's social position at birth with no opportunity for upward social mobility. The subordination of women in these societies is very pronounced; women are commonly denied education, land ownership, and a voice in public affairs.

Traditionalism

The cultures of LDCs generally place great value on traditional ways of life passed down, virtually unchanged, from generation to generation. Traditionalism also means the acceptance of one's life and one's fate, however poor. It also means resisting innovation and change.

High Fertility

Birthrates are generally very high in the LDCs. Family reliance on human labor, high infant mortality rates, the low status of women, and the ab-

[a]A note on terminology: Less-developed countries (LDCs) were once referred to as the "Third World." This term was used during the Cold War (see Chapter 14) to distinguish between industrialized Western democracies ("First World"); the stagnating communist economies of Eastern Europe ("Second World"); and poorer, nonindustrialized societies in Asia, Africa, and Latin America ("Third World").

not belong to many organizations other than union and church. In their views toward others in the community, they are "private-regarding"; they believe they work hard for a living and feel others should do the same. They tend to look down on people who accept welfare unless those people are forced to do so by circumstances over which they have no control. When they vote, they generally vote Democratic, but they are often apathetic about politics. The working-class position in politics is motivated not by political ideology but by ethnic and party loyalties, by the appeal of personalities, or by occasional favors. For recreation the working-class individual turns to bowling, stock-car racing, circuses, fairs, and carnivals.

sence of birth control information or technology all contribute to high birthrates. China has attempted to force families to have only one child; sterilization and abortion are common, but so also are abortion of female fetuses only and female infanticide.

Primitive Technology

Most energy in these societies is directly supplied by human and animal muscle power. A lifetime of hard manual labor, just to meet minimum needs, confronts most of the people of the world. Animal labor is more common than farm machinery.

LIFE IN THE LESS-DEVELOPED WORLD

	GNP per capita (U.S. $)	Birthrate*	Life expectancy (years)	Infant mortality rate†
United States	29,080	14.2	76.3	6.7
Mexico	3,700	24.5	72.4	23.4
Colombia	2,180	24.0	70.9	23.2
Venezuela	3,480	21.5	73.3	25.5
Egypt	1,200	26.3	62.7	65.7
Nigeria	280	41.1	53.1	68.2
Kenya	340	29.9	46.5	58.8
Ghana	390	30.8	57.5	74.8
China	860	14.6	70.3	41.1
India	370	24.9	63.9	58.5
Pakistan	500	32.6	59.7	90.3
Bangladesh	360	24.8	61.1	67.1

*Live births per 1,000 population per year.
†Number of deaths of children under one year of age per 1,000 live births per year.

SOURCE: U.S. Bureau of the Census, *Statistical Abstract of the United States 1999,* 836, 841.

THE LOWER CLASS

Lower-class individuals must live from day to day. They have little confidence in their ability to influence what happens to them. Things happen *to* them; they do not *make* them happen. When they work, it is often from payday to payday, and they frequently drift from one unskilled job to another. Their self-confidence is low; they feel little attachment to community; and they tend to resent authority (for example, that of policemen, social workers, teachers, landlords, and employers). (For a look at the lower class in other countries, see Cross-National Perspective, "Global Inequalities.")

The working class generally finds entertainment of a different nature, such as this carnival.

The lower-class family is frequently headed by a woman. For the male off-spring of a lower-class matriarchal family, the future is often depressing, with defeat and frustration repeating themselves throughout his life. He may drop out of school in the eighth or ninth grade because of lack of success. Without parental supervision, and having little to do, he may get into trouble with the police. The police record will further hurt his chances of getting a job. With limited job skills, little self-discipline, and low aspiration levels, the lower-class male is not likely to find a steady job that will pay enough to support a family. Yet he yearns for the material standard of living of higher classes—a car, a television set, and other conveniences. Frequently, to compensate for defeat and frustration, the lower-class male will resort to risk taking, conquest, and fighting to assert his masculinity. Entertainment may be limited to drinking and gambling. Many aspects of lower-class culture are unattractive to women. Sociologist Herbert Gans wrote: "The woman tries to develop a stable routine in the midst of poverty and deprivation; the action-seeking man upsets it."[9]

SOCIAL CLASSES: CONFLICT AND CONCILIATION

class consciousness
believing that all members of one's class have similar political and economic interests, adverse to those of other classes

An awareness of class membership is not the same as class consciousness. **Class consciousness** is the belief that all members of one's social class have similar economic and political interests that are adverse to the interests of other classes and ought to be promoted through common action. As we

MASTERS OF SOCIAL THOUGHT
Karl Marx and the Class Struggle

Conflict between social classes is a central feature of communist ideology. In the opening of his famous *Communist Manifesto,* Karl Marx wrote:

> The history of all hitherto existing society is the history of class struggles. Freeman and slave, patrician and plebeian, lord and serf, guild-master and journeyman, in a word, oppressor and oppressed, . . . [a]

Karl Marx was born in Prussia in 1818. His parents were Jews who converted to Christianity when Marx was a child. He studied history, law, and philosophy at Bonn, Berlin, and Jena and received his doctor of philosophy degree in 1841. Soon after, he entered revolutionary socialist politics as a journalist and pamphleteer; he was expelled from Prussia and engaged in conspiratorial activities in France and Belgium from 1843 to 1849. *The Communist Manifesto,* written with Friedrich Engels, appeared in 1848 as a revolutionary pamphlet. In 1849 Marx fled to London, where he spent the remainder of his life writing occasional pamphlets on socialism, advising socialist leaders, and setting forth his views in a lengthy work, *Das Kapital.*

According to Marx, social classes develop on the basis of the different positions that individuals fulfill in the prevailing "mode of production"—that is, the economy. In an agricultural economy, the principal classes are landowner and tenant, serf, or slave; and in an industrial economy, the capitalist or "bourgeois" (owner of the factory) and the non-property-owning worker or "proletarian." The bourgeoisie have an interest in maximizing profit and seek to keep for themselves the surplus of profit that has been created by the worker. Workers are exploited in that they produce more than they receive in wages; this "surplus value" is stolen from the workers by the capitalists.

Marx viewed class consciousness as an important prerequisite to successful proletarian revolution. Class consciousness would increase as the proletariat grew in numbers, as workers communicated among themselves and achieved solidarity in unions and political organizations, and as conflict between workers and owners intensified.

The bourgeoisie would not relinquish their control over the means of production without a fight, and therefore violent revolution was necessary and inevitable. Marx said little about the details of revolution; this aspect of communist ideology was developed later by Lenin (see Chapter 9). But after the successful proletarian revolution, Marx envisioned a society without social classes. This *classless society* would be a "dictatorship of the proletariat" with all other social classes eliminated. The state would control the means of production, and everyone would be in the same relationship to the state as everyone else. Eventually, the state, which functions in bourgeois society to help the bourgeoisie oppress the masses, would gradually "wither away" in a communist society.

The truth is, of course, that neither capitalist societies nor communist societies conformed to Marx's analysis. (See "Why Communism Collapsed" in Chapter 9). Yet much of the history of the twentieth century centered on the rise and fall of communism in the world.

[a]Karl Marx, *The Communist Manifesto,* ed. A. J. P. Taylor (New York: Penguin, 1967), 79.

have already seen, Americans are *aware* of class membership, but members of the same class do not always share political interests, feel that collective class action is necessary, or see themselves as locked in a struggle against opposing classes. Few Americans believe in the militant ideology of class struggle. Americans do not have a strong sense of class consciousness.

Nonetheless, there is some evidence of awareness of class interest in voting behavior. Although Democratic and Republican candidates draw their support from all social classes in America, social-class bases of the Democratic and Republican parties are slightly different (see Chapter 7). Professional and managerial groups and other white-collar employees give greater support to the Republican Party than do skilled, semiskilled, and unskilled workers. Likewise, people with some college education tend to vote Republican more often than persons with a high school or grade school education do. Of course, not all the upper-class vote goes to the Republican Party, and not all the lower-class vote goes to the Democratic Party. In fact, the differences in voter support are not very great. But there is some indication that class has an impact on voting behavior.

ABSENCE OF CLASS CONFLICT

class conflict
conflict between upper and lower social classes over wealth and power

Why is there no militant class consciousness or **class conflict** in America? This is a difficult question to answer precisely, but we can summarize some of the factors that appear to help stabilize the existing class system in America and reduce class conflict:

factors in American life reducing class conflict
high standard of living

upward mobility

large middle class

widespread belief in the system

many cross-cutting allegiances

- a relatively high standard of living of Americans of all social classes
- a great deal of upward mobility in the American system, which diverts lower-class attention away from collective class action and focuses it toward individual efforts at "getting ahead"
- the existence of a large middle-income, middle-prestige class
- widespread belief in the legitimacy of the class structure and the resulting acceptance of it
- many cross-cutting allegiances of individuals to churches, communities, races, unions, professional associations, voluntary organizations, and so forth, which interfere with class solidarity

In stabilizing the class system, these factors also stabilize the existing distribution of power in America.

The American system has produced a high level of material comfort for the great majority of the population. The real possibilities of acquiring greater income and prestige have reinforced efforts to strive within the system rather than to challenge it. Even individuals who realize that their own social mobility is limited can transfer their hope and ambition to their children. A large middle class, diverse in occupation and ambiguous in political orientation, helps to blur potential lines of class identification and conflict. This class stands as a symbol and an embodiment of the reality of opportunity. A widely accepted set of ideologies, beliefs, and attitudes supports the existing system. Finally, cleavages caused by religious affiliations, ethnic backgrounds, and racial categories, as well as by other types of diversity (region, skill level, occupational group), have all worked against the development of unified class movements.

SOCIAL CLASS AND POLITICAL POWER

Government leadership is recruited mainly from the upper and upper-middle social classes. Most government officials, particularly at the national level (cabinet officers, presidential advisers, congressional representatives, Supreme Court judges, and so on), are members of the well-educated, prestigiously employed, successful, and affluent classes. With few exceptions, they are the children of professionals, business owners and managers, or successful farmers and landowners. Only a small minority are the children of hourly wage earners. The occupational characteristics of representatives also show that they are generally of higher social standing than their constituents; professional and business occupations dominate the halls of Congress. One reason is, of course, that congressional candidates are more likely to win the election if their occupations are socially "respectable" and provide opportunities for extensive public contacts. The lawyer, insurance agent, and real estate agent establish in their businesses the wide circle of friends necessary for political success. Another, subtler reason is that candidates and elected legislators must come from occupational groups with flexible work responsibilities. Lawyers, landowners, and business owners can adjust their work to the campaign and legislative schedules, whereas office and factory workers cannot.

social class and legislative power

LAWYERS IN POLITICS

The overrepresentation of lawyers as an occupational group in Congress and other public offices is particularly marked. (Lawyers constitute no more than two-tenths of 1 percent of the labor force.) Lawyers have always played a prominent role in the American political system. Twenty-five of the fifty-two signers of the Declaration of Independence and thirty-one of the fifty-five members of the Continental Congress were lawyers. The legal profession has also provided 70 percent of the presidents, vice presidents, and cabinet officers of the United States and one-third to one-half of all U.S. senators and members of the House of Representatives (see Table 4-7). Lawyers are in a reasonably high-prestige occupation, but so are physicians, businesspeople, and scientists. Why, then, do lawyers, rather than members of those other high-prestige groups, dominate the halls of Congress?

It is sometimes argued that lawyers bring a special kind of skill to Congress. Since their occupation is the representation of clients, they make no great change in occupation when they move from representing clients in private practice to representing constituents in Congress. Also, they are trained to deal with public policy as it is reflected in the statute books, so they may be reasonably familiar with public policy before entering Congress. But professional skills alone cannot explain the dominance of lawyers in public office. Another answer is that of all those in high-prestige occupations, only lawyers can really afford to neglect their careers for political activities. For the physician, the corporate businessperson, and the scientist, such slighting of their vocations is very costly. However, for the lawyer, political activity can be a positive advantage in

TABLE 4-7

Occupational Backgrounds of Congress Members

	House	Senate	Congress
			Total
Actor/Entertainer	1	1	2
Aeronautics	1		1
Agriculture	22	6	28
Artistic/Creative	2		2
Business/Banking	159	24	183
Clergy	1	1	2
Education	84*	13	97
Engineering	9		9
Health Care	3		3
Journalism	9*	8	17
Labor Organizing	1		1
Law	163	55	218
Law Enforcement	10		10
Medicine	15	2	17
Military	1	1	2
Professional Sports	2	1	3
Public Service/Politics	106	18	124
Real Estate	20	4	24
Technical/Trade	3		3
Miscellaneous	6		6

Because some members have more than one occupation, totals are higher than total memberships
Includes Rep. Bernard Sanders, 1-Vt.

SOURCE: *Congressional Quarterly,* figures for 106th Congress, 1999–2001.

terms of occupational advancement; free public advertising and opportunities to make contacts with potential clients are two important benefits. Yet another answer is that lawyers naturally have a monopoly on public offices in the legal and judicial system, and the office of judge or prosecuting attorney often provides a steppingstone to higher public office, including Congress. Finally, inasmuch as the tradition of lawyers in public office is well known, many politically ambitious young people enter law school, not so much with the expectation of practicing law in the future, but rather with the notion of using their law school experience as a springboard to a career in politics.

Social Class and Executive Power

Power in the *executive branch,* which most analysts now see as more important than Congress in policy formulation, is also exercised by individuals from the upper and upper-middle classes. Cabinet secretaries, undersecretaries, and top

TABLE 4-8

Social Backgrounds of Cabinet-Level Appointees
in Presidential Administrations

	Truman through Carter	Reagan	George Bush	Clinton	George W. Bush
Education					
Advanced degree	69%	68%	80%	89%	69%
Law degree	40	26	40	67	38
Ivy League degree	48	58	50	50	31
Ph.D.	19	16	25	22	15
No college degree	0	0	0	0	0
Women	4%	5%	10%	17%	23%
African Americans	4%	5%	5%	17%	15%

SOURCES: For Reagan, Bush, and Clinton administrations, see Thomas R. Dye, *Who's Running America? The Clinton Years*, 6th ed. (Englewood Cliffs, N.J.: Prentice-Hall, 1995); for Truman through Carter, see Phillip H. Burch, Jr., *Elites in American History*, vol. 3 (New York: Holmes and Meier, 1980).

civil servants tend to come disproportionately from Ivy League schools; most are lawyers or businesspeople at the time of their appointment; many accept lower salaries out of a sense of obligation to perform "public service"[10] (see Table 4-8).

UPPER-CLASS RULE?

We know that political power is largely in the hands of individuals from upper social classes, but what does this really mean for the great majority of Americans? We might *infer* that people drawn from upper social classes share values and interests different from those of the majority of people. On the other hand, several factors may modify the impact of upper social classes in politics. First, there may be considerable conflict among members of upper social classes about the basic directions of public policy—that is, despite similarity in social backgrounds, individuals may *not* share a consensus about public affairs. Competition rather than consensus may characterize their relationships. Second, the elite may be very "public-regarding" in their exercise of power; they may take the welfare of the masses into account as an aspect of their own sense of well-being. Indeed, there is a great deal of evidence that America's upper classes are liberal and reformist and that "do-goodism" is a widespread impulse. Many public leaders from very wealthy families of the highest social status (for instance, Franklin D. Roosevelt, Adlai Stevenson, and John F. Kennedy) have championed the interests of the poor and the downtrodden. Thus, upper-class values may foster public service rather than political exploitation. Third, upper-class leaders, whatever their values, can be held accountable for their exercise of power by the majority in elections. Our system of parties and elections forces public officials to compete for mass support to acquire public office and the political power that goes with it. This competition requires them to modify their public

upper-class power
modified by competition

public-regarding values

electoral accountability

MASTERS OF SOCIAL THOUGHT

C. Wright Mills and the Power Elite

The most popular and controversial analysis of power in the United States is *The Power Elite*, by sociologist C. Wright Mills. Since its appearance in 1956, most writers have been unable to discuss national power without reference to this important study.

According to Mills, power in the United States is concentrated at the top of the nation's corporate, governmental, and military organizations, which closely interlock to form a single structure of power: *a power elite*. Power rests in these three domains: "the corporation chieftains, the political directorate, and the warlords." Occasionally there is tension among them, but they share a broad consensus about the general direction of public policy. Other institutions (the family, churches, schools, and so forth) are subordinate to the three major institutions of power.

The power elite holds power because of its position at the top of the institutional structures of society. These people are powerful *not* because of any individual qualities—wealth, prestige, skill, or cunning—but because of the *institutional positions* they occupy. As society has concentrated more and more power in a few giant institutions, the people in command of these institutions have acquired enormous power over all of us. As Mills put it:

> *The history of modern society may readily be understood as the story of the enlargement and the centralization of the means of power—in economic, in political, and in military institutions.*[a]

Mills is aware that his description of power in the United States conflicts with the "pluralist" interpretation. But he believes that notions of powerholders who balance and compromise interests or who engage in competition between parties and groups apply to middle-level powerholders in America and not to the top power elite.

The *unity* of the top elite rests on several factors. First of all, these people are recruited from the same upper social classes; they have similar education, wealth, and upbringing. Moreover, they continue to associate with each other, reinforcing their common feelings. They belong to the same clubs, attend the same parties, meet at the same resorts, and serve on the same civic, cultural, and philanthropic committees.

Factions exist and individual ambitions clash, but their community of interest is far greater than any divisions among them. Perhaps what accounts for their consensus more than anything else is their experience in command positions in giant institutions. "As the requirements of the top places in each of the major hierarchies become similar, the types of men occupying these roles at the top—by selection and by training in the jobs—become similar."

Mills and his work are frequently cited by radical critics of American society. According to Mills, the power elite is guilty of "a higher immorality," that is, not necessarily personal corruption or even mistaken policies and deeds, but rather the moral insensitivity of institutional bureaucracy. More important, it is the failure of the power elite to be responsive and responsible to "knowledgeable publics." Mills implies that true democracy is possible only where persons in power are truly responsible to "men of Knowledge." He is not very specific about who the "men of Knowledge" are, but the reader is left with the impression that he means intellectuals like himself.

[a]C. Wright Mills, "The Structure of Power in American Society," in *Power, Politics and People: The Collected Writings of C. Wright Mills,* ed. Irving L. Horowitz (New York: Oxford University Press, 1963), 24.

statements and actions to fit popular preferences. Hence, in a democracy, the fact that the upper social classes tend to hold public office does not necessarily mean that the masses are oppressed, exploited, or powerless.

ON THE WEB

EXPLORING SOCIOLOGY

Sociology covers a very broad range of subject matter—social life, social change, and the social causes and consequences of human behavior. While this chapter has focused on power and social class, the subject matter of social class ranges from the intimate family to the hostile mob, from organized crime to religious cults, from the sociology of work to the sociology of sports.

American Sociological Association/Society for Applied Sociology. For a better understanding of the full range of sociology, one might begin by visiting the Web sites maintained by the American Sociological Association (ASA, www.asanet.org) and the Society for Applied Sociology (SAS, www.appliedsoc.org). The ASA site is oriented toward academic sociology, primarily teachers of sociology in colleges and universities, but it also provides student career information, including "Job Prospects for the BA Graduate." The SAS site is oriented toward practicing sociologists in government, health care, law enforcement, and human resources. It includes information on "Becoming a Sociolgist" and "Sociology Job Listings."

U.S. Census Bureau. Current information on income, education, and occupation of Americans, as well as information on poverty and inequality, can be found in U.S. Census Bureau data (www.census.gov). An "A to Z" index includes direct links to data on "income," "poverty," "inequality," and so on.

ABOUT THIS CHAPTER

After traveling to the new American nation in 1835, the French social commentator Alexis de Tocqueville wrote: "When it is birth alone, independent of wealth, which classes men in society, every one knows exactly what his own position is upon the social scale; he does not seek to rise, he does not fear to sink. . . . [But in America] as the social importance of men is no longer ostensibly and

permanently fixed by blood, and is infinitely varied by wealth, ranks still exist, but it is not easy clearly to distinguish at a glance those who respectively belong to them."* Thus, Tocqueville acknowledged that there were social classes in America, but unlike Europe at the time, class membership was based on wealth and achievement, not birth, and individuals could rise or fall in social position.

In this chapter, we looked at how Americans "stratify" themselves into social classes, how sociologists measure this stratification, and the relationship between social class and lifestyle and power. Now that you have read Chapter 4, you should be able to

- describe the stratification system and the methods that sociologists use to identify and measure stratification
- describe functional and conflict explanations of social classes
- define class consciousness and identify the factors that help to stabilize the existing class system in America
- discuss the basic notions set forth by Karl Marx about social classes and describe what some of the problems are in Marxist analysis
- discuss the relationships between social class and lifestyle and between social class and political power

DISCUSSION QUESTIONS

1. Discuss the social stratification system. Include in your discussion a description of the bases used for stratification, as well as the characteristics associated with the stratification system.
2. Describe the functional and conflict theories of social class.
3. If you were studying social class, what methods might you use to identify and measure social stratification? If in the course of your study you were to ask average Americans how they see themselves in the class system, what class would they choose, and why? How

*Alexis de Tocqueville, *Democracy in America* (New York: New American Library, 1956), p. 40.

might the respondents' subjective evaluations differ from the results you as a social scientist obtained? What are the objective criteria you would use to identify social class?

4. Choose two of the American social classes and contrast them according to orientation toward life, individual self-confidence, women's roles, activities and interests, and political participation and party identification.

5. Contrast class consciousness with class awareness. Discuss the factors that appear to stabilize the existing class system in the United States and reduce class conflict.

6. Distinguish between inequality and social mobility. How is inequality usually measured? How can we measure mobility?

7. Discuss Karl Marx's views of economic roles and class consciousness in the struggle for power among social classes.

8. Define the *power elite* that was identified by C. Wright Mills and describe the factors that contribute to the emergence of such an elite. What is its actual base of power, and on what factors does its unity rest? How does Mills's interpretation of power in the United States conflict with the "pluralist" interpretation?

Chapter 5

Power and Personality

PERSONALITY AND INDIVIDUAL RESPONSES TO POWER

Individuals react toward power and authority in characteristic ways. In many different situations, their responses to power and authority are fairly predictable. Some individuals regularly seek power and authority, whereas others avoid seeking them. Some individuals are submissive to authority, whereas others are habitually rebellious. Some individuals try to conform to the expectations of other people, and others are guided by internalized standards. Some individuals feel powerless, helpless, and isolated; they believe they have little control over their own lives. Other individuals are self-assured and aggressive; they speak out at meetings, organize groups, and take over leadership positions. Some individuals are habitually suspicious of others and are unwilling to compromise; they prefer simple, final, and forceful solutions to complex problems. Some individuals are assertive, strong-willed, and self-confident; others are timid, submissive, and self-conscious. There are as many different ways of responding to power as there are types of personalities.

Personality *is all the characteristic ways of behaving that an individual exhibits; it is the enduring and organized sets of responses an individual habitu-*

personality
characteristic ways of behaving; the enduring and organized responses that individuals habitually make to particular stimuli

91

ally makes when subjected to particular stimuli. By *characteristic* and *habitual,* we mean that individuals tend to respond in a similar fashion to many separate situations. For example, their attitudes toward authority in general may affect their response to any number of different leaders, supervisors, directors, or other authority figures in different situations. By *enduring,* we mean that these characteristic ways of behaving may operate over a long time, perhaps through youth, young adulthood, and maturity. Attitudes toward authority in the home may carry over to school, university, job, church, government, and so forth. By *organized,* we mean that there are relationships between various elements of an individual's personality. A change in one element (let us say, a growing need for social approval) would bring about a change in another element (let us say, an increased willingness to conform to group norms). Thus, personality is not just a bundle of traits but an *integrated pattern of responses.*

NATURE VERSUS NURTURE

Children often have the same personality characteristics as their parents. Is the similarity a result of what they learned in the home? Or do children inherit personality characteristics from their parents? Actually, this is not an "either/or" question: Psychologists generally acknowledge that personality is shaped by *both* heredity and environment. The only question is: What is the relative influence of these factors on personality?

The question of the relative influence of heredity versus environment on personality is part of a larger controversy about the influence of genetics on behavior. Some psychologists attribute greater influence to heredity in determining many personality characteristics by chemical and hormonal balances, the functioning of the senses (sight, hearing, smell, taste, touch), and physique. Other psychologists attribute greater influence to environment. The influence of the environment may begin even before birth, depending, for example, on whether the mother has a good diet; avoids smoking, alcohol, and drugs; is active or inactive; and is in good emotional health. Infants respond to their earliest environment and acquire characteristic ways of responding—that is, personality—very early in life.

It is very difficult to determine whether a specific personality characteristic shared by a parent and child has been genetically inherited or transferred through social interaction in the home.[1] However, some studies of twins have suggested that heredity plays an important role in personality. **Identical twins** (who have the same genetic composition) score more alike on standard personality tests than **fraternal twins** (whose genetic composition is different).[2] Identical twins reared in separate families tend to share more personality and behavior characteristics than fraternal twins raised in the same household. According to various studies, separated identical twins shared the same smoking and eating habits and scored similarly on tests of intelligence, extroversion, and neuroticism.[3] (For more information on research in genetics, see Focus, "DNA: Blueprint to Life.")

identical twins
twins who develop from a single fertilized egg and who are genetically identical

fraternal twins
twins who develop from separate eggs and are no closer genetically than brothers and sisters

Research on the behavior of identical twins suggests the importance of genetic influences. Identical twins Gerald Levey and Mark Newman, for example, were separated at birth and raised in different homes. When reunited at age 31, they discovered that they had both become firefighters.

"GENES R US"

Every cell of the human body contains **genes** that instruct its growth and development. Genes contain **DNA**—the complex code of instructions that determine the cell's structure and appearance. It is difficult to estimate how much of our personality can be attributed to our genes versus our environment. A common estimate is that heritability—differences among people that are attributable to genetics—accounts for about fifty percent of the variation in personalities among people. This does *not* mean that fifty percent of any individual's personality is inherited, but rather that fifty percent of *differences among* people are inherited.

genes
inherited units of life found in every cell; genes contain DNA

DNA
code of instructions to cells determining their structure, appearance, and function

SEXUALITY

How much of the differences in the behaviors of men and women can be attributable to genetic differences between males and females? "With few exceptions anywhere in the world, males are more likely than females to initiate sexual activity."[4] Most hard-core pornography readers are males, while most romance novel readers are females. Men are much more accepting of casual sex and report masturbating more often than women.[5] Men rate youth and attractiveness higher in assessing women, while women rate maturity, affluence, and

FOCUS

DNA: Blueprint to Life

In recent years, scientific advances in genetics have influenced all of the social sciences. Genes are hereditary units of life. They contain DNA (deoxyribonucleic acid)—a complex code of instructions to cells of plants, animals, and humans that determines the cells' structure, appearance, and function. Each gene has a DNA of slightly different chemical components that determine the inheritance of specific tracts. (In 1953 geneticists James Watson and Francis Crick discovered the double helix structure of DNA that resembles a spiral staircase. See Figure 5-1.) Every living organism has different kinds and numbers of genes, ranging from a small number for simple forms of life to a very large number for complex organisms such as humans. Genes with their DNA codes determine everything from the color of eyes, hair, and skin to the number of arms and legs and whether the organism will have a tail or not.

In 2000, two groups of scientists—(Celera Genomics and the Human-Genome Project)—announced the completion of the genetic code in the DNA of human beings. The genetic code is a sequence of over *three billion* letters, representing the chemical components guanine, thymine, cytosine and adenine (GTCAs). This mammoth task required the efforts of thousands of scientists working over twenty-five years with powerful supercomputers. In the future, this research will enable medical scientists to identify particular genes that predispose people to particular diseases such as breast cancer and colon cancer.

Every human has a unique DNA code. Indeed, DNA evidence, derived from hair, skin, or bodily fluids, can be used to identify or exclude suspects in criminal cases. Genes are arranged in units called chromosomes. Humans normally have forty-six chromosomes arranged in matching pairs—twenty-three are inherited from the mother and twenty-three from the father. Human offspring appear somewhat different from either parent be-

cause of the reshuffling of inherited genes.

Normally DNA is very stable, that is, not subject to change. But occasionally a change does occur, and a slightly different code of instructions is transmitted to later generations. Such permanent genetic change is known as mutation. Geneticists do not really know all of the causes of mutation but suspect that radiation, certain chemicals, and heat may contribute to its occurrence.

Genetic Research

Genetic research has led to genetic engineering, deliberately rearranging genetic material to create new or different forms of life. Initially food grains were altered to make them grow faster and resist disease better. Some fruits have been genetically altered to keep them fresh and unspoiled long after they have been picked. Mice are often genetically altered—making them stronger, larger, more or less aggressive, and even longer lived—to observe the function of specific genes. In 1997 sheep were

resourcefulness higher in assessing men. (For an explanation based on evolutionary psychology, see Focus, "Evolutionary Psychology: The Mating Game.")

INTELLIGENCE

Perhaps no other aspect of the nature versus nurture argument generates as much controversy as that of intelligence. There are serious political implications in the nature versus nurture argument over intelligence: If mental abili-

"cloned"—that is, offspring were produced with the exact same genetic structure.

Genetic Engineering

Genetic engineering has led to speculation and debate about its future uses. Controversies have arisen regarding the ethics of engineering specific characteristics of humans. "Cloning" of humans or creating a "superrace" is well beyond the capabilities of geneticists today. But "gene splicing" to assist humans in fighting disease is a real possibility. And so is the identification of genes likely to create medical conditions. Should insurance companies be allowed to discriminate against people whose DNA indicates the likely occurrence of cancer, diabetes, anemia, or immune deficiencies?

FIGURE 5-1

A REPRESENTATION OF GENES AND THEIR LOCATION

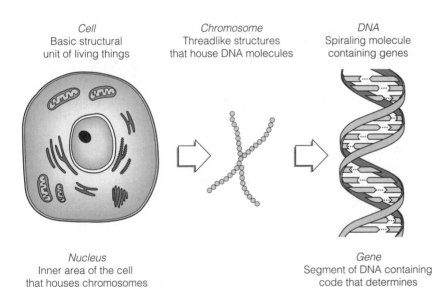

Cell
Basic structural unit of living things

Chromosome
Threadlike structures that house DNA molecules

DNA
Spiraling molecule containing genes

Nucleus
Inner area of the cell that houses chromosomes

Gene
Segment of DNA containing code that determines biological development

ties are primarily inherited, then efforts to equalize education are not likely to be successful and might as well be abandoned. If, on the other hand, mental abilities are primarily nurtured by the environment, then efforts to erase disadvantaged educational environments are worthwhile (see Controversies in Social Sciences, "The Bell Curve" in Chapter 4 on pages 76–77).

Research on twins again suggests that genetics contributes heavily to intelligence: Identical twins raised together are closer in intelligence scores than fraternal twins raised together. Indeed, identical twins raised apart are closer in intelligence scores than fraternal twins raised together. And by inserting an "intelligence" gene into fertilized mouse eggs, researchers have produced smarter mice.[6]

However, early experiences of newborns and even unborn fetuses can have profound effects on mental abilities. Malnutrition, sensory deprivation (absence of cuddling, talking to, and stimulating babies), and social isolation have profound effects on brain development.

NURTURE AND HUMAN DEVELOPMENT

The mother is the single most important influence in anyone's early environment. We cannot deprive human babies of contact with their mothers for the sake of experimentation, but psychologists have placed newborn monkeys in isolation and observed their development. The results showed abnormal and irreversible behavior: extreme fear, anxiety, avoidance of all social contact with other monkeys, and emotional and intellectual retardation.

NEWBORN INSTINCTS

Some psychologists argue that early mother-child relationships are instinctual. Newborns possess five instinctual responses: sucking, crying, smiling, clinging, and following. Together these responses bind the child to the mother and the mother to the child. Some psychologists contend that these inherited responses were acquired over millions of years by natural selection. There is also evidence that clinging and following are inherited responses. Infant monkeys reared in isolation from their mothers were supplied with two surrogate mother figures. One was made of wire mesh, while the other was made of soft "cuddly" cloth. The baby monkeys chose to be near the soft surrogate, even when the wire mesh surrogate had a bottle attached to it for feeding.

NURTURE AND BRAIN ACTIVITY

But newer technology, notably PET (positron-emission tomography) scanning of brain activity in infants, has provided convincing evidence of the significance of very early learning. Simple activities, like cuddling and rocking, and singing and talking to babies, stimulate electrical activity in a baby's brain and actually build neuron connections. In the first few months of life, the number of these connections (synapses) increases over twentyfold from 100 billion to more than 1 trillion. An infant's earliest experiences exert a dramatic impact on the brain's growth, physically determining the number and strength of neural connections. These connections govern everything from language and music to mathematics and emotions. The brain of a baby not only grows bigger, but its actual wiring is set in place. Infants who are deprived of human interaction fail to develop as

FIGURE 5-2

PET SCANS OF HEALTHY AND ABUSED BRAINS

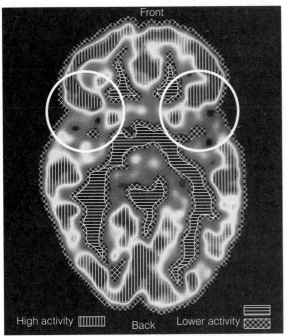

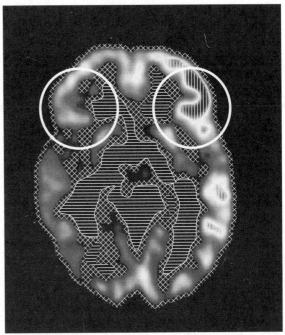

a. PET scan of the healthy brain of a normal child shows regions of high and low activity. Circles show temporal lobes.

b. This PET scan of the brain of a Romanian orphan institutionalized shortly after birth shows the effects of extreme deprivation; areas of high activity are few. Circles show temporal lobes.

many active areas of the brain and as many neural connections as infants who experience more stimulation.

Early traumas elevate stress hormones in an infant's brain. These hormones actually reduce electrical activity. Abused children have smaller brains than normal children and fewer neural connections (see Figure 5-2). These conditions are associated with later language, cognitive, learning, and emotional problems.

APPROACHES TO PSYCHOLOGY AND PERSONALITY

Psychologists differ over the precise meaning of *personality*. Definitions tend to be linked to major approaches to individual behavior and to the major approaches within psychology itself. These approaches are not necessarily

FOCUS

Inside the Brain

A newborn's brain is already wired for rudimentary behaviors—breathing, heartbeat, reflexes, crying, sucking, etc. But in higher regions of the brain, neural connections are still being created (see Figure 5-3). These connections are stimulated and reinforced by an infant's exposure to language, images, sounds, and even facial expressions. Because no two babies have the exact same experience, no two brains are wired exactly the same.

As we examine personality in this chapter, we should remember that both heredity and environment, "nature" and "nurture," play important roles in shaping human beings. We will examine some theories of personality that emphasize instincts and heredity, others that emphasize early childhood experiences, and still others that emphasize continuing growth and development over a lifetime. There is no single "right" theory of personality.

FIGURE 5-3

BRAIN FUNCTION IN NEWBORNS

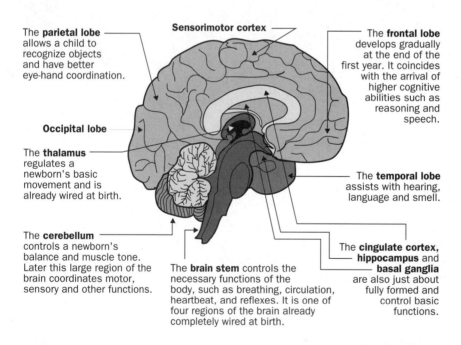

The **parietal lobe** allows a child to recognize objects and have better eye-hand coordination.

Sensorimotor cortex

The **frontal lobe** develops gradually at the end of the first year. It coincides with the arrival of higher cognitive abilities such as reasoning and speech.

Occipital lobe

The **thalamus** regulates a newborn's basic movement and is already wired at birth.

The **temporal lobe** assists with hearing, language and smell.

The **cerebellum** controls a newborn's balance and muscle tone. Later this large region of the brain coordinates motor, sensory and other functions.

The **brain stem** controls the necessary functions of the body, such as breathing, circulation, heartbeat, and reflexes. It is one of four regions of the brain already completely wired at birth.

The **cingulate cortex, hippocampus** and **basal ganglia** are also just about fully formed and control basic functions.

FIGURE 5-4

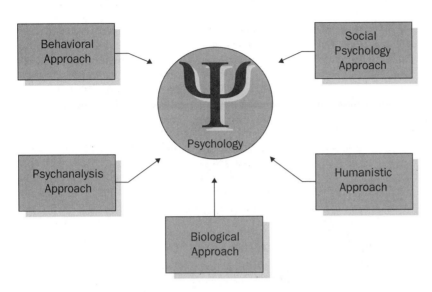

APPROACHES TO PSYCHOLOGY

The Greek letter *psi,* ψ, is sometimes used as an abbreviation for *psychology.*

exclusive; many psychologists employ more than one approach in their efforts to understand behavior (see Figure 5-4).

BIOLOGICAL PSYCHOLOGY

Biological psychology attempts to relate specific behaviors to electrical and chemical events taking place within the brain and nervous system. The human brain contains well over ten *billion* nerve cells and an almost infinite number of connections between them. Electrical and chemical processes, known as **neurotransmitters,** make connections between these cells. Electrical stimulation and chemical therapies are known to change mental processes and behaviors.

Personality traits as varied as shyness, curiosity, risk-taking, and aggressiveness have been identified in genetic research. And there appears to be genetic predispositions to alcoholism, schizophrenia, depression, and other mental disorders.

A related field of **evolutionary psychology** describes relationships between biological needs, genetic coding, and psychological traits of humans. It assumes that psychological traits have evolved over millions of years through the process of natural selection; that is, the development of genetic traits that improve survival and are passed on to future generations.

But genes provide only a probability for a specific personality trait. A neurotransmitter must be "turned on" before genes can do their job. The effect of early childhood experiences can be profound. Genetics may increase the

biological psychology
the study of electrical and chemical events in the brain and nervous system

neurotransmitters
electrical and chemical connections between brain cells

evolutionary psychology
the study of relationships between biological needs, genetic coding, and psychological traits of humans

FOCUS

Evolutionary Psychology: The Mating Game

Understanding sexual behavior has long posed a challenge to psychologists as well as the rest of us. Why do men ogle women's breasts and evaluate women so much on their physical attractiveness? Why do women judge men more on their power, resources, and earnings potential? Why are men more likely to engage in short-term and extramarital affairs than women?

Evolutionary psychologists are proposing answers to these and similar questions about sexual behavior by reference to the mating concerns of our prehistoric ancestors. They argue that human sexual behavior, and human behavior generally, has been shaped by biological challenges confronting men and women and the evolutionary development of mental devices for coping with these challenges.

Evolutionary psychologists contend that men and women are as different psychologically as they are physically. In every culture, men consistently value youth and physical attractiveness in a mate more than women do. Women are consistently more concerned with a man's power, status, and resources. These preferences evolved from the different biological challenges facing men and women. Women invest far more time and energy in child rearing than men; human infants require years of nurturing. Over millions of years, women evolved a psychology that preferred men who appeared to have the power and resources to offer protection and assistance in the tasks of child rearing. In contrast, men's reproductive success depends on the fertility of their mates. So men have developed a mind-set that searches for signs of fertility—youth, large breasts, good looks. (Cultures where food is less plentiful may prefer heavier women, while more affluent cultures may prefer slimness. But in all cultures, the hips should be roughly one-third larger than the waist, a ratio that suggests high fertility and good health.) Women also appreciate men's physical attractiveness because it promises good genes for their offspring. Thus men as well as women in most cultures, modern as well as ancient, "beautify" themselves. However, women must balance good looks against men's willingness and ability to provide continuing subsistence for the nest. Women must be concerned with men's commitment to a relationship long enough to nurture children.

While men have a stake in maintaining a long-term relationship with women in order to help ensure the survival of offspring, another strategy available to men is to impregnate as many women as possible to increase the likelihood that their genes will be continued. Thus, men, even those with long-term mates, are psychologically more disposed toward short-term anonymous affairs. Women in long-term relationships may also engage in affairs, but it is likely to be part of a search for a new, more attractive, more resourceful, or more committed mate.

Male-oriented erotica, as in pornographic videos, feature lust-driven females willing to engage in sex acts with multiple partners with no emotional attachment. Female-oriented erotica, as in romance novels, feature handsome, powerful males with fiercely passionate commitments to the heroines.

Evolutionary psychology does not offer any solution to the battle between the sexes. But it suggests that a better understanding of the contrasting psychologies of men and women might lessen the damages arising from the war.

probability of personality traits—and even predict the likelihood of various mental illnesses. But experiences largely determine whether the wiring for these genes will be developed or not. It is very difficult to estimate what proportion of an adult's personality is determined by genes versus that which is developed by interaction with his or her environment.

BEHAVIORAL PSYCHOLOGY

Behavioral psychology, another major approach to psychology, is concerned with the scientific study of the behavioral responses of human beings to various stimuli. Behavioral psychology focuses on observed behavior; frequently its setting is the academic laboratory, and rats and pigeons are often subjects of experimentation. There is an emphasis on careful observation, quantitative data, and statistical methods. Behavioral psychology relies heavily on *learning theory* (stimulus-response theory), which views all behavior as a product of learning or conditioning. Behavioral patterns are learned through a process whereby a stimulus evokes a response that is either rewarded or punished, and habits are formed. The behavioral approach to personality views personality as a *pattern of learned, reinforced responses.*

behavioral psychology
the study of how people and animals learn to respond to different stimuli

PSYCHOANALYTIC OR FREUDIAN PSYCHOLOGY

Psychoanalytic or Freudian psychology views behavior as a product of the interaction between biologically based instincts (for example, hunger, sex, survival, aggression) and our efforts to satisfy these instincts in socially acceptable fashions. Early childhood experiences that forbid immediate gratification of instinctual drives tend to force them into the unconscious, where they remain to affect dreams, speech, and mannerisms, and to create anxieties, some of which may develop into emotional problems or mental illness.

Psychoanalysis is a type of insight-oriented therapy that encourages patients to think about themselves—their problems, dreams, memories—so they can gain insight into the causes of their own difficulties. Psychoanalysis encourages patients to talk about early childhood experiences and thus to reveal unconscious motivations, emotions, and conflicts. The psychoanalytic approach to personality emphasizes *childhood experiences* and *unconscious feelings* as determining factors in personality development. Although traditionally the practice of psychoanalysis has been the domain of the Freudian-trained psychiatrist, many clinical psychologists do use psychoanalytic psychology in their approach to therapy.

psychoanalytic or Freudian psychology
A theory in psychology that explains behavior as a product of the interaction of biological instincts and social learning, especially early childhood experiences. Named for its founder, Sigmund Freud.

psychoanalysis
insight-oriented therapy, often focused on early childhood experiences

SOCIAL PSYCHOLOGY

Social psychology is concerned with the individual's relationships with other individuals and groups. The social psychologist studies the whole person and

social psychology
the study of the individual's relationships with other individuals and groups

the impact of the social world on the person—the world of social interaction and group life, which constantly shapes and modifies the individual's goals, perceptions, attitudes, and behavior. The social-psychological approach to personality emphasizes the individual's *socialization*—the development of individual identity through *interpersonal experiences* and the *internalizing of the expectations of significant others.*

HUMANISTIC PSYCHOLOGY

humanistic psychology
the study of human experience and human fulfillment

Humanistic psychology focuses on human experience and human fulfillment; it emphasizes the individual's innate potential to grow and develop. According to the humanists, human beings are unique among animals because they alone have psychological as well as biological needs. The individual is internally motivated to fulfill those needs, to grow and develop, and to expand the capacity for creativity. Humanistic psychology views personality development as a *continuous process of positive growth* in which the individual, having fulfilled a lower need, pursues the fulfillment of a higher one.

In the following pages, we will see how each of these approaches can contribute to our understanding of personality and individual reactions to power and authority.

THE AUTHORITARIAN PERSONALITY

The Freudian approach to power relationships focuses on early childhood determinations of habitual responses to power and authority. Power motives—for example, a need to dominate others or, the opposite, comfort in accepting direction—are organized into the personality early in life.

An early influential study of power, authority, and personality, one that was conducted mainly within the framework of Freudian theory, was the landmark study *The Authoritarian Personality.*[7] This study was undertaken after World War II by a group of psychologists who sought to identify potentially antidemocratic individuals—those whose personality structures render them particularly susceptible to authoritarian appeals. One of the tools developed in the course of the study was the F (fascism) Scale, now widely used by social scientists to identify authoritarianism. Part of the original F Scale is reproduced in Table 5-1. Persons who agree with all or most of the items in the F Scale are said to be authoritarian.

characteristics of the authoritarian personality
dominance and submission

orientation toward power

rigidity

exaggerated concern with strength

cynicism

ethnocentrism

The central attitudes of authoritarianism are *dominance* and *submission*—dominance over subordinates in any power hierarchy and submissiveness toward superiors. Authoritarians are highly ambivalent in their attitudes toward authority. They are outwardly servile toward those they perceive as their superiors, but in fact they also harbor strong negative feelings toward these same people. Their repressed rage toward their superiors is redirected into hostility toward the weak and inferior.

TABLE 5-1

COMPONENTS OF THE F (FASCISM) SCALE WITH SAMPLE ITEMS

Conventionalism   Rigid adherence to conventional middle-class values.
- Obedience and respect for authority are the most important virtues children should learn.
- A person who has bad manners, habits, and breeding can hardly expect to get along with decent people.

Authoritarian submission   Submissive, uncritical attitude toward idealized moral authorities of the in-group.
- What this country needs most, more than laws and political programs, is a few courageous, tireless, devoted leaders in whom the people can put their faith.

Authoritarian aggression   Tendency to be on the lookout for and to condemn, reject, and punish people who violate conventional values.
- What the youth needs most is strict discipline, rugged determination, and the will to work and fight for family and country.
- An insult to our honor should always be punished.

Anti-introception   Opposition to the subjective, the imaginative, the tender-minded.
- When people have problems or worries, it is best for them not to think about it, but to keep busy with more cheerful things.
- Nowadays more and more people are prying into matters that should remain personal and private.
- If people would talk less and work more, everybody would be better off.

Power and "toughness"   Preoccupation with the dominance-submission, strong-weak, leader-follower dimension; identification with power figures; overemphasis upon the conventionalized attributes of the ego; exaggerated assertion of strength and toughness.
- No weakness or difficulty can hold us back if we have enough willpower.
- What the youth needs most is strict discipline, rugged determination, and the will to work and fight for family and country.
- People can be divided into two distinct classes: the weak and the strong.

Destructiveness and cynicism   Generalized hostility, vilification of the human.
- Human nature being what it is, there will always be war and conflict.
- Familiarity breeds contempt.

SOURCE: Abridgement of Table 7 (pp. 255–257), "The F (Fascism) Scale," from T. W. Adorno et al., *The Authoritarian Personality.* Copyright © 1950 by The American Jewish Committee. Reprinted by permission of HarperCollins, Inc.

Authoritarians are *oriented toward power.* They tend to think in power terms, to be acutely sensitive in any situation to questions of who dominates whom. They are very uncomfortable when they do not know what the chain of command is. They need to know whom they should obey and who should obey them.

Authoritarians are *rigid.* They are "intolerant of ambiguity." They like order and are uncomfortable in the presence of disorder. When matters are complex, they impose their own rigid categories on them. Their thinking, therefore, is largely in stereotypes.

Authoritarians show *exaggerated concern with strength.* Feelings of personal weakness are covered with a facade of toughness. They are unusually preoccupied with masculine virtues, and they stereotype women as feminine and soft.

MASTERS OF SOCIAL THOUGHT

Sigmund Freud and Psychoanalytic Theory

Viennese psychiatrist Sigmund Freud (1856–1939) was principally responsible for the development of psychoanalytic theory. He first studied hypnosis because he learned that neurotic symptoms could be removed during hypnotic trance. But he soon found that patients did not really need to be in a full hypnotic trance so long as they felt relaxed and uninhibited. He encouraged them to engage in *free association*—that is, to say anything that came into their minds without regard to organization, logic, or embarrassment over socially unacceptable ideas. He wanted to make the patient's *unconscious* motives, drives, feelings, and anxieties *conscious* ones. The goal of psychoanaly-

sis, as it was called, was to help patients attain *insight*, or self-knowledge. Once that was achieved, the neurotic symptoms tended to disappear.

According to Freud, the personality is composed of three major systems: the *id*, the *ego*, and the *superego*. The *id* is the basic system of life instincts, or drives—hunger, thirst, sex, rest, pain avoidance, and so on. The id is in close touch with the body's needs; these needs produce psychic energy, which is experienced as uncomfortable states of tension. A newborn's personality is almost pure id. It seeks immediate gratification of bodily urges and has no knowledge of reality or morals. The *ego* is the part of the personality that is in contact with objective

reality. It directs the energies of the id toward real-world objects that are appropriate for the satisfaction of the urge and the reduction of tension. The *superego*, the last part of the personality to develop, is the internal representative of the values, standards, and morals that the child is taught.

Anxiety is a state of tension that results from an apprehension of impending pain or danger, whether physical or psychological. Anxiety reduction is a drive like hunger or thirst, the difference being that it results from psychological, rather than bodily, discomfort. When its intensity and nature are appropriate to the real situation, the anxiety is *normal*. When there does not seem to

---

Authoritarians are *cynical*. They distrust the motives of others and are generally pessimistic about human nature. They are disposed to believe that the world is a jungle and that various conspiracies exist to threaten them and their ways of life.

Authoritarians are *ethnocentric*. They view members of social groups other than their own as outsiders who are different, strange, unwholesome, and threatening. They hold an exalted opinion of their own groups. They reject outsiders and project many of their own aggressive impulses onto them. They place stereotyped labels on outsiders.

criticisms of *The Authoritarian Personality*

educated persons recognize bias in the F Scale

fails to identify left-wing authoritarians

not really a complete and separate syndrome

A great deal of research followed *The Authoritarian Personality* study, much of it using the F Scale to identify authoritarians and then observing related attitudes, environments, and behaviors. Some of the subsequent research on authoritarianism raised serious criticisms and reservations about the original work. First, it was observed that poorly educated persons tend to agree with F Scale statements more frequently than do well-educated persons. This finding does not necessarily mean that a lack of education causes authoritarianism, but it does suggest that differences in F Scale scores may be be adequate cause for it in the real world, when it is caused by unconscious or irrational fears, and when it interferes with the person's functioning, the anxiety is *neurotic.*

The most important of the *defense mechanisms* that the body uses, often unconsciously, to reduce anxiety and tension is *repression:* The ego protects the individual from unbearable impulses by forcing these impulses out of consciousness. This defensive maneuver may occur when an impulse would endanger life, risk punishment, or risk feelings of guilt. But there are costs to repression. A severely repressed individual who has denied many strong impulses may suffer fatigue, nervousness, or depression. Freud's seeming emphasis on sex was a product not of his belief that this drive was any more powerful than others but of his view that it was the most repressed and therefore the source of many personality disorders.

Perhaps no other social science theory has been subjected to such searching and bitter criticism as Freudian theory. The criticism ranges from charges that Freud was a "sex maniac" to more serious scientific reservations. (Freud was a dedicated father and husband whose marriage lasted a lifetime; Freud's daughter, Anna, became a distinguished psychoanalyst herself.) One criticism centers on psychoanalytic therapy: It can be long and costly, and it is not always successful. Drugs and behavioral therapy frequently produce more complete results in less time and at less expense. Another criticism is that Freud's observations were based on abnormal, clinical cases rather than on normal adults; most of his patients were middle-class Europeans; and he worked in a cultural period when sexual repression in society was much greater than it is today. Another problem with Freudian theory is that it is difficult to test scientifically. Freudian explanations proceed from observed behavior *back* to unconscious feelings and childhood experiences, but they do not permit exact predictions of future behavior from these factors.

a product of education and *not* of personality development. Well-educated persons, whether they are authoritarian or not, simply know enough not to agree with the obviously biased statements on the F Scale.

Another problem is that the F Scale tests only for *right-wing* (fascist) authoritarianism and fails to identify *left-wing* authoritarianism. Yet there is ample evidence of exaggerated submission to authority in revolutionary and communist movements; aggression and sadism practiced by left-wing authoritarians against the hated out-group, the "bourgeoisie"; rigidity, toughness, and an orientation toward power among revolutionaries; extreme cynicism toward society among leftists as well as conspiratorial views about politics; and rigid conformity to stereotyped Marxist ideas. Unfortunately, the F Scale equates authoritarianism with only fascist ideas. (For an interesting look at authority, see the Case Study, "Authority and Obedience: The 'Shocking' Experiments.")

Despite these reservations, *The Authoritarian Personality* provides us with valuable insights into the psychological mechanisms by which some individuals adjust themselves to power and authority.

CASE STUDY

Authority and Obedience: The "Shocking" Experiments

A significant theme in the study of human behavior has been the reaction of individuals who were commanded to inflict pain, injury, or death upon others. An estimated six million Jews—men, women, and children—were murdered in Nazi death camps in World War II by individuals who frequently claimed they were "only carrying out orders."

Authority, as we have noted, is a form of power that is perceived as legitimate by society. Doubtless, throughout the ages, more pain, injury, and death have been inflicted on humanity by "authorities" than by recognized "criminals." The criminal's claim to power is sanctioned only by guns, knives, fists, or fraud, not by "legitimacy." But what are the psychological mechanisms that provide legitimacy to the exercise of power, and how far will ordi-

nary Americans go in inflicting pain, injury, or even death if they believe they are acting legitimately?

These are some of the questions explored by psychologist Stanley Milgram in a series of classic experiments in which experimenters told subjects to administer electric shocks to other people.[a] The subjects in these experiments were all adult males of various ages and represented a cross section of occupations. Each subject was told that he was participating in a "learning experiment"; the "learner" (actually an associate of the experimenter) was strapped into an "electric chair" and given a list of questions and answers to memorize. The subject was told by the experimenter to administer an ever-increasing electric shock every time the "learner" made a mistake. Thirty separate voltage levers were used, with signs reading from 15 to 450

volts. Signs also announced that the shocks ranged from "Slight Shock" to "Danger: Severe Shock." Actually the "learner" did not receive any shocks at all, but the subject did not know this. Moreover, the subject could watch the "learner" through a window and hear any sounds the "learner" made. Starting with 75 volts, the "learner" began to twitch, grunt, and groan with each shock. At 150 volts, the "learner" demanded that he be let out of the experiment. At 180 volts, the "learner" screamed that he could no longer stand the pain. At 300, volts the "learner" slumped over, refused to provide any more answers to questions, and appeared in dire distress. In response to each of the acts by the "learner," the experimenter told the subject, who was administering the shocks, "You have no choice, you must go on!"

[a] Stanley Milgram, "Some Conditions of Obedience and Disobedience to Authority," *Human Relations* 18 (February 1965): 57–76.

BEHAVIORISM AND LEARNING THEORY

Behavioral psychology is heavily indebted to learning theory or, more precisely, stimulus-response (SR) theory. It is not an overstatement to say that rats have had more to do with shaping this theory than human beings; SR theory grew out of experimental laboratory studies with animals. Academic psychology is based largely on SR theory; many college courses in psychology are oriented toward this approach. Behavioral psychology asserts that the goal of psychologists should be to study **behavior** by employing the same *scientific* tests as the natural sciences. Behavioral psychologists discount Freudian notions about the mind or the personality, which cannot be directly observed. For the behaviorists, one is what one does; personality *is* behavior, a pattern of learned, reinforced responses.

behaviorism
an approach to psychology that asserts that only observable behavior can be studied

150 volts	"You want me to keep going?"
165 volts	"That guy is hollering in there. He's liable to have a heart attack. You want me to go on?"
180 volts	"He can't stand it. I'm not going to kill that man in there! You hear him hollering. He's hollering. He can't stand it. What if something happens to him? . . . I mean who is going to take the responsibility if something happens to that gentleman?" (The experimenter says he will accept responsibility.)
195 volts	"You see he's hollering. Hear that? Gee, I don't know." (The experimenter says, "The experiment requires that you go on.")
210 volts	
225 volts	
240 volts	"Aw, no. You mean I've got to keep going up the scale? No, sir. I'm not going to kill that man! I'm not going to give him 450 volts!" (The experimenter repeats, "The experiment requires that you go on.") The subject proceeds to the highest shock level, 450 volts.[b]

The shocking results of Milgram's "shocking" experiments were that 62 percent of the subjects obeyed the experimenter's commands completely and proceeded to administer the highest shock level on the board (450 volts). Only 38 percent of the subjects broke off the experiment when the "learner" groaned, screamed, demanded to be released, and finally pretended to be near death.

Many subjects expressed concern about their "learner" victims and about their part in the experiments but continued the experiment anyway.

One point made in these experiments is that the subjects were not simply sadistic. They were average men selected from all walks of life. Most objected verbally to what they were doing at some point in the experiment. But

in the context of *authority* (an experimenter who told them to continue no matter what happened) and *legitimacy* (the idea that they were participating in a scientific experiment at a prestigious university), these individuals performed acts of brutality that they would not otherwise consider doing.

It is not clear how far we can generalize from these experiments. But it is certainly not far-fetched to suspect that under the right conditions otherwise normal people can become unusually cruel. If those who are invested with authority and legitimacy encourage sadistic behavior toward others, we can reasonably expect that a substantial proportion of the population will engage in such behavior. Another holocaust is not impossible.

[b] Excerpt from *Obedience to Authority*, by Stanley Milgram. Copyright © 1974 by Stanley Milgram. Reprinted by permission of Harper-Collins, Inc.

CONDITIONED RESPONSES

The founder of modern stimulus-response theory was the Russian physiologist Ivan Petrovich Pavlov (1849–1936), who had already won a Nobel Prize for his studies of digestive glands before he undertook his landmark experiments with salivating dogs. Pavlov's early experiments established the notion of *conditioning*. Saliva flows when meat is placed in a dog's mouth. If a bell is consistently sounded just a moment before the meat is placed in its mouth, the dog will soon begin to salivate merely upon hearing a bell even if the meat is not given. Dogs do not normally salivate at the sound of a bell, so such a response is a **conditioned response.** The bell and the meat have become associated in the dog's mind by their occurring together.

Pavlov's dogs

conditioned response
a behavior that is elicited by a previously neutral stimulus

conditioned SR linkage requires
drive

cue

response

reinforcement

The learning process is a bit more complex than it first appears. *To establish a linkage between a conditioned stimulus and response,* there must be a *drive,* a *cue,* a *response,* and *reinforcement.* Learning depends on the establishment of this SR linkage. In simple terms, in order to learn, one must want something as a result of one's action (*drive*). For example, for a rat that is placed in a box and given electric shocks through a wire grid floor, reinforcement is the relief of pain. Pain provides the *drive,* which is the first factor that must be present if learning is to occur. Hunger, thirst, or curiosity may also provide the drive to learn. In our example, the electric shocks that the rat receives are accompanied by a buzzer. The buzzer provides the *cue,* the stimulus associated with the response. The stimulus may be visual (objects, colors, lights, designs, printed words), auditory (bells, whistles, spoken words), or related to any of the other senses. Of course, for a response to be linked to a cue, a response must first occur. A critical stage in the learning process is the production of the *appropriate response.* The rat experiencing an electric shock and hearing the buzzer will make a variety of responses; eventually it may pull on the lever that turns off the current. The particular response that satisfies the drive is likely to recur the next time the same situation is encountered. Learning takes place not so much through "trial and error" as through "trial and success." The rat's first success in pulling the lever will be an accident. After several shocking experiences, however, the rat will learn to pull the lever immediately to stop the current.

REINFORCEMENT

reinforcement
repeating conditioned stimulus and response

The key to the learning process is the **reinforcement** of the appropriate behavior. Reinforcement occurs each time the behavior is accompanied by reduction in the drive. The cue itself will eventually elicit the same response as the original drive. Thus, the rat will pull the lever when it hears the sound of the buzzer whether it is shocked or not. In this way, a previously neutral stimulus (the buzzer) becomes a *conditioned stimulus,* the rat having learned to respond to it in a particular way.

strength of SR linkage depends on
strength of drive

immediate drive reduction

number of trials

The *strength* of the SR linkage depends on (1) the strength of the original drive, (2) the closeness of the drive reduction to the response, and (3) the number of consistently reinforced trials. Thus, the combination of a strong shock, the quick elimination of the shock after the rat pulls the lever, and a large number of trials makes a well-trained rat.

BEHAVIORAL THERAPY

In recent years, behavioral psychologists have come out of the laboratory to engage in some types of treatment for mental disorders. Behaviorists define disorders in terms of the undesirable behaviors that are exhibited. Behavioral psychologists seldom talk about anxiety or repression; they talk in terms of *functional* (desirable) and *dysfunctional* (undesirable) behaviors. They believe neurotic behavior has been learned—generally by inconsistent use of rewards

This rat's stimulus-response behavior is reinforced with food pellets.

and punishment. (Hungry rats that are shocked when they pull a lever that previously produced food develop symptoms similar to nervous breakdowns.) Undesirable behaviors can be extinguished by withholding rewards or by administering punishment. Neurotic behavior can be unlearned by the same combination of principles by which it was taught. **Behavioral psychotherapy** establishes a set of conditions by which neurotic habits are unlearned and nonneurotic habits are learned. The behavioral therapist is regarded as a kind of teacher and the patient as a learner. Thus, the behavioral therapist may reward patients in mental hospitals for good behavior with tokens to be used to buy small luxuries. A therapist of this school believes that smokers can learn avoidance reaction by having thick, obnoxious cigarette smoke blown in their faces; or that bed wetters can unlearn their habit by sleeping on a wire blanket that produces a mild shock when it becomes wet. Even repression (viewed by the behaviorists as "learned nonthinking") can be overcome by forcing individuals to confront situations, events, or experiences they have repressed.

behavioral psychotherapy
treatment based on learning or unlearning behavior

MASTERS OF SOCIAL THOUGHT
B. F. Skinner and the Control of Human Behavior

Power is the capacity to control human behavior. Behavioral psychologist B. F. Skinner (1904–1990) believed that society could no longer afford individual freedom and self-determination. He argued that human behavior must be controlled to ensure the survival of humanity and that *behavioral conditioning* must be employed on a massive scale to remold human beings and human culture. In the Skinnerian world, people would be conditioned to be humanitarian rather than selfish and to refrain from polluting, overpopulating, rioting, and making war. Outmoded ideas of individual freedom and self-determination would be discarded in favor of a scientifically designed culture that would condition people to be "good."

Skinner believed that the freedom and dignity of an autonomous human being are "illusions" anyhow. All behavior is determined by prior conditioning. The apparent freedom of human beings is merely inconspicuous control: A permissive government is simply relying on other sources of control—family, church, schools, values, ideologies. There is, however, ample evidence—war, crime, poverty, racism—that existing control mechanisms are inadequate for survival. Behavioral conditioning replaces imperfect and haphazard control methods with a more effective technology of behavioral control. *Brainwashing* is attacked by scholars who otherwise support changing people's minds by less obvious control mechanisms. Yet, according to Skinner, brainwashing is an effective means of accomplishing *behavioral modification.*

> *A common technique is to build up a strong aversive condition, such as hunger or lack of sleep, and, by alleviating it, to reinforce any behavior which "shows a positive attitude" toward a political or religious system. A favorable "opinion" is built up simply by reinforcing favorable statements.*[a]

Skinner developed his ideas through a lifetime of laboratory research on behavioral conditioning. He was the inventor of the famous "Skinner box," a soundproof enclosure with a food dispenser that can be operated by a rat pressing a lever or a pigeon pecking at a bar. He was a pioneer in the development of teaching machines and programmed instruction, which employ conditioning principles by reinforcing correct answers with a printed statement that the student's response is correct.

Serious dilemmas of power are raised by Skinner's proposals. Who is to determine what is "good" and "bad" behavior? In Skinner's utopia, immense power would be placed in the hands of the behavioral scientist who designs the culture. Skinner's utopia, although benevolent, is totalitarian. Can the behavioral scientist always be trusted to be "good"? How can the power entrusted to the scientist be checked if the scientist has full capacity to manipulate human behavior? Moreover, what kind of human beings would be produced under a system that manipulates behavior, choices, tastes, and desires? If we believe individual freedom and dignity are essential components of humanity, then behavioral conditioning on a massive scale is dehumanizing. Giving up freedom and dignity to achieve a secure, comfortable, unpolluted, egalitarian world may be too high a price to pay.

[a] B. F. Skinner, *Beyond Freedom and Dignity* (New York: Knopf, 1971), 5.

SOCIAL PSYCHOLOGY—THE SELF IN RELATION TO OTHERS

Social psychology is concerned primarily with interpersonal interactions—how the individual interacts with others. The social psychologist studies the individual as a whole person interacting with the environment rather than studying particular responses, behaviors, or reflexes. Many social psychologists are critical of the "reductionism" of behavioral psychology—the tendency to reduce individual behavior to a series of stimulus-response linkages. Social psychology is strongly influenced by early **Gestalt psychologists,** who argued that the whole person is an entity that cannot be understood by breaking it into sensory elements. (The German word *Gestalt* means "whole," "pattern," or "configuration.")

Gestalt psychology
the study of the whole individual

SELF-AWARENESS

Social psychologists view *interpersonal interaction* as the critical determinant of personality development. Indeed, an individual develops an awareness of **self** only by interaction with the environment. The newborn cannot distinguish its own body from the outer world. It acquires an identity—a sense of self—only by moving out into the world and relating to other people. As the infant observes and responds to its mother, the mother becomes a meaningful object, bringing pleasure, frustration, pain, and so on. The infant becomes aware of itself only in relation to others. An infant who is totally ignored withdraws to a corner of its crib, does not talk or develop in any way, and withers away physiologically and psychologically. The emergence of self-identity requires interpersonal interaction; without others, there is no self.

self
the individual's awareness of himself or herself derived from interpersonal interaction

SOCIALIZATION

The process by which an individual internalizes the values, attitudes, and judgments of others is called **socialization.** By *interacting* with others, people come to understand what is expected of them and *internalize* these expectations as part of their personalities. George Herbert Mead conceived the notion of *roles* to explain how the individual internalizes the expectations of others and acquires the values of society. The essential process in the development of self is the individual's taking on the roles of others.

socialization
assuming the roles expected of us by others

Through interaction with its parents, the child learns that certain sounds, such as "Mama" and "Daddy," gain favorable attention. The child begins to repeat these sounds because of the response they evoke in others and in this way begins to learn language. Children also learn that the things they do are meaningful to those around them, and thus they develop a sense of *self.* Infants who are ignored fail to develop either language or self-identity. Later the small child at play tries on a variety of **roles**—"mother,"

role playing
developing a sense of self by trying on a variety of roles

CROSS-NATIONAL PERSPECTIVE
The Self in Individualist and Collectivist Cultures

Cross-cultural psychologists have observed that "self" is perceived differently across cultures, ranging from individualism in the United States to collectivism in Asia.

In more collectivist cultures, people give priority to their family and communal identities. (Chinese names begin with the family name followed by the individual's name, as in Lee, Li Peng; whereas Western names place the family name last, as in Robert E. Lee.) In collectivist cultures, people value many things; avoid direct confrontation; give great respect to others, especially elders and superiors; value politeness and humility; and view reciprocal favors as social necessities. The family is stable, and divorce is rare. But the price of devaluing individual initiative and enterprise may be slower economic progress. And the emphasis on collectiveness devalues individual human rights.

In contrast, in individualist cultures, happiness is usually perceived as personal achievement and well-being. People value personal identity, aspire to self-fulfillment, resist family and peer group pressures, celebrate innovation and creativity, and emphasize individual rights. But the price of individualism may be more loneliness, more divorce, more crime, and more stress-related diseases.

	Individualism	Collectivism
Self	Independent (identity from individual traits)	Interdependent (identity from belonging)
What matters	Me—personal achievement and fulfillment; rights and liberties; self-esteem	We—group goals and solidarity; social responsibilities and relationships
Coping method	Change reality	Accommodate to reality
Morality	Defined by individuals (self-based)	Defined by social networks (duty-based)
Relationships	Many, often temporary or casual; confrontation acceptable	Few, close and enduring; harmony valued

SOURCE: Derived from "Individualism" in U. S. Ramachandran, ed., *Encyclopedia of Human Behavior* (San Diego, CA: Academic Press, 1994).

"father," "firefighter," "soldier"—and increases self-realization in the process. Even such basic social roles as male and female may be viewed as products of socialization rather than biology. Masculine and feminine traits develop through the child's internalization of the expectations of others and through role playing. Schools, games, and group activities provide more and more role-playing opportunities. Of course, not all the "others" in one's life are equally influential in shaping self-identity; each person has some *significant others* whose judgments carry more weight than the judgments of others. As socialization continues, knowledge of roles and attitudes of others becomes more generalized, and we gradually unify and consolidate the many roles we have played into a generalized self-conception. At this point, the mature personality emerges.

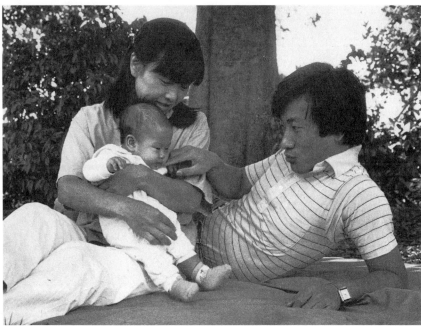

Self-awareness develops through early interpersonal interactions.

PERSONALITY AS INTERPERSONAL RESPONSE TRAITS

Over time, an individual acquires a distinctive pattern of **interpersonal response traits,** relatively consistent and stable dispositions to respond in a distinctive way toward others. These interpersonal response traits constitute the *personality*. They represent the sum of one's socialization, one's role experiences, and one's history of successes and failures with various interpersonal responses. Table 5-2 presents twelve interpersonal response traits.

Many social psychologists believe that interpersonal-interaction theory provides a basis for the treatment of *personality disorders*. They define an *integrated personality* as one in which the individual plays fairly well-defined and stable roles that are not incompatible or conflicting and that are consistent with the values of the groups and culture in which the individual lives. *Personality disorganization* occurs when people find themselves in highly conflicting roles. Most people can handle mildly conflicting roles, such as being mother and office worker simultaneously, but serious role conflicts, such as an inability to assume fully either a male or a female identification, may create deeper problems. Another source of personality disorganization may be an abrupt change in roles—caused, for example, by the loss of a job by a breadwinner, the loss of a wife or husband, even war and natural disaster. Failure to be adequately "socialized" in the first place is another recognized source of personality disorder—for example, the adult who exhibits childlike behavior, or adolescents who cannot "find themselves," that is, find

interpersonal response traits
the sum of all of an individual's socializing experience, or personality

causes of personality disorder
conflicting role expectations

abrupt changes in roles

inadequate socialization

desocialization: consistent defeat, frustration, and withdrawal

TABLE 5-2

SOME INTERPERSONAL RESPONSE TRAITS

Role dispositions
- Ascendance (*social timidity*): defends one's rights; does not mind being conspicuous; is not self-reticent; is self-assured; forcefully puts self forward
- Dominance (*submissiveness*): assertive; self-confident; power-oriented; tough; strong-willed; order-giving or directive leader
- Social initiative (*social passivity*): organizes groups; does not stay in background; makes suggestions at meetings; takes over leadership
- Independence (*dependence*): prefers to do own planning, to work things out in own way; does not seek support or advice; emotionally self-sufficient

Sociometric dispositions
- Acceptance of others (*rejection of others*): nonjudgmental in attitude toward others; permissive; believing and trustful; overlooks weaknesses and sees best in others
- Sociability (*unsociability*): participates in social affairs; likes to be with people; outgoing
- Friendliness (*unfriendliness*): genial, warm; open and approachable; approaches other people easily; forms many social relationships
- Sympathy (*lack of sympathy*): concerned with the feelings and wants of others; displays kindly, generous behavior; defends underdog

Expressive dispositions
- Competitiveness (*noncompetitiveness*): sees every relationship as a contest in which other people are rivals to be defeated; self-aggrandizing; noncooperative
- Aggressiveness (*nonaggressiveness*): attacks others directly or indirectly; shows defiant resentment of authority; quarrelsome; negativistic
- Self-consciousness (*social poise*): embarrassed when entering a room after others are seated; suffers excessively from stage fright; hesitates to volunteer in group discussions; bothered at work when people watch; feels uncomfortable if different from others
- Exhibitionism (*self-effacement*): is given to excess and ostentation in behavior and dress; seeks recognition and applause; shows off and behaves in odd ways to attract attention

Note: Opposite trait appears in parentheses.

mature responsible roles for themselves in society. *Desocialization* occurs when an individual, encountering consistent defeat and frustration in interpersonal situations, withdraws from contacts with others. Thus, social psychologists tend to view mental disorders in terms of people's relationships to their social environment—whether they are well adjusted and capable of functioning in a socially acceptable fashion. (See the Cross-National Perspective, "Suicide.")

HUMANISTIC PSYCHOLOGY—THE INNATE HUMAN POTENTIAL

humanistic psychology
focuses on individual
development and self-fulfillment

Humanistic psychology, like social psychology, focuses on the *whole* person, rather than on particular defensive structures or behavioral responses. However, while social psychology focuses on the process of socialization as the key factor in determining personality, humanistic psychology emphasizes the individual's innate potential for development, the human need for self-fulfillment.

Humanistic psychology represents a reaction against behaviorism and psychoanalytic theory, the two forces that dominated psychology for many years. Humanistic psychology rejects behaviorism's insistence on using the strictly scientific, objective, value-free methods of the natural sciences. It views behaviorism, with its narrow focus on behavior itself and its disregard of the subjective human experience, as unable to explain the totality of the person. Humanistic psychology also rejects the Freudian emphasis on the biological needs, or drives, of the body and on the defensive structure of the personality. For the humanists, the basic "self" is not a negative force that must be repressed or controlled; the self is good and has the innate and unique capacity to grow and to develop and expand its creativity.

humanistic psychology as an alternative to psychoanalysis and behaviorism

THE NEED TO SELF-ACTUALIZE

According to the humanists, our needs include the need for safety and security, for friendships and intimacies, for self-esteem and self-expression. The highest psychological need is the need for *"self-actualization."* Human beings are internally motivated to fulfill these needs, to realize their potential; they have an innate propensity toward self-actualization. Personality development is the continuous process of positive growth in search of fulfilling ever-higher needs, the ultimate goal being self-actualization.

the need to "self-actualize"

Self-actualization requires first of all that individuals be aware of their own feelings; without such self-awareness, they can never know themselves, let alone realize their innate potential. In addition, self-actualization is affected by social, or environmental, factors. Like the social psychologists, humanistic psychologists believe that an individual's concept of "self" is in large measure socially determined, that others in one's world have an important impact on the way one feels about oneself. If one is fully and unconditionally accepted as a person, then one develops positive feelings about oneself; if, on the other hand, acceptance is contingent on certain types of behavior, then one may experience anxiety and the need to function defensively, to close oneself off from feelings and a subjective experience of the world. This type of functioning interferes with the process of self-actualization.

factors in personality development

HIERARCHY OF NEEDS

From the point of view of humanistic psychology, the ultimate power of the individual might be regarded as the ability to achieve self-actualization. Abraham Maslow, one of the foremost spokespersons of the humanistic movement, devised a **hierarchy of needs** that distinguishes between the "higher" and "lower" needs inherent in each individual. The highest need is, of course,

hierarchy of needs
the arrangement of needs from lowest to highest in potency

CROSS-NATIONAL PERSPECTIVE
Suicide

Suicide is an individual act. At first glance, it would appear to be solely a product of internal conflicts within the individual. But the pioneering sociologist Emile Durkheim, writing a century ago, argued convincingly that social relations played a major role in the incidence of suicide. Durkheim studied records of suicide in various regions of Europe and observed that some categories of people were much more likely than others to commit suicide. Durkheim found that males, Protestants, wealthy people, and unmarried people all had higher suicide rates than females, Catholics and Jews, poor people, and married people. Durkheim theorized that differences in social integration—the strength of social attachments—explained differences in suicide rates. Lower rates were found among people who forged stronger bonds with others, and higher rates were found among people whose lifestyles were typically individualistic and autonomous. Durkheim reasoned that because men have more autonomy in most societies than women, they are more likely to kill themselves. Because Catholic life fosters family, church, and community ties, Catholics are less likely to commit suicide than Protes-

tants, whose doctrine emphasizes individual and autonomous life. The wealthy have more independence than the poor, who are frequently dependent on others, but the result of this independence is a higher suicide rate. Finally, Durkheim reasoned that single people's suicide rates were higher because they usually had fewer and weaker social attachments than married people.

A century later, Durkheim's general observations still hold true. In the United States, the suicide rate for white males (21.4 per 100,000 persons) is much higher than black males (12.5), and the rates for both white and black males are

higher than those for white females (5.0) and black females (2.1).

Cross-national comparisons also tend to confirm Durkheim's original theory (see table). Suicide rates are higher for men than for women. (Women are more likely to *attempt* suicide, but men are four times more likely to succeed.) Suicide rates are generally higher in richer and predominantly Protestant nations. Suicide rates are higher among single, widowed, and divorced people. And suicide rates are higher among the elderly, especially men, who may choose suicide as an alternative to current or future suffering.

SUICIDE RATES (RATE PER 100,000 POPULATION)

United States	11.8	Japan	15.1
(male)	(19.9)	Netherlands	9.2
(female)	(4.6)	New Zealand	12.6
Australia	12.6	Norway	12.1
Austria	20.2	Poland	14.6
Bulgaria	15.9	Portugal	7.5
Canada	13.0	Romania	12.6
Czech Republic	18.1	Russia	41.2
Denmark	20.4	Spain	7.4
Finland	26.1	Sweden	14.2
France	19.3	Switzerland	19.6
Germany	13.9	United Kingdom	11.9
Hungary	30.9		
Italy	7.2		

SOURCE: U.S. Bureau of the Census, *Statistical Abstract of the United States 1999* (Washington, D.C.: U.S. Government Printing Office, 1999), 837.

self-actualization. However, before one can fulfill the higher needs, one must first satisfy the lower needs. Individual behavior at any time is determined by the individual's strongest need at that time. The higher needs reflect later stages of personality development. Figure 5-5 shows Maslow's formulation of the hierarchy of needs. (Note that the peak of an earlier main class of needs must be passed before the next "higher" need can begin to assume a dominant role. Note also that as psychological development takes place, the number and variety of needs increase.)

At the base of Maslow's hierarchy are **physiological needs** (food, clothing, shelter). These basic needs must be satisfied first. Once they have been satisfied, other levels of needs become important and begin to motivate individual behavior. Above physiological needs are the needs for safety and security. These needs may not always be apparent to the individual; they may be subconscious and not easily identified. A need for **safety** or **security** may become highly motivating, depending on early childhood experiences. The insecure child may later prefer occupations that offer insurance, retirement, protection from layoffs, and a predictable life. In contrast, the adult who had a secure childhood may prefer occupations that offer continuing challenges to imagination and ingenuity and that penalize failure.

Once physiological and safety needs are fairly well satisfied, **social needs** become dominant. The individual, according to Maslow, now seeks group acceptance, friendships, and intimacies. Indeed, studies of group dynamics

physiological needs
the most basic cluster of needs, including water, food, oxygen, sleep, elimination, and sex

safety needs
include order, security, and predictability

belongingness and love needs
include affiliation with others and the feeling of being loved

FIGURE 5-5

MASLOW'S HIERARCHY, SHOWING PROGRESSIVE CHANGES IN NEEDS

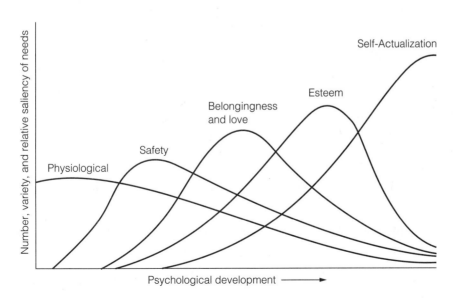

Self-Actualization

Esteem

Belongingness and love

Safety

Physiological

Number, variety, and relative saliency of needs

Psychological development ⟶

suggest that group approval may occasionally become so important that it tends to override realistic appraisal of other sources of action. The individual may actually become a victim of group pressures in his or her search to satisfy social needs and find acceptance in life.

Assuming that an individual's social needs are reasonably well satisfied, a fourth need comes into prominence: **esteem.** Failure to understand this need may lead parents to complain, "We've given our child everything—a good home, stable family, all the things he asked for, even our own time and assistance—yet he is still dissatisfied." However, it may be that it is precisely because such children have had the three basic needs sufficiently satisfied that a fourth need emerges—recognition of worth as an individual. Like the need for security or social needs, the need for personal esteem appears in a variety of forms; a search for *recognition* is one manifestation of the need for personal esteem. Evidence from studies of large corporate and governmental organizations suggests that recognition or symbols of prestige are often more important in motivating management employees than money. Salary carries some prestige value, but often an impressive-sounding title (for example, "vice-president for operations," "director of planning," or "deputy secretary") is even more important. Many individuals will sacrifice salary to achieve these symbols of esteem.

esteem needs
include status, prestige, competence, and confidence

SELF-ACTUALIZATION   When the first four needs are more or less satisfied, we can expect to witness the emergence of Maslow's fifth and final need: the need for **self-actualization.** It is not always clear what self-actualization really is. According to Maslow, "Self-actualizing people are, without one single exception, involved in a cause outside of their own skin, in something outside of themselves."[8] Despite problems in defining self-actualization, it does seem true that at some point in life, frequently in the late thirties or early forties, many individuals feel a vague sense of dissatisfaction. This "mid-life crisis" may be related to the need for self-actualization. Individuals who have provided well for themselves and their families; who face no serious threats to their security; who are well accepted by their family, friends, and neighbors; and who have won recognition in their field of work may nonetheless feel that something is missing. These individuals may have been content while striving to achieve their position in life, but once they have achieved this position, they ask, "Is that all there is?" According to Maslow, these individuals have reached a point at which they must turn to their fifth and final need, self-actualization.

self-actualization
the highest level in the hierarchy, reached only if the preceding need levels have been adequately satisfied; the self-actualizing individual operates at full capacity

THE SELF-ESTEEM CONTROVERSY

Self-esteem has emerged as a policy issue in education, especially minority education. Many educators believe that children who feel good about themselves learn more easily, are more persistent at difficult tasks, and are less likely to use drugs. These educators, therefore, recommend programs to improve self-esteem. Among minority children, these efforts involve, among other things, an emphasis on minority history, language, and contributions to society. The self-esteem argument also contributes to the emphasis on multiculturalism in schools and in colleges and universities (see Chapter 3).

However, it is not clear that self-esteem can be inflated by these efforts. That is, self-esteem may come only with meeting challenges, achieving goals, and surmounting difficulties. Telling children that they are wonderful may do little to improve their levels of achievement. Moreover, various studies of minority children reveal that their self-esteem is as high as or higher than that of nonminority children.

Most people express a great deal of self-esteem. Self depreciation is usually limited to truly depressed individuals. In national surveys, 80 to 90 percent of respondents rate their own performance, attractiveness, ethics, and positive attributes at least above average. Failures are frequently attributed to others, circumstances, or bad luck. (After receiving poor grades, most students criticized the exam, the professor, or the subject, not themselves.) People are quick to believe flattering descriptions of themselves and filter out criticisms.

TREATING MENTAL ILLNESS

It is not always easy to distinguish mental health from mental illness. Generally, people are said to have a mental disorder when they feel distressed by their condition *and* it impairs their ability to pursue their normal functions in life (see the Case Study, "Diagnosing Mental Illness"). Brief stresses and strains of daily living usually do not require treatment, while severe, lasting, and incapacitating mental suffering clearly does so. But most symptoms of mental illness are less than completely incapacitating. How much sadness indicates depression? How much suspicion indicates paranoia? How much self-confidence indicates mania? Most of us bear some mental stress without seeking professional help. But some people do not recognize their need for treatment even in the midst of acute mental illness.

CLINICAL PSYCHOLOGY

Clinical psychology focuses on the treatment of psychological disorders. It is closely related to *psychiatry* in that both clinical psychologists and psychiatrists deal with the diagnosis and treatment of psychological disorders. (The psychiatrist, however, is also a medical doctor.) Clinicians deal with real people with real psychological problems. They enter the patient's world and concern themselves with the subjective human experience, including wishes, fears, anxieties, ambitions. Clinical psychology stresses therapy, ranging from chemical therapy and shock treatment to various behavior therapies and insight therapies.

clinical psychology
focuses on treatment of psychological disorders

CASE STUDY

Diagnosing Mental Illness

The American Psychiatric Association has tried to increase public awareness of the symptoms of mental illness as well as to remove the social stigma that surrounded mental illness in the past. Mental illness is not a character weakness but a treatable illness.

Schizophrenia

Schizophrenia is one of the most debilitating mental illnesses. Often characterized by distorted thinking, hallucinations, delusions, and a dulling of normal emotions, schizophrenia is considered a brain disease. An estimated 1.5 million Americans suffer from this mental illness.

The following symptoms are sometimes associated with schizophrenia:

- hearing nonexistent sounds
- seeing nonexistent images
- thoughts that dart uncontrollably from subject to subject

- unfounded fears that one is being plotted against or watched
- loss of self-esteem
- withdrawal from friends and family
- inappropriate reactions to situations
- deteriorating work and school performance
- neglect of social relationships and personal appearance

Depression

The most common and treatable mental illness, depression affects eight million to fourteen million Americans each year. Characterized by feelings of sadness, helplessness, hopelessness, and irritability, depression affects one in four women and one in ten men at some point during their lifetime.

If four or more of the following symptoms persist for more than two weeks, an indi-

vidual should seek professional help:

- change in appetite (significant weight loss or gain)
- change in sleeping patterns
- loss of interest in pleasurable activities
- loss of energy; fatigue
- feelings of worthlessness
- feelings of inappropriate guilt
- inability to concentrate; indecisiveness
- recurring thoughts of death or suicide
- melancholia (overwhelming feelings of sadness and grief)
- disturbed thinking (out of touch with reality)
- physical symptoms (headaches or stomachaches)

Manic Depression

Manic depression (bipolar illness) is a more severe form of depression. An estimated two to three million people will suffer from this disorder

---

psychiatrist
an M.D. who specializes in the treatment of mental disorders

clinical psychologist
a therapist with a Ph.D. in psychological treatment and testing

psychological counselor
a therapist with graduate training in psychology or related fields

PROFESSIONAL CARE

Professional assistance can be rendered by a **psychiatrist**—a medical doctor (M.D.) who specializes in the diagnosis and treatment of mental disorders; or a **clinical psychologist**—a therapist with graduate training, usually a Ph.D., in psychological testing and treatment; or a **psychological counselor**—often a person with graduate training in psychology, marriage and family life, alcohol and drug abuse treatment, social work, or related fields.

Diagnosing mental illness requires psychiatrists and psychologists to recognize a pattern of symptoms that correspond to an illness. This is often done by asking questions or giving written tests concerning a person's mental state. The American Psychiatric Association publishes *The*

at some time in their lives. People with manic depression experience mood swings from euphoria to depression.

All symptoms of depression can also be symptoms of manic depression. These are some of the typical symptoms of the manic (euphoric) phase of the disorder:

- an "on top of the world" mood that appears overly euphoric
- expressions of unwarranted optimism
- lack of judgment
- grandiose delusions of connections with God, celebrities, or political leaders
- hyperactivity and excessive participation in numerous activities
- racing, uncontrollable thoughts
- decreased need for sleep
- attention easily diverted to inconsequential or unimportant details

- sudden irritability, rage, or paranoia

Anxiety Disorders

There are several types of anxiety disorders, each with somewhat different symptoms. Anxiety disorders are very common, affecting an estimated 10 to 15 percent of the population.

- *social phobia:* an intense fear of being scrutinized or evaluated by others
- *simple phobia:* an intense fear of a particular object or situation
- *posttraumatic stress disorder:* undesired recollections or reexperiences of a prior intense experience, often accompanied by chronic anxiety, angry outbursts, sleep disturbances, and emotional distress
- *panic disorder:* repeated bouts of intense anxiety not necessarily related to any particular situation, often

causing shortness of breath, dizziness, sweating, fainting, vomiting, racing and pounding heart

- *obsessive/compulsive disorder:* obsessions are recurrent and persistent ideas, thoughts, or images that cannot be ignored or suppressed or stopped; compulsions are repetitive and persistent behaviors usually performed in a ritualistic manner that are not connected in any reasonable fashion with subjective circumstances
- *generalized anxiety disorder:* generalized anxiety experienced for six months or longer that is not associated with life circumstances or a particular stimulus; symptoms include shakiness, restlessness, fatigue, shortness of breath, heart palpitations, sweating, dizziness, hot flashes, difficulty concentrating, irritability

Diagnostic and Statistical Manual (DSM), which defines various mental disorders, describing typical observable behavior and responses to examiners' questions. While the *DSM* can be very helpful, seldom do patients' symptoms and responses fit perfectly with a recognized disorder. Indeed, sometimes fully qualified professionals render very different diagnoses of the same patients.

Treatment may come in the form of psychotherapy or drug therapy or some combination of the two. **Psychotherapy,** or "talk" therapy, involves communication between patient and therapist designed to help the patient better understand and deal effectively with troubling feelings and behavior. Psychotherapy includes a wide variety of techniques—some that depend on developing the patient's understanding of deeply ingrained motives and

psychotherapy
"talk" therapy, involving communication between patient and therapist; includes a wide variety of techniques

conflicts, and others that help patients cope with their problems without necessarily exploring their underlying causes.

PSYCHOANALYSIS

Traditional psychoanalysis is a therapy based on the Freudian notion that mental illness is most often a product of unconscious conflicts. If patients can acquire an insight into their own motives and needs, presumably they can develop more effective ways of handling their problems. When patients can freely express previously repressed emotions or relive intense emotional experiences, they are believed to be better equipped to face their current problems effectively. Sometimes insights are found in spontaneous talk or "free association," or in the interpretation of dreams, or in hypnosis. But psychoanalysis is very time-consuming and expensive. It may require weekly sessions over several years.

BEHAVIORAL THERAPIES

Behavioral therapy assumes that disturbed behavior has been learned and that it can be unlearned or modified by new conditioning techniques. Behavioral therapists are more concerned with changing specific behavioral patterns than with understanding or analyzing a patient's personality. For example, in relaxation training, people learn to relax various muscles and eventually learn to relax their entire body. After learning to relax, they may be asked to confront a previously anxiety-producing stimulus. "Desensitization" occurs when people are able to maintain their relaxed condition while gradually encountering fears and phobias. "Assertiveness training" is another form of behavioral therapy in which people are taught to "speak up" or "say no" when others try to take advantage of them. Positive reinforcement is sometimes employed in mental hospitals when patients are rewarded for socially acceptable behavior. Negative reinforcement, or adverse conditioning, is occasionally employed in modifying alcohol and substance abuse.

HUMANISTIC THERAPIES

Humanistic therapies tend to emphasize "client-centered" solutions to individual problems. The humanistic therapist does not try to interpret patients' behavior (as would a psychoanalyst) or modify it (as would a behavioral therapist) but, rather, allows patients to develop their own self-actualizing solution to their problems. The therapist does not render judgments or opinions but, rather, tries to create an open and tolerant atmosphere for the patient's self-expression. The goal is to enable patients to clarify their feelings.

Group therapy is a means of encouraging people to express their feelings in the presence of others with similar problems. Group therapy saves time and money because one therapist can work with six to twelve patients at once. People may derive some comfort and support from observing others with similar or perhaps even worse problems. And people may learn vicariously—by watching how others deal with their problems.

DRUG THERAPIES

Drug therapy has had a revolutionary impact on mental health care. Beginning in the late 1950s, psychiatric drugs dramatically improved the effectiveness of treatment for a vast array of disorders. Prior to the advent of drug therapies, mental hospitals were very dismal places; physicians were able to offer little more than custodial care. Hallucinating patients talked to "voices"; catatonic patients sat in stupors; and manic patients paced the floors. The most agitated patients were sedated or placed in restraints. There were few "cures." But drug therapies changed these scenes. Currently, hospital stays are relatively brief; patients are medically and psychologically evaluated; drug therapies are initiated and are closely supervised. Patients who pose no danger to themselves or others are released.

The impact of the drug revolution is apparent in the depopulation of mental hospitals. During the first half of the century, the number of mental hospital patients rose steadily. But the introduction of drug therapies reversed this trend, and mental hospitals were emptied of all but temporary patients and a few very severe cases.

Indeed, the drug revolution was exploited as a means of reducing public spending for mental health care. Many patients are being released into the community with instructions for drug therapies and outpatient care. But they often have been unable to follow their instructions, and community care frequently has been lacking. It is estimated that one-quarter to one-third of the nation's street-wandering "homeless" population suffers from serious mental illness.

Schizophrenia, mania, and depression are the categories of mental illness that are frequently and successfully treated with drugs.[9] Four classes of drugs are commonly used in psychiatry today: antianxiety drugs, antipsychotics, antidepressants, and mood stabilizers. These drugs frequently provide immediate and effective relief for symptoms of mental illness. Patients are medically monitored for potential unwanted side effects. But the newer drugs have proven very effective with only minimal side effects.

THE SOCIOLOGY OF PSYCHOLOGICAL DISORDERS

Psychological disorders appear to vary by ethnicity and gender (see Table 5-3).

Men are much more likely than women to suffer alcohol abuse and dependence. Women are more likely to report mood disorders. Men are more likely to develop antisocial personalities (see "A Psychological Perspective on Crime—The Antisocial Personality" in Chapter 12 on page 317).

TABLE 5-3

THE SOCIOLOGY OF PSYCHOLOGICAL DISORDERS

	Total*	Gender		Ethnicity		
		Men	Women	White	Black	Hispanic
Alochol Abuse	13.8%	23.8%	4.8%	13.6%	13.8%	16.7%
Anxiety	3.8	2.4	5.0	3.4	6.1	3.7
Phobias	14.3	10.4	17.7	9.7	23.4	12.2
Mood disorder	7.8	5.2	10.2	8.0	6.3	7.8
Schizophrenia	1.5	1.2	1.7	1.4	2.1	0.8
Antisocial personality	2.6	4.5	0.8	2.6	2.3	3.4

*Percentage of Americans who have *ever* experienced a disorder.

SOURCE: Data derived from L. Robbins and D. Regier, *Psychiatric Disorders in America* (New York: Free Press, 1991), 564–565.

Psychological disorders of various sorts are somewhat more prevalent among minorities in America. Minorities are also more likely to experience poverty (see Focus, "Who Are the Poor?" in Chapter 11 on page 285). Poverty, therefore, may be the real factor affecting ethnic differences in disorders. The stress of poverty may precipitate psychological disorders, especially depression among women and alcoholism among men.[10]

POWERLESSNESS AND MENTAL HEALTH

There is a common adage that "power tends to corrupt, and absolute power corrupts absolutely." It reflects our negative view of power and our association of power with abuse. But the distinguished psychologist Rollo May, whose contributions to the humanistic movement are highly significant, contends that power is a fundamental aspect of the life process. Indeed, he believes that *powerlessness* corrupts the human personality by robbing the individual of a sense of meaning and significance.

power is functional

power to be

power as self-affirmation

power as self-assertion

power as aggression

power as violence

Rollo May's argument is that power occurs in an individual's life in five functional forms.[11] The first is the *power to be*. The word *power* comes from the Latin root meaning "to be able." The newborn must have the power to make others respond to its needs—it cries and waves its arms violently as signs of its discomfort. An infant who cannot elicit a response from others fails to develop as a separate personality. *Power as self-affirmation* is the recognition of one's own worth and significance in life. Some power is essential for self-esteem and self-belief. *Power as self-assertion* makes it clear who we are and what we believe. It gives us the potential to react to attack and protect ourselves from becoming victims. Power also occurs in everyone's life as *aggression*—thrusting out against a person or thing seen as an adversary. The constructive aspects of aggression include cutting through barriers to initiate relationships; confronting another person, not with the intent to hurt, but in order to penetrate that individual's consciousness; and actualizing one's own self in a hostile environment. The destructive side of aggression, of course, includes thrusting out to inflict injury and taking power simply to increase one's own range of control. Finally, power occurs as *violence.* May believes that violence is an attempt to exercise power. Violence may result from a failure at self-affirmation or self-assertion, or it may accompany aggression. Nonetheless, it can be regarded as functional to the individual if there is no other way for that person to gain significance in life.

It is May's belief that modern mass society impairs the individual's self-esteem and self-worth. The feeling of personal powerlessness is widespread.

> *To admit our own individual feelings of powerlessness—that we cannot influence many people; that we count for little; that the values to which our parents devoted their lives are to us insubstantial and worthless; that we feel ourselves to be "faceless others," insignificant to other people and therefore not worth much to ourselves—that is, indeed, difficult to admit.*[12]

May believes that much irrational violence—riots, assassinations, senseless murders—is a product of feelings of powerlessness.

ON THE WEB

EXPLORING PSYCHOLOGY

Psychology encompasses a wide variety of subjects. The official site of the American Psychological Association lists fifty-two "branches" of psychology, most with their own Web sites.

American Psychological Association. The best place to begin your exploration of psychology is the official site of the American Psychological Association (APA; www.apa.org). It provides information for students, parents, teenagers, the media, and others about a wide variety of topics related to psychology, including common psychological disorders. For students, this site provides career-planning information employment data, programs and degrees in graduate education, financial assistance, and more relating to psychology. Student membership in the APA is inexpensive and includes subscriptions to *Monitor on Psychology* and *American Psychologist.* The APA site includes links to some fifty-two fields of psychology, including developmental, personality, clinical, educational, behavioral, experimental, and humanistic psychology; psychoanalysis; psychopharmacology; and sport. And a search engine at the site provides an index of topics from "addiction" to "women."

Psychoanalysis Division, APA. Among the more interesting subfield sites of the American Psychological Association is that of its Psychoanalysis Division (www.divapa.org). This site is designed to provide the public with an understanding of psychoanalysis. It even includes a tour of the Freud Museum in London.

Psychology.com. Several commercial sites invite browsers to view topics in psychology. Psychology.com (www.psychology.com) contains current articles, psychological tests, the directory of therapists, and even an "Ask a therapist" interactive link. Another commercial site, Evolution Voyage (www.evoyage.com), focuses on evolutionary psychology.

Personality Theories. A professor of psychology at Pennsylvania's Shippensburg State University has compiled an online introduction to the theories of many prominent psychologists, including those mentioned in this chapter—Freud, Skinner, Maslow, and May (www.ship.edu/~cgboeree).

DNA Learning Center. The DNA Learning Center (www.vector.cshl.org) provides introductory information for students, teachers, and nonscientists who wish to learn more about genetics. It is sponsored by the Cold Spring Harbor Laboratory, the center for molecular genetics research.

ABOUT THIS CHAPTER

An understanding of personality, of individual behavioral responses and their determinants, is essential to a full understanding of power in society. In this chapter, we have explored the meaning of personality and various psychological theories regarding the determinants of personality. We also saw what various schools of psychology have to say about the relationship between personality and power. Now that you have read Chapter 5, you should be able to

- describe the "nature versus nurture" controversy in the shaping of personality
- discuss how psychoanalytic (Freudian) theory views personality and its development and how this theory interprets individual responses to power and authority
- discuss behavioral psychology's use of learning theory in its approach to the study of personality and B. F. Skinner's ideas for the control of human behavior
- describe humanistic psychology's view of the "self," Abraham Maslow's construction of a "hierarchy of needs," and Rollo May's concept of powerlessness
- discuss how power in the form of authority and legitimacy can command obedience and the implications of such obedience

DISCUSSION QUESTIONS

1. Describe the "nature versus nurture" controversy over the determination of personality. How does research on the personality characteristics of identical twins help us learn more about the relative effects of heredity versus environment on human behavior?

2. Discuss the psychoanalytic (Freudian) view of the determinants of behavior. Identify the three major systems that Freudians believe compose the personality and describe the roles played by each of these systems. Differentiate between normal and neurotic anxiety and describe the functions of identification.

3. Describe the authoritarian personality. What are some psychoanalytic explanations of the authoritarian personality? Discuss the criticisms of the *Authoritarian Personality* study.

4. How would a behavioral psychologist define personality and the goal of psychology? Describe how a linkage between a conditioned stimulus and response is established.

5. Describe how a social psychologist would approach the study of personality. Identify the processes that social psychologists believe are critical determinants of personality development.

6. Discuss humanistic psychology's view of the individual, Rollo May's formulation of the functions of power, and Abraham Maslow's "hierarchy of needs."

7. Discuss the results of the experiments that psychologist Stanley Milgram carried out at Yale University. What do these results tell us about the power of authority and legitimacy to command obedience? What are the implications of such obedience?

8. If you were interested in becoming a clinical psychologist, which type of therapy do you think you would want to practice—psychoanalytic therapy, behavioral therapy, a therapy based on the principles of interpersonal-interaction theory, or one that uses the approach of humanistic psychology? Describe how the theory you would choose views "personality disorder."

9. Which of the theories studied do you think provides the most cogent view of personality and the relationship between personality and power? Discuss your reasoning, including any criticisms you may have about any of these theories.

Chapter 6

Power and the Economic Order

POWER AND ECONOMIC ORGANIZATION

A great deal of power in the United States is centered in large economic organizations—corporations, banks, utilities, investment firms, and government agencies charged with the responsibility of overseeing the economy. Not all power, it is true, is anchored in or exercised through these institutions; power is also embodied in class, cultural, political, and ideological institutions and processes, as discussed elsewhere in this volume. *But control of economic resources provides a continuous and important base of power in any society.*

Economics is the study of the production and distribution of scarce goods and services. Economics decides the following questions:

- *What should be produced?* What goods and services should be produced and in what quantities? Should we produce more automobiles or more trains and subways, more food and fertilizer or more clean air and water, more police protection or higher Social Security benefits? Should we produce more for immediate consumption, or should we save and invest more now in order to be able to enjoy even more later? Every economic system must answer questions like these.

economics
the study of the production and distribution of scarce resources

economic decisions
what to produce
how to produce it
for whom it will be produced

127

- *How will goods and services be produced?* The decision to produce particular goods and services does not accomplish the task. Resources must be organized and allocated, and people must be motivated to work. Various combinations of resources—land, labor, capital (factories, machinery, supplies), and technology—might be used to produce a particular item. All these resources must be organized for production, either by providing economic incentives (wages and profits) or by threats of force.
- *For whom will goods and services be produced?* Who will consume these products and services? Economists refer to this question as the question of *distribution*. Should people be paid according to their skills, knowledge, or contribution to the production of goods and services? Or should everyone be paid equally regardless of their skills, knowledge, or contribution to production? Should people be allowed to bid for goods and services, with the most going to the highest bidders? Or should goods and services be distributed by government, with the most going to those who are best able to influence government decisions?

economic decision making
markets: individually through voluntary exchange
governments: collectively through coercion

In general, there are two ways of making these economic decisions: (1) individually, through the market system; or (2) collectively, through governments.

The *market* system allows individuals and firms to make their own decisions about who gets what and how. Markets implement decisions through voluntary exchange. Markets work through decentralized decisions of many separate individuals and businesses.

Governments also decide who gets what and how by *collective decision making*. Governments implement decisions through coercion (fines, penalties, imprisonment) and threats of coercion. In democracies, collective decisions are influenced by individual voters, interest groups, and parties; in nondemocratic governments, the decisions are influenced primarily by ideology and the interests of government leaders themselves.

In most economies, including that of the United States, economic decisions are made by *both* the market system and the government.[1]

THE MARKET SYSTEM, HARD-BOILED AND IMPERSONAL

economic system
institutions and processes by which society produces and distributes scarce resources

The **economic system** consists of the *institutions and processes by which a society produces and distributes scarce resources.* There is not enough of everything for all of us to have all we want. If nature provided everything that everyone wanted without work, there would be no need for an economic system. But resources are "scarce," and some scheme must be created to decide who gets what. Scarcity, together with the problem of choice it raises, is the fundamental question of economics.

Markets can be small sidewalk enterprises. Here, a fruit vendor sells grapes in Chinatown, New York City.

The American economic system is a market, or free enterprise, system. It is largely "unplanned"; no government bureau tells all 115 million workers in the United States where to work, what to do, or how to do it. On the whole, the **private enterprise economy** organizes itself, with a minimum of centralized planning or direction. The American system relies chiefly on private individuals, in search of wages and profits, to get the job done. No government agency directs that shirts be produced: If people want shirts, then there is profit to be made in producing them, and businesspeople who recognize the potential profit will begin turning them out. No government agency directs how many shirts will be produced: As shirt output increases, a point is reached at which there are so many shirts that the price that people are willing to pay falls below the cost of producing them, and businesspeople then begin curtailing their production of shirts. This same production-in-search-of-profits goes on as well for thousands of other products simultaneously.

private enterprise economy
private individuals in search of wages and profits, acting on their own, without government direction

MARKETS

A private enterprise economy decides what is to be produced, how it is to be produced, and how it is to be distributed, all in a fashion that is for the most part impersonal. Everyone, by following self-interest, decides who gets what. The absence of planning and control does not mean chaos. Rather, it means a complex system of production and distribution that no single mind, and probably no government planning agency, could organize or control in all its infinite detail.

market

arrangement that enables people to exchange money for goods, services, and labor

consumer demand

preferences for goods and services, expressed by willingness to pay

profits

motivate producers to satisfy consumer demand and to produce goods and services in the most efficient way possible

A **market** is any place or arrangement that enables people to exchange money for goods, services, or labor. The exchange rate is called the *price.* Under the private enterprise system, the *market determines what is to be produced, how much it will cost, and who will be able to buy it.* Consumers decide what should be produced by expressing their preferences in terms of the amount of money they spend on various goods and services (**consumer demand**). When consumers *are willing to pay* for something, they will bid up the *price* of that item. The price is an indication of how much of the item consumers want produced.[2]

PROFITS

Business firms are out to make **profits.** Profits motivate producers to satisfy consumer demands. Profits drive the free enterprise system. Profits occur when selling prices are higher than the costs of production. Businesspeople move into industries in which consumers bid up prices. Where consumer demand bids up prices, businesspeople can afford to pay higher wages; and workers tend to move toward those industries with higher pay and better working conditions. Thus, consumer demand shifts both business and labor into industries in which prices are high. Business firms play a key role in a private enterprise system because they channel production toward industries having the strongest consumer demand and organize productive activity in the most efficient (lowest-cost) way possible. Profits are the mainspring of the market system. In seeking profits, business firms perform a vital economic function.

PRICES

Who gets the goods that are produced? The price system allocates goods to those who have both the *willingness to pay* and the *ability to pay.* The willingness to pay determines the desirability of producing a certain item. No government agency determines whether we "need" goods and services; the market reveals whether individuals are willing to pay for them. Consumers, however, must also have the ability to pay: They must earn incomes by working to produce goods and services that consumers want. The *labor market* largely determines where people will work and how much they will be paid. The income received for their labor depends primarily on their worth to the businesses that employ them. They are worth more when they contribute more to production and profit. Where production and profits are low, wages will be low and individuals will be frequently unemployed.

The market is hard-boiled and impersonal. If a business produces too much of a particular item—more than consumers are willing to buy at a particular price—the price will have to be lowered or production (supply) will have to be cut back. Competition among businesses also checks prices, for a business that sets a price higher than that set by competitors will lose sales. Thus, *consumer demand, product supply, and competition determine prices.* In the absence of interfering factors, the **price** depends on a relationship of supply and demand at any given time. If demand increases, prices tend to rise; if demand decreases, prices tend to fall. If supply increases, prices tend to fall; if supply decreases, prices tend to rise.

prices
allocate goods and services by willingness and ability to pay

determined by consumer demand, product supply, and competition

THE IDEAL MARKET

The market reconciles the interests of buyers and sellers, labor and business, in the process of getting people to agree on prices. The market in a free enterprise system undertakes this reconciliation automatically, without assistance from outside individuals or forces. The ideal conditions for a market operation are these:

- *Competition:* The existence of a perfect competition, in which the market has so many buyers and sellers that no single trader has any control over the price of the good or service being exchanged, and the price is made by the market through the impersonal forces of supply and demand. (If one or a few sellers have control over supply, the market is said to be *monopolistic;* if one or a few buyers have control over demand, the market is said to be *monopsonistic.*)
- *Exclusion:* The ability of a buyer of the good to exclude others from the satisfactions that good provides so no one can enjoy the benefits of someone else's purchase. (When people benefit from the purchases of others, there are said to be *spillover effects,* as, for example, in the case of national defense products, which cannot be sold on the open market.)
- *Mobility:* The complete mobility of resources and labor so they can move in response to changes in prices. In a completely mobile economy, each individual and business is prepared to alter the pattern of spending and working in response to changes in prices of goods and labor.

ideal conditions for a market operation
competition among many buyers and sellers

ability of buyer to exclude others from benefits of purchase

mobility of resources and labor

In other words, in an ideal market there is a great deal of competition, and prices are determined solely by supply and demand. All must pay for the goods and benefits they receive, and resources and labor shift easily in response to changes in prices and wages.

SUPPLY, DEMAND, AND THE MARKET PRICE

In order to understand the market, we must consider the decisions of both suppliers and consumers simultaneously. In other words, we must consider supply and demand and how both are reconciled by price.

An Example of Market Pricing

Let us illustrate what happens in a true market economy, where price is governed by supply and demand.

Along with many other commodities, millions of bushels of wheat are bought and sold every day at the Chicago Board of Trade. Let us suppose that the first buyer of the day offers $2 per bushel for wheat. Let us also suppose that there are buyers for twenty million bushels of wheat at this low price (demand). However, few owners are willing to sell at this price, and therefore, there are only ten million bushels of wheat offered at $2 per bushel (supply). The result is an imbalance in supply and demand, a ten-million-bushel shortfall in supply at the low $2 price. Those still wishing to buy must therefore raise their price to attract more wheat to the market. Let us suppose that the price then shoots up to $4 per bushel. At this price, there are fewer buyers (let us say only an eight-million-bushel demand) and many more sellers (let us say an eighteen-million-bushel supply). The result is an excess supply of ten million bushels at the high price; this excess will eventually push prices back down.

The New York Stock Exchange is a market on a larger scale.

FIGURE 6-1

An Example of Supply, Demand, and Price

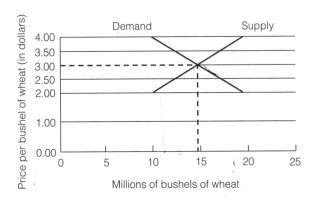

Thus, the price tends to stabilize at a point low enough to attract sufficient demand for wheat but high enough to attract an equivalent supply of wheat. In our example, this price is $3 per bushel, where fourteen million bushels are demanded and fourteen million bushels are offered.

Figure 6-1 shows our example of supply and demand in graphic form. The supply curve is low at a low price, but it increases as the price increases. Demand is high at a low price, but it declines as the price increases. The two lines for supply and demand intersect at a price where the amount demanded just matches the amount supplied. This will tend to be the market price. In our example, it is set at $3 per bushel. Any other price will produce either an excess supply (at a higher price) or an excess demand (at a lower price).

Product, Labor, and Capital Markets

Consumer products are only one type of market.[3] The **labor market** consists of the decisions of employers and employees to offer and accept jobs at specified wages. Wages represent the price of labor in the labor market. The **capital market** refers to money made available by banks and other lenders as loans, primarily to business firms but to consumers as well. The interest rate charged by lenders is really the price of money. It is the price that businesses and consumers are willing to pay lenders in order to borrow money.

All three of these types of markets—product, labor, and capital markets—function simultaneously in the economy. Prices, wages, and interest rates regulate the supply and demand for products, labor, and capital, respectively. We can envision the economy as the interaction of supply and demand in all three of these types of markets (see Figure 6-2).

labor market
decisions of employers and employees to offer and accept jobs at specified wages (prices)

capital markets
decisions of lenders and borrowers to make and accept loans at specified interest rates (prices)

FIGURE 6-2

PRODUCT, LABOR, AND CAPITAL MARKETS

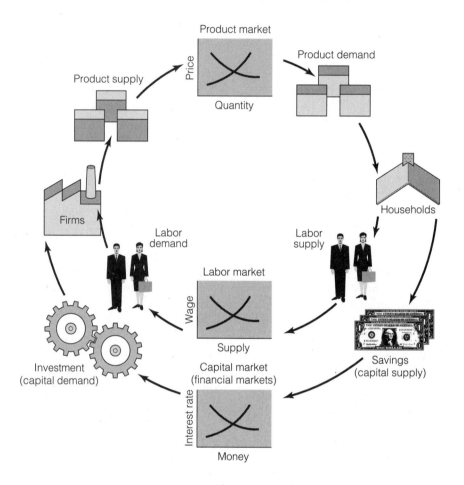

MEASURING AMERICA'S WEALTH

national income accounting
data collected by government
that describes the nation's
income and output

**GDP (gross domestic
product)**
total value of nation's production
of goods and services for a year

Underlying the power of nations is the strength of their economy—their total
productive capacity. The United States can produce $10 trillion worth of
goods and services in a single year for its 281 million people. To understand
America's vast wealth, we must learn how to measure it. We need to know
where the wealth comes from and where it goes. The system of **national income accounts** provides these measures. The U.S. government, as well at the
governments of other advanced industrialized nations, collects extensive data
on economic activity.

Let us begin with the gross domestic product. *The **GDP** is the nation's total
production of goods and services for a single year valued in terms of market*

Adam Smith and Laissez-Faire Economics

In the same year the Declaration of Independence was signed, Adam Smith, a Scottish professor of philosophy, published his *The Wealth of Nations* and thereby secured recognition as the founder of free enterprise economics. Today, the economic model set forth by Adam Smith is frequently referred to as *classical economics* or *laissez-faire economics* (from the French phrase meaning "allow to do as one pleases"). Smith wrote *The Wealth of Nations* as an attack on the *mercantilism* of nations in his day, that is, the attempt of governments to intervene in the economy with special tariffs, regulations, subsidies, and exclusive charters to businesses, all designed to maximize the accretion of gold and silver in government treasuries. Smith argued against mercantilism and for *free competition* in the marketplace. He believed that a worldwide market, *unfettered by government restrictions or subsidies,* would result in lower prices and high standards of living for all. A free market would allow the businesses and nations most capable of producing particular goods cheaply and efficiently to do so. The outcome of the specialization and efficiency created by free competition would be a high standard of living for everyone. Thus, pursuit of private profit was actually in the public interest.

Laissez-faire economics is based on the idea that people are rational, that they will pursue their own economic self-interest, and that they are mobile and able to shift their resources and labor as the market demands. According to this economic system, there should be no artificial blocks to the most efficient use of people and materials. The market has a large number of competitors buying and selling products, services, and labor; and no one alone has control over supply, demand, or price. Buyers buy from producers who make the best goods at the lowest price. Thus, efficiency is rewarded and inefficiency is driven out of the economy. As competition increases supply and lowers prices, some producers shift to more lucrative lines. The market continuously corrects unproductive use of resources. The system is self-adjusting and self-regulating.

Smith objected to government interference in the natural operations of the marketplace. Government should do only two things: (1) create an environment for an orderly marketplace, that is, maintain law and order, protect private property, enforce contracts, and provide a monetary system; and (2) supply those services the marketplace cannot provide, such as defense, public works, and care of widows, orphans, and other helpless people.

Today many "classical" economists echo Adam Smith's ideas. Although it is now widely recognized that government must play an important role in stabilizing the economy (avoiding both inflation and depression), protecting consumers, regulating business and labor practices, and assisting individuals who cannot care for themselves, classical economists nonetheless argue that economic planning by government is incompatible with *personal freedom*. They contend that bureaucratic intervention in the economy not only is inefficient and wasteful but also gradually erodes individual freedom and initiative.

Thus, the appeal of laissez-faire economics is based not only on the efficiency of the marketplace in channeling labor and resources into their most productive uses, but also on the personal freedom this system guarantees.

*prices.** It is the sum of all the goods and services that people have been willing to pay for, from wheat production to bake sales, from machine tools to maid service, from aircraft manufacturing to bus service, from automobiles to chewing gum, from wages and salaries to interest on bank deposits.

COMPUTING THE GDP

To compute the GDP, economists sum up all the expenditures on goods and services, plus government purchases. Care is taken to count *only the final product* sold to consumers so that raw materials will not be counted twice, that is, in the original sale to a manufacturer and in the final price of the product. Business investment includes *only new investment goods* (buildings, machinery, and so on) and does not include financial transfers such as the purchase of stocks and bonds. Government purchases for goods and services include the money spent on *goods* (weapons, roads, buildings, parks, and so on), as well as the *wages* paid for the *services* of government employees. "Transfer payments" such as welfare payments, unemployment insurance, and Social Security payments are *not* part of the GDP because they are not payments for currently produced goods or services. The GDP ignores *all* transactions of money and goods in which *no new* goods or services are produced. Thus, the GDP becomes a measure of the nation's production of goods and services. It can be thought of as the total national economic pie for a given year.

GDP AS CIRCULAR FLOW

National income accounting describes a complex circular flow that includes both an *income* and *expenditure* side of the GDP. Figure 6-3 shows this circular flow of goods and services. Note that the GDP is composed of consumer outlays, plus business investment and government purchases of goods and services. Each of these components is measured and valued each year by the U.S. Bureau of Economic Analysis in the Department of Commerce.

CURRENT DOLLARS VERSUS CONSTANT DOLLARS

constant dollars
dollars valued from a particular year in order to account for changes in the value of dollars; that is, inflation

Because prices have increased over time through inflation, to get a meaningful measure of actual growth in output, we must view the gross domestic product in **constant dollars.** Doubling the GDP merely by doubling prices signifies no real gain in production, so in order to separate *real increases* in

---

* Occasionally, economists use a slightly different measure of national output: the gross national product. The GNP measures output attributable to U.S. residents; the GNP measures total output attributable to production located in the United States. The GNP is often used in cross-national comparisons.

FIGURE 6-3

CIRCULAR FLOW OF GDP

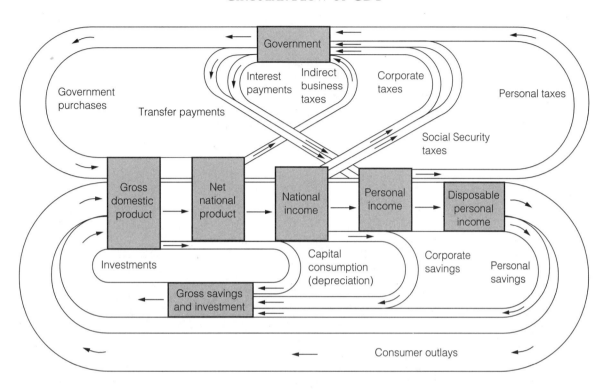

the GDP from mere *dollar increases,* we must adjust for changes in the value of the dollar over the years. Economists account for changes in the value of a dollar by establishing the value of a dollar in a particular time base (for example, 1992) and then using *constant dollars* to measure the value of goods over time. Figure 6-4 shows that the GDP has grown both in current dollars *and* in constant dollars. Thus, America's economic growth is not just a product of inflation.

PER CAPITA GDP

The GDP is sometimes measured in per capita terms—the gross national product divided by the population. **Per capita GDP** is a better measure of the well-being of the average person in a country. Cross-national comparisons are generally made in gross national product (GNP)—a slightly different measure that includes goods and services produced by citizens outside of their own country (see Cross-National Perspective, "GNP and Standards of Living").

per capita GDP
gross domestic product divided by the population; a measure of economic well-being

FIGURE 6-4

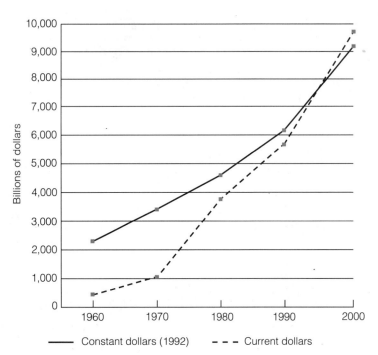

GDP GROWTH IN THE UNITED STATES

SOURCE: Drawn from data in *Statistical Abstract of the United States 1999*; and *Budget of the United States Government 2001*.

LIMITATIONS OF THE GDP MEASURE

The GDP does *not* measure nonmarket activities, for example, household work or child rearing (unless these tasks are performed by paid employees). It does not measure well-being as it is reflected in leisure time. Indeed, an increase in leisure may be associated with a decrease in GDP because less time is devoted to producing goods and services. Yet we might consider ourselves better off for having more time for leisure activities. Moreover, the GDP does not directly measure social ills, for example, crime or pollution. And it does not measure the *distribution* of income or output among individuals in a society. It is not a measure of inequality; it does not tell us what proportion of people are wealthy or poor.

The GDP values all goods and services equally in dollar items. It does not distinguish, for example, between cigarette sales, Bible sales, football-game ticket sales, grocery-store sales, or handgun sales. Arguably, some goods and services benefit society more than others, yet the GDP is neutral in its valuation of all goods and services.

GNP and Standards of Living

National income accounting is highly refined in the western industrialized nations. But figures for less-developed nations are often estimates by agencies of the United Nations or the United States. We can compare the relative size of national economies, as well as the distribution of some key consumer items, by observing the table.

The United States is the world's largest national economy. However, the European Economic Community, which promises to eliminate national trade barriers between the western European nations and to create a single united economy, may eventually create a larger market than the United States. Less-developed nations, despite accounting for three-fourths of the world's population, have very modest GNPs.

Productivity, or economic output per person, is frequently measured by GNP per capita. Note that although the United States has the largest overall economy, productivity in several nations equals or exceeds productivity in the United States. Japan, for example, has an economy slightly over half the size of the United States; but Japan has a population of only 125 million, compared to 275 million in the United States. This means that productivity in Japan, measured by GNP per capita, is greater than in the United States.

The United States is the most consumer-oriented society in the world. Americans enjoy more consumer items—cellular telephones, television sets, and many other goods—than any other people. Note that the Japanese, despite their high per capita aggregate output, do not generally enjoy the same high standard of living as the average American. Many consumer items that Americans consider necessities are rarities in less-developed countries. For example, although there is one automobile for every 1.8 Americans, there is only one automobile for every 1,075 Chinese.

GNP AND STANDARDS OF LIVING IN SELECTED NATIONS

	GNP billions $1997	GNP (per capita 1994)	Cellular telephones (per 100,000 people)	Televisions (per 1,000 people)
United States	7,783	29,080	12,800	776
Brazil	784	4,790	795	229
Canada	595	19,640	8,647	649
China	1,055	860	302	250
France	1,542	26,300	2,375	579
Germany	2,321	28,280	4,275	550
India	357	370	15	61
Italy	1,160	20,170	6,738	436
Japan	4,812	38,160	8,149	619
Mexico	349	3,700	699	192
Pakistan	65	500	33	22
Philippines	64	1,200	730	121
Poland	139	3,590	194	408
South Korea	485	10,550	3,659	323
Spain	570	14,490	2,408	490
United Kingdom	1,231	20,870	9,799	612

SOURCE: *Statistical Abstract of the United States 1999*, (Washington, D.C.: U. S. Government Printing Office, 1999), 841, 846.

underground economy
economic activities that are unreported and not counted in GDP

Finally, some economic activities escape measurement. The **underground economy** involves activities that are unreported to government and therefore not counted in the GDP. For example, illegal drug transactions are not counted as part of the GDP, even though they may constitute a significant portion of economic activity in the nation. Likewise, income that is not reported for tax purposes, that is, tax-evasion income, generally goes unreported into GDP. For example, cash received in private transactions, including tips, is often unreported or underreported. Studies estimate that the size of the U.S. underground economy is anywhere from 5 to 30 percent of the GDP.

GOVERNMENT IN A FREE MARKET ECONOMY

reasons for government intervention in the economy
protect property

enforce contracts

provide money

assure fair competition

set minimum wages

regulate public industries

protect consumers

provide public services

care for persons not in the marketplace

stabilize the market

The free enterprise system that was previously described is subject to major modifications by the activities of government. In fact, government is now so involved in the economy that we might call the American economic system a *mixed* economy rather than a *private enterprise* economy. Government intervenes in the free market for many reasons:

- To protect private property and enforce contracts
- To provide a stable money supply
- To assure competition among businesses by breaking up monopolies and prohibiting unfair competitive practices
- To set minimum standards for wages and working conditions
- To regulate industries (like banking, communications, broadcasting, and transportation) in which there is a strong public interest
- To protect the consumer from phony goods and services and false or misleading advertising
- To provide a wide range of public services (defense, education, highways, police protection) that cannot be reasonably provided on a private-profit basis
- To provide support and care (welfare, Social Security, unemployment compensation, health care, and so forth) to individuals who cannot supply these things for themselves through the market system
- To ensure that the economic system functions properly and avoids depression, inflation, or unemployment

Employment Act of 1946
pledges the federal government to promote maximum employment, production, and purchasing power

CUSHIONING THE UPS AND DOWNS

The U.S. government is committed to preserving economic prosperity and using fiscal and monetary policies to try to offset the effects of inflation and recession (see Case Study, "Achieving Economic Stability"). The **Employment Act of 1946** specifically pledges the federal government "to promote maximum employment, production, and purchasing power." The act created the **Council of Economic Advisers** (CEA) to "develop and recommend to

Council of Economic Advisers
advises the president on national economic policies

CASE STUDY

Achieving Economic Stability

Socialist critics of free market economies have long argued that the "internal contradictions of capitalism" would eventually bring about the downfall of free markets. They contended that economic cycles of inflation and depression would undermine public support for free markets and pave the way for socialism. And indeed, before 1950, economic cycles in the United States produced extreme ups and downs, with double-digit swings in real gross domestic product (GDP). In recent decades, however, economic fluctuations have been more moderate. We still experience economic cycles, but many economists believe that countercyclical government fiscal and monetary policy has succeeded in achieving greater stability (see figure).

ECONOMIC CYCLES SINCE 1910

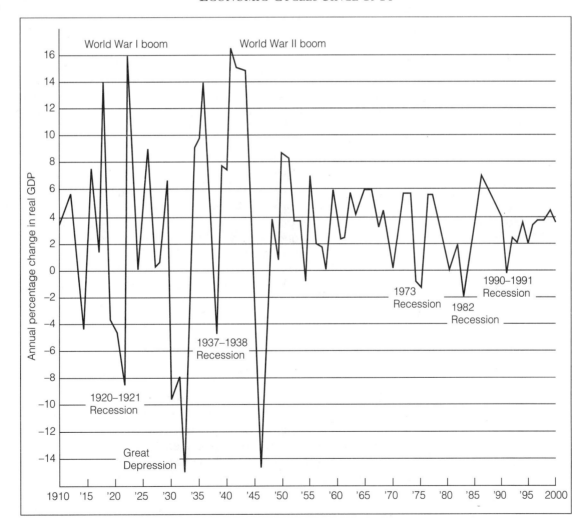

the president national economic policies." The CEA is composed of three economists, appointed by the president, and a staff of analysts who collect data on the economy and advise the president on what to do to offset cycles of inflation or recession. The act also requires the president to submit to Congress an annual economic report assessing the state of the economy and recommending economic legislation.

FISCAL POLICY

fiscal policy
effects of government taxing, spending, and deficits on the economy

Fiscal policy refers to the effects of government taxing, spending, and deficits on the economic condition of the nation. In Keynesian theory (see Masters of Social Thought, "John M. Keynes and the Mixed Economy"), during recessions when consumer demand must be increased, Congress should increase government spending, thereby adding to the total demand, or it should cut taxes, thereby putting more money into the pockets of consumers. Conversely, during inflation, when strong consumer demands are pushing prices up, Congress should cut its own spending, thereby reducing total demand, or it should raise taxes, thereby restricting the spending power of consumers. During recessions, the government must run a deficit (debt) in order to pour money into the economy. During inflation, the government must cut its spending or raise taxes and create a surplus in its budget: That is, it must take money out of the economy and reduce its debt in order to lower consumer demand and stabilize prices.

AUTOMATIC STABILIZERS

automatic stabilizers
government programs that act to counter economic cycles

Automatic stabilizers are government programs that act automatically to counter the effects of economic cycles. For example, since income taxes increase in proportion to one's earnings, the income tax automatically restricts spending habits in times of prosperity by taking larger bites of income. In times of adversity and low earnings, taxes drop automatically. Welfare programs also act automatically to counter economic cycles: In recessions, more people apply for welfare and unemployment payments, and those payments help offset declines in income.

MONETARY POLICY

monetary policy
government's influence over the supply of money and credit and interest rates

Federal Reserve Board
controls the supply of money and credit and interest rates (sets monetary policy)

Monetary policy refers to the government's influence over the supply of money and credit and over interest rates. Because banks are the major source of money and credit, the government can influence investment spending by making it easy or difficult to borrow money from banks. The **Federal Reserve Board** (the Fed) was created in 1913 to regulate the nation's supply of money through its *power to control the amount of money that commercial banks can lend.* The Fed is headed by a seven-person board of governors, appointed by the president, for overlapping terms of fourteen years.

MASTERS OF SOCIAL THOUGHT

John M. Keynes and the Mixed Economy

The Great Depression of the 1930s significantly altered American thinking about laissez-faire economics. It is difficult to realize today what a tremendous economic disaster befell the nation in those days. Following the stock market crash of October 1929, the American economy virtually collapsed. Businesses failed, factories shut down, new construction practically ceased, banks closed, and millions of dollars in savings were wiped out. One out of four American workers was unemployed, and one out of six was receiving welfare relief. Many lost faith in the free enterprise system and urged the abandonment of the market economy. The "solutions" of fascism in Italy and Germany and communism in the Soviet Union were looked to as alternatives to a "doomed" capitalist system.

In 1936 John M. Keynes, a British economist, wrote a landmark book called *The General Theory of Employment, Interest and Money*. Keynes attacked the basic notion of classical economics—that the free enterprise system was a self-adapting mechanism that tended to produce full employment and maximum use of resources. He believed that not all savings went into investment. When there was little prospect of profit, savings were likely to be hoarded and not used. This removal of money from the economy brought depression. Moreover, he argued, low interest rates would not necessarily stir businesses to reinvest; the expectation of *profit*, not the availability of money, motivated investment. Keynes believed that as confidence in the future diminishes, investment will decline, regardless of interest rates.

In Keynes's view, only *government* can reverse a downward economic cycle. Private businesses cannot be expected to invest when consumer demand is low and there is no prospect of profit. And consumers cannot be expected to increase their purchases when their incomes are falling. So the responsibility rests on the government to take *countercyclical* action to increase income and consumption. In recessions government can in-crease its own expenditures or lower taxes or do both in order to raise total demand and private income. Of course, increasing expenditures or lowering taxes or both means an *increase in government debt*, but only in this fashion can government pump money into the economy.

Keynes also argued that governments should pursue countercyclical fiscal policies to offset inflation as well as depression. *Inflation* means a general rise in the price level of goods and services. Inflation occurs when total demand exceeds or nears the productive capacity of the economy. An excess of demand over supply forces prices up. Keynes believed that when inflation threatens, government should gear its fiscal policy toward *reducing its own expenditures or increasing taxes or both*.

Keynes was no revolutionary. On the contrary, he wished to preserve the private enterprise system by developing effective governmental measures to overcome disastrous economic cycles.

In periods of *recession*, the Fed can *loosen controls* on lending and encourage banks to lend more money to businesspeople at lower interest rates. During *inflation*, the Fed can pursue *tight money policies*, policies that make it more difficult for banks to lend money, and thus reduce inflationary pressures.

SUPPLY-SIDE ECONOMICS

Keynesian economics emphasizes the *demand side* of the economy—increasing government spending and expanding the money supply in periods of recession and doing the opposite in periods of inflation. In other words, Keynesian economics calls for government manipulation of aggregate (total) demand for goods and services. However, other economists call for increased attention to the **supply side** of the economy—to government activities that affect the aggregate supply of goods and services. High government tax rates and costly regulations reduce incentives for Americans to work, save, invest, and produce. Supply-side economists believe that government should act to increase incentives to produce. Increased production will keep prices down (reduce inflation) and open up new employment opportunities (avoid recession).

supply-side economics
government policies designed to increase the supply of goods and services through incentives to work, save, and produce

REDUCING TAX RATES

marginal tax rates
tax rates applied to additional income

Central to supply-side economics is the idea of reducing **marginal rates of taxation.** (The marginal rate of taxation is the rate at which *additional* income is taxed.) Before 1981, the marginal rates of the federal personal income tax ranged from 14 to 70 percent. Supply-side economists argued that these high marginal rates of taxation (especially the 50- to 70-percent brackets) reduced economic output and productivity. People prefer leisure time over extra work if, for example, 50 percent of the additional money they make from the extra work is "snatched away" by income taxes. Individuals avoid risking their money in new business investments if, for example, 70 percent of the income from the investment will be taken away by income taxes. High marginal tax rates also encourage people to seek out "tax shelters," unproductive investments that are favored by special provisions in the tax laws that reduce personal income taxes. In addition, a large underground economy flourishes when tax rates are high; in the underground economy people hide their real incomes and/or trade goods and services rather than conduct transactions out in the open where they will be subject to taxation.

results of high marginal tax rates
less work

less investment risk

more unproductive "tax shelters"

a large underground economy hiding income

REAGAN TAX CUTS

tax cut results
economic growth

more jobs

huge government deficits

When the Reagan administration arrived in Washington in 1981, its first priority was to reduce high marginal rates of income taxation in the hope of stimulating economic growth. In two tax cut acts (1981 and 1986) pushed through Congress by President Ronald Reagan, the top marginal tax rate came down from 70 to 28 percent (see Figure 6-5). These tax rate reductions succeeded in stimulating the economy. Runaway inflation was halted, unemployment was reduced from double-digit levels, and the number and proportion of Americans with jobs reached all-time highs. However, the incentive effects of the tax cuts did not produce enough new tax revenues to make up for lower rates. Tax revenues lagged far behind federal expenditures. Neither

FIGURE 6-5

TOP MARGINAL INCOME TAX RATES

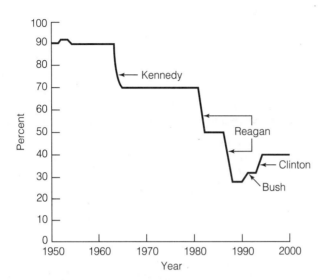

President Reagan, President Bush, nor Congress was willing to cut expenditures enough to reduce the gap between lower taxes and continued high spending levels. This resulted in the largest deficits in the nation's history.

BUSH AND CLINTON TAX INCREASES

Neither President George Bush nor President Bill Clinton was fully convinced by the arguments of supply-side economics. At the Republican National Convention in 1988, George Bush made a firm pledge to the American people that he would veto any tax increase passed by the Democratic-controlled Congress. "Read my lips. No new taxes." But the pressure of continuing high deficits, and the unwillingness to cut spending, caused President Bush to reverse course and agree to an increase in the top marginal income tax rate to 31 percent, thereby abandoning the supply-side economic policies of his predecessor Ronald Reagan. By breaking his solemn pledge on taxes, Bush contributed heavily to his own defeat in the 1992 presidential election.

Bill Clinton won the presidency largely on his pledge to revive the economy. (At his campaign headquarters, aides reportedly posted a large sign, "It's the economy, stupid" to help maintain the focus of the campaign.) Clinton repeatedly referred to the supply-side economics of the Reagan years as "failed, trickle-down" economics. Soon after taking office, he presented Congress with a new economic plan calling for a large tax increase; cuts in defense spending; increases in spending for health, education, communications, and transportation, and a schedule for gradually lowering annual federal deficits. Clinton succeeded in getting the Democratic-controlled Congress to raise top marginal income tax rates to 36 and 39.6 percent on high income earners.

PROSPERITY

The United States experienced its longest continuous period of GDP growth beginning in 1991. The economic prosperity of the 1990s created more jobs and lowered the **unemployment rate**—the percentage of the workforce not working but looking for jobs or waiting to return to a job. At the same time **inflation**—rises in the general level of prices—was kept in check (see Case Study, "The Recent Performance of the American Economy"). This prosperity confounded supply-side economic theory, inasmuch as it came after *increases* in marginal tax rates. And economic growth in the 1990s, combined with increases in tax rates, succeeded in turning annual federal deficits into annual surpluses.

unemployment rate
the percentage of the labor force not working but looking for work or waiting for a job to open

inflation
a rise in the general level of prices, not just prices or some products

GOVERNMENT MONEY: WHERE IT COMES FROM AND WHERE IT GOES

The U.S. government currently receives about two *trillion* dollars each year in revenues, an amount equal to about 22 percent of the GDP.[4] It currently spends somewhat less than it receives (see Figure 6-6).

REVENUES

Where does all this money come from? Federal revenues come primarily from the federal personal income tax (48 percent) and the Social Security payroll tax (34 percent). These taxes are paid to the federal government directly by the American people. The corporate income tax has declined as a source of federal revenue (11 percent) over the years. Federal excise taxes on various products, including alcohol, tobacco, and gasoline, provide an additional source of revenue (4 percent); and the government also collects miscellaneous revenues, including customs' duties on imported goods, fines, penalties, and forfeitures.

EXPENDITURES

Most U.S. government spending goes into "entitlement" programs. These programs provide classes of people with legally enforceable rights to government benefits. Entitlements now account for over 60 percent of all federal spending, including Social Security (23 percent), Medicare (12 percent), Medicaid (7 percent), and various welfare entitlements (6 percent), including

The Recent Performance of the American Economy

The U.S. Economy performed very well in the 1990s. Economic prosperity is reflected in growth each year in real output of goods and services—annual percentage increases in GDP. Early in the decade, the United States experienced a recession; real GDP actually declined by about 1 percent in 1991. But beginning in 1992, real GDP rose each year (see top figure).

In order to produce more goods and services, American businesses began to hire more workers. The unemployment rate began a long decline in 1993 (see middle figure). (Generally, the unemployment rate lags slightly behind growth in the GDP, as businesses wait before hiring new workers to ensure that demand for their products continues to rise.) Many economists once believed that an unemployment rate of 6 percent was normal even in an expanding economy; they believed that this percentage of people was likely to be temporarily out of work and looking for new jobs. But recent experience has indicated that the unemployment rate can drop below 5 percent. A very low unemployment rate suggests a labor shortage and likely increases in wages.

In the past, economic prosperity has frequently led to inflation. But the nation's recent economic growth has been accompanied by low inflation—on average only about 3 percent a year (see bottom figure). This success is generally credited to prudent monetary policy decisions by the Federal Reserve Board. The Fed has kept the money supply in balance with growth in the economy, raising interest rates just enough to avoid inflation but not so much as to adversely affect economic growth.

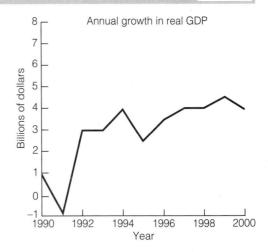

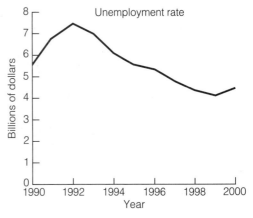

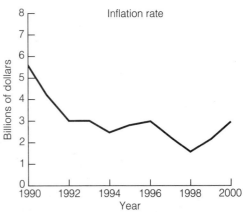

FIGURE 6-6

U.S. GOVERNMENT REVENUES AND EXPENDITURES

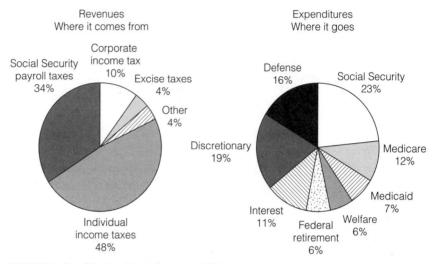

SOURCE: *Budget of the United States Government 2001.*

food stamps, supplemental security income, and tax credits. These entitlement programs were enacted by past Congresses and represent continuing commitments of federal spending. Of course, future Congresses could reduce or cancel these previously promised benefits, but doing so would be regarded by many voters as a failure of trust. Social Security and Medicare benefits are especially sacrosanct. In addition to these entitlement programs, the federal government is committed to other "mandatory" spending, including interest payments on the national debt.

Each year as more people become entitled to Social Security and Medicare—the two largest entitlement programs—federal government spending rises accordingly.

Spending for national defense has declined dramatically since the end of the Cold War (see Chapter 18). At one time, defense spending accounted for more than half of the federal budget; today, it accounts for only about 16 percent.

federal deficits
the annual negative imbalances between revenues and expenditures of the U.S. government

national debt
the accumulated debt of the U.S. government of over $5 trillion owed to purchasers of U.S. bonds

GOVERNMENT DEBT, DEFICITS, AND SURPLUSES

For many years the federal government spent more than it received in revenues (see Figure 6-7). These annual **deficits** drove up the accumulated debt of the U.S. government to well over $5 *trillion.* The **national debt** now exceeds $18,000 for every man, woman, and child in the nation, or about $68,000 for every one of America's sixty-six million families.

FIGURE 6-7

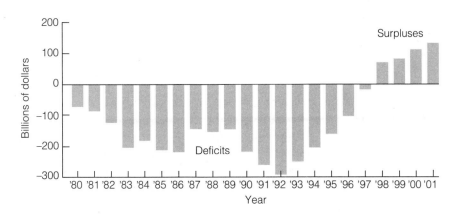

ANNUAL FEDERAL DEFICITS AND SURPLUSES

The U.S. government debt is owed mostly to American banks and financial institutions and private citizens who buy Treasury bonds. Only about 20 percent of this debt is owed to foreign banks, firms, and individuals. As old debt comes due, the Treasury Department sells new bonds to pay off the old; that is, it continues to "roll over" or "float" the debt. The debt today is smaller as a percentage of the gross national product than at some periods in U.S. history. Indeed, in order to pay the costs of fighting World War II, the U.S. government ran up a debt of 110 percent of GDP; the current debt is the highest in history in dollar terms but only about 60 percent of the GDP. This suggests that the debt is manageable because of the size and strength of the U.S. economy.

The ability to float such a debt depends on public confidence in the U.S. government—confidence that it will continue to pay interest on its debt, that it will pay off the principal of bond issues when they come due, and that the value of the bonds will not decline over time because of inflation.

DEBT BURDENS

Interest payments on the national debt come from current taxes and divert money from *all* other government programs. Even if the federal government manages to continue to balance its current annual budgets, these payments will remain obligations of the children and grandchildren of the current generation of policymakers and taxpayers.

The federal debt requires the U.S. Treasury Department to borrow large amounts of money. This money is diverted from the private sector, where it would otherwise be available as loans for new and expanding businesses, for modernizing industrial plants and equipment, and for financing the purchase of homes, cars, appliances, and other credit items for consumers. In other words, the federal government's borrowing "crowds out" capital markets. The less capital available in the private sector, the slower the growth rate of the economy.

THE POLITICS OF DEFICITS

For many years, despite pious rhetoric in Washington about the need to "balance the budget," neither presidents nor Congresses, Democrats nor Republicans were willing to reduce expenditures or raise taxes enough to produce a balanced budget. Congressional leaders consistently sidetracked proposed amendments to the U.S. Constitution that would require a balanced budget. It was politically more expedient to shift the burden of current government spending to future generations by incurring deficits than it was to cut favorite programs or raise taxes. Politicians were (and still are) especially reluctant to challenge the politically powerful older citizens who receive the largest proportions of federal spending through the Social Security and Medicare programs.

The nation's booming economy in the 1990s added more revenues to the federal treasury and gradually reduced annual deficits. In 1998 President Clinton was able to present the first balanced federal budget in thirty years to the Congress and to project surpluses for future years. The political question became: What to do with the surplus? (Of course, the question assumes that the economy continues its rapid growth and that surpluses actually result.) The president and both Republicans and Democrats in Congress pledged to "save Social Security first" before adding new spending programs or cutting taxes (see Controversies in Social Science, "What Should We Do with Budget Surpluses?).

THE CONCENTRATION OF ECONOMIC POWER

Economic power in America is highly concentrated. Large economic and financial institutions decide what will be produced in the United States and increasingly what will be produced outside of it. They decide how many people will be employed and what their wages will be. They determine how goods and services will be distributed and what new products will be developed. They decide how much money will be available for capital investment and where these investments will be made. Decisions made in the boardroom of these institutions affect out lives as much as those typically made by governments (see Focus, "The Concentration of Corporate Power").

POWER IN THE CORPORATION

governing the corporation
"inside" and "outside" directors

The modern corporation is governed by its board of directors. The directors include the chairman of the board, the president or CEO (chief executive officer), selected senior vice presidents, and some "outside" members

CONTROVERSIES IN SOCIAL SCIENCE
What Should We Do with Budget Surpluses?

After decades of deficit spending, Americans are skeptical that the federal government can continue to balance its annual budgets and produce surpluses. Over two-thirds of Americans doubt that the federal budget will stay in balance in future years. Nonetheless, under current tax laws and expenditure policies, and assuming continued economic growth, federal budget surpluses are projected for at least the next decade.

Of course, projected surpluses could quickly disappear in the event of a major recession, and Washington could return to its habit of deficit spending. Moreover, the long-term financial problem confronting the federal government currently is the expected rise in the cost of Social Security and Medicare entitlements when the "baby boom" generation begins to retire after 2010.

The American public appears to be aware that Social Security and Medicare will require strengthening in future years. Indeed, among the various choices offered Americans in opinion polls regarding what to do with the budget surplus, strengthening Social Security and Medicare appeared to be the public's first priority. It is not surprising that both Democrats and Republicans echo the slogan "Save Social Security First."

Question: Which of these do you think should be the top priority for any surplus money in the federal budget: Cut federal income taxes, put it toward reducing the national debt, strengthen the Social Security system, or increase spending in other domestic programs?

Strengthen Social Security	47%
Cut federal income taxes	22
Reduce national debt	19
Increase domestic spending	10
No opinion	2

Finally, it is interesting to note that more Americans credit "good economic conditions" (77 percent) for reducing deficits than they credit either President Clinton (63 percent) or a Republican-run Congress (54 percent).

SOURCE: ABC News Poll, as reported in *The Polling Report,* August 2, 1999.

who are not managers of the corporation. The "inside" directors, who are also full-time presidents or vice presidents of the corporation, tend to dominate board proceedings because they know more about the day-to-day operations of the corporation than do the outside directors. Outside directors may sit on the corporate board as representatives for families who still own large blocks of stock or as representatives for banks that have lent money to the corporation. Occasionally, outside directors are prominent citizens, members of minority groups, or representatives of civic associations. Outside directors are usually chosen by the CEO and the inside directors. All directors are officially elected by the corporation's stockholders. However, the CEO and inside directors draw up the "management slate," which usually wins, because top management casts many proxy votes, which they solicit in advance from stockholders. Corporate power does *not* rest in the hands of masses of corporate employees or even in the hands of millions of middle- and upper-middle-class Americans who own corporate stock.

FOCUS

The Concentration of Corporate Power

Control over the nation's economic resources is becoming increasingly concentrated in the hands of very few people, largely because of the *consolidation of economic enterprise* into a small number of giant corporations. The following statistics can only suggest the scale and concentration of modern corporate enterprise in the United States: There are over 200,000 industrial corporations in the United States, but the 100 largest corporations hold over two-thirds of the nation's industrial assets. Indeed, just ten industrial corporations hold one-third of the nation's industrial assets (see table). Banking is also highly concentrated. There are nearly 15,000 banks in the United States, but the 10 largest banks hold over one-third of all banking assets. The rate of corporate and banking mergers in recent years suggests that this concentration of economic resources is increasing.

The largest U.S. industrial corporations (ranked by revenues)	The largest U. S. commercial banks (ranked by assets)
1. General Motors	1. Citigroup
2. Ford Motor	2. BankAmerica
3. Wal-Mart	3. Chase Manhattan
4. Exxon	4. First Union
5. General Electric	5. Wells Fargo
6. IBM	6. J. P. Morgan
7. Philip Morris	7. Bankers Trust
8. Boeing	8. Fleet Financial
9. AT&T	9. National City Corp.
10. Mobil	10. PNC Bank

SOURCE: Derived from data in *Fortune*, April 26, 1999.

When confronted with mismanagement, these stockholders simply sell their stock, rather than try to challenge the power of the directors.

MANAGERIAL POWER

Following the Industrial Revolution in America in the late nineteenth century and well into the twentieth century, the nation's largest corporations were controlled by the tycoons who created them—Andrew Carnegie (Carnegie Steel, later United States Steel, and today USX), Andrew Mellon (Alcoa and Mellon banks), Henry Ford (Ford Motor), J. P. Morgan (J. P. Morgan), and John D. Rockefeller (Standard Oil Company, later broken into Exxon, Mobil, Chevron, Atlantic Richfield, and other large oil companies). But by the 1930s, control of most large corporations had passed from owners to professional managers. The theory of **managerialism** became the conventional wisdom about corporate governance.[5]

It was recognized early on that corporate managers might run their firms to best serve their own interests rather than those of the owners—for example, paying themselves multimillion-dollar annual salaries and providing

managerialism
control of the corporation by professional managers rather than stockholders

themselves with lavish corporate-paid lifestyles. But for decades, individual and institutional stockholders largely ignored this potential **principal-agent problem.** Stockholders' power was fragmented and dispersed; there was not much the stockholders could do, other than sell their stock, even if they knew that managers were taking personal advantage of their position. But perhaps a more important reason that managers were largely unchallenged was that the American economy prospered from the 1940s through the 1970s. Governance of the U.S. corporation seemed to be working well, rewarding both managers and owners.

principal-agent problem
ensuring that managers (agents) operate firms in the best interest of the owners (principals) rather than themselves

CORPORATE COUNTERREVOLUTION

Traditionally, the top managers of large corporations were considered impregnable; nothing short of bankruptcy could dislodge them. Corporate managers ran the American economy, perpetuating themselves in office; they ruled without much interference from outside directors, stockholders, employees, or consumers. But beginning in the 1980s, new challenges to the imperial position of top management arose, most notably from: (1) a new activism by outside directors and large stockholders, checking the power of corporate chief executives and occasionally forcing their retirement; and (2) a rise in **hostile takeovers** led by corporate raiders, who acquire corporate stock and voting power in order to force the ouster and replacement of existing management.

managerial challenges
new activism by outside directors representing financial institutions

hostile takeovers by corporate raiders

hostile takeover
the purchase of stock in a corporation by an outsider and the subsequent ousting of the prior management

   The new activism by outside directors and large stockholders, particularly those representing large financial institutions—pension funds, mutual funds, insurance companies, and banks—is largely attributable to slower economic growth in recent years and the failure of some American corporations to remain competitive in global markets. Mutual and pension funds, as well as banks and insurance companies, are more likely than small individual investors to take action against the managers of poorly performing corporations in which they have invested funds.[6]

CORPORATE RAIDERS

A hostile takeover involves the purchase of enough stock in a publicly held corporation to force the ouster and replacement of existing corporate management. Usually a hostile takeover begins with a **corporate raider** buying the stock of a corporation on the open market, often with money borrowed for this purpose. After establishing a stock ownership position in the corporation, the raider may then offer a takeover bid to existing management. Management may reject the bid outright or try to buy back the stock purchased by the raider at a higher price, that is, to offer the raider "greenmail." If the raider and management cannot reach an agreement, the hostile takeover proceeds. The raider arranges to borrow additional

corporate raiders
investors who arrange to purchase stock in a hostile takeover effort

money—perhaps several billion dollars—to make a purchase offer to the target corporation's stockholders, usually at a price higher than the current stock exchange price. If the raider wins control of the corporation, the old managers are replaced.

Following a successful takeover, the corporation is heavily laden with new debt. The raider may have borrowed billions to buy out shareholders. The investment firms that provided the loans to finance the corporation's purchase may issue "junk bonds" with high interest rates to attract investors to these risky ventures. The corporation must pay off these bonds with its own revenues. Additionally, there may be many millions of dollars in bond-sale commissions and attorneys' fees to pay out. The raider may be forced to sell off parts of the corporation or some of its valuable assets in order to help pay off part of the debt. Thus, the target corporation itself must eventually bear the burden of the takeover battle.

Are corporate takeovers good or bad for America? The raiders claim that their activities force improvements in efficiency and productivity. Even the potential threat of a takeover forces corporate managers to streamline their operations, eliminate waste, increase revenues, raise profits, and distribute profits to their shareholders rather than spend them on the management comforts. The raiders argue that American management has grown soft, lazy, and self-satisfied—that, as a result, the American corporation has lost its competitive edge in the world marketplace.

Opponents of the corporate takeover movement argue that fear of the raider forces management to focus on short-range profits at the expense of long-range research and development. Management must keep the current price of its stock high in order to deter a takeover attempt. Even worse, management often resorts to "poison pills" to deliberately weaken its own corporation to make it unattractive to raiders: It may increase its debt, buy other poorly performing corporations, devalue stockholders' voting powers, or provide itself with "golden parachutes" (rich severance benefits) in the event of ouster. While the original stockholders are paid handsomely by the raider, the corporation must labor intensively to pay off the debt incurred. The corporation may be broken apart and its separate pieces sold, which may disrupt and demoralize employees. If the corporation cannot meet the high interest payments, bankruptcy threatens. And the diversion of American capital from productive investments to takeovers threatens to weaken national productivity.

THE GLOBALIZATION OF ECONOMIC POWER

Today, almost one-quarter of the world's total economic output is sold in a country other than the country in which it was produced. The United States currently exports about 11 percent of the value of its gross domestic product (GDP) and imports about 12 percent. Exports and imports were only about 3 percent of GDP as late as 1970.[7]

Historically, America's corporate and financial institutions supported high tariffs in order to protect their domestic marketplace. **Tariffs** on foreign imports forced prices up and gave U.S. firms sheltered markets. Not only did this improve the profit margins of U.S. corporations, but this also allowed them to operate less efficiently: Management became top-heavy; its products, especially automobiles, were frequently poor in quality; and the workforce was larger, and wages for workers were higher than they otherwise would be if U.S. firms had to face foreign competition.

tariffs
taxes on goods imported into a country

EXPANDING WORLD TRADE

But America's corporate and financial powers gradually came to see the economic advantages of expanding world trade (see Figure 6-8). U.S. firms that dominated the domestic market in the 1950s and 1960s—steel, automobiles, aircraft, computers, drugs, electronics, agriculture, and so on—began to look abroad to expand their own sales. American corporations became multinational corporations. They began by expanding their sales and distribution staffs worldwide and then later began to shift manufacturing itself to low-wage, low-cost countries.

Globalization of economic power required reductions in tariffs and trade barriers around the world. America's corporate and financial elites began to lobby Congress for reductions in U.S. tariffs. The result was a dramatic decline in average U.S. tariff rates. In effect, the United States became an open market.

FIGURE 6-8

THE GROWTH OF WORLD TRADE IN THE U.S. ECONOMY

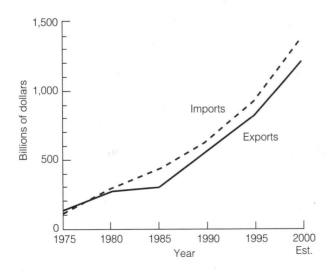

CROSS-NATIONAL PERSPECTIVE
The Multinationals' Global Economic Power

The concentration of economic power in relatively few large institutions is not an exclusively American phenomenon. On the contrary, the trend toward corporate concentration of resources is worldwide. It is not only large American corporations that have expanded their markets throughout the world, invested in overseas plants and banks, and merged with foreign corporations; large European and Japanese firms compete very effectively for world business. Just as American companies have greatly expanded investments abroad, so too have foreign companies sharply increased their business in the United States. The result is the emergence of truly "multinational" corporations, which not only trade worldwide but also build and operate plants in many nations.

The world's largest corporations are listed in the table. General Motors and Ford are the world's largest non-banking corporations. But only nine of the world's twenty-five largest corporations are headquartered in the United States; eleven are Japanese corporations. Germany's Daimler-Benz recently bought America's third largest automaker, Chrysler.

In brief, the central feature of the American and world economy is the concentration of resources in relatively few large corporations.

WORLD'S LARGEST CORPORATIONS

Rank	Corporation	Country
1	General Motors	United States
2	Ford Motor	United States
3	Mitsui	Japan
4	Mitsubishi	Japan
5	Exxon	United States
6	Itochu Shoji	Japan
7	Marubeni	Japan
8	Sumitomo	Japan
9	Toyota Motor	Japan
10	Wal-Mart Stores	United States
11	Mobil	United States
12	General Electric	United States
13	Nissho Iwai	Japan
14	Nippon Telegraph and Telephone	Japan
15	IBM	United States
16	British Petroleum	United Kingdom
17	Hitachi	Japan
18	Philip Morris	United States
19	Matsushita Electric Industrial	Japan
20	Royal Dutch Petroleum	Netherlands
21	Chrysler	United States
22	Daimler-Benz	Germany
23	Nissan Motor	Japan
24	Volkswagen	Germany
25	Unilever	United Kingdom

SOURCE: Derived from *Fortune,* July 15, 1999.

"COMPARATIVE ADVANTAGE"

The classic argument for free trade is based on the principle of **"comparative advantage."** If nations devote more of their resources to the production of those goods that they produce most efficiently, then all trading nations benefit.[8] Comparative advantage focuses on what each nation does *relatively* better than the other. Trade shifts resources (investment capital, jobs, technology, raw materials, etc.) in each nation toward what each does best. (Imagine a lawyer who is also a faster typist than her secretary. Even though the lawyer is better than her secretary at both law *and* typing it makes more sense for her to concentrate on law and leave the typing to her secretary. Their combined output of lawyering and typing will be greater than if each did some of the other's work.)

"comparative advantage"
the argument that countries benefit most when they concentrate on producing the goods that they are most efficient at producing

THE BENEFITS OF TRADE

The efficiencies achieved by trading are said to directly benefit consumers by making available cheaper imported goods. Export industries also benefit when world markets are opened to their products. American exporters benefit directly from sales abroad, and they also benefit indirectly when foreign firms are allowed to sell in the American market. This is because sales of foreign goods in America provide foreigners with U.S. dollars that they can use to purchase the goods of America's exporting industries.

It is also argued that the pressure of competition from foreign-made goods in the American marketplace forces out domestic industries to become more efficient—cutting their costs and improving the quality of their own goods. Trade also quickens the flow of ideas and technology, allowing nations to learn from each other. Finally, trade expands the menu of goods and services available to trading countries. American consumers gain access to everything from exotic foods and foreign language movies to Porsches, BMWs, and Jaguars.

WORLD TRADE ORGANIZATION

International economic agreements and organizations have been arranged in order to facilitate the new global economy. The **World Trade Organization** (WTO) was created in 1993 with 117 member nations. The WTO has been given power to adjudicate trade disputes among countries and monitor and enforce trade agreements.

The most important worldwide trade agreement is the multinational **General Agreement on Tariffs and Trade** (GATT). Initially created after World War II, GATT has undergone various revisions. The latest version—the Uruguay Round—was completed in 1993. Among other things, it eliminated quotas on textile products; established more uniform standards for proof of dumping; set rules for the protection of intellectual property rights (patents

World Trade Organization (WTO)
an international organization that adjudicates trade disputes among countries and monitors and enforces trade agreements

General Agreement on Tariffs and Trade (GATT)
a multinational agreement covering trade relations among nations

and copyrights on books, movies, videos, and so on); reduced tariffs on wood, paper, and some other raw materials; and scheduled a gradual reduction of government subsidies for agricultural products.

NAFTA

North American Free Trade Agreement (NAFTA)
an agreement in which the United States, Mexico, and Canada agree to eliminate all barriers to trade

In 1993 the United States, Canada, and Mexico signed the **North American Free Trade Agreement** (NAFTA). Objections by labor unions in the United States (and independent presidential candidate Ross Perot) were drowned out in a torrent of support by the American corporate community, Democrats and Republicans in Congress, President Bill Clinton, and former President George Bush. NAFTA envisions the removal of tariffs on virtually all products by all three nations over a period of ten to fifteen years. It also allows banking, insurance, and other financial services to cross these borders.

TRADE DEFICITS

trade deficit
the difference that results when a country imports more goods than it exports

The United States imports more goods then it exports. The difference is referred to as a **trade deficit.** The trade deficit is made up by the transfer of American dollars, government bonds, and corporate securities, etc., to foreign firms. U.S. banks, as well as the U.S. Treasury, actually benefit from the deficit because it means that foreigners are accepting U.S. paper—currency, bonds, and securities—in exchange for their products. This makes it easier for the U.S. government to fund its own debt—selling bonds to foreign investors. Approximately 15 percent of the total U.S. government debt of over $5 trillion is owned by foreign banks and investors.

THE CASE FOR PROTECTIONISM

protectionism
maintaining high tariffs in order to protect domestic producers from foreign competition

Although most economists favor worldwide free trade, arguments can also be made for **protectionism**—maintaining high tariffs in order to protect domestic producers from foreign competition. The principal argument for protectionism is that unlimited foreign competition costs Americans their jobs. When Americans buy Japanese or Korean steel, steelworkers in Pittsburgh lose their jobs. When Americans buy shoes from Taiwan or Hong Kong, millworkers in South Carolina become unemployed.

Some foreign producers, especially those in the less-developed world, gain comparative advantage by paying their workers extremely low wages. American producers cannot compete effectively with companies that pay wages that may be less than a quarter of those paid in the United States. Moreover, foreign producers are not subject to the same environmental protection laws as producers in the United States. These laws raise the cost of production in the United States and, thereby, give comparative advantage to foreign producers who do not incur such costs.

ON THE WEB

EXPLORING ECONOMICS

News and information about business and economics abounds on the Web. Individual corporations, business and trade associations, securities firms, labor unions, and a variety of government agencies all post valuable economic information on the Web.

Bureau of Economic Analysis. Probably the best place to start browsing for economic information is the site maintained by the Bureau of Economic Analysis of the U.S. Department of Commerce (www.bea.doc/gov). It provides up-to-date information on GDP, prices, income, exports and imports, government revenues and expenditures, etc., in current and constant dollars, annually and for the last four quarters, and by industry and by region of the United States. Its page "Overview of the U.S. Economy" is a good starting place.

Bureau of Labor Statistics. Information on careers in economics is available at the Web site maintained by the Bureau of Labor Statistics of the U.S. Department of Labor entitled "Occupational Outlook Handbook." It describes the work of economists (as well as that of other occupations from A to Z), their training and employment opportunities, earnings, and job outlook (www.bls.gov/oco). Employment opportunities for economics majors are usually much better than those for majors in other social sciences. Average earning for economists are also higher. Applied economics is useful in business and in a wide variety of other organizations, including labor unions and governments.

National Bureau of Economic Research. Historical data on the U.S. economy, including data on economic cycles, can be found at the Web site maintained by the National Bureau of Economic Research (www.nber.org.).

Office of Management and Budget. Information on the federal government's role in the economy is available at the Web Site maintained by the Office of Management and Budget (OMB, www.omb.gov). It includes a helpful "Citizen's Guide to the Federal Budget," as well as the lengthy, annual *Budget of the United States Government* and the annual *Economic Report of the President* prepared by the Council of Economic Advisers.

Business Roundtable. The views of American businesspeople on a wide variety of topics, including views on corporate governments, government regulation, fiscal policy, and international trade, are presented by the Business Roundtable, an organization of chief executive officers of the nation's largest corporations (www.brtable.org).

AFL-CIO. The views of organized labor are summarized by the American Federation of Labor Congress of Industrial Organizations (AFL-CIO, www.aflcio.org). This site includes information on the global economy, the minimum wage, Social Security and Medicare issues, and instruction on "Common Sense Economics." A particularly interesting page is their "Executive Pay Watch" that compares the exploding compensation of corporate chiefs to that of working men and women.

ABOUT THIS CHAPTER

In this chapter, we have examined power in the economy. Economic power is deciding about the production and distribution of goods and services—what will be produced, how it will be produced, and to whom it will be distributed. After reading Chapter 6, you should be able to

- describe the operation of a free market
- identify the ideal conditions for market operations
- show how prices reflect supply and demand
- define the gross domestic product (GDP), and describe the difference between constant and current dollars
- describe the reasons for government intervention in the economy and the major tools of government intervention
- compare the ideas of Keynesian economics with modern "supply-side" economic ideas
- describe how power is exercised in the corporation, contrasting the positions of managers, outside directors, large stockholders, and "corporate raiders"

DISCUSSION QUESTIONS

1. Discuss how the market in a private enterprise economy determines what is to be produced, how much it will cost, and who will be able to buy it. Comment on the roles that the following factors play in a market

operation: consumer demands, profits, prices, willingness to pay and ability to pay, labor market, competition, product supply.

2. Describe the ideal conditions for a market operation in a free enterprise system. What are the reasons for government interference in such a system?

3. Discuss the similarities between laissez-faire (classical) economics and a traditional democratic political system. Describe the conflict between laissez-faire economics and Keynesian economics over the self-adaptability of the free enterprise system.

4. Describe the kinds of fiscal and monetary policies that a Keynesian economist would recommend during a recessionary period and an inflationary period. How do the automatic stabilizers work during each of these periods?

5. Define supply-side economics. What government policies are proposed by supply-side economists?

6. Explain how economists compute the gross domestic product (GDP). Differentiate between actual increases in the GDP and "dollar" increases in GDP.

7. What proportion of the GDP is produced by all governments—federal, state, and local—in the United States? What are the major sources of revenue of the *federal* government, and what are its major spending categories?

8. Describe the power of managers, directors, and large institutional stockholders in corporate governance. What challenges have arisen to the power of managers? Why is the corporate raider feared by management? Are corporate takeovers good or bad for the economy as a whole?

9. Distinguish between annual federal government deficits and the national debt. What are the major burdens created by a large national debt?

Chapter 7

Power and Government

POLITICS, POLITICAL SCIENCE, AND GOVERNMENTAL POWER

A distinguished American political scientist, Harold Lasswell, defined **politics** as "who gets what, when, and how." "The study of politics," he said, "is the study of influence and the influential. The influential are those who get the most of what there is to get. . . . Those who get the most are the *elite;* the rest are *mass.*"[1] He went on to define *political science* as the study of "the shaping and sharing of power." Admittedly, Lasswell's definition of political science is very broad. Indeed, if we accept Lasswell's definition of political science as the *study of power,* then political science includes cultural, economic, social, and personal power relationships—topics we have already discussed in chapters on anthropology, economics, sociology, and psychology.

Although some political scientists have accepted Lasswell's challenge to study power in all its forms in society, most limit the definition of political science to *the study of government.*

What distinguishes **governmental power** from the power of other institutions, groups, and individuals? The power of government, unlike that of other institutions in society, is distinguished by (1) *the legitimate use of physical force* and (2) *coverage of the whole society* rather than only segments of it. Because governmental decisions extend to the whole of society and because only government can legitimately use physical force, government has the

politics
the study of power

distinguishing governmental power
the legitimate use of force; coverage of the whole society

primary responsibility for maintaining order and for resolving differences that arise *between* segments of society. Thus, government must regulate conflict by establishing and enforcing general rules by which conflict is to be carried on in society, by arranging compromises and balancing interests, and by imposing settlements that the parties in the dispute must accept. In other words, government lays down the "rules of the game" in conflict and competition between individuals, organizations, and institutions within society.

THE MEANING OF DEMOCRACY

democracy's meaning:
popular participation in government majority rule, with minority rights

the value of individual dignity equality of opportunity

Ideally, **democracy** means *individual participation* in the decisions that affect one's life. In traditional democratic theory, popular participation has been valued as an opportunity for individual self-development. Responsibility for governing one's own conduct develops character, self-reliance, intelligence, and moral judgment—in short, dignity. Even if a benevolent king could govern in the public interest, the true democrat would reject him.[2]

Procedurally, popular participation was to be achieved through *majority rule* and *respect for the rights of minorities.* Self-development means *self-government,* and self-government can be accomplished only by encouraging each individual to contribute to the creation of public policy and by resolving conflicts over public policy through majority rule. Minorities who had had the opportunity to influence policy but whose views had not succeeded in

Democracy means individual participation in government.

winning majority support would accept the decisions of majorities. In return, majorities would permit minorities to attempt openly to win majority support for their views. Freedom of speech and press, freedom to dissent, and freedom to form opposition parties and organizations are essential to ensure meaningful individual participation.

The underlying value of democracy is *individual dignity.* Human beings, by virtue of their existence, are entitled to life, liberty, and the pursuit of happiness. Governmental control over the individual should be kept to a minimum; this means the removal of as many external restrictions, controls, and regulations on the individual as possible without infringing on the freedom of other citizens.[3]

Another vital aspect of classic democracy is a belief in the *equality* of all people. The Declaration of Independence expresses the conviction that "all men are created equal." The Founders believed in equality *before the law,* notwithstanding the circumstances of the accused. A person was not to be judged by social position, economic class, creed, or race. Many early democrats also believed in *political equality,* that is, equal opportunity to influence public policy.[4] Political equality is expressed in the concept of "one person, one vote."

Over time, the notion of equality has also come to include *equality of opportunity* in all aspects of American life—social, educational, and economic, as well as political—and to encompass employment, housing, recreation, and public accommodations. All people are to have equal opportunity to develop their individual capacities to their natural limits.

In summary, democratic thinking involves the following ideas:

- Popular participation in the decisions that shape the lives of individuals in a society
- Government by majority rule, with recognition of the rights of minorities to try to become majorities; these rights include the freedoms of speech, press, assembly, and petition, and the freedom to dissent, to form opposition parties, and to run for public office
- A commitment to individual dignity and the preservation of the liberal values of liberty and property
- A commitment to equal opportunity for all to develop their individual capacities

POWER AND THE AMERICAN CONSTITUTION

A **constitution** establishes government authority. It sets up governmental bodies (such as the House of Representatives, the Senate, the presidency, and the Supreme Court in the United States). It grants them powers. It determines how their members are to be chosen. And it prescribes the rules by which they make decisions.

Constitutional decision making is deciding how to decide; that is, it is deciding on the rules for policy making. It is not policy making itself. Policies will be decided later, according to the rules set forth in the Constitution.[5]

constitution
establishment of governmental authority; creation of governmental bodies, granting their powers, determining how their members are selected; establishment of the rules by which government decisions are to be made. Considered basic or fundamental, a constitution cannot be changed by ordinary acts of governmental bodies.

A constitution cannot be changed by the ordinary acts of governmental bodies; change can come only through a process of general popular consent. The U.S. Constitution, then, is superior to ordinary laws of Congress, orders or the president, decisions of the courts, acts of the state legislatures, and regulations of the bureaucracies. Indeed, the Constitution is "the supreme law of the land."

CONSTITUTIONALISM: LIMITING GOVERNMENTAL POWER

constitutionalism
a government of laws, not people; the principle that governmental power must be limited and government officials should be restrained in their exercise of power over individuals

Constitutions govern government. **Constitutionalism**—a government of laws, not of people—means that those who exercise governmental power are restricted in their use of it by a higher law. To place individual freedoms beyond the reach of government and beyond the reach of majorities, a constitution must truly limit and control the exercise of authority by government. It does so by setting forth individual liberties that the government—even with majority support—cannot violate.

THE BILL OF RIGHTS

Bill of Rights
first ten amendments to the U.S. Constitution listing individual freedoms and restrictions on governmental power.

The American Constitution contains many specific written restrictions on governmental power. The original text of the Constitution that emerged from the Philadelphia convention in 1787 did *not* contain a **"Bill of Rights"**—a listing of individual freedoms and restrictions on governmental power. The nation's Founders originally argued that a specific listing of individual freedoms was unnecessary because the national government possessed only enumerated powers; the power to restrict free speech or press or religion was not an enumerated power, so the national government could not do these things. But anti-Federalists in the state ratifying conventions were suspicious of the power of the new national government.[6] They were not satisfied with the mere inference that the national government could not interfere with personal liberty; they wanted specific written guarantees of fundamental freedoms. The Federalist supporters of the new Constitution agreed to add a "Bill of Rights" as the first ten amendments to the Constitution in order to win ratification in the state conventions. This is why our fundamental freedoms—speech, press, religion, assembly, petition, and due process of law—appear in the Constitution as *amendments*.

STRUCTURAL LIMITS ON POWER IN THE CONSTITUTION

The Constitution that emerged from the Philadelphia convention on September 17, 1787, founded a new government with a unique structure. That structure was designed to implement the Founders' belief that government rested on the consent of the people, that government power must be limited, and that the purpose of government was the protection of individual liberty and property. But the Founders were political realists; they did not have any

MASTERS OF SOCIAL THOUGHT
John Locke and Constitutionalism

The potential power of governments has worried people for a long time.

Constitutionalism is the belief that governmental power should be *limited*. A fundamental ideal of constitutionalism—"a government of laws and not of men"—suggests that those who exercise governmental authority are restricted in their use of it by a higher law. A *constitution* governs government.

A famous exponent of the idea of constitutional government was the English political philosopher John Locke (1632–1704). Perhaps more than anyone else, Locke inspired the political thought of our nation's Founders in that critical period of American history in which the new nation won its independence and established its constitution. Locke's ideas are written into both the Declaration of Independence and the Constitution of the United States.

According to Locke, all people possess natural rights.

These rights are not granted by government but derive from human nature itself. Governments cannot deprive people of their "inalienable rights to life, liberty, and property." People are rational beings, capable of self-government and able to participate in political decision making. Locke believed that human beings formed a contract among themselves to establish a government in order to better protect their natural rights, maintain peace, and protect themselves from foreign invasion. The *social contract* that established government made for safe and peaceful living and for the secure enjoyment of one's life, liberty, and property. Thus, the ultimate *legitimacy* of government derived from a contract among the people themselves and not from gods or kings. It was based on the *consent* of the governed. To safeguard their individual rights, the people agreed to be governed.

Because government was instituted as a contract to secure the rights of citizens, government itself could not violate individual rights. If government did so, it would dissolve the contract establishing it. Revolution, then, was justified if government was not serving the purpose for which it had been set up. However, according to Locke, revolution was justified only after a long period of abuses by government, not over any minor mismanagement.

Thomas Jefferson eloquently expressed Lockean ideals in the Declaration of Independence:

> *We hold these truths to be self-evident, that all men are created equal, that they are endowed by their Creator with certain inalienable rights, that among these are life, liberty, and the pursuit of happiness. That to secure these rights, governments are instituted among men, deriving their just powers from the consent of the governed.*

romantic notions about the wisdom and virtue of "the people." James Madison wrote: "A dependence on the people is, no doubt, the primary control on the government; but experience has taught mankind the necessity of auxiliary precautions."[7] The **key structural arrangements** in the Constitution—national supremacy, federalism, republicanism, separation of powers, checks and balances, and judicial review—all reflect the Founders' desire to create a strong national government while at the same time ensuring that it would not become a threat to liberty or property.

key structural arrangements in American Constitution

national supremacy

federalism

republicanism

separation of powers

checks and balances

judicial review

CROSS-NATIONAL PERSPECTIVE
The Role of Government

The idea of *limited* government, found in the writings of John Locke and echoed by the Founders of the American nation, continues to influence American politics. Indeed, public opinion in the United States about the role of government in society differs significantly from public opinion in other nations, even in other advanced Western industrial nations.

Americans generally believe they are individually responsible for their own well-being, while Europeans tend to look toward government as their protector and benefactor. For example, Americans are much less likely than Europeans to believe that government "should provide everyone with a guaranteed basic income," or that government "should provide a job for everyone who wants one." Americans are more likely than Europeans to believe their taxes are "too high," even though taxes in the United States are generally lower than those in European nations. Americans are also generally less supportive of governmental regulation, even for purposes of public safety and health. Americans seem to prefer that individuals, rather than governments, make the decisions that shape their lives (see table).

RESULTS OF SURVEYS RELATED TO THE ROLE OF GOVERNMENT (PERCENTAGE WHO "STRONGLY AGREE" OR "AGREE" WITH EACH STATEMENT)

	Government should provide everyone with a guaranteed basic income	Government should provide a job for everyone who wants one	Taxes are much too high
Switzerland	43	50	51
Great Britain	61	59	41
Netherlands	50	75	60
West Germany	56	77	52
Austria	57	80	47
Italy	67	82	62
Hungary	77	92	39
United States	**21**	**45**	**70**

SOURCE: Derived from international surveys reported in *The American Enterprise* (March/April 1990): 113–115.

NATIONAL SUPREMACY

The heart of the Constitution is the National Supremacy Clause of Article VI:

> *This Constitution, and the Laws of the United States which shall be made in Pursuance thereof; and all Treaties made, or which shall be made, under the Authority of the United States, shall be the supreme Law of the Land; and the Judges in every State shall be bound thereby, any Thing in the Constitution or Laws of any State to the Contrary notwithstanding.*

This sentence ensures that the Constitution itself is the supreme law of the land. Laws made by Congress must not conflict with the Constitution. The Constitution and the laws of Congress supersede state laws.

FEDERALISM

The Constitution *divides power* between the nation and the states. It recognizes that both the national government and the state governments have independent legal authority over their own citizens: Both can pass their own laws, levy their own taxes, and maintain their own courts.[8] The states have an important role in the selection of national officeholders—in the apportionment of congressional seats and in the allocation of electoral votes for president. Most important, perhaps, both the Congress and three-quarters of the states must consent to changes in the Constitution itself.

federalism
the division of power between states and nations

REPUBLICANISM

To the Founders, a **republican** government meant the delegation of powers by the people to a small number of representatives "whose wisdom may best discern the true interest of their country, and whose patriotism and love of justice, will be least likely to sacrifice it to temporary or partial considerations." The Founders believed that government rests ultimately on "the consent of the governed." But their notion of republicanism envisioned decision making by *representatives* of the people, not the people themselves. The U.S. Constitution does not provide for **direct democracy** voting by the people on national questions; that is, unlike many state constitutions today it does not provide for national *referenda* (see Controversies in Social Science, "Direct versus Representative Democracy"). Moreover, in the original Constitution of 1787 only the House of Representatives (sometimes referred to even today as "the people's house") was to be elected directly by voters in the states. Members of the Senate were to be elected by state legislatures; not until the ratification of the Seventeenth Amendment in 1913 would voters directly elect their U.S. senators. The president was to be elected by "electors" (chosen in a way prescribed by state legislatures) and the Supreme Court and other federal judges were appointed by the president with the consent of the Senate.

republicanism
government by elected representatives of the people

direct democracy
people themselves vote directly on issues, rather than their representatives

These republican arrangements may appear undemocratic from our perspective today, but in 1787 this Constitution was more democratic than any other governing system in the world. Most other nations of that time were governed by monarchs, emperors, chieftains, and hereditary aristocracies. Later democratic impulses in America greatly altered the original Constitution and reshaped it into an even more democratic document.

THE SEPARATION OF POWERS

The **separation of powers** in the national government—separate legislative, executive, and judicial branches—was intended by the nation's Founders as an additional safeguard for liberty. *The Federalist* paper Number 51 expresses

separation of powers
the principle of dividing governmental powers among the executive, legislative, and judicial branches

CONTROVERSIES IN SOCIAL SCIENCE
Direct versus Representative Democracy

"Democracy" means popular participation in government. (The Greek roots of the word mean "rule by the many.") But "popular participation" can have different meanings. To our nation's Founders, who were quite ambivalent about the wisdom of democracy, it meant that the voice of the people would be *represented* in government. "Representational democracy" means the selection of government officials by vote of the people in periodic elections open to competition in which candidates and voters can freely express themselves.

"Direct democracy" means that the people themselves can initiate and decide policy questions by popular vote. The Founders were profoundly skeptical of this form of democracy. *The U.S. Constitution has no provision for direct voting by the people on national policy questions.* It was not until over one hun-

dred years after the U.S. Constitution was written that widespread support developed in the American states for direct voter participation in policy making. Direct democracy developed in states and communities, and it is to be found today *only* in state and local government.

Initiative and Referendum

The *initiative* is a form of direct democracy whereby a specific number or percent of voters, through the use of petition, may have a proposed state constitutional amendment or state law placed on the ballot for adoption or rejection by the electorate of a state. This process bypasses the legislature and allows citizens to both propose and adopt laws and constitutional amendments. The *referendum* is a device by which the electorate must approve citizen initiatives or decisions of the legislature before

these become law or become part of the state constitution. Most states require a favorable referendum vote for a state constitutional amendment. Referenda on state laws may be submitted by the legislature (when legislators want to shift decision-making responsibility to the people), or referenda may be demanded by popular petition (when the people wish to change laws passed by the legislature).

Arguments for Direct Democracy

Proponents of direct democracy make several strong arguments on behalf of the initiative and referendum devices.

- Direct democracy enhances government responsiveness and accountability. The threat of a successful initiative and referendum drive— indeed, sometimes the mere

SOURCE: See Thomas E. Cronin, *Direct Democracy* (Cambridge, MA.: Harvard University Press, 1989).

the logic behind creating separate branches of government and giving them checks over each other:

> *Ambition must be made to counteract ambition. . . . It may be a reflection on human nature, that such devices should be necessary to control the abuses of government. But what is government itself, but the greatest of all reflections on human nature? If men were angels, no government would be necessary. If angels were to govern men, neither external nor internal controls on government would be necessary. In framing a government which is to be administered by men over men, the great difficulty lies in this: you must first enable the government to control the governed; and in the next place oblige it to control itself.[9]*

circulation of a petition—encourages officials to take the popular actions.

- Direct democracy allows citizen groups to bring their concern directly to the public. Taxpayer groups, for example, who are not especially well represented in state capitols, have been able through the initiative and referendum devices to place their concerns on the public agenda.
- Direct democracy stimulates debate about policy issues. In elections with important referendum issues on the ballot, campaigns tend to be more issue-oriented.
- Direct democracy stimulates voters' interest and improves election-day turnout. Controversial issues on the ballot—the death penalty, abortion, gun control, taxes, gay rights, a ban on racial preferences, and so on—bring out additional voters.

Arguments for Representative Democracy

Opponents of direct democracy, from our nation's Founders to the present, argue that representative democracy offers far better protection for individual liberty and the rights of minorities than direct democracy. The Founders constructed a system of checks and balances not so much to protect against the oppression of a ruler, but to protect against the tyranny of the majority. Opponents of direct democracy echo many of the Founders' arguments:

- Direct democracy encourages majorities to sacrifice the rights of individuals and minorities. This argument supposes that voters are generally less tolerant than elected officials.
- Voters are not sufficiently informed to cast intelligent ballots on many issues.

Many voters cast their vote in a referendum without ever having considered the issue before going into the polling booth.

- A referendum does not allow consideration of alternative policies or modifications or amendments to the proposition set forth on the ballot. In contrast, legislators devote a great deal of attention to writing, rewriting, and amending bills, and seeking out compromises among interests.
- Direct democracy enables special interests to mount expensive initiative and referendum campaigns. Although proponents of direct democracy argue that these devices allow citizens to bypass legislatures dominated by special-interest groups, in fact, only a fairly well-financed group can mount a statewide campaign on behalf of a referendum issue.

CHECKS AND BALANCES

Each of the major decision-making bodies of American government possesses important **checks and balances** (see Figure 7-1) over the decisions of the others. No bill can become law without the approval of both the House and the Senate. The president shares in legislative power through the veto and the responsibility of the office to "give to the Congress information of the State of the Union, and recommend to their consideration such measures as he shall judge necessary and expedient." The president can also convene sessions of Congress. But the president's powers to make appointments and treaties are shared by the Senate. Congress can also override executive vetoes.

checks and balances
the principle whereby each branch of the government exercises a check on the actions of the others, preventing too great a concentration of power in any one person or group of persons

FIGURE 7-1

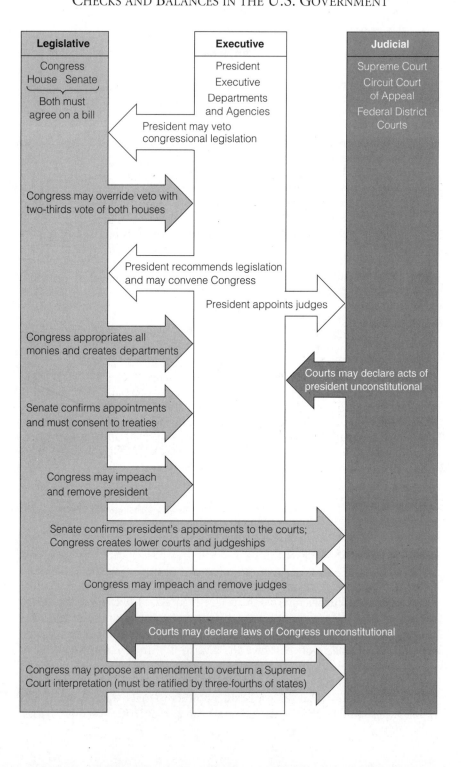

CHECKS AND BALANCES IN THE U.S. GOVERNMENT

The president must execute the laws, but to do so he or she must rely on the executive departments, and they must be created by Congress. Moreover, the executive branch cannot spend money that has not been appropriated by Congress.

Federal judges, including members of the Supreme Court, must be appointed by the president, with the consent of the Senate. Congress must create lower and intermediate courts, establish the number of judges, fix the jurisdiction of lower federal courts, and make "exceptions" to the appellate jurisdiction of the Supreme Court.

JUDICIAL REVIEW

Perhaps the keystone of the system of checks and balances is the idea of **judicial review,** an original contribution by the nation's Founders to the science of government. Judicial review is the power of the courts to strike down laws that they believe conflict with the Constitution. Article VI grants federal courts the power of judicial review of *state* decisions, specifying that the Constitution and the laws and treaties of the national government are the supreme law of the land, superseding anything in any state laws or constitutions. However, nowhere does the Constitution specify that the Supreme Court has power of judicial review of *executive* action or of laws enacted by *Congress.* This principle was instead established in the case of *Marbury v. Madison* in 1803, when Chief Justice John Marshall argued convincingly that the Founders had intended the Supreme Court to have the power of invalidating not only state laws and constitutions, but also any laws of Congress or executive actions that came into conflict with the Constitution of the United States. Thus, the Supreme Court stands as the final defender of the constitutional principles against the encroachments of popularly elected legislatures and executives.

judicial review
power of the Supreme Court or any court to declare federal or state laws unconstitutional

FEDERALISM AND THE GROWTH OF POWER IN WASHINGTON

Over the nation's history, power has flowed toward the national government and away from the states.[10] Major developments in the history of American federalism have contributed to national power:

sources of growing national power:

EXPANSION OF IMPLIED NATIONAL POWER

Chief Justice John Marshall added immeasurably to national power in *McCulloch v. Maryland* (1819) when he broadly interpreted the "necessary and proper" clause of Article I, Section 8, of the Constitution. In approving

1. broad interpretation of national power in the Constitution

the establishment of a national bank (a power not specifically delegated to the national government in the Constitution), Marshall wrote:

> *Let the end be legitimate, let it be within the scope of the Constitution, and all means which are appropriate, which are plainly adopted to that end, which are not prohibited but consistent with the letter and the spirit of the Constitution, are constitutional.*

Since then, the "necessary and proper" clause has been called the "implied powers" clause or even the "elastic" clause, suggesting that the national government can do anything not specifically prohibited by the Constitution. Given this tradition, the courts are unlikely to hold an act of Congress unconstitutional simply because no formal constitutional grant of power gives Congress the power to act.

NATIONAL VICTORY IN THE CIVIL WAR

2. national military force

The Civil War was the nation's greatest crisis in federalism. Did a state have the right to oppose federal action by force of arms? This issue was decided in the nation's bloodiest war. (Combined military and civilian casualties in the Civil War exceeded U.S. casualties in World War II, even though the U.S. population in 1860 was only one-quarter of the population in 1940.) The same issue was at stake when the federal government sent troops to Little Rock, Arkansas, in 1957; to Oxford, Mississippi, in 1962; and to Tuscaloosa, Alabama, in 1963, to enforce desegregation; however, in these confrontations it was clear which side held the military advantage.

GROWTH OF INTERSTATE COMMERCE

3. broad interpretation of interstate commerce

The growth of national power under the interstate commerce clause is also an important development in American federalism. The Industrial Revolution created a national economy governable only by a national government. Yet, until the 1930s, the Supreme Court placed many obstacles in the way of government regulation of the economy. Finally, in *National Labor Relations Board v. Jones & Laughlin Steel Corporation* (1937), the Supreme Court recognized the principle that Congress could regulate production and distribution of goods and services for a national market under the interstate commerce clause. As a result, the national government gained control over wages, prices, production, marketing, labor relations, and all other important aspects of the national economy.

FEDERAL CIVIL RIGHTS ENFORCEMENT

4. development of national system of civil rights enforceable in federal courts

Over the years, the U.S. Supreme Court has built a national system of civil rights based on the Fourteenth Amendment. This amendment rose out of the Civil War: "No State shall . . . deprive any person of life, liberty, or property, without due process of law; nor deny to any person within its jurisdiction the equal protection of the laws." In early cases, the Supreme Court held that the general guarantee of *liberty* in the first phrase (the "due process" clause) prevents state and local governments from interfering with free speech, press, religion, and other personal liberties. Later, particularly after *Brown v. Board of Education of Topeka* in 1954, the Supreme Court also used the "equal protection" clause to prohibit state and local government officials from denying equality of opportunity.

FEDERAL GRANTS-IN-AID MONEY

Money and power go together. The income tax (established in 1913) gave the federal government the authority to raise large sums of money, which it spent for the "general welfare," as well as for defense. Gradually the federal government expanded its power in states and communities by use of **grants-in-aid.** During the Great Depression of the 1930s, the national government used its taxing and spending powers in a number of areas formerly reserved to states and communities. Congress began grants-in-aid programs to states and communities for public assistance, unemployment compensation, employment services, child welfare, public housing, urban renewal, highway construction, and vocational education and rehabilitation.

5. growth of federal grants-in-aid money

federal grants-in-aid
payments of funds from the national government to state or local governments, usually with conditions attached to their uses

FEDERALISM TODAY

Today, federal grants-in-aid are the principal source of federal power over states and communities. Nearly one-quarter of all state and local government revenues are from federal grants. These grants almost always come with detailed conditions regarding how the money can be used. "Categorical" grants specify particular projects or particular individuals eligible to receive funds; "block" grants provide some discretion to state or local officials in using the money for a particular governmental function, such as law enforcement. Federal grant money is distributed in hundreds of separate programs, but welfare (including Assistance to Needy Families) and health (including Medicaid) account for nearly two-thirds of federal aid money (see Figure 7-2).

Federal mandates to state and local governments also centralize power in Washington. Often the federal government by law requires state and local governments to perform functions or undertake tasks that Congress deems in the public interest. Many of these federal mandates are "unfunded"—that is, Congress does not provide any money to carry out these mandated functions or tasks even though they impose costs on states and communities. For example, environmental protection laws passed by Congress require local governments to provide specified levels of sewage treatment; the Americans with Disabilities Act requires state and local governments to build ramps and alter curbs in public streets and buildings.

federal mandates
directions to state and local governments from the national government

FIGURE 7-2

PURPOSES OF FEDERAL GRANTS-IN-AID TO STATE AND LOCAL GOVERNMENTS

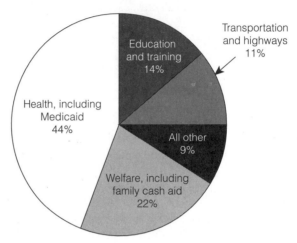

SOURCE: *Budget of the United States Government 2001.*

In its 1985 *Garcia* decision, the U.S. Supreme Court appeared to remove all constitutional barriers to direct federal legislation in matters traditionally "reserved" to the states.[11] The case arose when Congress mandated that state and local governments pay federal minimum wages to their own employees. The Supreme Court dismissed arguments that the "reserved power clause" of the Tenth Amendment prevented Congress from directly legislating in state and local affairs. The Court said that the only protection for state powers was to be found in the states' role in electing U.S. House and Senate members and the president—a concept known as **representational federalism.**

DEVOLUTION?

Over the years various efforts have been made to return power to states and communities. President Ronald Reagan was partially successful in his "New Federalism" efforts; many categorical grant programs were consolidated into block grants with greater discretion given to state and local governments. But today state and local government reliance on federal aid remains high; about 25 percent of all state-local revenue comes from federal grants-in-aid.

Recently, Congress has considered the **devolution** of some governmental responsibilities from the national government to the states and their local governments. So far, welfare cash assistance is the only major federal program to "devolve" back to the states. Since Franklin D. Roosevelt's New Deal, with its federal guarantee of cash Aid to Families with Dependent

representational federalism
an argument that there are no constitutional barriers to Congress's legislating in state affairs, and the only protection for states is their role in electing Congress members and the president

devolution
the transfer of federal programs to state and local governments

Children (AFDC), low-income mothers and children had enjoyed a legal "entitlement" to welfare payments. But welfare reform in 1996, by devolving responsibility for determining eligibility to the state, ended this sixty-year federal entitlement. This is a major change in federal social welfare policy (see Chapter 11) and may become a model for future shedding of federal entitlement programs.

FEDERALISM REVIVED?

In some recent decisions, the U.S. Supreme Court appears to be somewhat more respectful of the powers of states and somewhat less willing to see these powers overridden by the national government. In a surprise ruling in 1995, the Supreme Court held that the federal Gun Free School Zones Act was unconstitutional because it exceeded Congress' powers under the Interstate Commerce Clause. The Court even cited James Madison with approval: "The powers delegated by the proposed Constitution to the federal government are few and defined. Those which are to remain in the state governments are numerous and indefinite."[12] The Court decided in 1997 that Congress could not command local law enforcement officers to conduct background checks on gun purchasers, as it tried to do in the Brady Handgun Violence Protection Act. And in 2000, the Court held that Congress invaded the reserve police powers of the states in the Violence Against Women Act.[13] But these cases reinforcing the principle of federalism were all made by the Supreme Court in close 5-to-4 decisions. A change in court personnel could reverse directions again and return to more limited notions of state power.

PRESIDENTIAL POWER

Americans look to their president for "greatness." Great presidents are those associated with great events—George Washington with the founding of the nation, Abraham Lincoln with the preservation of the Union, Franklin D. Roosevelt with the nation's emergence from economic depression and victory in World War II (see Focus, "Rating the Presidents"). People tend to believe that the president is responsible for "peace and prosperity" as well as "change." They expect their president to present a "vision" of America's future and to symbolize the nation.

PROVIDING NATIONAL LEADERSHIP

The president personifies American government for most people.[14] People expect the president to act decisively and effectively to deal with national problems. They expect the president to be "compassionate"—to show concern for problems confronting individual citizens. The president, while

FOCUS

Rating the Presidents

From time to time, historians and political scientists have been asked to rate U.S. presidents. The ratings given the presidents have been remarkably consistent. Abraham Lincoln, George Washington, Franklin Roosevelt, Woodrow Wilson, and Thomas Jefferson are universally recognized as the greatest American presidents.

Schlesinger (1948)	Schlesinger (1962)	Dodder (1970)	Murray (1982)	Ridings & McIver (1996)
Great	**Great**	**Accomplishments of Administration**	**Presidential Rank**	**Overall Ranking**
1. Lincoln	1. Lincoln	1. Lincoln	1. Lincoln	1. Lincoln
2. Washington	2. Washington	2. F. Roosevelt	2. F. Roosevelt	2. F. Roosevelt
3. F. Roosevelt	3. F. Roosevelt	3. Washington	3. Washington	3. Washington
4. Wilson	4. Wilson	4. Jefferson	4. Jefferson	4. Jefferson
5. Jefferson	5. Jefferson	5. T. Roosevelt	5. T. Roosevelt	5. T. Roosevelt
6. Jackson	**Near Great**	6. Truman	6. Wilson	6. Wilson
Near Great	6. Jackson	7. Wilson	7. Jackson	7. Truman
7. T. Roosevelt	7. T. Roosevelt	8. Jackson	8. Truman	8. Jackson
8. Cleveland	8. Polk	9. L. Johnson	9. J. Adams	9. Eisenhower
9. J. Adams	Truman (tie)	10. Polk	10. L. Johnson	10. Madison
10. Polk	9. J. Adams	11. J. Adams	11. Eisenhower	11. Polk
Average	10. Cleveland	12. Kennedy	12. Polk	12. L. Johnson
11. J. Q. Adams	**Average**	13. Monroe	13. Kennedy	13. Monroe
12. Monroe	11. Madison	14. Cleveland	14. Madison	14. J. Adams
13. Hayes	12. J. Q. Adams	15. Madison	15. Monroe	15. Kennedy
14. Madison	13. Hayes	16. Taft	16. J. Q. Adams	16. Cleveland
15. Van Buren	14. McKinley	17. McKinley	17. Cleveland	17. McKinley
16. Taft	15. Taft	18. J. Q. Adams	18. McKinley	18. J. Q. Adams
17. Arthur	16. Van Buren	19. Hoover	19. Taft	19. Carter
18. McKinley	17. Monroe	20. Eisenhower	20. Van Buren	20. Taft
			21. Hoover	21. Van Buren

These ratings result from surveys of scholars ranging in numbers from 55 to 950.

SOURCES: Arthur Murphy, "Evaluating the Presidents of the United States," *Presidential Studies Quarterly* 14 (1984): 117–26; William J. Ridings, Jr., and Stuart B. McIver, *Rating the Presidents* (Secaucus, N.J.: Citadel Press, 1997).

playing these roles, is the focus of public attention and is the nation's leading celebrity. Presidents receive more media coverage than any other person in the nation, for everything from their policy statements to their favorite foods.

The nation looks to the president for leadership. The president has the capacity to mobilize public opinion, to communicate directly with the American people, to offer direction and reassurance, and to advance policy initiatives in both foreign and domestic affairs.

It is more difficult for historians to rate recent presidents; the views of historians are influenced by current political controversies. Often the passage of time allows scholars to make more objective evaluations. Richard Nixon may be evaluated higher by future historians than he is today. How would you rate Bill Clinton?

Schlesinger (1948)	Schlesinger (1962)	Dodder (1970)	Murray (1982)	Ridings & McIver (1996)
Average	**Average**	**Accomplishments of Administration**	**Presidential Rank**	**Overall Ranking**
19. A. Johnson	18. Hoover		22. Hayes	22. Bush
20. Hoover	19. B. Harrison	21. A. Johnson	23. Arthur	23. Clinton
21. B. Harrison	20. Arthur	22. Van Buren	24. Ford	24. Hoover
Below Average	Eisenhower (tie)	23. Arthur	25. Carter	25. Hayes
22. Tyler	21. A. Johnson	24. Hayes	26. B. Harrison	26. Reagan
23. Coolidge	**Below Average**	25. Tyler	27. Taylor	27. Ford
24. Fillmore	22. Taylor	26. B. Harrison	28. Tyler	28. Arthur
25. Taylor	23. Tyler	27. Taylor	29. Fillmore	29. Taylor
26. Buchanan	24. Fillmore	28. Buchanan	30. Coolidge	30. Garfield
27. Pierce	25. Coolidge	29. Fillmore	31. Pierce	31. B. Harrison
Failure	26. Pierce	30. Coolidge	32. A. Johnson	32. Nixon
28. Grant	27. Buchanan	31. Pierce	33. Buchanan	33. Coolidge
29. Harding	**Failure**	32. Grant	34. Nixon	34. Tyler
	28. Grant	33. Harding	35. Grant	35. W. Harrison
	29. Harding		36. Harding	36. Fillmore
				37. Pierce
				38. Grant
				39. A. Johnson
				40. Buchanan
				41. Harding

Presidential popularity with the American people is an important asset in providing national leadership. Popular presidents cannot *always* transfer their popularity into policy successes, but popular presidents usually have more success than unpopular presidents. Presidential popularity is regularly tracked in national opinion polls. Over the years, national surveys have asked the American public the following: "Do you approve or disapprove of the way the current president is handling his job?" (See Focus, "Explaining

FOCUS

Explaining Presidential Approval Ratings

President watching is a favorite pastime among political scientists. Regular surveys of the American people ask the question: "Do you approve or disapprove of the way the current president is handling his job?" By asking this same question over time about presidents, political scientists can monitor the ups and downs of presidential popularity. Then they can attempt to explain presidential popularity by examining events that correspond to changes in presidential approval ratings.

One hypothesis that helps explain presidential approval ratings centers on the election cycle. The hypothesis is that presidential popularity is usually highest immediately after election or reelection, but it steadily erodes over time. Note that this hypothesis tends to be supported by the survey data in the figure. This simple graph shows, over time, the percent-

age of survey respondents who say they approve of the way the president is handling his job. Presidents usually begin their administrations with high approval ratings. Presidents and their advisers generally know about this "honeymoon" period hypothesis and try to use it to their advantage by pushing hard for their policies in Congress early in the term.

Another hypothesis centers on the effects of international

PRESIDENTIAL APPROVAL RATINGS

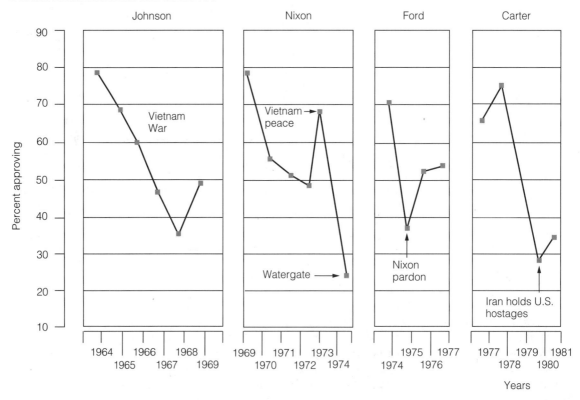

crises. Initially, people "rally 'round the flag" when the nation is confronted with an international threat and the president orders military action. President Bush registered an all-time high in presidential approval ratings during the Persian Gulf War. But prolonged, indecisive warfare erodes popular support for a president. The public approved of President Johnson's handling of his job when he first sent U.S. ground combat troops into Vietnam in 1965; but support for the president waned over time as military operations mounted.

Major scandals may hurt presidential popularity and effectiveness. The Watergate scandal produced a low of 22-percent approval for Nixon just prior to his resignation. Reagan's generally high approval ratings were blemished by the Iran-Contra scandal in 1987. Yet Clinton's ratings continued their upward trend despite a White House sex scandal and a vote for impeachment by a Republican-controlled House of Representatives.

Finally, it is widely hypothesized that economic recessions erode presidential popularity. Every president in office during a recession has suffered loss of popular approval, including President Reagan during the 1982 recession. But no president suffered a more precipitous decline in approval ratings than George Bush, whose popularity plummeted from its Gulf War high of 89 percent to a low of 37 percent in only a year, largely as a result of recession.

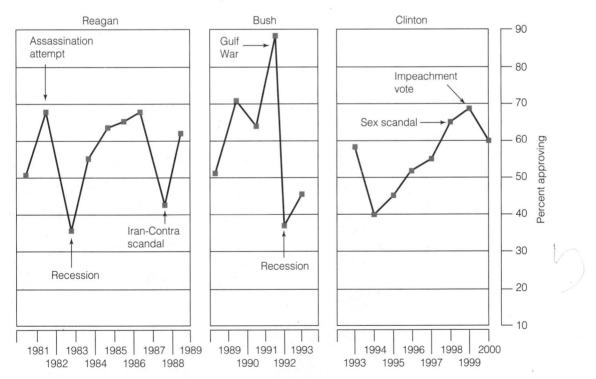

Presidential Approval Ratings.") Generally, presidents have been more successful in providing leadership in both foreign and domestic affairs when they have enjoyed high approval ratings.[15]

MANAGING CRISES

In time of crisis, the American people look to their president to take action, to provide reassurance, and to protect the nation and its people. It is the president, not the Congress nor the courts, who is expected to speak on behalf of the people in time of national triumph and tragedy. The president gives expression to the nation's pride in victory. The nation's heroes are welcomed and its championship sports teams are feted in the White House Rose Garden. The president also gives expression to the nation's sadness in tragedy and strives to help the nation go forward.

PROVIDING POLICY LEADERSHIP

The president is expected to set policy priorities for the nation. Most policy initiatives originate in the White House and various departments and agencies of the executive branch, then are forwarded to Congress with the president's approval. Presidential programs are submitted to Congress in the form of messages, including the president's annual State of the Union Address, and

George W. Bush won the presidency in 2000 by winning a majority of the electoral votes of the states, despite losing the nationwide popular vote to Al Gore. Florida's 25 electoral votes were crucial to Bush's election.

the Budget of the United States Government, which the president presents each year to Congress.

As a political leader, the president is expected to mobilize political support for policy proposals. It is not enough for the president to send policy proposals to Congress. The president must rally public opinion, lobby members of Congress, and win legislative battles. To avoid being perceived as weak or ineffective, presidents must get as much of their legislative proposals through Congress as possible. Presidents use the threat of a veto to prevent Congress from passing bills they oppose; when forced to veto a bill, they fight to prevent an override of the veto. The president thus is responsible for "getting things done" in the policy arena.

Managing the Economy

The American people hold the president responsible for maintaining a healthy economy. Presidents are blamed for economic downturns, whether or not government policies had anything to do with market conditions. The president is expected to "Do Something!" in the face of high unemployment, declining personal income, high mortgage rates, rising inflation, or even a stock market crash. Herbert Hoover in 1932, Gerald Ford in 1976, Jimmy Carter in 1980, and George Bush in 1992—all incumbent presidents defeated for reelection during recessions—learned the hard way that the general public holds the president responsible for hard economic times. Presidents must have an economic "game plan" to stimulate the economy—tax incentives to spur investments, spending proposals to create jobs, plans to lower interest rates. In today's economy, they must also develop programs to improve America's international "competitiveness."

Presidents themselves are partly responsible for these public expectations. Incumbent presidents have been quick to take credit for economic growth, low inflation, low interest rates, and low unemployment. And presidential candidates in recessionary times invariably promise "to get the economy moving again."

Managing the Government

As the chief executive of a mammoth federal bureaucracy with 2.8 million civilian employees, the president is responsible for implementing policy—that is, for achieving policy goals. Policy making does not end when a law is passed. Policy implementation involves issuing orders, creating organizations, recruiting and assigning personnel, disbursing funds, overseeing work, and evaluating results. It is true that the president cannot perform all of these tasks personally. But the ultimate responsibility for implementation—in the words of the Constitution, "to take Care that the Laws be faithfully executed"—rests with the president. Or as the sign on Harry Truman's desk put it: "The Buck Stops Here."

The Global President

Nations strive to speak with a single voice in international affairs; for the United States, the global voice is that of the president. As commander-in-chief of the armed forces of the United States, the president is a powerful voice in foreign affairs.[16] Efforts by Congress to speak on behalf of the nation in foreign affairs and to limit the war-making power of the president have been generally unsuccessful. It is the president who orders American troops into combat. It is the president's finger that rests on the nuclear trigger.

Commander-in-Chief

Global power derives primarily from the president's role as commander-in-chief of the armed forces of the United States. Presidential command over the armed forces is not merely symbolic; presidents may issue direct military orders to troops in the field. As president, Washington personally led troops to end the Whiskey Rebellion in 1794; Abraham Lincoln issued direct orders to his generals in the Civil War; Lyndon Johnson personally chose bombing targets in Vietnam; and George Bush personally ordered the Gulf War cease-fire after one hundred hours of ground fighting. All presidents, whether they are experienced in world affairs or not, soon learn after taking office that their influence throughout the world is heavily dependent upon the command of capable military forces.

Modest Constitutional Powers

Popular expectations of presidential leadership far exceed the formal constitutional powers granted to the president. Compared with the Congress, the president has only modest constitutionally expressed powers (see Table 7-1). Nevertheless, presidents over the years have consistently exceeded their specific grants of power in Article II, from Thomas Jefferson's decision to double the land area of the United States in the Louisiana Purchase, to William Jefferson Clinton's decision to send U.S. troops to keep the peace in Bosnia and Kosovo.

Limits on Presidential Power

Despite the great powers of the office, no president can monopolize policy making. The president functions within an established political system and can exercise power only within its framework.[17] The president cannot act outside existing political consensus, outside the "rules of the game" (see Case Study, "Watergate and the Limits of Presidential Power").

TABLE 7-1

CONSTITUTIONAL POWERS OF THE PRESIDENT

Chief Administrator

Implement policy: "take Care that the Laws be faithfully executed" (Article II, Section 3)

Supervise executive branch of government

Appoint and remove executive officials (Article II, Section 2)

Prepare executive budget for submission to Congress (by law of Congress)

Chief Legislator

Initiate policy: "give to the Congress Information of the State of the Union, and recommend to their Consideration such Measures as he shall judge necessary and expedient" (Article II, Section 3)

Veto legislation passed by Congress, subject to override by a two-thirds vote in both houses

Convene special session of Congress "on extraordinary Occasions" (Article II, Section 3)

Chief Diplomat

Make treaties "with the Advice and Consent of the Senate" (Article II, Section 2)

Exercise the power of diplomatic recognition: "receive Ambassadors" (Article II, Section 3)

Make executive agreements (by custom and international law)

Commander-in-Chief

Command U.S. armed forces: "The president shall be Commander in Chief of the Army and Navy" (Article II, Section 2)

Appoint military officers

Chief of State

"The executive Power shall be vested in a President" (Article II, Section 1)

Grant reprieves and pardons (Article II, Section 2)

Represent the nation as chief of state

Appoint federal court and Supreme Court judges (Article II, Section 2)

ELECTING THE PRESIDENT

Americans were given a dramatic reminder in 2000 that the president of the United States is *not* elected by nationwide popular vote but rather by a majority of the electoral votes of the states. Democrat Al Gore won 500,000 more votes nationwide (out of over 100 million cast) than his opponent Republican George W. Bush. But Bush won a majority of the states' electoral votes—271 to 267—the narrowest margin in modern American history. And Florida's crucial 25 electoral votes were decided by the Supreme Court of the United States more than a month after election day.

THE ELECTORAL COLLEGE

The U.S. Constitution provides that the president shall be chosen by the majority of the number of "Electors" chosen by the states. Article II says "Each

CASE STUDY

Watergate and the Limits of Presidential Power

Richard Nixon was the only president ever to resign from office. His forced resignation in 1974 was not merely a product of specific misdeeds; it also grew out of his failure to cooperate with Congress and the courts, and his disregard for the general "rules of the game."

On the night of June 17, 1972, five men with burglary and wiretapping tools were arrested in the offices of the Democratic National Committee in the Watergate apartments in Washington, together with E. Howard Hunt and G. Gordon Liddy, who directed the break-in. All pleaded guilty and were convicted, but U.S. District Court Judge John J. Sirica believed that the defendants were shielding whoever had ordered and paid for the bugging and break-in. Judge Sirica threatened the defendants with heavy sentences, and soon James W. McCord confessed to secret payments and a cover-up.

The Senate formed a Special Select Committee on Campaign Activities—the so-called Watergate Committee—headed by Senator Sam J. Ervin, to delve into Watergate and related activities. The national press, led by "investigative reporters" Bob Woodward and Carl Bernstein of *The Washington Post,* launched a series of damaging stories, re-

ported nightly on the national television networks, involving Nixon's campaign director and former Attorney General John Mitchell, White House chief of staff H. R. Haldeman, and White House adviser John Ehrlichman.

President Nixon might have been able to stay in office if he had publicly repented his own actions and cooperated in the Watergate investigation by Congress and the courts. But Nixon increasingly viewed the Watergate affair as a test of his own strength and character; he perceived it as a conspiracy among liberal opponents in Congress and the news media to reverse the 1972 election outcome.

When the Senate Watergate Committee learned that the president regularly taped conversations in the Oval Office, it issued subpoenas for tapes that would prove or disprove charges of a cover-up. In response, President Nixon chose to argue that the constitutional separation of powers permitted the president to withhold information from both Congress and the courts. But the Supreme Court, in *The United States v. Richard M. Nixon,* denied the president the power to withhold information that was essential to a criminal investigation. President Nixon

publicly released the transcripts of the subpoenaed White House tapes in a national television broadcast in which he claimed innocence of any wrongdoing. The conversations on the tapes are rambling and inconclusive but the most common interpretation is that President Nixon approved a payoff to silence the convicted burglars.

The Judiciary Committee of the House of Representatives passed articles of impeachment accusing the president of obstructing justice in the Watergate investigation. Shortly thereafter, Nixon was informed by congressional leaders of his own party that impeachment by a majority of the House and removal from office by two-thirds of the Senate was assured. On August 9, 1974, President Nixon resigned his office—the first U.S. president ever to do so.

On September 8, 1974, new President Gerald R. Ford pardoned former President Richard Nixon "for all offenses against the United States which he, Richard Nixon, has committed or may have committed or taken part in" during his presidency. President Ford stated that his purpose in granting the pardon was to end "bitter controversy and divisive national debate."

state shall appoint, in such Manner as the Legislature thereof may direct, a Number of Electors, equal to the whole Number of Senators and Representatives to which the State may be entitled in the Congress. . . ." Because Representatives are apportioned to the states on the basis of population, the electoral vote of the states is subject to change after each ten-year census (see Figure 7-3). The Twenty-third Amendment granted three electoral votes to the District of Columbia even though it has no voting members in Congress. So winning the presidency requires winning in the states with at least 270 of the 538 total electoral votes.

The Constitution specifically gives state *legislatures* the power to determine how electors in their states are to be chosen. By 1840 the spirit of Jacksonian democracy (see Chapter 8) had inspired state legislatures to allow the voters of their states to choose slates of presidential electors pledged to vote for one or another party's presidential and vice presidential candidates. (The names of electors seldom appear on the ballot, only the names of the

FIGURE 7-3

ELECTORAL SHAPE OF THE STATES, 2000

Note: States drawn in proportion to number of electoral votes in 2000. Total electoral votes: 538

SOURCE: Holly Idelson, "Count Adds Seats in Eight States," *Congressional Quarterly Weekly Report* 48 (December 29, 1990), p. 4220.

candidates and parties.) The slate that wins a plurality of the popular vote in a state (more than any other slate, but not necessarily a majority) casts all of the state's vote in the Electoral College.

It is possible for a presidential candidate to win more popular votes nationwide and yet lose the election by failing to win a majority of the electoral votes. That is, a candidate could win by large margins of the popular vote in some states, yet lose by small margins in states with a majority of electoral votes, and thus lose the presidency despite having more popular votes nationwide.

The Constitution specifies that if no candidate wins a majority of the electoral votes, the House of Representatives chooses the president, with each state delegation casting one vote. But the Constitution does not specify what happens if competing slates of electors are submitted by one or more states. This problem is left up to the full Congress to resolve.

THE HISTORICAL RECORD

Only two presidential elections have ever been decided formally by the House of Representatives. In 1800 Thomas Jefferson and Aaron Burr tied in the Electoral College because the Twelfth Amendment had not yet been adopted to separate presidential from vice presidential voting; all the Democratic-Republican electors voted for both Jefferson and Burr, creating a tie. In 1824 Andrew Jackson won the popular vote and more electoral votes than anyone else but failed to get a majority. The House chose John Quincy Adams over Jackson, causing a popular uproar and ensuring Jackson's election in 1828.

In addition, in 1876, the Congress was called on to decide which electoral results from the southern states to validate; a Republican Congress chose to validate enough Republican electoral votes to allow Republican Rutherford B. Hayes to win, even though Democrat Samuel Tilden had won more popular votes. Hayes promised the Democratic southern states that in return for their acknowledgement of his presidential claim, he would end the military occupation of the South.

In 1888, the Electoral College vote failed to reflect the popular vote. Benjamin Harrison received 233 electoral votes to incumbent president Grover Cleveland's 168, even though Cleveland won about 90,000 more popular votes than Harrison. Cleveland was elected for a second time in 1892, the only president to serve two nonconsecutive terms.

ELECTORAL VOTE STRATEGIES

Presidential candidates are well aware of the necessity to garner a majority of the electoral votes of the states. So in their campaigns they generally concentrate their efforts on the "swing" states—those that are adjudged to be close—and give less attention to states they feel are solidly in their column or hopelessly lost.

The Bush campaign conceded New York, California, and most of the northeastern states to Gore. The Gore campaign conceded Texas and most of the southern and mountain states to Bush. The battleground states were Pennsylvania, Ohio, Michigan, Illinois, Wisconsin, and especially Florida. Bush's younger brother, Jeb Bush, had been elected governor of Florida in 1998 and Republicans controlled both houses of the legislature. Early in the campaign, Bush had been so certain of winning Florida that he made very few appearances there. Only late in the campaign, when Gore was showing a lead in the Florida polls, did Bush mount a serious effort in that state.

Early in the evening the television networks "called" all of the battleground states for Gore, in effect declaring him the winner. But by 9 p.m. Florida was yanked back into the undecided column; the Electoral College vote looked like it was splitting down the middle. Around 1 a.m., Florida was "called" for Bush, and the networks pronounced him the next president of the United States. Gore telephoned Bush to concede, but after learning that the gap in Florida was closing fast, Gore called again and withdrew his concession. For the second time, the television networks pulled Florida back into the "Too Close to Call" column.

The Battle after the Bell

The morning after election day, it was clear that Al Gore had won the nationwide popular vote. But the Electoral College outcome depended on Florida's 25 electoral votes. Bush's lead in Florida, after several machine recounts and the count of absentee ballots, was 930 votes out of six million cast in that state.

Armies of lawyers descended on Florida. The Gore campaign demanded *hand* recounts of the votes in the state's three most populous and Democratic counties—Miami-Dade, Broward (Fort Lauderdale), and Palm Beach. Bush's lawyers argued that the hand counts in these counties were late, unreliable, subjective, and open to partisan bias. Gore's lawyers argued that the Palm Beach "butterfly" ballot was confusing (the Gore/Lieberman punch hole was positioned third instead of second under Bush/Cheney; Pat Buchanan's punch hole was positioned second). They also argued that partially detached and indented "chads" (small perforated squares in the punch cards that should fall out when the voter punches the ballot) should be inspected to ascertain the "intent" of the voter.

A President Chosen by the Supreme Court

Gore formally protested the Florida vote, expecting that his protest would eventually be decided by the Florida Supreme Court, with its seven Democratic-appointed justices. And, indeed, by a 4-to-3 vote the Florida high court agreed. It ordered a hand recount of all "undervotes" in the state—ballots that failed to register a presidential selection on machines—to determine the "intent" of the voter.

FOCUS

Bush v. Gore in the U.S. Supreme Court

From the Majority Opinion

On December 8, 2000, the Supreme Court of Florida ordered that the Circuit Court of Leon County tabulate by hand 9,000 ballots in Miami-Dade County. . . . The court further held that relief would require manual recounts in all Florida counties where so-called "undervotes" had not been subject to manual tabulation. The court ordered all manual recounts to begin at once. . . .

The [Bush] petition presents the following questions: whether the Florida Supreme Court established new standards for resolving Presidential election contests, thereby violating *Art. II, Section 1, cl. 2, of the United States Constitution* and failing to comply with 3 U.S.C. Section 5, and whether the use of standardless manual recounts violates the Equal Protection and Due Process Clauses.

With respect to the equal protection question, we find a violation of the Equal Protection Clause. . . .

Much of the controversy seems to revolve around ballot cards designed to be perforated by a stylus but which, either through error or deliberate omission, have not been perforated with sufficient precision for a machine to count them.

In some cases a piece of the card—a chad—is hanging, say, by two corners. In other cases there is no separation at all, just an indentation. The Florida Supreme Court has ordered that the intent of the voter be discerned from such ballots. . . .

The recount mechanisms implemented in response to the decisions of the Florida Supreme Court do not satisfy the minimum requirement for nonarbitrary treatment of voters necessary to secure the funda-

mental right (of equal protection). Florida's basic command for the count of legally cast votes is to consider the "intent of the voter." . . . This is unobjectionable as an abstract proposition and a starting principle. The problem inheres in the absence of specific standards to ensure its equal application.

From Justices Rehnquist, Scalia, and Thomas Concurring with the Majority

Moreover, the court's interpretation of "legal vote," and hence its decision to order a contest-period recount, plainly departed from the legislative scheme. Florida statutory law cannot reasonably be thought to require the counting of improperly marked ballots. Each Florida precinct before election day provides instructions on how properly to cast a vote; each polling

However, Bush appealed to the Supreme Court of the United States, arguing that the Florida Supreme Court had overreached its authority under the U.S. Constitution when it substituted its own deadline for the deadline enacted by the state's legislature. (Article II, Section 1, declares that "Each State shall appoint [presidential electors] in such Manner as the *Legislature* thereof may direct. . . .") Bush's lawyers also argued that without specific standards to determine the "intent" of the voter, different vote-counters would use different standards (counting or not counting "dimpled," "pregnant," "indented," etc. chads). Without uniform rules, such a recount would violate the Equal Protection Clause of the Fourteenth Amendment.

place on election day contains a working model of the voting machine it uses; and each voting booth contains a sample ballot. In precincts using punch-card ballots, voters are instructed to punch out the ballot cleanly:

"AFTER VOTING, CHECK YOUR BALLOT CARD TO BE SURE YOUR VOTING SELECTIONS ARE CLEARLY AND CLEANLY PUNCHED AND THERE ARE NO CHIPS LEFT HANGING ON THE BACK OF THE CARD."

No reasonable person would call it "an error in the vote tabulation," or a "rejection of legal votes," when electronic or electromechanical equipment performs precisely in the manner designed, and fails to count those ballots that are not marked in the manner that these voting instructions explicitly and prominently specify.

From Dissenting Opinions, Justice Stevens

What must underlie petitioners' entire federal assault on the Florida election procedures is an unstated lack of confidence in the impartiality and capacity of the state judges who would make the critical decisions if the vote count were to proceed. Otherwise, their position is wholly without merit. The endorsement of that position by the majority of this Court can only lend credence to the most cynical appraisal of the work of judges throughout the land. It is confidence in the men and women who administer the judicial system that is the true backbone of the rule of law. Time will one day heal the wound to that confidence that will be inflicted by today's decision. One thing, however, is certain. Although we may never know with complete certainty the identity of the winner of this year's presidential election, the identity of the loser is perfectly clear. It is the nation's confidence in the judge as an impartial guardian of the rule of law.

From Dissenting Opinions, Justice Breyer

Halting the manual recount, and thus ensuring that the uncounted legal votes will not be counted under any standard, this Court crafts a remedy out of proportion to the asserted harm. And that remedy harms the very fairness interests the Court is attempting to protect. The manual recount would itself redress a problem of unequal treatment of ballots . . . I fear that in order to bring this agonizing long election process to a definitive conclusion, we have not adequately attended to that necessary "check upon our own exercise of power," "our own sense of self-restraint."

In *Bush v. Gore* the U.S. Supreme Court agreed (by a 7-to-2 vote) that the Florida court had created "constitutional problems" involving the Equal Protection Clause, and the Court ordered (by a 5-to-4 vote) that the hand count be ended altogether (see Focus: *Bush v. Gore* in the U.S. Supreme Court). The effect of the decision was to reinstate the Florida Secretary of State's certification of Bush as the winner of Florida's 25 electoral votes and consequently the winner of the Electoral College vote for president by the narrowest of margins—271-to-267.

For the first time in the nation's history, a presidential election was decided by the Supreme Court of the United States. Perhaps only the Supreme Court possesses sufficient legitimacy in the mind of the American public to bring about a resolution to the closest presidential electoral vote in history.

THE POWER OF CONGRESS

What are the powers of Congress in the American political system? Policy proposals are usually initiated *outside* Congress; it is the role of Congress to respond to proposals from the president, executive agencies, and interest groups. Congress does not merely ratify or "rubber-stamp" decisions; it plays an independent role in the policy-making process. But this role is essentially a deliberative one in which Congress accepts, modifies, or rejects the policies initiated by others. Congress functions as an *arbiter* rather than an *initiator* of public policy.

Congress as arbiter rather than initiator of policy

DOMESTIC AFFAIRS

Congress more influential in domestic policy than in foreign or military affairs

Congress is more influential in *domestic* than in foreign and military affairs. It is much freer to reject presidential proposals regarding business, labor, agriculture, education, welfare, urban affairs, civil rights, taxation, and appropriations. The president and executive departments must go to Congress for needed legislation and appropriations. Congressional committees can exercise power in domestic affairs by giving or withholding the appropriations and the legislation these executive agencies want.

FOREIGN AND MILITARY AFFAIRS

In the Constitution, the president and Congress share power over foreign and military affairs. The president is "Commander in Chief of the Armed Forces," but Congress "declares war." The president "sends and receives ambassadors" and "makes treaties," but the Senate must confirm appointments and "advise and consent" to treaties. Nevertheless, strong presidents have generally led the nation in both war and peace. (See the Case Study in Chapter 8, "Vietnam: A Political History," and the Case Study in Chapter 14, "American Military Power: 'Desert Storm.'")

WAR POWERS ACT

War Powers Act
Congress' effort to limit presidential war-making power

Until Vietnam, no congressional opposition to undeclared war was evident. But military failure and public opposition to the war in Vietnam led Congress to try to curtail the war power of the president. Congress passed the controversial War Powers Act in 1973 over a weakened President Nixon's veto. The act specifies that if the president sends U.S. troops into combat, this must be reported to Congress within forty-eight hours. American forces can remain in a combat situation for only sixty days unless Congress by specific legislation authorizes their continued engagement. The act also states that Congress can withdraw troops at any time by passing a resolution in both houses, and the president cannot veto a resolution. Obviously the War Powers Act raises very serious constitutional questions, but they may never be tested in court. The U.S. Constitution makes the president, not Congress, commander-in-chief of the armed forces, and commanders may order their troops to go anywhere at any time. The act did not prevent President Ford from sending troops to Cambodia during the *Mayaguez* incident; or President Carter from attempting a military rescue of the Iranian-held U.S. hostages; or President Reagan from sending U.S. troops to Lebanon and Grenada; or President Bush from sending military forces to Panama and ordering U.S. forces into "Operation Desert Storm" to liberate Kuwait; or President Clinton from ordering U.S. forces into Haiti, Bosnia, and Kosovo.

THE POWER OF THE COURTS

The Founders of the United States viewed the federal courts as the final bulwark against threats to individual liberty. Since *Marbury v. Madison* first asserted the Supreme Court's power of judicial review over congressional acts, the federal courts have struck down more than eighty congressional laws and uncounted state laws that they believed conflicted with the Constitution. *Judicial review and the right to interpret the meaning and decide the application of the Constitution and laws of the United States* are great sources of power for judges.[18]

KEY COURT DECISIONS

Some of the nation's most important policy decisions have been made by courts rather than by executive or legislative bodies. The federal courts took the lead in eliminating racial segregation in public life, ensuring the separation of church and state, defining relationships between citizens and law enforcers, and guaranteeing voters equal voice in government. Today the federal courts grapple with the most controversial issues facing the nation: abortion, affirmative action, the death penalty, religion in schools, the rights of criminal defendants, and so on. Courts are an integral component of America's governmental system, for sooner or later most important policy questions are brought before them.[19]

key policy decisions by federal courts
eliminating racial segregation

ensuring separation of church and state

guaranteeing voters equal voice

establishing abortion rights

defining affirmative action

determining rights of criminal defendants

DEMOCRACY AND THE SUPREME COURT

The undemocratic nature of judicial review has long been recognized in American politics. Nine Supreme Court justices—who are not elected to office, whose terms are for life, and who can be removed only for "high crimes and misdemeanors"—possess the power to void the acts of popularly elected presidents, Congresses, governors, and state legislators. Why should the

judicial review of federal laws

views of an appointed court about the meaning of the Constitution prevail over the views of *elected* officials? Presidents and members of Congress are sworn to uphold the Constitution, and it can reasonably be assumed they do not pass laws they believe to be *un*constitutional. Why should the Supreme Court have judicial review of the decisions of these bodies?

The answer appears to be that the Founders distrusted both popular majorities and elected officials who might be influenced by popular majorities. They believed government should be limited so it could not attack principle and property, whether to do so was the will of the majority or not. So the courts were deliberately *insulated* against popular majorities; to ensure their independence, judges were not to be elected, but appointed for life terms. Only in this way, the writers of the Constitution believed, would they be sufficiently protected from the masses to permit them to judge courageously and responsibly. Insulation is, in itself, another source of judicial power.

insulation of the courts
appointed, not elected

judges serve life terms

JUDICIAL RESTRAINT

The power of the courts, especially the U.S. Supreme Court, is limited only by the justices' own judicial philosophy. The doctrine of **judicial restraint** argues that because justices are not popularly elected, the Supreme Court should defer to the decisions of Congress and the president unless their actions are in clear conflict with the plain meaning of the Constitution. Justice Felix Frankfurter once wrote: "The only check upon our own exercise of

judicial restraint
judges should defer to the decision of elected representatives unless it is in clear conflict with the plain meaning of the Constitution

Custom, rather than the Constitution, dictates a nine-member Supreme Court of the United States.

power is our own sense of self-restraint. For the removal of unwise laws from the statute books, appeal lies not with the Courts but to the ballot and to the processes of democratic government."[20] One should not confuse the wisdom of a law with its constitutionality; the courts should decide only the constitutionality of laws, not the wisdom or fairness.

A related limitation on judicial power is the principle of ***stare decisis,*** which means the issue has already been decided in earlier cases. Reliance on precedent is a fundamental notion in law; it gives stability to the law. If every decision ignored past precedents and created new law, no one would know what the law is from day to day.

stare decisis
reliance on precedent to give stability to the law

JUDICIAL ACTIVISM

However, much of the history of the Supreme Court has been one of **judicial activism,** not restraint. The dominant philosophy of the Supreme Court under Chief Justice Earl Warren (1953–1969) was that judges should interpret the meaning of the Constitution to fit the needs of contemporary society. By viewing the Constitution as a broad and flexible document, the nation can avoid new constitutional amendments and still accomplish changes in society. Precedents can be overturned as society grows and changes.

judicial activism
judges may interpret the meaning of the Constitution to fit the needs of contemporary society

Judicial activism was reflected in the Supreme Court's famous *Brown v. Board of Education of Topeka* decision in 1954 that declared that racially segregated schools violated the equal protection clause of the Fourteenth Amendment. The Supreme Court also overturned precedent in requiring that the states apportion their legislatures so as to guarantee equal voter representation in *Baker v. Carr* in 1962. It struck down long-established practices of prayer and Bible reading in public schools in *Engle v. Vitale,* also in 1962. The Court under Earl Warren also greatly expanded the rights of criminal defendants.

The Supreme Court under President Richard Nixon's appointee, Chief Justice Warren Burger (1969–1986), was only slightly less activist. The Court's 1973 decision in *Roe v. Wade,* declaring that abortion was a constitutional right of women, was perhaps the most sweeping reinterpretation of individual liberty in the Court's history.

Presidents Ronald Reagan and George Bush sought to strengthen the doctrine of judicial restraint in their appointments to the Supreme Court. Chief Justice William Rehnquist (first appointed to the Court by President Nixon in 1971 and later elevated to chief justice by President Reagan in 1986) has been less activist than his predecessors. However, none of the major decisions of the Warren or Burger Courts has been reversed.

Liberals worried that the appointment of conservative Clarence Thomas by President Bush in 1991 would result in an emergence of a conservative majority on the Supreme Court. But despite the fears of liberals, no solid conservative majority emerged on the Court. Rather, moderates (including Sandra Day O'Connor, David Souter, and Anthony Kennedy) appeared to prevail in key cases over conservatives (Rehnquist, Scalia, and Thomas). For example, in the important abortion case of *Planned Parenthood v. Casey,*

TABLE 7-2

MEMBERS OF THE U.S. SUPREME COURT

	Law school from which graduated	President who appointed
Rehnquist, William Hubbs*	Stanford	Nixon (1971)
		Reagan (1986)
Stevens, John Paul	Chicago	Ford (1975)
O'Connor, Sandra Day	Stanford	Regan (1981)
Scalia, Antonin	Harvard	Reagan (1986)
Kennedy, Anthony McLeod	Harvard	Reagan (1988)
Souter, David H.	Harvard	Bush (1990)
Thomas, Clarence	Yale	Bush (1991)
Ginsburg, Ruth Bader	Columbia	Clinton (1993)
Breyer, Stephen G.	Harvard	Clinton (1994)

*Rehnquist was nominated to the U.S. Supreme Court in 1971 by Richard Nixon; he was nominated as chief justice by Ronald Reagan in 1986.

Sandra Day O'Connor led the Court in upholding *Roe v. Wade* abortion rights while at the same time allowing state restrictions that do not "unduly burden" women in the exercise of their rights[21] (see Chapter 10). President Clinton's appointments of Ruth Bader Ginsburg (the second woman to serve on the Court) and Stephen Breyer further strengthen the moderate to liberal voice of the current Supreme Court (see Table 7-2).

POLITICAL BEHAVIOR IN THE UNITED STATES

Popular participation in the political system is the very definition of democracy. Individuals in a democracy may run for public office; participate in marches and demonstrations; make financial contributions to political candidates and causes; attend political meetings, speeches, and rallies; write letters to public officials and newspapers; belong to organizations that support or oppose particular candidates and take stands on public issues; wear political buttons and place bumper stickers on their cars; attempt to influence friends while discussing candidates and issues; vote in elections; or merely follow an issue or campaign in the mass media. This list of activi-

forms of political participation

ties constitutes a ranking of the **forms of political participation**, in inverse order of their frequency. The activities at the beginning of the list require greater expenditure of time and energy and greater personal commitment; consequently, far fewer people engage in those activities (see Figure 7-4). Fully one-third of the population are politically apathetic: They do not vote, and they are largely unaware of and indifferent to the political life of the nation.

FIGURE 7-4

POLITICAL PARTICIPATION

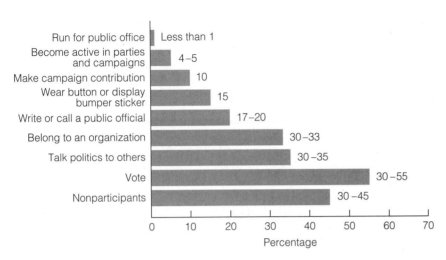

VOTER TURNOUT

Voter turnout is greatest in presidential elections, but even in those contests turnout is only about 50 to 55 percent of eligible people. "Off-year" congressional elections—congressional elections held in years in which there is no presidential election—attract only 35 or 40 percent of eligible people to the polls. Yet in these "off-year" contests, the nation chooses all of its U.S. representatives, one-third of its U.S. senators, and about one-half of its governors. Local government elections—for mayor, council members, school board, and so forth—frequently attract only one-quarter to one-third of eligible voters.

NONVOTING

Who votes and who doesn't?[22] Some groups of people are more likely to vote than others. Education appears to be the most important determinant of voter turnout. It may be that schooling promotes an interest in politics, instills the ethic of citizen participation, or gives people a better awareness of public affairs and an understanding of the role of elections in a democracy. Education is associated with a sense of confidence and political "efficacy"—the feeling that one can indeed have a personal impact on public affairs.

Age is another factor affecting voter participation. Perhaps because young people have more distractions, more demands on their time in schooling, work, or new family responsibilities, nonvoting is greatest among those age eighteen to twenty-one. In contrast, older Americans are politically influential in part because candidates know they turn out at the polls.

High-income people are more likely to vote than are low-income people. Most of this difference is a product of the fact that high-income people are more likely well educated and older. But poor people may also feel alienated from the political system. The poor may lack a sense of political efficacy—they may feel they have little control over their own lives, let alone over public affairs. Or the poor may simply be so absorbed in the problems of life that they have little time or energy to spend on registering and voting.

Historically, race was a major determinant of nonvoting. Black voter turnout, especially in the South, was markedly lower than white voter turnout. But today, blacks and whites at the *same* educational and income levels register and vote with the same frequency. The greatest racial disparity in voter turnout is between Hispanics and others. Low voter participation by Hispanics may be a product of language differences, late cultural assimilation, or noncitizenship status.

THE VOTER DECIDES

Perhaps no other area of political science has been investigated so thoroughly—by political candidates, campaign strategists, and political scientists—as the **reasons behind the voters' choices** at the polls.[23] Voters cast ballots for and against candidates for a variety of reasons, including their party affiliation, their membership in social and economic groups, their positive and negative evaluations of the images of the candidates, their view of the goodness or badness of the times (especially the economy), and sometimes even the positions of the candidates on important issues.

Although party ties have weakened somewhat over time, party affiliation remains an important influence over voter choice. People who identify themselves as Democrats or Republicans usually vote for their party's candidate (see "Politics" in Table 7-3). Membership in various social and economic groups also affects voting; for example, black voters regularly give much greater support to Democratic candidates (see "Race" in Table 7-3).

Candidates spend a great deal of time and money during a campaign trying to project a favorable image of themselves (or a negative image of their opponent) through television and the press. (See Focus, "Media Power: The Presidential Debates.") Challengers attack the record of **incumbents** seeking reelection, holding them responsible for anything bad that happened during their term, especially any weaknesses that developed in the economy. Incumbents are more likely to be reelected when the nation enjoys "peace and prosperity." Relatively few voters cast their ballot exclusively on a particular policy position of a candidate, although some "hot button" issues—abortion, for example—influence the choice of some voters.

reasons behind voters' choices

party affiliation

group membership

candidate image

nature of the times, especially the economy

issues

incumbent
a candidate currently in office seeking reelection

TABLE 7-3

Voting by Groups in Recent Presidential Elections

2000

	Democrat Gore	Republican Bush	Green Nader
National	**48%**	**48%**	**3%**
Gender			
Male	42	53	3
Female	54	43	2
Race			
White	42	54	3
Black	90	8	1
Hispanic	62	35	2
Age			
Under 30 years	48	46	5
30–49	48	49	2
50 years & older	51	47	2
Religion			
Protestants	42	56	2
Catholics	50	47	2
Jewish	79	19	1
Politics			
Republicans	8	91	2
Democrats	86	11	1
Independents	45	47	6

		1996			1992		
		Democrat Clinton	Republican Dole	Independent Perot	Democrat Clinton	Republican Bush	Independent Perot
National		**49%**	**41%**	**8%**	**43%**	**38%**	**19%**
Gender	Male	43	44	10	41	38	21
	Female	54	38	7	46	37	17
Race	White	43	46	9	39	41	20
	Nonwhite	84	12	4	82	11	7
Age	Under 30 years	53	34	10	44	34	22
	30–49	48	41	9	42	38	20
	50 years & older	48	41	9	45	40	15
Religion	Protestants	41	50	8	33	46	12
	Catholics	53	32	9	44	36	20
Politics	Republicans	13	80	6	10	73	17
	Democrats	84	10	5	77	10	13
	Independents	43	35	17	38	32	30

SOURCE: Based on data from the *Gallup Poll* surveys, and voter exit polls, 2000.

FOCUS

Media Power: The Presidential Debates

Presidential debates attract more viewers than any other campaign activity. Debates allow people to directly compare the responses of each candidate. Even if issues are not really discussed in depth, people see how presidential candidates react as human beings under pressure.

Kennedy-Nixon

Televised presidential debates began in 1960 when John F. Kennedy and Richard M. Nixon confronted each other on a bare stage before an America watching on black-and-white television sets. Nixon was the vice president in the popular presidential administration of Dwight Eisenhower; he was also an accomplished college debate team member. He prepared for the debates as if they were college debates, memorizing facts and arguments. But he failed to realize that image triumphs over substance on television. Nixon was shifty-eyed and clearly in need of a shave or more makeup to hide his pronounced "five o'clock shadow." By contrast, Kennedy was handsome, cool, confident. Television viewers preferred the glamorous young Kennedy. The polls shifted in Kennedy's direction after the debate, and he won in a very close general election. Nixon blamed his makeup man.

Carter-Ford

President Lyndon Johnson avoided debating in 1964, and Nixon, having learned his lesson, declined to debate in 1968 and 1972. Thus, televised presidential debates did not resume until 1976, when incumbent President Gerald Ford, perceiving that he was behind in the polls, agreed to debate challenger Jimmy Carter. Ford made a series of verbal slips—saying, for example, that the nations of eastern Europe were free from Soviet domination. Carter was widely perceived as having "won" the debates, and he went on to victory in the general election.

Reagan-Carter and Reagan-Mondale

It was Ronald Reagan who demonstrated the true power of television. Reagan had lived his life in front of a camera. Carter talked rapidly and seriously about programs, figures, and budgets. But Reagan was master of the stage; he was relaxed, confident, joking. He appeared to treat the president of the United States as an overly aggressive, impulsive younger man, regrettably given to exaggeration. ("There you go again.") When the debate was all over, it was clear to most viewers that Carter had been bested by a true professional in media skills.

However, in the first of two televised debates with Walter Mondale in 1984, Reagan's skills of a lifetime seemed to desert him. He stumbled over statistics and groped for words. His poor performance raised the only issue that might conceivably defeat him—his age. The president had looked and sounded *old*.

In preparation for the second debate, Reagan decided, without telling his aides, to lay the perfect trap for his questioners. When asked about his age and capacity to lead the nation, he responded with a serious deadpan expression to a hushed audience and waiting America: "I want you to know that I will not make age an issue in this campaign. I am not going to exploit for political purposes [pause] my opponent's youth and inexperience." The studio audience broke into uncontrolled laughter. Even Mondale had to laugh. With a classic one-liner, the president buried the age issue and won not only the debate but the election.

Bush-Dukakis

In 1988, Michael Dukakis ensured his defeat with a cold, detached performance in the presidential debates, beginning with the very first question. When CNN anchor Bernard Shaw asked: "Governor, if Kitty Dukakis were raped and

SOURCE: Thomas R. Dye, *Politics in America*, 2nd ed. (New York: Prentice-Hall, 1997), pp. 276—277.

murdered, would you favor an irrevocable death penalty for the killer?" The question demanded an emotional reply. Instead, Dukakis responded with an impersonal recitation of his stock positions on crime, drugs, and law enforcement. Bush seized the opportunity to establish an intimate, warm, and personal relationship with the viewers: "I do believe some crimes are so heinous, so brutal, so outrageous . . . I do believe in the death penalty." Voters responded to Bush, electing him.

Clinton-Bush-Perot

The three-way presidential debates of 1992 drew the largest television audiences in the history of presidential debates. In the first debate, Ross Perot's Texas twang and down-home folksy style stole the show. But it was Bill Clinton's smooth performance in the second debate, with its talk-show format, that seemed to wrap up the election. Ahead in the polls, Clinton appeared at ease walking about the stage and responding to audience questions with sympathy and sincerity. By contrast, George Bush appeared stiff and formal, and somewhat ill at ease with the "unpresidential" format.

Clinton-Dole

A desperate Bob Dole, running twenty points behind, faced a

Al Gore and George W. Bush debating in 2000.

newly "presidential" Bill Clinton in their two 1996 debates. (Perot's poor standing in the polls led to his exclusion.) Dole tried to counter his image as a grumpy old man in the first encounter; his humor actually won more laughs from the audience than the president's more stately comments. Dole injected more barbs in the second debate, complaining of "ethical problems in the White House" and repeating the mantra "I keep my word," suggesting that Clinton did not. But Clinton remained cool and comfortable, ignoring the challenger and focusing on the nation's economic health. Viewers, most of whom were already in Clinton's court, judged him the winner of both debates.

Bush-Gore

Separate formats were agreed upon for three debates—the traditional podium, a conference table, and a town hall setting. Gore was assertive, almost to the point of rudeness, but both candidates focused on policy differences rather than personal attacks. Viewers gave Gore the edge in these debates, but they found Bush more likable. Bush appeared to benefit more in the post-debate polls. An estimated 47 million people watched the first debate, viewership fell to 36 million for the second and third debates. Most observers rated the single vice-presidential debate between Dick Cheney and Joe Lieberman as friendlier and more informative than the Bush-Gore encounters.

DEMOCRATS AND REPUBLICANS—
WHAT'S THE DIFFERENCE?

functions of political parties

organize majorities

identify candidate's coalition of interests

structure choices

define issues

criticize officeholders

Democracy is ultimately based on majority rule, and one function of political parties is to *put majorities together*. Political parties organize voters for effective political expression at the polls. Voters, in turn, use party labels to help them identify the general political viewpoints of the candidates.[24]

Because American parties are necessarily rather loose coalitions of interests, they do not command the total loyalty of every officeholder elected under a party's banner. The fact that candidates run under a Republican or Democratic label does not clearly indicate where they will stand on every public issue. Even so, these coalitions do have considerable cohesion and historical continuity. The party label *discloses the coalition of interests and the policy views* with which candidates have generally associated themselves. At the least, the party label tells more about a candidate's politics than would a strange name, with no party affiliation, on the ballot.

Especially in two-party systems, such as we have in the United States, parties also *structure the choice of candidates* for public office and thus relieve voters of the task of choosing among dozens of contending candidates on election day. The preliminary selecting and narrowing of candidates, by conventions and primary elections, are indispensable in a large society.

Political parties help *define the major problems and issues* confronting society. In attempting to win a majority of the voters, parties inform the public about the issues facing the nation. The comparisons parties make during political campaigns have an important educational value: Voters come to "know" the opposing candidates for public office, and the problems of national interest are spotlighted.

Finally, the party *out* of office performs an important function for democratic government by *criticizing officeholders*. Moreover, the very existence of a recognized party outside the government helps make criticism of government legitimate and effective.

Party Differences

evidence of party differences

differing coalitions of voter groups

differing views of party leaders

differing voting records in Congress

It is sometimes argued that there are few significant differences between the two main American parties. It is not uncommon in European nations to find authoritarian parties competing with democratic parties, capitalist parties with socialist parties, Catholic parties with secular parties, and so on. However, within the context of American political experience, the Democratic and Republican Parties can be clearly differentiated. There are at least three ways in which to discern the differences: (1) by examining differences in the *coalitions of voters* supporting each party, (2) by examining differences in the *policy views of the leaders* in each party, and (3) by examining differences in the *voting records of the representatives and senators* of each party.

SOCIAL GROUP DIFFERENCES IN PARTY SUPPORT

In ascertaining party differences according to support from different groups of voters, we must note first that major groups are seldom *wholly* within one party or the other. For example, in presidential elections all major social groups divide their votes between the parties. Yet differences between the parties are revealed *in the proportions of votes given by each major group to each party* (see "Race" and "Religion" in Table 7-3). Thus, the Democratic Party receives a disproportionate amount of support from Catholics, Jews, African Americans, lower-income groups, blue-collar workers, union members, and big-city residents. The Republican Party receives disproportionate support from Protestants, whites, higher-income groups, professionals and managers, white-collar workers, nonunion members, and rural and small-town residents.

DIFFERENCES IN VIEWS OF PARTY LEADERS

The second way of discerning Democratic and Republican Party differences involves an examination of the political opinions of the leaders of each party. Political scientists have studied party differences by presenting a series of policy questions to the delegates to the Democratic and Republican national conventions. They have found substantial differences of opinion between Democratic and Republican leaders on important public issues. Political scientist Herbert McClosky concludes:

> *Democratic leaders typically display the stronger urge to elevate the low-born, the uneducated, the deprived minorities, and the poor in general; they are also more disposed to employ the nation's collective power to advance humanitarian and social welfare goals (e.g., Social Security, immigration, racial integration, a higher minimum wage, and public education). They are more critical of wealth and big business and more eager to bring them under regulation. Theirs is the greater faith in the wisdom of using legislation for redistributing the national product and for furnishing social services on a wide scale. Of the two groups of leaders, the Democrats are more "progressively" oriented toward social reform and experimentation. The Republican leaders, while not uniformly differentiated from their opponents, subscribe in greater measure to the symbols and practices of individualism,* laissez-faire, *and national independence. They prefer to overcome humanity's misfortunes by relying upon personal effort, private incentives, frugality, hard work, responsibility, self-denial (for both men and government), and the strengthening rather than the diminution of the economic and status distinctions that are the "natural" rewards of the differences in human character and fortunes.*[25]

PARTY DIFFERENCES IN CONGRESSIONAL VOTING

The third indication of party differences in the United States is the roll-call voting behavior of the representatives and senators of each party on controversial issues. About half of all roll-call votes in Congress are **party votes**—votes in which a majority of Democrats oppose a majority of Republicans. Party votes occur most frequently on well-publicized, high-conflict issues (see Table 7-4). Party voting also occurs on presidential recommendations, with the president's party in Congress supporting the president's position and the opposition party opposing it. Bipartisan votes, those roll calls in which party majorities are found on the same side, usually occur on less-publicized, low-conflict issues. On many issues, voting follows party lines during

TABLE 7-4

PARTY CONFLICT ON SELECTED ROLL-CALL VOTES

	House votes			
	Republicans		Democrats	
	yes	no	yes	no
Reagan income tax cuts (1981)	189	1	48	196
Clinton tax increase (1993)	0	175	218	38
Brady law, gun control (1993)	56	116	182	70
Balanced Budget Constitutional Amendment* (1995)	228	2	72	129
Ban late-term abortions† (1996)	218	15	70	121
Welfare reform (1996)	226	4	30	165
Impeach President Clinton (1998)	223	5	5	200

	Senate votes			
	Republicans		Democrats	
	yes	no	yes	no
Reagan income tax cuts (1981)	51	0	20	26
Clinton tax increase (1993)	0	44	50	6
Brady law, gun control (1993)	16	28	47	8
Balanced Budget Constitutional Amendment* (1995)	52	1	14	33
Ban late-term abortions† (1996)	45	6	12	35
Welfare reform (1996)	51	1	23	33
Remove President Clinton from office‡ (1999)	45	10	0	45

*Required two-thirds vote for passage. Dole vote shown as "yes" although officially cast as "no" to preserve option of calling for another vote.
†Vote to override President Clinton's veto; fails to win necessary two-thirds vote of both houses.
‡Required two-thirds vote for removal

SOURCE: *Congressional Quarterly Weekly Report,* "Key Votes," in various issues.

roll calls on preliminary amendments but swings to a bipartisan vote on the final legislation. This occurs when the parties disagree on certain aspects of a bill but compromise on its final passage.

ON THE WEB

EXPLORING GOVERNMENT AND POLITICS

The Internet overflows with information about government, politics, and public affairs. The real problem with finding specific information is that of sorting through the overabundance of political news and commentary. Internet users should be cognizant of the *sources* of political information and be prepared to adjust for political bias.

White House. A frequent starting place for browsing through government and politics is with the White House itself (www.whitehouse.gov). The news, speeches, reports, etc., carried on this site reflect the political views of the president. But the site also links with all other executive departments and agencies.

Congress. Congress, both the House of Representatives and the Senate, also maintains Web sites (www.house.gov and www.senate.gov). These sites not only provide current information on congressional activity but also link directly to the Web pages of individual representatives and senators. It is interesting to check out the site of one's own state representative; many of these Web pages are quite elaborate, featuring the legislator's photo, biography, policy positions, key votes, speeches, etc.

Supreme Court. Supreme Court decisions, including those issued most recently, can be viewed at the Web site maintained by Cornell University Law School (www.supct.law.cornell.edu/supct). This site describes pending cases, all Supreme Court decisions since 1990, and selected historic decisions of the Court.

Democratic and Republican Parties. The Democratic and Republican national party organizations welcome browsers to their Web sites (www.democrats.org and www.rnc.org). These sites provide histories of their respective parties, party positions on issues, and, not surprisingly, invitations to contribute money.

News Organizations. All major news organizations—ABC News, CBS News, NBC News, CNN—give prominent space to political news, usually under their

"Washington News" title. Independent organizations also maintain political Web sites. Politics.com is a very popular site for obtaining political news (www.politics.com).

Candidate Sites. During election campaigns, virtually all candidates for state and national office now set up Web sites, touting their own abilities, polishing their own résumés, setting forth their policy positions, and requesting campaign contributions. These sites can usually be accessed by inserting their names into search engines.

American Political Science Association. The American Political Science Association maintains a Web site oriented toward both faculty and students (www.apsa.net) that describes training and careers in government, politics, and public affairs.

ABOUT THIS CHAPTER

The power of government is truly awesome. Government power influences every facet of our lives "from the cradle to the grave." We eat government-inspected foods, which have been transported on government-regulated railroads and highways and grown on government-subsidized farms. We live in government-inspected homes, paid for by government-subsidized mortgages from government-regulated banks. We attend government-subsidized schools, or work in government-inspected shops, or manage government-regulated businesses. The awesome powers of government have worried people for centuries. How can governmental power be limited? How can we enjoy the benefits and protections of government yet not become slaves to it? How can government leaders be restrained? How can we guarantee that our personal liberties will not be threatened by governments?

These questions are the province of political science, and in this chapter, we have examined the answers that political science provides. Now that you have read Chapter 7, you should be able to

■ discuss the meaning of *democracy*—its underlying values and rules of decision making

- describe the separation of powers in American government and the system of checks and balances, and discuss the reasons the Founders designed these amendments
- discuss the meaning of *federalism*, and describe how and why power has flowed though Washington over the years
- describe the growth of presidential power as well as the limits on such power
- contrast the power of Congress in foreign and domestic affairs, and outline the arguments for and against term limits
- define the power of judicial review and discuss judicial activism and judicial restraint
- define the principal forms of political participation in American government
- identify differences between the Democratic and Republican Parties
- discuss the impact of television on presidential elections

DISCUSSION QUESTIONS

1. Define *political science* and describe its areas of concern.
2. Describe John Locke's views on constitutionalism and constitutional government, natural law, and the social contract. Discuss the influence of Locke's ideas on the authors of the U.S. Constitution.
3. Define *democracy*.
4. What are the foundations of national power, and how does the Constitution define and limit them?

Contrast *expressed* (delegated) powers with *implied* powers and identify the clause on which implied powers are based.
5. Define *federalism* and discuss the changes that have taken place in the American federal structure. Include in your discussion a definition of *grants-in-aid*.
6. Discuss the rationale the Founders used for structuring the government around a separation of powers. Identify the separate power structures the Constitution created. Describe the principal checks and balances each structure exercises over the others.
7. Discuss the sources of presidential power and the factors contributing to the growth of that power in the twentieth century. Briefly describe how Richard Nixon overstepped the boundaries or limitations of presidential power.
8. Define *judicial review* and explain why the nation's Founders were in favor of this principle. Describe how and why the courts are "insulated." Contrast the arguments for "judicial restraint" and "judicial activism."
9. Discuss participation and nonparticipation in democracy. Who participates, and how is it possible to participate? What are the principal forms of participation? What groups of people are more likely to vote?
10. Describe the functions of political parties. How is it possible to identify real party differences in America?
11. What has been the impact of television on politics, especially presidential elections?

Chapter 8

Power and History

HISTORY AND SOCIAL SCIENCE

Can history inform the social sciences? The purpose of this chapter is not to teach American history, but rather to examine the work of historians to see what contribution they can make to our understanding of power and the social sciences.

History refers to all *past human actions and events.* The study of history is the *recording, narrating, and interpreting of these events.* History includes the discovery of facts about past events, as well as the interpretation of the events. Many historians contend that their primary responsibility is the reporting of facts about the past: the accurate presentation of what actually happened, unbiased by interpretive theories or philosophies.

But however carefully historians try to avoid bias, they cannot report *all* the facts of human history. Facts do not select and arrange themselves. The historians must select and organize facts that are worthy of interest, and this process involves personal judgment of what is important about the past. The historian's judgment about the past is affected by present conditions. So the past is continually reinterpreted by each generation of historians. History is "an unending dialogue" between the present and the past; it is "what one age finds worthy of note in another."

In selecting and organizing their facts, historians must consider the causes of wars and revolutions, the reasons for the rise and fall of civilizations, the consequences of great events and ideas. They cannot marshal their facts

history
the recording, narrating, and interpreting of all past human actions and events

without some notion of *interrelations* among human events. Because they must consider what forces have operated to shape the past, they become involved in economics, sociology, psychology, anthropology, and political science. Historian Henry Steele Commager has observed that "no self-respecting modern historian is content merely with recording what happened; he wants to explain why it happened."[1] Thus, history and social science are intimately related.

HISTORY AND THE AMERICAN EXPERIENCE

approaches to American history

the "great man" approach

the democratic institutions approach

critical approaches

There is a great temptation to romanticize national history. Many national histories are self-congratulating, patriotic exercises. Many historical biographies paint their subjects as larger-than-life figures, free of the faults of common people, who shape the course of events themselves rather than merely respond to the world in which they live. National leaders of the past—Washington, Jefferson, Jackson, Lincoln, Franklin D. Roosevelt—are portrayed as noble people superior in character and wisdom to today's politicians. Even with the myth of the cherry tree discarded, generations of historians have looked with awe on the gallery of national heroes.

Some national histories do not rely on "great man" explanations, but instead emphasize the origin and growth of democratic institutions. Democracy is traced from its ancient Greek beginnings, through English constitutional development, to the colonies and the American constitutional system. Frequently, these national histories reinforce reverence for existing political and governmental institutions.

But historians have also been critical of American institutions. At the beginning of the twentieth century, reform politicians and muckraking journalists brought a new skepticism to American life. The Progressive era was critical of the malfunctioning of many governmental institutions that had become sacred over time, and even of the Olympian position of the nation's Founders. In 1913, Charles A. Beard created an uproar by suggesting that economic motives played a part in leading the Founders to write the Constitution (see Controversies in Social Science, "Charles Beard and the Economic Interests of the Founders").

Nevertheless, for the most part the quest for the American past has been carried on in a spirit of sentiment and nostalgia, rather than of critical analysis. Historical novels, fictionalized biographies, pictorial collections, and books on American regions all appeal to our fondness for looking back to what we believe was a better era. Americans have a peculiar longing to recapture the past, to try to recover what seems to have been lost.

POWER AND CHANGE OVER TIME

Our own bias about the importance of power in society leads us to focus attention on *changing sources of power over time* in American history and on the characteristics of the people and groups who have acquired power. We contend that the Constitution, and the national government it established, reflected the beliefs, values, and interests of the people of power—the elite—of the new republic. If we are to have a true understanding of the Constitution, we must investigate the political interests of the Founders and the historical circumstances surrounding the Philadelphia convention in 1787.

CHANGES IN POWER OVER TIME

Power structures change over time. As an expanding American economy created new sources of wealth, power in the United States shifted to those groups and individuals who acquired the new economic resources. First, Western expansion and settlement; then industrialization, immigration, urbanization; and now technological and information innovation created new sources of wealth, new bases of power, and new powerholders.

But power in the United States has changed hands, without any serious break in the ideas and values underlying the American political and economic system. The nation has never experienced a true revolution, in which national leadership is forcefully replaced by groups or individuals who do not share the values of the system itself. Instead, **changes have been slow and incremental.** New national leaders have generally accepted the national consensus about private enterprise, limited government, and individualism.

Historian Richard Hofstadter argues effectively that many accounts of the American past overemphasize the political differences in every era:

> *The fierceness of the political struggles has often been misleading; for the range of vision embraced by the primary contestants in the major parties has always been bounded by the horizons of property and enterprise. However much at odds on specific issues, the major political traditions have shared a belief in the rights of property, the philosophy of economic individualism, the value of competition; they have accepted the economic virtues of capitalist culture as necessary qualities of man. Even when some property right has been challenged—as it was by followers of Jefferson and Jackson—in the name of the rights of man or the rights of the community, the challenge, when translated into practical policy, has actually been urged on behalf of some other kind of property.*[2]

THE RISE OF WESTERN ELITES

According to historian Frederick Jackson Turner, "The rise of the New West was the most significant fact in American history."[3] Certainly the American West had a profound impact on the political system of the new nation. People went west because of the vast wealth of fertile lands that awaited them there; nowhere else in the world could one acquire wealth so quickly. Because landed families of the eastern seaboard seldom had reason to migrate westward, the western settlers were mainly middle- or lower-class immigrants. With hard work and good fortune, a penniless migrant could become a rich plantation owner or cattle rancher in a single generation. Thus, the West meant rapid upward social mobility.

incremental change
slow and continuous rather than rapid or revolutionary

American beliefs shared over time
individualism

private property

enterprise

competition

influence of the West on American history
new wealth and opportunity

upward social mobility

more open elite system

CONTROVERSIES IN SOCIAL SCIENCE
Charles Beard and the Economic Interests of the Founders

Charles Beard, historian and political scientist, provided the most controversial historical interpretation of the origin of American national government in his landmark book, *An Economic Interpretation of the Constitution.*[a] Beard argued that to understand the Constitution we must understand the economic interests of the national elite, which included the writers of the document:

> *Did the men who formulated the fundamental law of the land possess the kinds of property which were immediately and directly increased in value or made more secure by the results of their labors in Philadelphia? Did they have money at interest [loans outstanding]? Did they own public securities [government bonds]? Did they hold Western lands for appreciation? Were they interested in shipping and manufactures?*[b]

Beard was *not* charging that the Founders wrote the Constitution exclusively for their own benefit. But he argued that they personally benefited immediately from its adoption and that they did not act only "under the guidance of abstract principles of political science." Beard closely studied old unpublished financial records of the U.S. Treasury Department and the personal letters and financial accounts

of the fifty-five delegates to the Philadelphia convention. The table summarizes his findings of the financial interests of the nation's Founders.

Beard then turned to an examination of the *Constitution* itself, in the original form in which it emerged from the Convention, to observe the *relationship between economic interests and political power.*

The first, and perhaps the most important, enumerated power is the power to "lay and collect taxes, duties, imposts, and excises." The *taxing power* was of great benefit to the holders of government bonds, particularly when it was combined with the provision in Article VI that "all debts contracted and engagements entered into, before the adoption of this Constitution, shall be as valid against the United States under this Constitution, as under the Confederation." This meant that the national government would be obliged to pay off all those investors who held bonds of the United States, and the taxing power would give the national government the ability to do so on its own.

Following the power to tax and spend, to borrow money, and to regulate commerce in Article I, there is a series of *specific powers designed to enable Congress to protect money and property.* Congress is given the power to make bankruptcy

laws, to coin money and regulate its value, to fix standards of weights and measures, to punish counterfeiting, to establish post offices and post roads, to pass copyright and patent laws to protect authors and inventors, and to punish piracies and felonies committed on the high seas. Each of these powers is a specific asset to bankers, investors, merchants, authors, inventors, and shippers.

The Constitution provided an explicit advantage to slaveholders in Article IV, Section 2 (later altered by the Thirteenth Amendment, which abolished slavery):

> *No person held to Service or Labour in one State, under the Laws thereof, escaping into another, shall, in Consequence of any Law or Regulation therein, be discharged from such Service or Labour, but shall be delivered up on Claim of the Party to whom such Service or Labour may be due.*

Many historians disagree with Beard's emphasis on the economic motives of the Founders. For example:

> *The Constitution was adopted in a society which was fundamentally democratic, not undemocratic; and it was adopted by people who were primarily middle-class property owners, especially farmers who owned realty,*

[a]Charles Beard, *An Economic Interpretation of the Constitution* (New York: Macmillan, 1913).
[b]Ibid., p. 73.

not just by the owners of personalty. . . . The Constitution was not just an economic document, although economic factors were undoubtedly important. Since most of the people were middle-class and had private property, practically everybody was interested in the protection of property.[c]

Moreover, in the struggle over ratification of the new Constitution, influential anti-Federalists deplored its undemocratic features, and their criticism about the omission of a Bill of Rights led directly to the inclusion of the first ten amendments.

BEARD'S CLASSIFICATION OF THE FOUNDERS OF THE AMERICAN NATION BY ECONOMIC INTERESTS

Public Security interests (owners of U.S. bonds)		Real estate and land speculation	Lending and banking investments	Mercantile, manufacturing and shipping interests	Plantations and slaveholdings
Major	Minor				
Baldwin	Bassett	Blount	Bassett	Broom	Butler
Blair	Blount	Dayton	Broom	Clymer	Davie
Clymer	Brearley	Few	Butler	Ellsworth	Jenifer
Dayton	Broom	FitzSimons	Carroll	FitzSimons	A. Martin
Ellsworth	Butler	Franklin	Clymer	Gerry	L. Martin
FitzSimons	Carroll	Gerry	Davie	King	Mason
Gerry	Few	Gilman	Dickinson	Langdon	Mercer
Gilman	Hamilton	Gorham	Ellsworth	McHenry	C. C. Pinckney
Gorham	L. Martin	Hamilton	Few	Mifflin	C. Pinckney
Jenifer	Mason	Mason	FitzSimons	G. Morris	Randolph
Johnson	Mercer	R. Morris	Franklin	R. Morris	Read
King	Mifflin	Washington	Gilman		Rutledge
Langdon	Read	Williamson	Ingersoll		Spaight
Lansing	Spaight	Wilson	Johnson		Washington
Livingston	Wilson		King		Wythe
McClurg	Wythe		Langdon		
R. Morris			McHenry		
C. C. Pinckney			Manson		
C. Pinckney			C. C. Pinckney		
Randolph			C. Pinckney		
Sherman			Randolph		
Strong			Read		
Washington			Washington		
Williamson			Williamson		

[c]Robert E. Brown, *Charles Beard and the Constitution* (Princeton, N.J.: Princeton University Press, 1956); 200.

JACKSONIAN DEMOCRACY

A new elite arose in the West and had to be assimilated into America's governing circles. This assimilation had a profound effect on the character of America's elite. No one exemplifies the new entrants better than Andrew Jackson. Jackson's victory in the presidential election of 1828 was not a victory of the common man over the propertied classes, but a victory of the new western elite over established leadership in the East. It forced the established elite to recognize the growing importance of the West and to open their ranks to the new rich who were settling west of the Alleghenies.

Jackson Democracy
"natural aristocracy" of self-made individuals

universal white male suffrage

no property restrictions on voting or office-holding

presidential nominations by party conventions

presidential electors chosen by popular vote

Because Jackson was a favorite of the people, it was easy for him to believe in the wisdom of the masses. But **Jacksonian Democracy** was by no means a philosophy of leveling egalitarianism. The ideal of the frontier society was the self-made individual, and wealth and power won by *competitive skill* were much admired. Wealth and power obtained through special privilege offended the frontierpeople. They believed in a *natural aristocracy,* rather than an aristocracy by birth, education, or special privilege. It was *not* absolute equality that Jacksonians demanded but a *more open elite system*—a greater opportunity for the rising middle class to acquire wealth and influence through competition.

SEEKING MASS SUPPORT

In their struggle to open America's elite system, the Jacksonians appealed to mass sentiment. Jackson's humble beginnings, his image as a self-made man, his military adventures, his frontier experience, and his rough, brawling style endeared him to the masses. As beneficiaries of popular support, the new western elite developed a strong faith in the wisdom and justice of popular decisions. The new western states that entered the Union granted universal white male suffrage, and gradually the older states fell into step. The rising elite, themselves often less than a generation away from the masses, saw in a widened electorate a chance for personal advancement they could never have achieved under the old regime. Therefore, the Jacksonians became noisy and effective advocates of the principle that all free men should have the right to *vote* and that no restrictions should be placed on *office-holding.* They also launched a successful attack on the congressional caucus system of nominating presidential candidates, substituting instead nomination by national party conventions. In 1832, when the Democrats held their first national convention, Andrew Jackson was renominated by acclamation.

Jacksonian Democracy also brought changes in the method of selecting presidential electors. The Constitution left to the various state legislatures the right to decide how presidential electors should be chosen, and in most cases the legislatures themselves chose the electors. But after 1832, all states elected their presidential electors by popular vote. In most states, the people voted for electors who were listed under the name of their party and their candidate and pledged to cast their electoral vote for the listed candidate.

THE CIVIL WAR AND ELITE DIVISION

Social scientists can gain insight into societal conflict and *the breakdown of elite consensus* through the study of history, particularly the history of the American Civil War. America's elite were in substantial agreement about the character and direction of the new nation during its first sixty years. In the 1850s, however, the role of African Americans in American society—the most divisive issue in the history of American politics—became an urgent question that drove a wedge between the elite groups and ultimately led to the nation's bloodiest war. The political system was unequal to the task of negotiating a peaceful settlement to the problem of slavery because America's elite were deeply divided over the question.

division among the elite

SOUTHERN ELITE

It was the white **southern elite** and not the white masses who had an interest in the slave and cotton culture. On the eve of the Civil War, probably not more than one in four southern families held slaves, and many of those families held only one or two slaves each. The number of great planters (men who owned fifty or more slaves and large holdings of land) was probably not more than seven thousand. Yet the views of these planters dominated southern politics.

southern elite
plantation owners dependent on slave labor

NORTHERN ELITE

The **northern elite** consisted of merchants and manufacturers who depended on wage labor. The northern elite had no direct interest in the abolition of slavery in the South. Some northern manufacturers were making good profits from southern trade, and with higher tariffs they stood a chance to make even better profits. Abolitionist activities imperiled trade relations between North and South and were often looked on with irritation in northern social circles.

northern elite
manufacturers dependent on wage labor

ELITE CONFLICT OVER WESTERN LAND

However, both the northern and the southern elite realized that control of the West was the key to future dominance of the nation. The northern elite wanted a West composed of small farmers who produced food and raw materials for the industrial and commercial East and provided a market for eastern goods. But southern planters feared the voting power of a West composed of small farmers and wanted western lands for the expansion of the cotton and slave culture. Cotton ate up the land, and because it required continuous cultivation and monotonous rounds of simple tasks, cotton growing was suited to slave labor. Thus, to protect the cotton economy, it was essential to expand westward and to protect slavery in the West. The conflict over western land eventually precipitated the Civil War.

The costs of preserving the Union. This photo, taken after the battle of Antietam, shows the "Bloody Lane" where two Union regiments trapped Confederates in a barrage of rifle fire. The photo was taken by the famous Civil War photographer Matthew Brady, whose images were the first that Americans had ever seen of the horrors of war.

ATTEMPTS AT COMPROMISE

underlying elite consensus: attempts at compromise

Missouri Compromise of 1820

Compromise of 1850

Kansas-Nebraska Act of 1854

Yet despite such differences, the underlying consensus of the American elite was so great that compromise after compromise was devised to maintain unity. Both the northern and the southern elite displayed a continued devotion to the principles of constitutional government and the protection of private property. In the *Missouri Compromise* of 1820, the land in the Louisiana Purchase exclusive of Missouri was divided between free territory and slave territory at 36°30′; and Maine and Missouri were admitted to the Union as free and slave states, respectively. After the war with Mexico, the elaborate *Compromise of 1850* caused one of the greatest debates in American legislative history, with Senators Henry Clay, Daniel Webster, John C. Calhoun, Salmon P. Chase, Stephen A. Douglas, Jefferson Davis, Alexander H. Stephens, Robert Toombs, William H. Seward, and Thaddeus Stevens all participating. Cleavage within the elite was apparent, but it was not yet so divisive as to split the nation. A compromise was achieved, providing for the admission of California as a free state; for the creation of two new territories, New Mexico and Utah, out of the Mexican cession; for a drastic fugitive slave law to satisfy southern planters; and for the prohibition of the slave trade in the District of Columbia. Even the *Kansas-Nebraska Act of 1854* was intended to be a compromise; each new territory was supposed to decide for itself whether it should be slave or free, the expectation being that Nebraska would vote free and Kansas slave. Gradually, however, the spirit of compromise gave way to divergence and conflict.

ELITE CONSENSUS BREAKS DOWN

Beginning in 1856, proslavery and antislavery forces fought it out in "bleeding Kansas." Senator Charles Sumner of Massachusetts delivered a condemnation of slavery in the Senate and was beaten almost to death on the Senate floor by Congressman Preston Brooks of South Carolina. Intemperate language in the Senate became commonplace, with frequent threats of secession, violence, and civil war. In 1857 a southern-dominated Supreme Court decided, in *Dred Scott v. Sanford,* that the Missouri Compromise was unconstitutional because Congress had no authority to forbid slavery in any territory. Slave property, said Chief Justice Roger B. Taney, was as much protected by the Constitution as was any other kind of property. In 1859 John Brown and his followers raided the U.S. arsenal at Harper's Ferry, as a first step to freeing the slaves of Virginia by force. Brown was captured by Virginia militia under the command of Colonel Robert E. Lee, tried for treason, found guilty, and executed. Southerners believed that northerners had tried to incite the horror of slave insurrection, whereas northerners believed that Brown died a martyr.

LINCOLN'S VIEWS AND SLAVERY

Abraham Lincoln never attacked slavery in the South; his exclusive concern was to halt the spread of slavery in the western territories. He wrote in 1845: "I hold it a paramount duty of us in the free States, due to the Union of the States, and perhaps to liberty itself (paradox though it may seem), to let the slavery of the other states alone."[4] Throughout his political career, Lincoln consistently held this position. On the other hand, with regard to the western territories, he said: "The whole nation is interested that the best use shall be made of these territories. We want them for homes and free white people. This they cannot be, to any considerable extent, if slavery shall be planted within them."[5] In short, Lincoln wanted the western territories to be tied economically and culturally to the northern system.

PRESERVING THE UNION

Historian Richard Hofstadter believed that Lincoln's political posture was essentially conservative: He wished to preserve the long-established order and consensus that had protected American principles and property rights so successfully in the past. He was not an abolitionist, and he did not seek the destruction of the southern elite or the rearrangement of the South's social fabric. His goal was to bring the South back into the Union, to restore orderly government, and to establish the principle that states cannot resist national authority with force. At the beginning of the Civil War, Lincoln knew that a great part of conservative northern opinion was willing to fight for the Union but might refuse to support a war to free slaves. Lincoln's great political skill was his ability to gather all the issues of the Civil War into one single overriding theme: *the preservation of the Union*. However, he was bitterly attacked throughout the war by radical Republicans who thought he had "no antislavery instincts."

As the war continued and casualties mounted, opinion in the North became increasingly bitter toward southern slaveowners. Many Republicans joined the abolitionists in calling for emancipation of the slaves simply to punish the "rebels." They knew that the power of the South was based on the labor of slaves. Lincoln also knew that if he proclaimed to the world that the war was being fought to free the slaves, there would be less danger of foreign intervention.

THE EMANCIPATION PROCLAMATION

On September 22, 1862, Lincoln issued his preliminary Emancipation Proclamation. Claiming his right as commander-in-chief of the army and navy, he promised that "on the first day of January, . . . 1863, all persons held as slaves within any State or designated part of a State the people whereof shall then be in rebellion against the United States shall be then, thenceforward, and forever free." Thus, one of the great steps forward in human freedom in this nation, the Emancipation Proclamation, did not come about as a result of demands by the people, and certainly not as a result of demands by the slaves themselves (see Focus, "Reconstruction and African-American History"). Hofstadter contended that *the Emancipation Proclamation was a political action taken by the president for the sake of helping to preserve the Union*. It was not a revolutionary action but a conservative one.

POWER AND THE INDUSTRIAL REVOLUTION

the rise of the industrial elite   The importance of the Civil War for the power structure of the United States lay in the commanding position that the new industrial capitalists won during the course of that struggle. Even before 1860, northern industry had been altering the course of American life; the economic transformation of the United States from an agricultural to an industrial nation reached the crescendo of a revolution in the second half of the nineteenth century. Canals and steam railroads had been opening up new markets for the growing industrial cities of the East. The rise of corporations and of stock markets for the accumulation of capital upset old-fashioned ideas about property. The introduction of machinery in factories revolutionized the conditions of labor and made the masses dependent on industrial capitalists for their livelihood. Civil War profits compounded the capital of the industrialists and placed them in a position to dominate the economic life of the nation. Moreover, when the southern planters were removed from the national scene, the government in Washington became the exclusive domain of the new industrial leaders.

SOCIAL DARWINISM

The new industrial elite found a new philosophy to justify its political and economic dominance. Drawing an analogy from Darwinian biology, Herbert Spencer undertook to demonstrate that, just as an elite was selected in nature through evolution, so also society would near perfection as it allowed a natural *social* elite to be selected by *free competition*. Spencer hailed the accumulation of new industrial wealth as a sign of "the survival of the fittest." The **social Darwinists** found in the law of survival of the fittest an admirable defense for the emergence of a ruthless ruling elite, an elite that defined its own self-interest more narrowly, perhaps, than any other in American history. It was a philosophy that permitted the conditions of the masses to decline to the lowest depths in American history.

social Darwinism
competition selects the best; a philosophy justifying great accumulations of wealth

The growth of industry, such as the mass production of automobiles, brought many people to urban areas.

Reconstruction and African-American History

Consciously or unconsciously, all historians are biased. There is bias in their choice of subject, in their selection of material, in their organization and presentation of the material, and, inevitably, in their interpretation of it.

Let us consider the historical interpretation of the African-American experience in America, particularly of the black experience in the Reconstruction era following the Civil War. Traditionally, historians viewed the Reconstruction Congress as vindictive. The period as a whole was considered destructive, oppressive, and corrupt. Military rule was imposed on the South. "Carpetbaggers" and "scalawags" confiscated the property of helpless southerners and retarded the economic progress of the South for decades. Maladministration and corruption in the federal government were portrayed as being greater than ever before in American history. The accomplishments of African Americans during this period were overlooked. Finally, it was suggested that the separation of the races—segregation—was the "normal" pattern of southern life. The belief was fostered that blacks and whites in the South had never known any other pattern of life than slavery and segregation.

A new awareness of African-American history in recent years has resulted in a thoroughgoing reinterpretation of the Reconstruction era. Historian C. Vann Woodward's work led the way in bringing new light to this important period. Woodward recorded the progress of blacks during Reconstruction, described the good-faith efforts of the Reconstruction Congress to secure equality for African Americans, and explained the reimposition of segregation in terms of class conflict among whites. (Alex Haley's popular book *Roots,* together with the dramatic television series based on it, is another example of historical interpretation. Whereas, many older histories of the pre-Civil War South romanticized plantation life, *Roots* described the cruelties and brutality of slavery.)

A Revised View of Reconstruction: African-American Progress

When the Republicans gained control of Congress in 1867, African Americans momentarily seemed destined to attain their full rights as U.S. citizens. Under military rule southern states adopted new constitutions that awarded the vote and other civil liberties to blacks. Black men were elected to state legislatures and to the U.S. Congress. In 1865, nearly 10 percent of all federal troops were black.[a]

The accomplishments of the Reconstruction Congress were considerable. Even before the Republicans gained control, the Thirteenth Amendment, which abolished slavery, had become part of the Constitution. But it was the Fourteenth and Fifteenth Amendments and the important Civil Rights Act of 1875 that attempted to secure a place for the blacks in the United States equal to that of the whites.

The Civil Rights Act of 1875 declared that all persons were entitled to the full and equal enjoyment of all public accommodations, inns, public conveniences, theaters, and other places of public amusement. In this act, the Reconstruction Congress committed the nation to a policy of nondiscrimination in all aspects of public life.

But by 1877, support for Reconstruction policies began to crumble. In what has been described as the "Compromise of 1877," the national government agreed to end military occupation of the South, thereby giving up its efforts to rearrange southern society and lending tacit approval to white supremacy in that region. In return, the southern states pledged their support for the Union, accepted national supremacy, and enabled the Republican candidate, Rutherford B. Hayes, to assume the presidency following the much-disputed election of 1876, in which his opponent,

Samuel Tilden, had received a majority of the popular vote.

The Development of the White Supremacy Movement

The withdrawal of federal troops from the South in 1877 did not bring about an instant change in the status of the blacks. Southern blacks voted in large numbers well into the 1880s and 1890s. Certainly we do not mean to suggest that discrimination was nonexistent during that period. Perhaps the most debilitating of all segregation—that in the public schools—appeared immediately after the Civil War under the sanction of Reconstruction authorities. Yet segregation took shape only gradually.

The first objective of the *white supremacy movement* was to disenfranchise blacks. The standard devices developed for achieving this feat were the literacy test, the poll tax, the white primary, and various forms of intimidation. Following the disenfranchisement of African Americans, the white supremacy movement established segregation and discrimination as public policy by the adoption of a large number of "Jim Crow" laws, designed to prevent the mingling of whites and blacks. (Jim Crow was a stereotypical African American in a nineteenth-century song-and-dance show.) Between 1900 and 1910, laws were adopted by southern state leg-

This Ku Klux Klan cross-burning is meant to intimidate.

islatures requiring segregation of the races in streetcars, hospitals, prisons, orphanages, and homes for the aged and indigent. In 1913 the federal government itself adopted policies that segregated the races in federal office buildings, cafeterias, and restroom facilities. Social policy followed (indeed, exceeded) public policy. Little signs reading "White Only" or "Colored" appeared everywhere, with or without the support of law.

Early Supreme Court Approval of Segregation

The Fourteenth Amendment had been passed by the Recon-

struction Congress and ratified in 1868. Its guarantee of "equal protection of the laws" was clearly designed to protect newly freed African Americans from discrimination in state laws. But in 1896, in the infamous case of *Plessy v. Ferguson*, the U.S. Supreme Court held that the separation of the races did *not* violate the Equal Protection Clause so long as people in each race received equal treatment. Schools and other public facilities that were "separate but equal" were held to be

Continued

constitutional. In the words of the Court:

> *The object of the amendment was undoubtedly to enforce the absolute equality of the two races before the law, but in the nature of things it could not have been intended to abolish distinctions based upon color, or to enforce social, as distinguished from political, equality, or a commingling of the two races upon terms unsatisfactory to either. Laws permitting, and even requiring, their separation in places where they are liable to be brought into contact do not necessarily imply the inferiority of either race to the other, and have been generally, if not universally, recognized as within the competency of the state legislatures in the exercise of their police power.[b]*

The effect of this decision was to give constitutional approval to segregation. The decision would not be reversed until *Brown v. Board of Education of Kansas* in 1954 (see Chapter 10).

Response of Blacks to Segregation

Many early histories of Reconstruction paid little attention to the response of blacks to the imposition of segregation. But there were at least three distinct types of response: (1) accommodation to a subordinate position in society, (2) the for-

mation of a black protest movement, and (3) migration out of the South to avoid some of the consequences of white supremacy.

The foremost African-American advocate of accommodation to segregation was the well-known educator Booker T. Washington. Washington enjoyed wide popularity among both white and black Americans. He was an adviser to two presidents (Theodore Roosevelt and William Howard Taft) and was highly respected by white philanthropists and government officials. In his famous Cotton States' Exposition speech in Atlanta in 1895, Washington assured whites that blacks were prepared to accept a separate position in society:

> *In all things that are purely social we can be as separate as the fingers, yet one as the hand in all things essential to mutual progress.[c]*

Booker T. Washington's hopes for African Americans lay in a program of self-help through education. He himself had attended Hampton Institute in Virginia, where the curriculum centered around practical trades for blacks. Washington obtained some white philanthropic support in establishing his own Tuskegee Institute in

Tuskegee, Alabama, in 1881. His first students helped build the school. Training at Tuskegee emphasized immediately useful vocations, such as farming, preaching, and blacksmithing. Washington urged his students to stay in the South, to acquire land, and to build homes, thereby helping to eliminate ignorance and poverty among their fellow African Americans. One of Tuskegee's outstanding faculty members was George Washington Carver, who researched and developed uses for southern crops. Other privately and publicly endowed black colleges were founded that later developed into major universities, including Fisk and Howard (both started by the Freedmen's Bureau) and Atlanta, Hampton, and Southern.

While Washington was urging blacks to make the best of segregation, a small band of blacks was organizing themselves behind a declaration of black resistance and protest that would later rewrite American public policy. The leader of this group was W. E. B. Du Bois, a brilliant historian and sociologist at Atlanta University. In 1905 Du Bois and a few other African-American intellectuals met in Niagara Falls, Canada, to draw up a black platform intended to "assail the ears" and sear the consciences of white Americans. In rejecting moderation and compromise, the Niagara statement proclaimed: "We refuse to allow the impression to remain that the Negro American assents to inferiority, is submissive under oppression and apologetic before insults." The platform listed the major injustices perpetrated against blacks since Reconstruction: the loss of voting rights, the imposition of Jim Crow laws and segregated public schools, the denial of equal job opportunities, the existence of inhumane conditions in southern prisons, the exclusion of blacks from West Point and Annapolis, and the failure on the part of the federal government to enforce the Fourteenth and Fifteenth Amendments. Out of the Niagara meeting came the idea for a nationwide organization dedicated to fighting for blacks, and on February 12, 1909, the one-hundredth anniversary of Abraham Lincoln's birth, the National Association for the Advancement of Colored People (NAACP) was founded.

Du Bois himself was on the original board of directors of the NAACP, but a majority of the board consisted of white liberals. In the years to follow, most of the financial support and policy guidance for the association was provided by whites rather than blacks. However, Du Bois was the NAACP's first director of research and the editor of its magazine, *Crisis*. The NAACP began a long and eventually successful campaign to establish black rights through legal action. Over the years, hundreds of court cases were brought at the local, state, and federal court levels on behalf of blacks denied their constitutional rights.

World War I provided an opportunity for restive blacks in the South to escape the worst abuses of white supremacy by migrating en masse to northern cities. In the years 1916 to 1918, an estimated half-million blacks moved to the North to fill the labor shortage caused by the war effort. Most migrating blacks arrived in big northern cities only to find more poverty and segregation. But

at least they could vote and attend better schools, and they did not encounter laws requiring segregation in public places.

The progressive "ghettoization" of African Americans—their migration from the rural South to the urban North and their increasing concentration in central-city ghettos—had profound political, as well as social, implications. The ghetto provided an environment conducive to political action. Even as early as 1928, the black residents of Chicago were able to elect one of their own to the House of Representatives. The election of Oscar de Priest, the first African-American congressman from the North, signaled a new turn in American urban politics by announcing to white politicians that they would have to reckon with the black vote in northern cities.

The black ghettos would soon provide an important element in a new political coalition that was about to take form: namely, the Democratic Party of Franklin Delano Roosevelt.

[a]For a general history of Reconstruction politics, see C. Vann Woodward, *Reunion and Reaction* (Boston: Little, Brown, 1951), and *The Strange Career of Jim Crow* (New York: Oxford University Press, 1957).
[b]*Plessy v. Ferguson* 163 U.S. 537 (1896).
[c]Quoted in Henry Steele Commager, ed., *The Struggle for Racial Equality: A Documentary Record* (New York: Harper & Row, 1967): 19.

INDUSTRIALISTS ACQUIRE POLITICAL POWER

After the Civil War, industrialists became more prominent in Congress than they had ever been. They had little trouble in voting high tariffs and hard money, both of which heightened profits. Very little effective regulatory legislation was permitted to reach the floor of Congress. After 1881 the Senate came under the spell of Nelson Aldrich, son-in-law of John D. Rockefeller, who controlled Standard Oil. Aldrich served thirty years in the Senate. He believed that geographical representation in that body was old-fashioned and openly advocated a Senate manned officially by representatives from the great business "constituencies"—steel, coal, copper, railroads, banks, textiles, and so on.

THE RISE OF THE MODERN CORPORATION

The *corporate form of business* facilitated the amassing of capital by limiting the liability of capitalists to their actual investments and thereby keeping their personal fortunes safe in the event of misfortunes to their companies. The corporate form also encouraged capitalists to take risks in expanding industrial capital through the stock market. "Wall Street," the address of the nation's busiest securities market, the New York Stock Exchange, became a synonym for industrial capitalism. The markets for corporation stocks provided a vast and ready money source for new enterprises or for the enlargement and consolidation of old firms.

THE NEW DEAL AND THE EMERGENCE OF THE "LIBERAL ESTABLISHMENT"

impact of the Great Depression

The *economic collapse of the Great Depression* undermined the faith of both rich and poor in the idea of social Darwinism. Following the stock market crash of October 1929, and in spite of assurances by President Herbert Hoover that prosperity lay "just around the corner," the American economy virtually stopped. Prices dropped sharply, factories closed, real estate values declined, new construction practically ceased, banks went under, wages were cut drastically, unemployment figures mounted, and welfare rolls swelled.

new era in elite thinking
reform and welfare to preserve American democracy

The election of Franklin D. Roosevelt to the presidency in 1932 ushered in a new era in American political philosophy. The Great Depression did *not* bring about a revolution; it did *not* result in the emergence of a new elite; but it did have an important impact on the **thinking** of America's governing circles. The economic disaster that had befallen the nation caused the elite to consider the need for economic reform. The Great Depression also reinforced the notion that the elite must acquire a greater public responsibility. The victories of fascism in Germany and communism in the Soviet Union and the growing restlessness of the masses in the United States made it plain that *reform and regard* *for the public welfare* were essential to the continued maintenance of the American political system and the dominant place of the elite in it.

THE NEW DEAL

Roosevelt sought to elaborate a **New Deal philosophy** that would permit government to devote much more attention to the public welfare than did the philosophy of Hoover's somewhat discredited "rugged individualism." The New Deal was not a revolutionary system but rather a necessary *reform* of the existing capitalist system. In the New Deal, the American elite accepted the principle that the entire community, through the agency of the national government, has a *responsibility for mass welfare.* Roosevelt's second inaugural address called attention to "one-third of a nation, ill housed, ill clad, ill nourished." Roosevelt succeeded in preserving the existing system of private capitalism and avoiding the threats posed to the established order by fascism, socialism, communism, and other radical movements.

Roosevelt and the New Deal
to reform capitalism, not replace it

Historian Richard Hofstadter commented on Roosevelt's liberal, public-regarding philosophy:

> At the beginning of his career he took to the patrician reform thought of the progressive era and accepted a social outlook that can best be summed up in the phrase "noblesse oblige." He had a penchant for public service, personal philanthropy, and harmless manifestos against dishonesty in government; he displayed a broad easy-going tolerance, a genuine liking for all sorts of people; he loved to exercise his charm in political and social situations.[6]

President Franklin D. Roosevelt signs the Social Security Bill in 1935.

CASE STUDY

Vietnam: A Political History

Histories of the Vietnam War, like all histories, reflect the historian's judgment about what facts are most important and how they should be interpreted. Perhaps the Vietnam experience is still too recent to expect dispassionate explanations—why it happened and why it turned out so badly for so many people. Histories of the war continue many of the same controversies that occurred during the war itself.

The account of the Vietnam War presented here reflects the writer's view that the war was a political, not a military, defeat, and that responsibility for the tragic results lies with the nation's political leadership—their failure to set forth clear objectives in Vietnam, to develop a strategy to achieve those objectives, and to rally mass support behind the effort.

Initially, the United States sought to resist communist aggression from North Vietnam and ensure a strong and independent democratic South Vietnamese government. President John F. Kennedy sent a force of more than twelve thousand advisers and counterinsurgency forces to assist in every aspect of training and support for the Army of the Republic of Vietnam (ARVN). President Kennedy personally inspired the development and deployment of Special Forces ("Green Berets") to deal directly with a guerrilla enemy and help

"win the hearts and minds" of the Vietnamese people.

By 1964, units of the North Vietnamese Army (NVA) had begun to supplement the communist guerrilla forces (Vietcong) in the South. President Lyndon B. Johnson, informed that the South Vietnamese government was on the "verge of collapse," authorized major increases in U.S. supporting forces and began planning for a U.S. combat role.

In February 1965, President Johnson ordered U.S. combat troops into South Vietnam and authorized a gradual increase in air strikes against North Vietnam. Marines landing on the beaches near Da Nang on March 8 in full battle gear were greeted by young girls selling flowers, souvenirs, and themselves; the heavy fighting would come later.

The fateful decision to commit U.S. ground combat forces to Vietnam was made without any significant effort to mobilize American public opinion, the government, or the economy, for war. On the contrary, President Johnson minimized the U.S. military effort, placed numerical limits on U.S. troop strength in Vietnam, limited bombing targets, and underestimated North Vietnam's military capabilities, as well as expected U.S. casualties. No U.S. ground troops were permitted to cross into North Vietnam, and only once (in Cambodia in 1970) were they

permitted to attack NVA forces elsewhere in Indochina.

By late 1967, more than 500,000 U.S. troops were committed to Vietnam. Washington committed these military forces to a war of attrition, a war in which U.S. firepower was expected to inflict sufficient casualties on the enemy to force them to negotiate a settlement. U.S. forces stressed mobility, and the helicopter became a principal instrument of U.S. ground forces in carrying troops into battle, waging war at treetop levels, and evacuating the wounded. But the enemy retained the initiative throughout the war. The enemy could attack, then quickly melt into the civilian population, hide in tunnels, or retreat back to "sanctuaries" in Cambodia and Laos. With attrition defined as the military objective, the enemy "body count" became notoriously unreliable.

The failure of the nation's leadership to set forth a clear military objective in Vietnam made "victory" impossible. The failure to achieve any decisive military victories eroded support for the war among both elites and masses. The *Pentagon Papers*,[a] composed of official memos and documents of the war, reveal increasing disenchantment with military results throughout 1967 by Secretary of Defense Robert McNamara and others who had originally initiated U.S.

military actions. But President Johnson sought to rally support for the war by claiming that the United States was "winning." The U.S. commander in Vietnam, General William Westmoreland, was brought home to tell Congress that there was light at the end of the tunnel. But these pronouncements only helped set the stage for the enemy's great political victory—the Tet offensive.

On January 30, 1968, Vietcong forces blasted their way into the U.S. embassy compound in Saigon and held the courtyard for six hours. The attack was part of a massive, coordinated Tet offensive against all major cities of South Vietnam. The offensive caught the United States and ARVN forces off guard. The ancient city of Hue was captured and held by Vietcong for nearly three weeks. But U.S. forces responded and inflicted very heavy casualties on the Vietcong. The Vietcong failed to hold any of the positions they captured, the people did not rise up to welcome them as "liberators," and their losses were high. By any *military* measure, the Tet offensive was a "defeat" for the enemy and a "victory" for U.S. forces.

Yet the Tet offensive was Hanoi's greatest political victory. "What the hell is going on?" asked a shocked television anchorman, Walter Cronkite. "I thought we were winning the war."[b] Television pictures of bloody fighting in Saigon and Hue seemed to mock the administration's reports of an early end to the war. The media, believing they had been duped by Johnson and Westmoreland, launched a long and bitter campaign against the war effort. Elite support for the war plummeted.

Deserted by the very elite who had initiated American involvement in the war, hounded by hostile media, and confronting a bitter and divisive presidential election, Lyndon Johnson made a dramatic announcement on national television on March 31, 1968: He halted the bombing of North Vietnam and asked Hanoi for peace talks, and concluded: "I shall not seek, and I will not accept, the nomination of my party for another term as your president."

American objectives in Vietnam shifted again with the arrival in Washington of the new president, Richard M. Nixon, and his national security adviser, Henry A. Kissinger. Nixon and Kissinger knew the war must be ended. But they sought to end it "honorably." The South Vietnamese could not be abruptly abandoned without threatening the credibility of American commitments everywhere in the world. They sought a peace settlement that would give South Vietnam a reasonable chance to survive. They hoped that "détente" with the Soviet Union, and a new relationship with communist China, might help to bring about "peace with honor" in Vietnam. But even in the absence of a settlement, they began the withdrawal of U.S. troops under the guise of "Vietnamization" of the war effort.

Unable to persuade Hanoi to make even the slightest concession at Paris, President Nixon sought to demonstrate American strength and resolve. He wished to make clear to Hanoi that he would not necessarily be bound by his predecessors' restraints. In the spring of 1970, Nixon authorized an attack on an NVA sanctuary inside the territory of Cambodia—an area known as the Parrot's Beak—not far from Saigon. The Cambodian operation was brief and probably achieved very little militarily. But it mobilized the antiwar movement in the United States. Demonstrations centered on American campuses, and four students were killed in an angry confrontation with National Guardsmen at Kent State University.

When North Vietnam launched a new, massive, conventional invasion of the South in March 1972, Nixon authorized the heaviest bombing campaign of the war, as well as a naval blockade of North Vietnam and the mining of its Haiphong Harbor. The NVA

Continued

CASE STUDY

Vietnam: A Political History *(Continued)*

suffered heavy casualties, and the attack was thrown back.

Meanwhile, National Security Adviser Henry Kissinger and Hanoi's Le Duc Tho had begun meeting secretly in Paris, away from the formal negotiations, to work out "the shape of a deal." U.S. prisoners of war were a major bargaining chip for Hanoi. In the presidential election of 1972, the war became a partisan issue. Democratic candidate George McGovern had earlier stated that he would "crawl on his hands and knees to Hanoi" for peace, while Nixon continued his "peace with honor" theme. Nixon's landslide reelection strengthened his position in negotiations.

The United States unleashed a devastating air attack directly on Hanoi for the first time in December 1972. U.S. B-52s from Guam joined with bombers based in Thailand to destroy factories, power plants, and transportation facilities in Hanoi itself. Critics at home labeled Nixon's action "the Christmas bombing," and congressional doves planned to end the war by law. But when negotiations resumed in Paris

On the Vietnam memorial in Washington, D.C., are engraved the names of all those Americans who died in combat during the Vietnam War.

in January, the North Vietnamese quickly agreed to peace on the terms that Kissinger and Le Duc Tho had worked out earlier. Both Nixon and Kissinger contended that the Christmas bombing secured the final peace.[c]

Roosevelt's personal philosophy was soon to become the prevailing ethos of the new liberal establishment.

The New Deal brought a lasting commitment of the national government to social welfare. The Social Security Act of 1935 established a basic framework of national social policy that remains in place today (see Chapter 11). It established a compulsory insurance program for workers to provide cash as-

The Paris Peace Agreement of 1973 called for a cease-fire in place, with NVA troops remaining in their areas of control in the South. The South Vietnamese government and its troops also remained in place. All U.S. forces were withdrawn from South Vietnam and U.S. prisoners returned.

The South Vietnamese government lasted two years after the Paris Agreement. Congress refused to provide significant military aid to the South Vietnamese. The Watergate affair forced Nixon's resignation in August 1974. In early 1975, Hanoi decided that the Americans would not "jump back in," and therefore "the opportune moment" was at hand. President Gerald Ford never gave serious consideration to the use of U.S. military forces to repel the new invasion, and his requests to Congress for emergency military aid to the South Vietnamese fell on deaf ears. U.S. Ambassador Graham Martin, embarrassed by his government's abandonment of Vietnam, delayed implementation of escape plans until the last moment. The United States abandoned hundreds of thousands of loyal Vietnamese who had fought alongside the Americans for years.[d] The spectacle of U.S. Marines using rifle butts to keep desperate Vietnamese from boarding helicopters on the roof of the U.S. embassy "provided a tragic epitaph for twenty-five years of American involvement in Vietnam."[e]

America's humiliation in Vietnam had lasting national and international consequences. The United States suffered 47,378 battle deaths and missing-in-action among the 2.8 million who fought in Vietnam. Perhaps one million Vietnamese, military and civilian, in both the North and South, were killed during the war years. But the "peace" was more bloody than the war. In Cambodia more than two million people were murdered by victorious communist forces in genocidal "killing fields." More than 1.5 million South Vietnamese were forcibly relocated to harsh rural areas and "reeducation camps." Nearly one-half million "boat people" tried to flee their country; eventually the United States took in nearly 250,000 Vietnamese refugees. Unlike past wars, there were no victory parades, and no one could answer the question of the mother whose son was killed in Vietnam: "What did he die for?"

SOURCE: Taken from Thomas R. Dye and Harmon Zeigler, *The Irony of Democracy,* 7th. ed. (Pacific Grove, CA.: Brooks/Cole, 1987): 78–88.

[a]*The New York Times, The Pentagon Papers* (New York: Bantam Books, 1971).

[b]George C. Herring, *America's Longest War* (New York: Random House, 1979): 188.

[c]Henry Kissinger, *The White House Years* (Boston: Little, Brown, 1979): 1461; Richard Nixon, *RN: The Memoirs of Richard Nixon,* vol. 2 (New York: Warner Books, 1978): 251.

[d]Frank Snepp, *Decent Internal* (New York: Random House, 1977).

[e]Herring, *America's Longest War,* 262.

sistance on retirement, disability, or death. It provided assistance to the states for cash welfare payments to the poor and to the unemployed. Building on the New Deal, President Lyndon B. Johnson's "Great Society" initiatives in 1965 added the federal Medicare program for the aged and the Medicaid program for the poor, as well as the food-stamp program. Modern American liberalism remains in debt to the legacy of Franklin D. Roosevelt.

THE ORIGINS OF MODERN LIBERALISM

Thus, *modern liberalism* in the United States is a product of elite response to economic depression at home and the rising threats of fascism and communism abroad. Its historical origin can be traced to elite efforts to *preserve* the existing political and economic system through reform. This historical perspective on the liberal tradition gives us a better understanding of the origins of change and reform within society.

ON THE WEB

EXPLORING HISTORY

An almost endless variety of Web sites is available to assist students in the study of history. Indeed, in using standard search engines, it is best to designate the category of history that you wish to review, for example, "U.S. History—Civil War."

Smithsonian Institution. The Smithsonian Institution in Washington, D.C., is one of the nation's most viable resources. Its National Museum of American History (www.americanhistory.si.edu) is an excellent place to begin browsing. A click to "Collections, Scholarship and Research" opens links to the museum's extensive archives, with specific categories listed for such things as social and cultural history, ethnic and religious history, historical photographs, the history of sports, entertainment, business, technology, and medicine.

American Historical Association. The American Historical Association serves professional and academic historians. Its Web site (www.theaha.org) includes information on careers for students of history, services for graduate students in history, current job listings. and links to the publications *American Historical Review* and *Journal of American History.*

Black History. African-American history can be accessed at the site maintained by Encyclopedia Britannica, "Guide to Black History" (www.blackhistory.eb.com), and at the site maintained by the Library of Congress, "The African-American Mosaic" (www.lcweb.loc.gov/exhibits/african).

ABOUT THIS CHAPTER

History is the recording, narrating, and interpreting of past human actions and events. History is not always considered a social science; but when historians seek to go beyond recording and narrating the human experience and try to explain relationships among human events, they become involved in the social sciences. And certainly the social sciences can learn a great deal from history.

Over the ages, history seems to have had a variety of meanings for people:

So very difficult a matter is it to trace and find out the truth of anything by history.
—Plutarch (46–120)

History is little else than a picture of human crimes and misfortunes.
—Voltaire (1694–1778)

Peoples and governments never have learned anything from history, or acted on principles derived from it.
—Hegel (1770–1831)

The history of the world is but the biography of great men.
—Thomas Carlyle (1795–1881)

The subject of history is the life of peoples and of humanity. To catch and pin down in words . . . to describe directly the life, not only of humanity, but even of a single people, appears to be impossible.
—Tolstoy (1828–1910)

Despite these somewhat gloomy views, we believe it is possible to learn something from history, and we hope you will agree. After you have read this chapter, you should be able to

- describe briefly the various approaches to American history
- describe historian Charles Beard's "economic interpretation" of the Constitution
- describe changes in the power elite of various periods of American history, from the Revolution through the New Deal
- discuss how the Jacksonian period in American history helped to advance our institutions of democracy.

- discuss the historical reinterpretation of the African-American experience during the Reconstruction era
- discuss the reasons for U.S. involvement in the Vietnam War and why the U.S. effort failed

DISCUSSION QUESTIONS

1. Describe the various approaches to studying history. Comment on the strengths or weaknesses of each.
2. What were Charles Beard's two main approaches to understanding the Constitution? Describe briefly how the following constitutional provisions were of immediate benefit to the nation's elite: taxing power; interstate commerce clause; congressional powers to protect money and property; Article IV, Section 2, which required the return of runaway slaves and indentured servants; prevention of laws impairing obligation of contracts. Discuss the criticisms of Beard's interpretation of the Constitution.
3. Describe how the power elite was changed by expansion into the American West. What factors contributed to the emergence of this elite, and what was its power base? Describe the philosophy of this new elite and the impact it had on both the elite system and the electoral system.
4. Describe the economic interests of the northern and southern elite on the eve of the Civil War. What were their points of conflict and of agreement? Discuss at least one of the compromises they attempted. Describe Lincoln's attitude toward slavery and his attempts at preserving consensus. Why was the Emancipation Proclamation a conservative, rather than a revolutionary, document?
5. Describe the new elite that emerged in the aftermath of the Civil War. What factors contributed to the rise of this elite? Discuss the philosophy this elite adopted, as well as the influence this elite had on Congress.
6. Discuss the impact the Great Depression had on both elite and nonelite philosophy and the kind of elite thinking that developed in this era. What foreign influences had an impact on this new thinking? Briefly describe Franklin Delano Roosevelt's New Deal philosophy.
7. Show how historical interpretations of the same historical events can radically differ by contrasting earlier interpretations of the Reconstruction era with the more recent interpretations of historian C. Vann Woodward.
8. What were the U.S. objectives in Vietnam? How did these objectives change over time? Do you agree with the author that America's political leadership was responsible for our nation's defeat?
9. In Chapter 14, Power among Nations, you will find a case study, "American Military Power: 'Desert Storm.'" Describe differences in military strategies and outcomes between the Vietnam War and the Persian Gulf War.

The Uses of Power

PART THREE

In Part Three we shall explore the major social problems confronting society. These problems are interdisciplinary in nature, not confined to any of the social science disciplines. The problem of crime and violence, for example, is of as much interest and concern to the psychologist as it is to the sociologist. Because it is a question of human behavior and its consequences, it is also of concern to the political scientist, the historian, the economist, and the anthropologist. Each of these social scientists would approach the study of crime and violence from a somewhat different perspective. Our unifying perspective will continue to be power in society, but our main focus here will be on how power can be used to confront the crises that afflict human societies, for the betterment or detriment of humanity.

Chapter 9

Power and Ideology

THE POWER OF IDEAS

ideology
an integrated system of ideas that rationalizes and justifies the exercise of power

Ideas have power. People are coerced by ideas—beliefs, symbols, doctrines—more than they realize. Indeed, whole societies are shaped by systems of ideas that we frequently refer to as **ideologies.** An ideology is an integrated system of ideas that provides society and its members with rationalizations for a way of life, guides for evaluating "rightness" and "wrongness," and emotional impulses to action. Power and ideology are intimately related. Ideology rationalizes and justifies the exercise of power. By providing a justification of power, ideology itself becomes a source of control over people. Without the added *legitimacy* provided by ideology, powerholders would be confronted by an aroused populace who strongly resented what they regarded as the naked power exercised over them. Nothing could be more dangerous to the stability of a power system. Yet the very ideology that legitimizes power also governs the conduct of powerholders. Once an ideology is deeply rooted in a society, powerholders themselves are bound by it if they wish to retain power.[1]

the functions of ideology
describes human character and society

rationalizes and justifies a way of life

provides standards of right and wrong

motivates people to social and political action

FUNCTIONS OF IDEOLOGY

Ideologies control people's behavior in several ways: (1) Ideologies affect perception. Ideas influence what people "see" in the world around them.

Ideologies frequently describe the character of human beings in society; they help us become aware of certain aspects of society but often impair our ability to see other aspects. Ideologies may distort and oversimplify in their effort to provide a unified and coherent account of society. (2) Ideologies rationalize and justify a way of life and hence provide legitimacy for the structure of society. An ideology may justify the status quo, or it may provide a rationale for change, or even for revolution. (3) Ideologies provide normative standards to determine "rightness" and "wrongness" in the affairs of society. Ideologies generally have a strong moral component. Occasionally, they even function as "religions," complete with prophets (Marx), scriptures (the *Communist Manifesto*), saints (Lenin, Stalin, Mao), and visions of utopia (a communist society). (4) Ideologies provide motivation for social and political action. They give their followers a motive to act to improve world conditions. Ideologies can even "convert" individuals to a particular social or political movement and arouse them to action.

THE RISK OF OVERSIMPLIFICATION

It is difficult to summarize a modern ideology in a few brief paragraphs. The risk of oversimplification is great. And because ideologies themselves are oversimplifications, the problem is compounded. Moreover, ideologies are constantly changing. When old utopian hopes are disappointed, they are frequently revised or replaced by new ones. New ideologies compete with older ones in various stages of revision. To unravel the ideological forces operating in society at any given time is a highly complex affair. With these warnings in mind, however, let us consider some of the major ideologies that influence our contemporary world.

CLASSICAL LIBERALISM: THE LEAST GOVERNMENT IS THE BEST GOVERNMENT

Classical **liberalism** asserted the worth and dignity of the **individual.** It emphasized the rational ability of human beings to determine their own destinies, and it rejected ideas, practices, and institutions that submerged individuals into a larger whole and deprived them of their essential dignity. Liberalism grew out of eighteenth-century Enlightenment, the Age of Reason in which great philosophers such as John Locke and Adam Smith affirmed their faith in reason, virtue, and common sense. Liberalism originated as an attack on hereditary prerogatives and distinctions of a feudal society, the monarchy, the privileged aristocracy, the state-established church, and the restrictions on individual freedom associated with the feudal order.

classical liberalism
asserting the dignity of the individual and limited government power

CLASSICAL LIBERAL IDEAS

classical liberal ideas:

inalienable rights
rights not granted by government but belonging to individuals by virtue of their natural human condition

natural law
the law, existing before government, or written laws, or constitutions, that governs human conduct and grants individual rights

social contract
the idea that government arises from an implied contract among people as a means of protecting their rights

limited government
the idea that government cannot violate the rights that it was established to protect; government power over the individual is limited

equality of opportunity but not absolute equality
the idea that individuals must not be confronted with artificial barriers to advancement, but that inequalities may arise from differences in individual initiative, talent, skill, merit, and hard work

capitalism
an economic system that protects private property, private ownership of businesses, and the freedom to buy and sell goods and services, with a minimum of government intervention

political freedom and economic freedom related

Classical liberalism helped motivate America's Founders to declare their independence from England, to write the American Constitution, and to establish the Republic.[2] It rationalized their actions and provided ideological legitimacy for the new nation. John Locke, the English political philosopher whose writings most influenced the Founders of the United States, argued that even in a "state of nature"—that is, a world in which there were no governments—an *individual* possesses **inalienable rights** to life, liberty, and property. Locke spoke of a **natural law,** or moral principle, that guaranteed every person these rights. They were not given to the individual by government, and no government could legitimately take them away. Locke believed that the very purpose of government was to protect individual liberty. Human beings form a **social contract** with one another to establish a government to protect their rights; they agree to accept governmental authority in order to better protect life, liberty, and property. Implicit in the social contract and the liberal notion of freedom is the belief that governmental activity and restrictions over the individual should be kept to a minimum.

Thus, classical liberalism included a belief in **limited government.** Because government is formed by the consent of the governed to protect individual liberty, it logically follows that government cannot violate the rights it was established to protect.

Classical liberalism also affirmed the equality of all human beings. The Declaration of Independence expressed the conviction that "all men are created equal." The Founders believed in equality for all *before the law,* notwithstanding the accused's circumstances. Over time, the notion of equality has also come to include *equality of opportunity* in all aspects of life—social, educational, and economic. Each person should have an equal chance to develop individual capacities to his or her natural limits; there should be no artificial barriers to personal advancement. It is important to remember, however, that classical liberalism has always stressed **equality of opportunity but not absolute equality.** Thomas Jefferson recognized a "natural aristocracy" of talent, ambition, and industry, and classical liberals have always accepted inequalities that are a product of individual merit and hard work. Absolute equality, or "leveling," is not a part of classical liberalism.[3]

CLASSICAL LIBERALISM AND CAPITALISM

Classical liberalism as a *political* ideology is closely related to **capitalism** as an *economic* ideology.[4] Capitalism asserts the individual's right to own private property and to buy, sell, rent, and trade in a free market. The economic version of freedom is the freedom to make contracts, to bargain for one's services, to move from job to job, to join labor unions, to start one's own business. Capitalism and classical liberal democracy are closely related as economic and political systems. Capitalism stresses individual rationality in economic matters; freedom of choice in working, producing, buying, and selling; and limited governmental intervention in economic affairs. Liberal democracy emphasizes individual rationality in voter choice; freedoms of speech, press, and political activity; and limitations on governmental power over individual liberty. In liberal politics, individuals are free to speak out, to form political parties, and to vote as they please—to pursue their political interests as they think best. In liberal economics, individuals are free to find work, to start businesses, and to spend their money as they please—to pursue their economic interests as they think best. The role of government is restricted to protecting private property, enforcing contracts, and performing only those functions and services that cannot be performed by the private market.

MODERN LIBERALISM: GOVERNMENTAL POWER TO "DO GOOD"

Modern liberalism rationalizes and justifies much of the growth of governmental power that occurred in the United States in the twentieth century. Modern liberalism emphasizes the importance of the social and economic security of a whole population as a prerequisite to individual self-realization and self-development. Classical liberalism looked with suspicion on government as a potential source of "interference" with personal freedom, but modern liberalism looks on the *power of government as a positive force* to be used to contribute to the elimination of social and economic conditions that adversely affect people's lives and impede their self-development. Modern liberals approve of the use of governmental power to ensure the general social welfare and to correct the perceived ills of society. They believe they can change people's lives through the exercise of governmental power: end discrimination, abolish poverty, eliminate slums, ensure employment, uplift the poor, eliminate sicknesses, educate the masses, and instill humanitarian values in everyone. The prevailing impulse is to *do good,* to perform public services, and to assist the least fortunate in society, particularly minorities and the poor.[5]

modern liberalism
governmental power, a positive force in protecting the individual

REFORMING CAPITALISM

Modern liberalism is frequently critical of certain aspects of capitalism, but it proposes to *reform* capitalism rather than replace it with socialism. Modern liberalism continues to recognize the individual's right to own private property, but it imposes on the property owner many social and economic obligations. It assumes that business will be privately owned but will be subject to considerable governmental regulation. Thus, the government intervenes to ensure fair labor standards, minimum wages, healthy working conditions, consumer protection, environmental protection, and so forth.

Classical Liberalism

To understand political power aright, and derive it from its original, we must consider what estate all men are naturally in, and that is, a state of perfect freedom to order their actions, and dispose of their possessions and persons as they think fit, within the bounds of the law of Nature, without asking leave or depending upon the will of any other man.

John Locke, *Treatise of Civil Government,* 1668

Modern Liberalism

The hard truth is that our economic system is partially blind. It "sees" some things and not others. It carefully measures and keeps track of the value of those things most important to buyers and sellers, such as food, clothing, manufactured goods, work, and, indeed, money itself. But its intricate calculations often completely ignore the value of other things that are harder to buy and sell: fresh water; clean air, the beauty of the mountains, the rich diversity of life in the forest, just to name a few. In fact, the partial blindness of our current economic system is the single most powerful force behind what seem to be irrational decisions about the global environment.

Fortunately, these shortcomings can be fixed—albeit with great difficulty.

Al Gore, *Earth in the Balance,* 1992

Modern Conservation

Economic arrangements play a dual role in the promotion of a free society. On the one hand, freedom in economic arrangements is itself a component of freedom broadly understood, so economic freedom is an end in itself. In the second place, economic freedom is also an indispensable means toward the achievement of political freedom.

Milton Friedman, *Free to Choose,* 1980

Fascism

The stronger must dominate and not blend with the weaker, thus sacrificing his own greatness. Only the born weakling can view this as cruel, but he after all is only a weak and limited man; for if this law did not prevail, any conceivable higher development of organic living beings would be unthinkable.

Adolf Hitler, *Mein Kampf,* 1925

Anti-individualistic, the Fascist conception of life

A LARGER ROLE FOR GOVERNMENT

Modern liberals are also committed to a significant *enlargement of the public (governmental) sector of society* in matters having to do with education, welfare, housing, the environment, transportation, urban renewal, medicine, employment, child care, and so on. Modern liberalism envisions a larger role for government in the future: setting new goals, managing the economy, meeting popular wants, and redirecting national resources from private wants toward public needs.

REDUCTION OF INEQUALITIES

Modern liberalism defines equality somewhat differently than classical liberalism. Classical liberalism stresses the value of *equality of opportunity:* Individuals should be free to make the most of their talents and skills, but differences in wealth or stresses the importance of the State and accepts the individual only in so far as his interests coincide with those of the State, which stands for the conscience and the universal will of man as a historic entity.

Benito Mussolini,
Fascism, 1925

Communism

The history of all hitherto existing societies is the history of class struggles. Freeman and slave, patrician and plebeian, lord and serf, guild-master and journeyman, in a word, oppressor and oppressed, stood in constant opposition to one another, carried on an uninterrupted, now hidden, now open fight, a fight that each time ended, either in a revolutionary reconstitution of society at large, or in the common ruin of the contending classes.

Karl Marx and
Friedrich Engels,
Communist Manifesto, 1888

Socialism

The aim of all socialist measures, even of those which appear outwardly as coercive measures, is the development and the securing of a free personality. Their more exact examination always shows that the coercion included will raise the sum total of liberty in society, and will give more freedom over a more extended area than it takes away. The legal day of a maximum number of hours' work, for example, is actually a fixing of a minimum of freedom, a prohibition to sell freedom longer than for a certain number of hours daily, and, in principle, therefore, stands on the same ground as the prohibi-

tion agreed to by all liberals against selling oneself into personal slavery.

Edward Bernstein,
Evolutionary Socialism, 1899

Radicalism

We would replace power rooted in possession, privilege, or circumstance by power and uniqueness rooted in love, reflectiveness, reason, and creativity. As a *social system* we seek the establishment of a democracy of individual participation, governed by two central aims: that the individual share in those social decisions determining the quality and direction of his life; that society be organized to encourage independence in men and provide the media for their common participation.

Students for a
Democratic Society,
Port Huron Statement, 1962

power that are a product of differences in talent, initiative, risk taking, and skill are accepted as natural. In contrast, modern liberalism contends that individual dignity and equality of opportunity depend in some measure on *reduction of absolute inequality* in society. Modern liberals believe that true equality of opportunity cannot be achieved where significant numbers of people suffer from hunger, remediable illness, or extreme hardships in the conditions of life. Thus, modern liberalism supports government efforts to reduce inequalities in society.

MODERN CONSERVATISM: INDIVIDUALISM AND TRADITIONAL VALUES

modern conservatism
classical liberalism

tradition

evolutionary change

morality

In the United States today, *conservatism* is associated with classical liberalism (see Focus, "How to Tell If You're Liberal or Conservative").

How to Tell If You're Liberal or Conservative

	You Are **Liberal** If You Agree That	You Are **Conservative** If You Agree That
Economic Policy	Government should regulate business to protect the public interest	Free-market competition is better at protecting the public than government regulation
	The rich should pay higher taxes to support public services for all	Taxes should be kept as low as possible
	Government spending for social welfare is a good investment in people	Government welfare programs destroy incentives to work
Crime	Government should place primary emphasis on alleviating the social conditions (poverty, joblessness, etc.) that cause crime	Government should place primary emphasis on providing more police and prisons and stop courts from coddling criminals
Social Policy	Government should protect the right of women to choose abortion and fund abortions for poor women	Government should restict abortion and not use taxpayer money for abortions
	Government should pursue affirmative action programs on behalf of minorities and women in employment, education, etc.	Government should not grant preferences to anyone based on race or gender
	Government should keep religious prayers and ceremonies out of schools and public places	Government should allow prayers and religious observances in schools and public places
National Security Policy	Government should support "human rights" throughout the world	Government should pursue the "national interest" of the United States
	Military spending should be reduced now that the Cold War is over	Military spending must reflect a variety of new dangers in this post–Cold War period
You Generally Describe Yourself As:	"caring" "compassionate" "progressive"	"responsible" "moderate" "sensible"
And You Describe Your Political Opponents As:	"extremists" "right-wing radicals" "reactionaries"	"knee jerks" "bleeding hearts" "left-wing radicals"

SOURCE: Adapted from Thomas R. Dye, *Politics in America,* 4th ed. (New York: Prentice-Hall, 2001).

Conservatives in this country retain the early liberal commitment to individual freedom from governmental controls; maximum personal liberty; reliance on individual initiative and effort for self-development, rather than on governmental programs and projects; a free-enterprise economy with a minimum of governmental intervention; and rewards for initiative, skill, risk, and hard work, in contrast to government-imposed "leveling" of income. These views are consistent with the early classical liberalism of Locke, Jefferson, and the nation's Founders. The result, of course, is a confusion of ideological labels: Conservatives today charge modern liberals with abandoning the principles of individualism, limited government, and free enterprise, and today's conservatives claim to be the true "liberals" in society.[6]

LAW AND TRADITION

Modern conservatism does indeed incorporate much of classical liberalism, but conservatism also has a distinct ideological tradition of its own. Conservatism is not as optimistic as liberalism about human nature. Traditionally, conservatives realized that human nature includes elements of irrationality, intolerance, extremism, ignorance, prejudice, hatred, and violence. Thus, they were more likely to place their faith in *law* and *tradition* than in the popular emotions of mass movements. Without the protection of law and tradition, people and societies are vulnerable to terror and violence. The absence of law does not mean freedom, but rather, exposure to the tyranny of terrorism and violence.

PREFERENCE FOR EVOLUTIONARY CHANGE

Conservatism sets forth an *evolutionary* view of social progress. Revolutionary change is far more likely to set society back than to improve it. But over time, people can experiment in small ways with incremental changes; continued from generation to generation, this process of evolutionary change leads to a progressive improvement in the condition of humanity. No government possesses the wisdom to resolve all problems, but the cumulative experience of society does produce certain workable arrangements for the amelioration of social ills. Gradual progress is possible, but only if people do not destroy the painfully acquired wisdom of the past in favor of new, untried utopian solutions that jeopardize the well-being of society.

TRADITION, FAMILY, AND CHURCH AS GUIDES

Conservatives hold that people are rational beings, but that they are also victims of passion. Without the guidance of *law, tradition,* and *morality,* people would soon come to grief by the unruliness of their passions, destroying both themselves and others in pursuit of selfish gain. Rationalism is far from a sufficient guide to action; law, tradition, and morality are also needed for the realization of human purposes. Strong institutions—*family, church,* and *community*—are needed to repress individuals' selfish and irrational impulses and to foster civilized ways of life.

tradition and morality as guides

family, church, and community

FIGURE 9-1

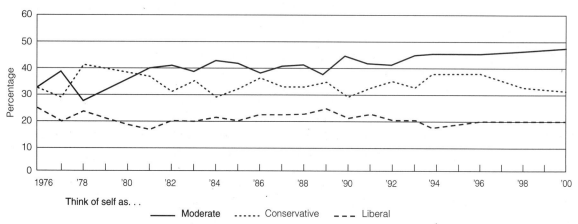

How Americans Describe Themselves

Question: How would you describe your views on most political matters?
Generally, do you think of yourself as liberal, moderate, or conservative?

SOURCES: Surveys by CBS News/*The New York Times* as reprinted in *The American Enterprise* (March/April 1993): 84; and (January/February 2000: 51.

How Americans Describe Themselves

The terms *liberal* and *conservative* have been used with different meanings over the years, so it is difficult to know whether Americans are really liberal or conservative on the issues. One way of determining their stance is to ask questions such as "How would you describe your own political philosophy—conservative, moderate, or liberal?" As can be seen from the results of recent surveys, self-described conservatives outnumber liberals, although it is important to note that many Americans prefer "moderate" and many others decline to label themselves at all (see Figure 9-1).

What do Americans mean when they label themselves "liberal," "moderate," or "conservative"? There is no clear answer to this question. People who called themselves "conservatives" did not consistently oppose social welfare programs or government regulation of the economy. People who called themselves "liberals" did not consistently support social welfare programs or government regulation of the economy.

FASCISM: THE SUPREMACY OF RACE AND NATION

fascism

the supremacy of the nation over the individual

Fascism is an ideology that asserts *the supremacy of the nation or race over the interests of individuals.* In the words of the former Italian fascist dictator, Benito Mussolini, "Everything for the state; nothing against the state; nothing outside of the state."

THE ORGANIC STATE

Fascism perceives the state as not merely a governmental bureaucracy but *the organic life* of a whole people. According to Mussolini, "The Italian nation is an organism having ends, life, and means of action superior to those of the separate individuals or groups of individuals which compose it." In *Mein Kampf*, written before his assumption of power in Germany in the 1930s, Adolf Hitler added to the concept of an organic state, with his idea of the *Volk* (people), in which race and nation are united.[7]

Hitler, *Mein Kampf*

Volk
race and nation united

FASCIST GOAL

The **goal of the fascist state** is not the welfare of the mass of people but the *development of a superior race of human beings.* The goal is the cultivation of bravery, courage, creativity, genius, intelligence, and strength. Fascism values the superior individual who rises out of the mire of mass mediocrity, and the superior nation that rises above the vast anthill of humankind. If life is a struggle for existence in which the fittest survive, then strength is the ultimate virtue and weakness is a fault. Good is that which survives and wins; bad is that which fails. War frequently brings out the best in a nation: unity, bravery, strength, and courage.

the goal of the fascist state
a superior race of human beings

MERGER OF NATIONALISM AND SOCIALISM

Fascism offers itself as a *merger of nationalism and socialism.* Before World War II, fascism in Italy and Germany put itself forward as a socialist regime adopted to national purposes. The party of Adolf Hitler was the National Socialist, or "Nazi," party. Under fascism the nation is an organic whole; therefore, the economy ought to be *cooperative* rather than competitive. Every class and every interest ought to work together for the *good of the nation.* Against the rights of liberty or equality, national socialism established the duties of *service, devotion,* and *discipline.*

TOTALITARIAN POWER STRUCTURE

The power structure of a fascist regime is **totalitarian.** The unity of the fascist state requires "one people, one party, one leader." The fascist believes that a natural, superior, self-made leadership will emerge to provide intelligence and direction to the nation. At the head of the fascist elite is the leader—*Il Duce* in Italy or *Der Fuehrer* in Germany—in whose name everything is done, who is said to be "responsible" for all, but whose acts can nowhere be called into question. The leader is neither a scholar nor a theorist, but a charismatic man of action. Fascism strives for a *totality of power* in which all sectors of society—education, labor, art, science—are incorporated into the state and serve the purposes of the state.

totalitarianism
incorporating all sections of society into the state

ANTI-SEMITISM

anti-Semitism
hatred and prejudice against Jews

The origins of **anti-Semitism**—hatred and prejudice directed against Jews—go back many centuries in Europe—through persecutions, exclusions, ghettoization, and attacks (pogroms) against Jewish communities. But the racial theories developed under fascism brought anti-Semitism to a historically unprecedented scale of horror. In *Mein Kampf,* Hitler depicts the Jews as defilers of German racial purity—not human beings, but "maggots" "contaminating" the nation and state. The Nazis exploited anti-Semitism in their rise to power, encouraging discrimination, exclusion from schools and businesses, forced ghettoization, and violent attacks against Jews and Jewish-owned property. Later Hitler implemented his "final solution" to the "Jewish problem"—the mass murder of an entire people or **genocide.**

genocide
mass murder of an entire people

GENOCIDE

Almost six million European Jews were systematically murdered during World War II, along with millions of other peoples styled as "inferior" by Nazi ideology. The killing began with mass shootings by special *Einsatzgruppen* squads and later escalated into the systematic transportation of millions of Jews and others to a huge network of death camps including Auschwitz, Belsen, Buchenwald, and Dachau. Huge gas chambers and furnaces for the burning of corpses enabled SS troops to kill many thousands in a single day; many others died from starvation, beatings, disease, and cruel medical exper-

At the Belsen, Germany, concentration camp, liberating troops discovered a mass grave—a scene they would encounter again at each concentration camp.

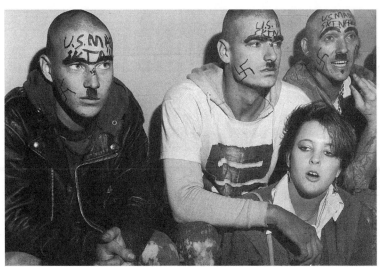

Fascist ideas are preserved in some extremist movements today. These "Skinheads" are emblazoned with Nazi swastikas.

imentation. Evidence of this **Holocaust** is preserved in photos, artifacts, documents, and personal accounts at the Yad Vashem memorial in Jerusalem, Israel, as well as the records of the International Military Tribunal held in Nuremberg, Germany, after the war to try Nazi war criminals.

Neofascism today can be observed in some extremist movements in Germany, France, Great Britain, and the United States. "Skinheads," often emblazoned with Nazi swastikas, preach and practice violence against nonwhites, Jews, and foreigners. Extremist parties and politicians frequently echo fascist themes in their aggressive patriotism, opposition to racial and ethnic minorities, and calls for national and racial unity.

Holocaust
the murder of millions of Jews and others in Nazi death camps during World War II

MARXISM: "WORKERS OF THE WORLD, UNITE"

Communism is a violent strain of the larger ideological movement of socialism. Both socialism and communism arose out of the Industrial Revolution and the "social evils" it generated. Even though the Industrial Revolution led to a rapid rise in standards of living in western Europe, what impressed many early observers of this revolution was the economic inequalities it engendered. Throughout much of the nineteenth century, the real beneficiaries of the new industrialism seemed to be the successful manufacturers, bankers, merchants, and speculators; the lot of the slum-dwelling working classes showed little improvement. This was a bitter disappointment to the humanitarian hopes of many who had earlier embraced liberalism in the expectation that the rewards of economic progress would be shared by everyone. It appeared that liberalism and capitalism had simply substituted an aristocracy of wealth for an aristocracy of birth.

KARL MARX

Communist Manifesto
political pamphlet describing
Marxism and calling for world
revolution

Like many other socialists, Karl Marx (1818–1883) was an upper-middle-class intellectual. When his radicalism barred academic advancement, he turned to journalism and moved from Berlin to Paris. There he met Friedrich Engels, a wealthy young intellectual who supported Marx financially and collaborated with him on many of his writings. The *Communist Manifesto* (1848) was a political pamphlet—short, concise, and full of striking phrases, such as "Workers of the world, unite. You have nothing to lose but your chains." It provided an ideology to what had previously been no more than scattered protest against injustices. The *Manifesto* set forth the key ideas of Marxism, which would be developed twenty years later in great detail in a lengthy work, *Das Kapital.*

ECONOMIC DETERMINISM

economic determinism
the nature of the economy
determines the social structure

Communists believe that the nature of the economy, or "mode of production," is basic to all the rest of society. The mode of production determines the class structure, the political system, religion, education, family life, law, and even art and literature. The economic structure of capitalism creates a class structure of a wealthy *bourgeoisie* (a property-owning class of capitalists) who control the government and exercise power over the *proletariat* (the propertyless workers).

CLASS STRUGGLE

class struggle
the basic conflict in any society is
between economic classes;
capitalists versus proletariat

The first sentence of the *Communist Manifesto* exclaims, "The history of all hitherto existing society is the history of class struggles." The class that owns the mode of production is in the dominant position and *exploits* the other classes. Such exploitation creates antagonism, which gradually increases until it bursts into revolution. The capitalist exploits the worker to the point at which the worker is forced to revolt against the oppressors and overthrow the capitalist state.

INEVITABILITY OF REVOLUTION

inevitability of revolution
by exploiting the workers,
capitalism inspires revolution

Marx asserted that the proletariat revolution was inevitable. As capitalists try to maximize their profits, the rich become richer and the poor become poorer. As capitalists drive wages down to maximize profits, capitalism becomes plagued by a series of crises or depressions, each one worse than the one before. The result of these "internal contradictions" in capitalism is a great deal of human misery, which eventually explodes in revolution. Thus, in their drive for profit, capitalists really dig their own graves by bringing the revolution ever closer.

Cuba's Fidel Castro is one of the last communist dictators in the world.

DICTATORSHIP OF PROLETARIAT

Although Marx claimed that the coming of the revolution was inevitable, he nonetheless urged workers to organize for revolutionary action. The capitalists will never peacefully give up their ruling position. Only a violent revolution will place the proletarians in power. When the proletarians come to power, they, like ruling classes before them, will set up a state of their own—a dictatorship of the proletariat—to protect their class interests. This proletariat dictatorship will seize the property of the capitalists and place ownership of the mode of production in the hands of the proletariat. The bourgeoisie will be eliminated as a class.

dictatorship of the proletariat
violent revolution will give all power to the workers and eliminate the bourgeoisie

THE CLASSLESS SOCIETY

After the revolution, as a result of *common ownership* of everything, a *classless* society will emerge. Because the purpose of government is to assist the ruling class in exploiting and oppressing other classes, once a classless society is established the government will have no purpose and will gradually "wither away." In the early stages of the revolution, the rule of distribution will be "from each according to his ability, to each according to his work." But after the victory of communism and the establishment of a full classless society, the rule of distribution will be "from each according to his ability, to each according to his need" (see Case Study, "The Rise and Fall of Communism in Russia").

withering away of the state
after the revolution, a classless society will emerge; the need for government will disappear

CASE STUDY

The Rise and Fall of Communism in Russia

The task fell to Lenin to reinterpret Marxism as a revolutionary ideology, to carry out a successful communist revolution, and to construct a communist state in the Soviet Union after the 1917 Revolution. Lenin contributed a great deal to communist ideology, so much so that contemporary communist ideology is frequently referred to as *Marxism–Leninism.*

The Totalitarian Party

According to Lenin, the *key to a successful revolution* was the creation of a new and revolutionary type of totalitarian political party composed of militant professional revolutionaries. This party would be organized and trained like an army to obey the commands of superior officers. While western European socialist parties were gathering millions of supporters in relatively democratic organizations, Lenin constructed a small, exclusive, well-disciplined, elitist party. According to Lenin, the Communist Party is the true "vanguard of the proletariat"— the most advanced and class-conscious sector of the proletariat—which has an exclusive right to act as spokesperson for the proletariat as a whole and to exercise the dictatorial powers—"dictatorship of the proletariat"—over the rest of society.

Communism in One Country

After Lenin came to power in the Soviet Union in 1917, he found himself no longer in the position of revolutionary leader; he was the leader of a nation. Gradually abandoning their original hopes for an immediate world revolution, Lenin and his successor, Stalin, turned to the task of creating "communism in one country." With the Communist Party more centrally disciplined than ever, the Soviet leaders turned to the achievement of rapid industrialization through a series of five-year plans designed to convert a backward agrarian country into a modern industrial nation. The sweeping industrialization, brought about by the repression and terror of a totalitarian regime, came at great cost to the people.

The Police State

The Stalinist period saw brutality, oppression, imprisonment, purges, and murders—later officially admitted by the Soviet leaders. The Soviet regime held down the production of consumer goods in order to concentrate on the development of heavy industry. In part, the ideology of communism made it possible to call on the people for tremendous sacrifices for the good of the communist state.

The state never withered away in communist Russia. Indeed, to maintain the communist government, a massive structure of coercion—informants, secret police, official terrorism, and a giant prison system—was erected. (The brutality of the system is described by Nobel Prize-winning author and former Soviet political prisoner Aleksandr Solzhenitsyn in *The Gulag Archipelago.*)

Militarism

Following the "Great Patriotic War"—the Russian name for World War II, in which more than twenty million Soviet citizens were killed and Nazi Germany was defeated—Stalin and his successors directed the Soviet economy primarily toward military purposes. The Soviets maintained the world's largest and most heavily armed military forces, and they built a nuclear missile force that surpassed that of the United States in size and numbers. (Their rapid progress in heavy missiles allowed them to place the first satellite in orbit in 1957 and the first man in space in 1962.) But the huge military establishment was a heavy economic burden; consumer goods in the Soviet Union were generally shoddy and always in short supply. Long waiting lines at state-run stores became the symbol of the Soviet economy.

This statue of Lenin, a symbol of communist rule, was torn down by the people of Riga, Latvia.

Perestroika and Glasnost

Mikhail Gorbachev ascended to power in the Soviet Union in 1985, committed to *perestroika* ("restructuring")—the reform and strengthening of communism in the nation. Gorbachev deviated from many of the earlier interpretations of Marxism–Leninism. He encouraged greater decentralization in industry and less reliance on centralized state direction. At the same time, he called for *glasnost* ("openness") in Soviet life and politics, removing many restrictions on speech, press, and religion and permitting elections with noncommunist candidates running for and winning elective office.

Gorbachev also reached agreements with the United States and western European nations on the reduction of both nuclear and conventional forces (see Chapter 14). Most importantly, he renounced the use of Soviet military force to keep communist governments in power in eastern Europe. As a result of this decision, communist governments were ousted in Poland, Czechoslovakia, Hungary, Bulgaria, Romania, and East Germany in 1989. The Berlin Wall was torn down and Germany was unified in 1990.

The Collapse of Communism

Gorbachev's economic and political reforms threatened powerful interests in the Soviet state—the Communist Party "apparatchiks" (bureaucrats) who were losing control over economic enterprises; the military leaders, who opposed the withdrawal of Soviet troops from Germany and eastern Europe; the KGB police, whose terror tactics were increasingly restricted; and central government officials, who were afraid of losing power to the republics. When these hardliners attempted the forcible removal of Gorbachev in August 1991, the democratic forces rallied to his support. Led by Boris Yeltsin, the first elected president of the Russian Republic, thousands of demonstrators took to the streets, Soviet military forces stood aside, and the coup crumbled. Gorbachev was temporarily restored as president, but Yeltsin emerged as the most influential leader in the nation. The failed coup hastened the demise of the Communist Party.

The Disintegration of the Soviet Union

Strong independence movements in the republics of the former Union of Soviet Socialist Republics (USSR) emerged as the authority of the centralized Communist Party in Moscow waned. Lithuania,

Continued

CASE STUDY

The Rise and Fall of Communism in Russia *(Continued)*

Estonia, and Latvia—nations that had been forcibly incorporated into the Soviet Union in 1939—led the way to independence in 1991. Soon all of the fifteen republics of the USSR declared their independence, and the USSR officially ceased to exist after December 31, 1991. Its president, Mikhail Gorbachev, no longer had a government to preside over. The red flag with its hammer and sickle atop the Kremlin in Moscow was replaced with the flag of the Russian Republic.

Russia after Communism

The transition from a centralized state-run economy to free markets turned out to be more painful for Russians than expected. Living standards for most people declined, alcoholism and death rates increased, and even average life spans shortened. President Boris Yeltsin was confronted by both extreme nationalists, who believed democracy weakened the power of Russia in the world, and the continuing efforts of communists to regain their lost power. Ethnic conflict and political separatism, especially in the largely Muslim province of Chechnya, added to Russia's problems. (Only in 2000, after prolonged fighting, did Russian troops finally take control of most of the province.) Yet Yeltsin was able to overcome these political challenges and win reelection as president in 1996. But corruption, embezzlement, graft, and organized crime continue to undermine democratic reforms. Ill health eventually forced Yeltsin to turn over power to Vladimir Putin, who himself won election as president of Russia in 2000.

The United States has a vital continuing interest in promoting democracy and economic reform in Russia. Russia remains the only nuclear power capable of destroying the United States.

SOCIALISM: GOVERNMENT OWNERSHIP, CENTRAL PLANNING

socialism
collective ownership of the means of production, distribution, and service

There are a bewildering variety of definitions of **socialism.** Occasionally critics of governmental programs in the United States label as "socialist" any program or policy that restricts free enterprise in any way. But fundamentally, socialism means *public ownership of the means of production, distribution, and service.* Socialists agree on one point: Private property in land, buildings, factories, and stores must be transformed into social or collective property. The idea of *collective ownership* is the core of socialism.

OPPOSITION TO CAPITALISM

socialism and communism
condemnation of capitalism

Socialism shares with communism a *condemnation of the capitalist system* as exploitive of the working classes. Communists and socialists agree on the evils of industrial capitalism: the exploitation of labor, the concentration of wealth, the insensitivity of the profit motive to human needs, the insecurities and sufferings brought on by the business cycle, the conflict of class interests, and the propensity of capitalist nations to involve themselves in war (see

Cross-National Perspective, "Capitalism and Socialism in the World"). In short, most socialists agree with the criticisms of the capitalist system set forth by Marx.

COMMITMENT TO DEMOCRACY

However, socialists are committed to the **democratic process** as a means of replacing capitalism with collective ownership of economic enterprise. They generally reject the desirability of violent revolution as a way to replace capitalism and instead advocate peaceful constitutional roads to socialism. Moreover, socialists have rejected the idea of a socialist "dictatorship"; they contend that the goal of socialism is a *free society* embodying the democratic principles of freedom of speech, press, assembly, association, and political activity. They frequently claim that socialism in the economic sector of society is essential to achieving democracy and equality in the political sector of society. In other words, they believe that true democracy cannot be achieved until wealth is evenly distributed and the means of production are commonly owned.

democratic socialism
replacing capitalism through democratic processes

GOVERNMENT OWNERSHIP

Wealth must be redistributed so that all persons can share in the benefits created by society. Redistribution means a transfer of ownership of all substantial economic holdings to the government. But the transfer must be accomplished in a democratic fashion, rather than by force or violence; and a socialist society must be governed as a true democracy.

government ownership of property

CENTRAL PLANNING

Socialism relies on central planning by government bureaucrats to produce and distribute goods and services. Free markets are either outlawed or restricted to a few consumer items. Government bureaucrats decide how many shirts, televisions, autos, and so on, should be produced. Factories are given quotas to meet, and their output is shipped to government stores. Workers' wages are also determined by government planners, as are decisions about new investments and developments. Government planners rely on their own judgment about what is needed, rather than relying on market demand. Planners set goals for each sector of the economy, usually in five-year plans.

central planning of economic activity

NATIONALIZATION

Socialists envision a gradual change from private to public ownership of property. Thus, socialists may begin by "nationalizing" the railroads, the steel industry, the automobile industry, privately owned public utilities, or other specific segments of the economy. **Nationalization** involves governmental seizure of these industries from private owners.

nationalization
government seizure of industries from private owners

CROSS-NATIONAL PERSPECTIVE

Capitalism and Socialism in the World

In reality all modern economies use some combination of capitalist and socialist economic organization. In primarily capitalist countries like the United States, the government protects private property, provides some public goods, and regulates and taxes business. In socialist countries, government ownership and central control of the economy exist side by side with a small but often significant free market.

The figure presents a rough classification of current world governments according to their reliance on capitalist or socialist economic organization. Hong Kong has long been among the most free and prosperous market systems in the

world. (In 1997 this British colony was returned by treaty to the People's Republic of China, an avowedly socialist state. The Chinese government has pledged to allow capitalism to continue in Hong Kong.) The Japanese economy is dominated by large private corporations, although social custom and government persuasion result in a high degree of central coordination. Approximately 35 percent of the gross national product of the United States is produced by governments—federal, state, and local combined. European nations generally have larger public sectors than the United States. Government in Sweden and Israel produces over half of the output of these nations.

The collapse of communism in Eastern Europe has led to the introduction of market reforms in all of the nations of the former Soviet empire. Russia under President Vladimir Putin is committed to market reforms, and that nation's economy is moving away from a centralized socialist system. In the past, 85 to 90 percent of the Russian economy was government-owned. China initiated market reforms in its agricultural sector as early as 1978, but movement toward a market economy in that nation has slowed since 1989. Communist Cuba and North Korea remain as socialist systems, wherein most private economic activity is suppressed by the government.

WHY COMMUNISM COLLAPSED

Speculation about the causes of communism's collapse is risky. The fact that before 1989 very few western social scientists had predicted these revolutionary events suggests that we do not fully understand their causes. Yet we can suggest some interesting hypotheses about the current crisis of communism.

DETERIORATING LIVING STANDARDS

Socialist economies cannot provide an adequate standard of living for their people. The democratic revolutions in Eastern Europe and the Soviet Union were inspired principally by the realization that free market capitalism was providing much higher standards of living in the western world. The economies of

ECONOMIC ORGANIZATION OF WORLD GOVERNMENTS

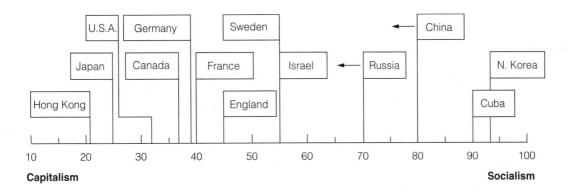

Capitalism

- Productive resources owned by private individuals and firms
- Workers employed by private individuals and firms or self-employed
- Investment undertaken by private individuals and firms in search of profit
- Allocation of goods by market forces
- Income determined by market forces that reward productivity and ownership

Russia, Eastern Europe, and China moving toward markets

Socialism

- Productive resources owned by government
- Workers employed by government
- Investment ordered by government planners according to their own goals
- Allocation of goods by government planners according to their own goals
- Income determined by government planners who may seek to reward productivity or achieve equality or any other goals they desire

the socialist-bloc nations were falling further and further behind the economies of the capitalist nations of the West. Similar comparative observations of the successful economies of the free market "Four Dragons"—South Korea, Taiwan, Singapore, and Hong Kong—inspired Chinese leaders to experiment with market forces.

INEFFICIENCIES AND SHORTAGES

Socialist bureaucracies cannot determine production and allocate goods and services as effectively as free markets. In a socialist system, central bureaucracies, not consumers, determine production. Production for elite goals (principally, a strong military) comes first; production for individual needs comes last. People serve the system instead of the other way around.

Consumer goods are shoddily made and always in short supply. This results in long lines at stores, rampant black marketeering, and frequent bribery of bureaucrats and managers to obtain necessary consumer items.

LACK OF INDIVIDUAL INCENTIVES

Socialism destroys the individual's incentive to work, produce, innovate, invent, save, and invest in the future. The absence of profit incentives leads to extravagant waste by enterprise managers. Employees have no incentives to work hard or to satisfy customers. Official prices are low, but shortages prevent workers from improving their standard of living. A common refrain among workers in socialist systems is: "The government pretends to pay me, and I pretend to work." Bureaucrats try to order innovation, but innovation requires individual creativity and reward, not conformity to a central plan.

POPULAR DISTRUST AND CYNICISM

Over time, *socialist systems lose the trust of the people.* Because the system promised a worker's paradise, the economic hardship imposed on the people inspires widespread *cynicism.* Because the system promised equality, the power and privilege enjoyed by the bureaucratic elite inspire resentment.

ABSENCE OF POLITICAL AND ECONOMIC FREEDOMS

The concentration of both economic and political decision making in the hands of a central government bureaucracy is *incompatible with democracy.* Democracy requires limited government, individual freedom, and dispersal of power in society. In socialist nations, the government exercises virtually *unlimited power over economic as well as political affairs,* individual economic freedoms are curtailed, and great power is accumulated by the government bureaucracy. In contrast, in capitalist nations, governmental intervention in the marketplace is limited, individuals are free to make their own economic decisions, and power is dispersed among many groups and institutions: governments, corporations, unions, press and television, churches, interest groups, and so forth.

COMMUNISM'S INCOMPATIBILITY WITH DEMOCRACY

Thus, democracy is closely tied to capitalism. Capitalism does not *ensure* democracy; some capitalist nations are authoritarian. But capitalism is a necessary condition for democracy. *All existing democracies have free market economies, and no socialist system is a democracy.* In other words, capitalism is a necessary, although not a sufficient, condition for democracy.

Can an individual confront the power of an authoritarian state? A lone citizen in Beijing, China, temporarily halted a column of tanks. Later, authoritarian rule was reimposed following a massacre of civilians in Tiananmen Square.

Above all, the socialist system denies individual freedom, political pluralism, and democracy. Force, repression, and indoctrination can be effective over many years. But at some point, the universal human aspiration for personal freedom and dignity emerges to challenge the socialist order.

ON THE WEB

EXPLORING IDEOLOGIES

There are many ideological-based organizations that maintain Web sites explaining their views and soliciting converts. You do not, however, have to agree with the views presented in order to learn something about their ideological positions.

Communist Party—U.S.A. The collapse of communism in Russia and in the other Eastern European countries a decade ago has not yet completely eradicated Marxist ideology. Indeed, a small Communist Party, known as Communist Party—U.S.A., continues to function within the United States. Its Web site (www.hartford-hwp.com/cp-usa) presents the views of "the Marxist–Leninist working-class party that unites black, brown, and

white." It offers press releases, position papers, the party's *Peoples Weekly* newspaper, and even an online copy of the *Communist Manifesto*.

Socialist Party. Likewise, a small Socialist Party maintains a Web site (www.thesocialistparty.org) that sets forth the history of the Socialist Party in America as well as its social and political views.

Americans for Democratic Action/American Conservative Union. Among the more prominent liberal and conservative organizations with informative Web sites are the Americans for Democratic Action (ADA) and the American Conservative Union (ACU). The ADA site (www.adaaction.org) describes the organization as "The voice of liberal activists" and provides liberal views on a wide variety of current social, economic, and political issues. The ACU described itself as "Your conservative voice in Washington"; its site (www. washtimes-weekly.com/conservative) provides pro-family, anti-crime, pro-free enterprise, anti-big government, and antitax views. *The Washington Times* newspaper also reflects conservative views.

Think Tanks. Among the more interesting liberal think tank sites are those of the Brookings Institution (www.brook.edu) and the Progressive Policy Institute (www.dlcppi.org). And among the more interesting conservative think tank sites are those of the Heritage Foundation (www.heritage.org) and the American Enterprise Institute (www.aei.org). These liberal and conservative organizations present their respective viewpoints on current issues, offer subscriptions and publications, and solicit memberships and contributions.

Libertarian Party. Classical liberalism is represented today by the Libertarian Party, whose Web site (www. lp.org) promotes a "free-market economy, individual liberty and personal responsibility, and a foreign policy of nonintervention, peace, and free trade." And classical liberalism is also promoted by a think tank, the CATO Institute (www.cato.org). This institute is named for *Cato's Letters,* libertarian pamphlets that helped lay the philosophical foundation for the American Revolution.

About this Chapter

When commanded by authority they perceive as legitimate, ordinary human beings may inflict extreme pain and suffering on their fellow humans. It is difficult for us to comprehend the atrocities of World War II—six million Jews murdered; entire villages of Europe eradicated in acts of indiscriminate retaliation; millions of men, women, and children condemned to slave labor; untold numbers suffering the horrors of concentration camps; still others suffering hideous "medical experiments." Incredibly enough, these were the acts of human beings. Not all of them could have been monsters. Many of them pleaded that they were just obeying "orders." Others revealed that despite their Nazi indoctrination, they felt a certain human aversion to their work. One German officer who had been in charge of an "extermination gang" testified at Nuremberg that to relieve the "psychological burden" on his men, he had had them

fire as a group, never as individuals, so they could avoid "personal responsibility."*

How is authority invested with such legitimacy that it has the power to command ordinary people to commit acts of such unthinkable brutality and inhumanity? At least part of the answer, but by no means all, may be found in the power of ideology. Ideology, it should be noted, may be used to further humanitarian as well as nonhumanitarian goals, but regardless of the purpose for which it is used, ideology can be an extremely powerful weapon. In this chapter, we have examined the nature of that power and described some of the major ideological conflicts in the contemporary world. Now that you have read Chapter 9, you should be able to

- define *ideology* and describe its power to influence people's behavior
- compare and contrast classical liberalism, modern liberalism, and modern conservatism
- discuss fascism, socialism, and communism
- describe the development of Marxism–Leninism in the Soviet Union and its subsequent collapse
- describe the relationships between capitalism, socialism, and democracy
- discuss the crisis of communism and the possible reasons for the collapse of communist regimes in Eastern Europe

Discussion Questions

1. Define *ideology* and describe its relationship to power. Discuss the ways in which ideology can control people's behavior. Identify the characteristics of modern ideologies.
2. Compare and contrast classical liberalism and modern liberalism. What is the attitude of each of these ideologies toward the individual? What is their approach to governmental power, the concept of equality, and the capitalist system?
3. Explain the confusion that arises from the ideological labels of "conservative" and "classical liberal."
4. Describe the goals of the fascist state. What is genocide?
5. Trace the development of socialism and communism. Discuss what Marx meant by economic determinism,

---

* William L. Shirer, *The Rise and Fall of the Third Reich* (New York: Simon and Schuster, 1960): 959.

class struggle, the inevitability of revolution, the dictatorship of the proletariat, and the "withering away" of the state.

6. Define *socialism* and discuss how this ideology differs from capitalism. How does democratic socialism differ from communism?

7. Describe how Lenin adapted the ideology of Marxism to conditions in the Soviet Union. Describe Lenin's totalitarian party and his theory of imperialism. How was the ideology of communism used during Stalin's regime? What changes did Mikhail Gorbachev introduce?

8. What explanations might be given for the collapse of communist regimes in Eastern Europe?

Chapter 10

Power, Race, and Gender

RACISM IN AMERICAN HISTORY

Race has been a central issue in American society throughout the nation's history. African slaves were introduced to the earliest colonial settlements in 1619. In 1863 the Emancipation Proclamation, issued by President Abraham Lincoln in the midst of the Civil War, applied to slaves living in the Confederate states, and slavery was constitutionally abolished in the United States by the Thirteenth Amendment in 1865. But within a generation, racial segregation replaced slavery as a means of subjugation (see Focus, "Reconstruction and African-American History" in Chapter 8). Segregation won constitutional approval by the U.S. Supreme Court in 1896; not until the historic *Brown v. Board of Education* case in 1954 did the Supreme Court formally reverse itself and declare segregation unconstitutional. Slavery and segregation left social scars that remain visible in American society today.[1]

Following the Civil War, Congress passed, and the states ratified, the Fourteenth Amendment to the U.S. Constitution, declaring that

> *no State shall make or enforce any law which shall abridge the privileges or immunities of citizens of the United States; nor shall any State deprive any person of life, liberty, or property, without due process of law; nor deny to any person within its jurisdiction the equal protection of the laws.*

The language and historical context leave little doubt that the purpose of the Fourteenth Amendment was to secure for blacks a place in American society equal to that of whites. Yet for a full century, these promises went unfulfilled. Segregation became the social instrument by which blacks were "kept in their place," that is, denied social, economic, educational, and political equality.

Segregation was enforced by a variety of private sanctions, from the occasional lynching mobs to country club admission committees. But government was a principal instrument of segregation both in the southern and in the border states of the nation. (School segregation laws in the United States in 1954 are shown in Figure 10-1.) In the northern states, government was seldom used to enforce segregation, but it was also seldom used to prevent it. The results were often quite similar.

The constitutional argument made on behalf of segregation—that the phrase "equal protection of the laws" did not prohibit the enforced separation of races so long as the races were treated equally—became known as the **separate-but-equal doctrine.** In 1896 the Supreme Court, in *Plessy v. Ferguson,* made this doctrine the official interpretation of the equal protection clause, thus giving segregation constitutional approval.

separate but equal
interpreting the equal protection clause of the Fourteenth Amendment to allow segregation of the races if facilities were equal (1896–1954)

The initial goal of the civil rights movement was the elimination of direct *legal segregation*. Discrimination and segregation practiced by governments had to be prohibited, particularly in voting and public education. Led by Thurgood Marshall, chief counsel for the National Association for the Advancement of Colored People—NAACP—(who was later to become the first African-American Supreme Court justice), the newly emerging civil rights

initial civil rights goal
elimination of segregation by law

Before the historic decision in Brown v. Board of Education *in 1954, Jim Crow laws separated blacks and whites.*

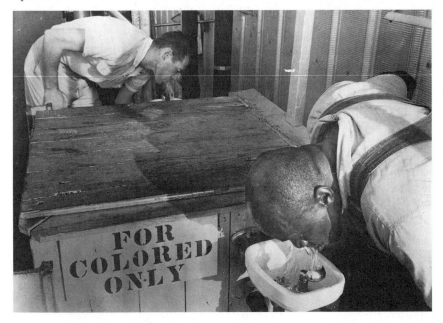

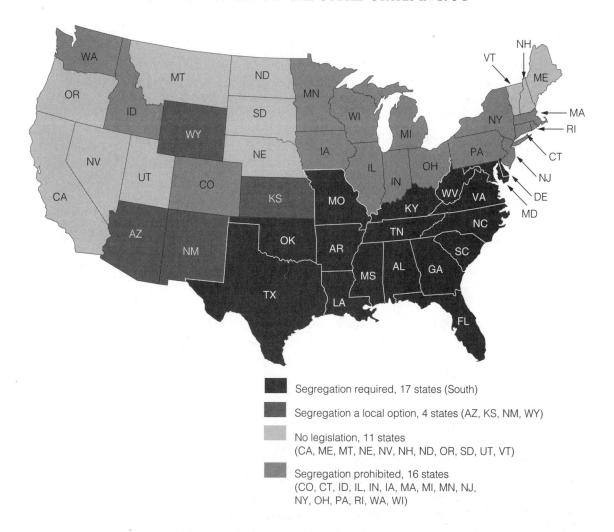

FIGURE 10-1

SEGREGATION LAWS IN THE UNITED STATES IN 1954

Segregation required, 17 states (South)

Segregation a local option, 4 states (AZ, KS, NM, WY)

No legislation, 11 states
(CA, ME, MT, NE, NV, NH, ND, OR, SD, UT, VT)

Segregation prohibited, 16 states
(CO, CT, ID, IL, IN, IA, MA, MI, MN, NJ,
NY, OH, PA, RI, WA, WI)

movement of the 1950s pressed for a court decision that direct lawful segregation violated the guarantee of "equal protection of the laws" of the Fourteenth Amendment. The civil rights movement sought a complete reversal of the separate-but-equal interpretation of *Plessy v. Ferguson;* it wanted a decision that *laws separating the races were unconstitutional.*

On May 17, 1954, the Court rendered its historic **Brown v. Board of Education of Topeka, Kansas:**

> *Segregation of white and colored children in public schools has a detrimental effect upon the colored children. The impact is greater when it has the sanction of law, for the policy of separating the races is usually interpreted as denoting the inferiority of the Negro group.*[2]

Brown v. Board of Education of Topeka, Kansas
landmark Supreme Court decision declaring that segregation itself violates the equal protection clause of the Fourteenth Amendment (1954)

The Supreme Court's decision in *Brown* was symbolically very important. Although it would be many years before any significant number of black children would attend previously all-white schools, the decision by the nation's highest court stimulated black hopes and expectations. Indeed, *Brown* started the modern civil rights movement. The African-American psychologist Kenneth Clark wrote: "This [civil rights] movement would probably not have existed at all were it not for the 1954 Supreme Court school desegregation decision which provided a tremendous boost to the morale of blacks by its *clear* affirmation that color is irrelevant to the rights of American citizens."[3]

THE CIVIL RIGHTS MOVEMENT

As long as the civil rights movement was combating *governmental* discrimination, it could employ the U.S. Constitution as a weapon in its arsenal and rely on *judicial* action to accomplish its objective. But when the civil rights movement turned its attention to combating *private discrimination,* it had to carry its fight into the *legislative* branch of government. *Only* Congress could restrict discrimination practiced by private owners of restaurants, hotels, and motels; private employers; and other individuals who were not government officials.

private discrimination

In the early 1960s, the civil rights movement stepped up its protests and demonstrations and attracted worldwide attention with organized sit-ins, freedom rides, picketing campaigns, boycotts, and mass marches. After the massive "March on Washington" in August 1963, led by Martin Luther King, Jr., President Kennedy asked Congress for the most comprehensive civil rights legislation it had ever considered. The Civil Rights Act of 1964 finally passed both houses of Congress by better than a two-thirds vote and with the overwhelming support of members of both the Republican and Democratic Parties. It can be ranked with the Emancipation Proclamation, the Fourteenth Amendment, and *Brown v. Board of Education* as one of the most important steps toward full equality for blacks in America.

the civil rights movement

The Act includes the following key provisions:

Civil Rights Act of 1964 provisions:

prohibits discrimination in public accommodations

prohibits discrimination in programs receiving federal funds

prohibits discrimination in employment

establishes EEOC to enforce its provisions

- It is unlawful to discriminate against or segregate persons on the grounds of race, color, religion, or national origin in any place of public accommodation, including hotels, motels, restaurants, movies, theaters, sports arenas, entertainment houses, and other places offering to serve the public.

- Each federal department and agency shall take appropriate action to end discrimination in all programs or activities receiving federal financial assistance in any form. These actions may include the termination of assistance.

- It is unlawful for any firm or labor union to discriminate against any individual in any fashion because of his or her race, color, religion, sex, or national origins; an Equal Employment Opportunity Commission shall be established to enforce this provision by investigation, conference, conciliation, or civil action in federal court.

MASTERS OF SOCIAL THOUGHT
Martin Luther King, Jr., and the Power of Protest

The civil rights movement invented new techniques for minorities to gain power and influence in American society. *Mass protest* is a technique by which groups seek to obtain a bargaining position for themselves that can induce desired concessions from established powerholders. It is a means of acquiring a bargaining leverage for those who would otherwise be powerless.

The nation's leading exponent of *nonviolent* protest was Dr. Martin Luther King, Jr. Indeed, King's contributions to the development of a philosophy of nonviolent, direct-action protest on behalf of African Americans won him international acclaim and the Nobel Peace Prize in 1964. King first came to national prominence in 1955, when he was only twenty-five years old; he led a year-long bus boycott in Montgomery, Alabama, to protest discrimination in seating on public buses. In 1957 he formed the Southern Christian Leadership Conference (SCLC)

to provide encouragement and leadership to the growing nonviolent protest movement in the South.

In 1963 a group of Alabama clergymen petitioned Martin Luther King, Jr., to call off mass demonstrations in Birmingham, Alabama. King, who had been arrested in the demonstrations, replied in his famous "Letter from Birmingham Jail":

One may well ask, "How can you advocate breaking some laws and obeying others?" The answer is found in the fact that there are unjust laws. I would be the first to advocate obeying just laws. One has not only a legal but a moral responsibility to obey just laws. Conversely, one has a moral responsibility to disobey unjust laws. . . .

One who breaks an unjust law must do it openly, lovingly . . . and with a willingness to accept the penalty. I submit that an individual who breaks a law that con-

science tells him is unjust, and willingly accepts the penalty by staying in jail to arouse the conscience of the community over its injustice, is in reality expressing the very highest respect for law.[a]

Nonviolent direct action is mass action directed against laws regarded as unjust. Mass demonstrations, sit-ins, and other nonviolent direct-action tactics often involve disobedience to state and local laws. The political purpose of nonviolent direct action and civil disobedience is to call attention or "to bear witness" to the existence of injustices. Only laws regarded as unjust are broken, and they are broken openly, without hatred or violence. Punishment is actively sought rather than avoided because punishment will further emphasize the injustices of the law. The object of nonviolent civil disobedience is to stir the conscience of an apathetic majority and to win support for measures that will eliminate

[a]A public letter by Martin Luther King, Jr., Birmingham, Alabama, April 16, 1963.

On April 4, 1968, Martin Luther King, Jr., was shot and killed in Memphis, Tennessee. The murder of the nation's leading advocate of nonviolence was a tragedy affecting all Americans. Before his death, King had campaigned in Chicago and other northern cities for an end to de facto segregation of blacks in ghettos and for the passage of legislation prohibiting discrimination in the sale or rental of houses and apartments. "Fair housing" legislation had con-

Martin Luther King, Jr., addresses a crowd of seventy thousand people in Chicago.

the injustices. By accepting punishment for the violation of an unjust law, persons practicing civil disobedience demonstrate their sincerity. They hope to shame the majority and to make it ask itself how far it will go to protect the status quo.

Perhaps the most dramatic application of nonviolent direct action occurred in Birmingham, Alabama, in the spring of 1963. Under the di-

rection of Martin Luther King, Jr., thousands of African Americans, including schoolchildren, staged protest marches. In response, police and firefighters, under the direction of Police Chief "Bull" Connor, attacked the demonstrators with fire hoses, cattle prods, and police dogs, all in clear view of national television cameras. Pictures of police brutality were flashed throughout the nation and the world,

doubtless touching the consciences of many white Americans. The demonstrators conducted themselves in a nonviolent fashion. Thousands were dragged off to jail, including King. (It was at this time that King wrote his "Letter from Birmingham Jail," explaining and defending nonviolent direct action.)

The most massive application of nonviolent direct action was the great "March on Washington" in August 1963, during which more than 200,000 black and white marchers converged on the nation's capital. The march ended in a formal program at the Lincoln Memorial in which Martin Luther King, Jr., delivered his most eloquent appeal, entitled "I Have a Dream."

I still have a dream. It is a dream deeply rooted in the American dream. I have a dream that one day this nation will rise up and live out the true meaning of its creed: "We hold these truths to be self-evident, that all men are created equal."

sistently failed in Congress; there was no mention of discrimination in housing even in the comprehensive Civil Rights Act of 1964; and the prospects of a national fair housing law at the beginning of 1968 were not promising. With the assassination of Martin Luther King, Jr., however, the mood of the nation and of Congress changed dramatically. Congress passed a fair housing law as a tribute to the slain civil rights leader.

Civil Rights Act of 1968
prohibits discrimination in the
sale or rental of a dwelling or in
advertising the sale or rental

The **Civil Rights Act of 1968** prohibited the following forms of discrimination:

- refusal to sell or rent a dwelling to any person because of race, color, religion, or national origin
- discrimination against a person in the terms, conditions, or privileges of the sale or rental of a dwelling
- indication of a preference or discrimination on the basis of race, color, religion, or national origin in advertising the sale or rental of a dwelling

CONTINUING INEQUALITIES

Despite progress toward equality in law, social and economic inequalities between blacks and whites persist. Median income of black families is only about 60 percent of that of white families, and this ratio has not improved over the past two decades (see Table 10-1). The black poverty percentage is three times higher than the white poverty percentage. Blacks have made notable progress in education but the proportion of college graduates is still smaller than that of the white population. Female-headed households have increased among both whites and blacks, but today nearly 46 percent of all black households are headed by a woman with no spouse present. Life expectancy among blacks lags behind that of whites, although the gap is closing over time. The infant mortality rate for blacks remains twice as high as for whites.

The civil rights movement opened many new opportunities for African Americans. But equality of *opportunity* is not the same as equality of *results.* What public policies should be pursued to achieve greater equality between

TABLE 10-1

CONTINUING RACIAL INEQUALITIES

		White	Black
Median family income	1970	$10,236	$6,279
	1998	$46.754	$26,602
Poverty (percentage below poverty line)	1970	9.9%	33.5%
	1998	11.0%	26.5%
College education (percentage of population twenty-five years and over)	1970	11.3%	4.4%
	1998	25.0%	14.7%
Female household, with children, no spouse present (percentage of all families with children)	1970	9%	33%
	1998	27%	62%
Life expectancy (years)	1970	71.7%	64.1
	2000	77.4	69.7
Infant mortality (deaths per one thousand live births)	1970	17.8	32.6
	1996	6.1	14.7

SOURCE: U.S. Bureau of the Census, *Statistical Abstract of the United States 1999* (Washington, D.C.: U.S. Government Printing Office, 1999).

the races? Is it sufficient that government eliminate discrimination, guarantee equality of opportunity, and apply "color-blind" standards to both blacks and whites? Or should government undertake **affirmative action**—preferential or compensatory treatment of minorities—to narrow the gap between whites and blacks in employment, education, and income?[4] (See Controversies in Social Science: "Affirmative Action and the Constitution.")

affirmative action
compensatory or preferential treatment of minorities

HISPANIC POWER

The term **Hispanic** refers to Mexican Americans, Puerto Ricans, Cubans, and others of Spanish-speaking ancestry and culture. Hispanics will soon become the nation's largest minority group (see Table 10-2). The largest subgroup is Mexican Americans. Some are descendants of citizens who lived in the Mexican territory annexed to the United States in 1848, but most have come to the United States in accelerating numbers in recent years. The largest Mexican-American populations are found in Texas, Arizona, New Mexico, and California. Puerto Ricans constitute the second-largest Hispanic subgroup. Many still retain ties to the commonwealth and move back and forth from the island to New York. Cubans make up the third-largest subgroup; most have fled from Castro's Cuba and live mainly in the Miami metropolitan area.

Hispanic
referring to Spanish-speaking ancestry and culture

Each of these Hispanic groups has encountered a different experience in American life. Indeed, there is some evidence that these groups identify themselves separately, rather than as Hispanics.[5] Many Cuban Americans, especially early refugees from Castro's revolution in 1959, were skilled professionals and businesspeople who rapidly set about rebuilding Miami's dormant economy. In politics Cuban Americans tend to vote Republican; they have succeeded in electing Cuban Americans to state and local offices in Florida and to the U.S. Congress.

Cuban Americans

TABLE 10-2

MINORITIES IN AMERICA*						
	2000		2020		2050	
	N	%	N	%	N	%
Total Population	274,634	100.0	322,742	100.0	393,931	100.0
African American	33,568	12.2	41,538	12.9	53,555	13.6
Hispanic	31,366	11.4	52,652	16.3	96,508	24.5
Asian/Pacific	10,584	3.9	18,557	5.7	32,432	8.2
Native American	2,054	0.7	2,601	0.8	3,534	0.9
White, non-Hispanic	197,061	71.8	207,393	64.3	207,901	52.8

*Resident population projections (middle series)

SOURCE: U.S. Bureau of the Census, *Statistical Abstract of the United States 1999*, (Washington, D. C.: U.S. Government Printing Office 1999): 19.

N = Numbers in thousands

CONTROVERSIES IN SOCIAL SCIENCE
Affirmative Action and the Constitution

The civil rights movement has opened new opportunities for minorities and women in America. But equality of *opportunity* is not the same as equality of *results*. The early emphasis of government policy was, of course, nondiscrimination. Over time, however, the goal of public policy shifted from the traditional aim of equality of opportunity through nondiscrimination to equality of results through "goals and timetables" established by affirmative action. Although carefully avoiding the term *quota*, the notion of affirmative action tests the success of equal opportunity by observing whether minorities and women achieve admissions, jobs, and promotions in proportion to their numbers in the population.

However, a *constitutional* question arises as to whether affirmative-action programs discriminate against whites and males and therefore violate the equal protection clause of the Fourteenth Amendment. The U.S. Supreme Court has wrestled with this question in several important cases.

The Bakke Case[a]

After several years of premedical courses and volunteer work in a hospital, Allan Bakke, a thirty-two-year-old white male who was also a Vietnam veteran, applied to the University of California at Davis Medical School. He was rejected two years in a row. He later learned that his college grades and medical aptitude test scores ranked well above those of many who had been accepted. All who had been accepted with lower scores were African or Mexican American. Bakke filed a lawsuit arguing that the university had discriminated against him because of race—a violation of the Fourteenth Amendment's guarantee of "equal protection of the laws." The university, which accepted one hundred applicants to medical school per year, admitted that it set aside sixteen places for "disadvantaged students," a category that never included any whites. Candidates for those sixteen positions were placed in a separate admissions pool and competed only against each other. White applicants with grade-point averages below 2.5 (out of a possible 4.0) were always rejected, but many minority students were accepted with averages as low as 2.1 and 2.2. Bakke's average was 3.5.

The university argued that using race as a favorable criterion was in the best interest of the state and the nation. By increasing the number of minority students, the university hoped eventually to improve medical care among the poor and the black. Minority doctors would also provide "role models" for young African and Mexican Americans, giving them something to aspire to in their career development. The university contended that its separation of black and white candidates was "benign" discrimination (meant to help) rather than "invidious" (meant to hurt).

However, the Supreme Court held that the affirmative-action program at the University of California at Davis Medical School violated Allan Bakke's rights to "equal protection of the laws" under the Fourteenth Amendment. The Court ordered the university to admit Bakke to medical school.

The Supreme Court was careful to specify the discriminatory aspects of the university's affirmative-action program:

> *The Davis special admission program involves the use of an explicit racial classification. . . . No matter how strong their qualifications . . . they [whites] are never afforded the chance to compete with applicants from the preferred groups for the special admission seats.*

The Supreme Court went on to describe how an affirmative-action program *could* be constitutional:

> *Race or ethnic background may be deemed a "plus" in a particular applicant's file, . . .*

[as long as] it does not insulate the individual from comparison with all other candidates for the available seats.

The Supreme Court generally approved of the goal of achieving racial and ethnic diversity in the student body. Thus, the *Bakke* case set some limits on affirmative-action programs, but it still permitted schools to consider race as a "plus" factor in competition for admission.

Since *Bakke,* the Supreme Court has considered many challenges to affirmative-action plans on a case-by-case basis. No clear or consistent policy has emerged. In some cases, racial quota systems have been upheld as constitutional, and in other cases, they have been struck down as violations of the U.S. Constitution or the Civil Rights Act. Many of these cases have been decided by close 5-to-4 votes of the justices.

Strict Scrutiny

In 1995, the Supreme Court held that racial classifications in law must be subject to "strict scrutiny." This means that race-based actions by government—any disparate treatment of the races by federal, state, or local public agencies—must be

found necessary to remedy past proven discrimination, or to further clearly identified, compelling, and legitimate government objectives. Moreover, it must be "narrowly tailored" so as not to adversely affect the rights of individuals. In striking down a federal construction contract "set-aside" program for small businesses owned by racial minorities, the Court expressed skepticism about governmental racial classifications: "There is simply no way of determining what classifications are 'benign' and 'remedial' and what classifications are in fact motivated by illegitimate notions of racial inferiority or simple racial politics."[b]

Later, the Supreme Court affirmed an appellate court decision that "diversity" in the student body of a university is *not* a sufficiently compelling interest to justify the use of race or ethnicity in admissions' decisions.[c]

The California Civil Rights Initiative

Opposition to racial and gender preferences inspired a citizen's initiative to be placed on the ballot in California in 1996. The California Civil Rights Initiative added the fol-

lowing key phrase to that state's constitution:

Neither the state of California nor any of its political subdivisions or agents shall use race, sex, color, ethnicity or national origin as a criterion for either discriminating against, or granting preferential treatment to, any individual or group in the operation of the State's system of public employment, public education or public contracting.

Supporters argued that this initiative extends protection to *all* of the state's citizens and eliminates racial preferences. The initiative was approved by 54 percent of California's voters. Opponents argued that it set back the civil rights movement and that it will end the progress of minorities in education and employment.

A federal Court of Appeals upheld the decision of California's voters to ban racial and gender preferences. "Impediments to preferential treatment do not deny equal protection. . . . That the Constitution permits rare race-based or gender-based preferences hardly implies that the state cannot ban them altogether."[d]

---

[a]*Regents of the University of California v. Bakke,* 438 U.S. 265 (1978).

[b]*Aderand Construction v. Pena,* 132 L. Ed. 158 (1995).

[c]*Hopwood v. Texas,* 78 F. 3d 932 (1996).

[d]*Coalition for Economic Equity et al. v. Pete Wilson et al.,* Ninth Circuit Court of Appeals, April 1997.

Mexican americans

The Mexican-American population in the southwestern United States is growing very rapidly. For many years, agricultural businesses encouraged immigration of Mexican farm laborers willing to endure harsh conditions for low pay. Many others came to the United States as undocumented or illegal aliens. In the Immigration Reform Act of 1987, Congress offered amnesty to all undocumented workers who had entered the United States prior to 1982. But the Act also required employers, under threat of penalties, to hire only people who could provide documentation of their legal status in the country. But the result has been a booming business in counterfeit green cards (employment) and Social Security cards. Economic conditions in Mexico and elsewhere in Central America continue to fuel immigration, legal and illegal, to the United States. Mexican Americans appear to work more than most groups; over 82 percent of adult Mexican-American males are in the workforce, compared to only 75 percent of the general population of adult males. But with lower educational levels, average incomes of Mexican-American families are lower, and the poverty rate is higher than the general population. While Mexican Americans have served as governors of Arizona and New Mexico and won election to the U.S. Congress, their political power does not yet match their population percentages. Mexican-American voter turnout is lower than other ethnic groups, perhaps because many are resident aliens or illegal immigrants not eligible to vote, or perhaps because of cultural factors that discourage political participation.[6]

Puerto Ricans

Residents of Puerto Rico are American citizens. Puerto Rico is a commonwealth of the United States with a government that resembles that of a state with a constitution and elected governor and legislature. However, Puerto Rico has no voting members of the U.S. Congress and no electoral votes for president. Median family income in Puerto Rico is higher than anywhere else in the Caribbean but only half that of the poorest state in the United States. As citizens, Puerto Ricans can move anywhere in the United States; many have immigrated to New York City.

IMMIGRATION TO AMERICA

The United States accepts more immigrants than all other nations of the world combined. The vast majority of immigrants in recent years come from less-developed nations of Asia and Latin America (see Figure 10-2). Most immigrants come to the United States for economic opportunity. Most personify the traits we typically think of as American: opportunism, ambition, perseverance, initiative, and a willingness to work hard. As immigrants have always done, they frequently take dirty, low-paying, thankless jobs that other Americans shun. When they open their own businesses, they often do so in blighted, crime-ridden neighborhoods long since abandoned by other entrepreneurs.

CULTURAL CHANGE?

The politics of immigration center on both cultural and economic issues. The nation's business and corporate leaders tend to view immigration in eco-

FIGURE 10-2

Sources of Legal Immigration

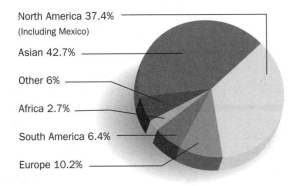

North America 37.4%
(Including Mexico)

Asian 42.7%

Other 6%

Africa 2.7%

South America 6.4%

Europe 10.2%

nomic terms, principally as an increase in the supply of low wage workers in the United States. Most middle-class Americans view immigration in cultural terms, principally its impact on the ethnic composition of their communities. Population projections based on current immigration and fertility (birth) rates suggest that the ethnic character of the nation will shift dramatically over time (see Table 10-2).

LEGAL IMMIGRATION

Immigration policy is a responsibility of the national government. It was not until 1882 that Congress passed the first legislation restricting entry into the United States of persons alleged to be "undesirable" as well as virtually all Asians. Following the end of World War I, Congress passed a comprehensive Immigration Act of 1921 that established maximum numbers of new immigrants each year and set a quota for each foreign country at three percent (later reduced to two percent) of the number of that nation's foreign born living in the United States in 1890. These restrictions reflected anti-immigration feelings that were generally directed at the large wave of southern and eastern European, Catholic and Jewish immigrants (Poland, Russia, Hungary, Italy, Greece) who had entered the United States prior to World War I. It was not until the Immigration and Nationality Act of 1965 that national origin quotas were abolished, replaced by preference categories for relatives and family members and professional and highly skilled persons.

Immigration "reform" was the announced goal of Congress in the Immigration Reform and Control Act of 1986, also known as the Simpson-Mazzoli Act. It sought to control immigration by placing principal responsibility on employers; it set fines for knowingly hiring an illegal alien, with prison terms

FIGURE 10-3

IMMIGRATION TO THE UNITED STATES BY DECADES

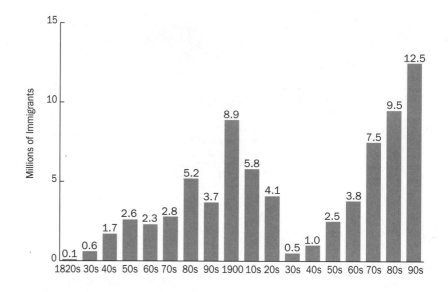

for repeat offenders. However, it allowed employers to accept many different forms of easily forged documentation, and subjected them to penalties for discriminating against legal foreign-born residents. To win political support, the Act granted amnesty to illegal aliens who had lived in the United States since 1982. But the Act failed to reduce the flow of either legal or illegal immigrants (see Figure 10-3).

CURRENT IMMIGRATION POLICY

Today, roughly one million people per year are admitted *legally* to the United States as "lawful permanent residents" (persons who have relatives who are U.S. citizens are lawful permanent residents, or who have needed job skills); or as "refugees" or "asylees" (persons with "a well-founded fear of persecution" in their country of origin). In addition, over twenty million people are awarded visas each year to enter the United States for study, pleasure, or business. Federal law recognizes the following categories of noncitizens admitted into the United States:

- *Legal immigrants* (also "lawful permanent residents" or "permanent resident aliens"). These immigrants are admitted to the United States under a ceiling of 675,000 per year, with some admitted on the basis of job skills but most coming as family members of persons legally residing in the United States. Legal immigrants may work in the United States and apply for citizenship after five years of continuous residence; they are eligible for all federal assistance programs.

- *Refugees and asylees.* These are persons admitted to the United States because of "a well-founded fear of persecution because of race, religion, nationality, political opinion, or membership in a social group." (Refugees are persons not yet in the United States; asylees are persons who have already arrived and apply for refugee protection.) They may work in the United States and are eligible for all federal assistance programs.

- *Parolees* (or persons enjoying "temporary protected status"). These are persons admitted to the United States for humanitarian or medical reasons or whose countries are faced with natural or man-made disasters.

- *Legalized aliens* (also called "amnesty aliens"). These formerly illegal aliens were given legal status (amnesty) under the Immigration Reform and Control Act of 1986. To qualify, they must show some evidence of having resided in the United States since 1982. They may work in the United States and are eligible for all federal assistance programs after five years.

- *Nonimmigrants* (also "nonresident legal aliens"). Over twenty million people are awarded visas to enter the United States for pleasure and business. Time limits are placed on these visas usually by stamping a passport. Additionally, students, temporary workers and trainees, transient aliens, and foreign officials are eligible for temporary visas.

ILLEGAL IMMIGRATION

The United States is a free and prosperous society with over five thousand miles of borders (two thousand with Mexico) and hundreds of international air and sea ports. In theory, a sovereign nation should be able to maintain secure borders, but in practice, the United States has been unwilling and unable to do so. Estimates of illegal immigration vary wildly, from the official U.S. Immigration and Naturalization Service (INS) estimate of 400,000 per year (about 45 percent of the legal immigration), to unofficial estimates ranging up to three million per year. The INS estimates that about four million illegal immigrants currently reside in the United States; unofficial estimates range up to ten million or more. Many illegal immigrants slip across U.S. borders or enter ports with false documentation, while many more overstay tourist or student visas (and are not counted by the INS as illegal immigrants).[7]

As a free society, the United States is not prepared to undertake massive roundups and summary deportations of millions of illegal residents. The Fifth and Fourteenth Amendments to the U.S. Constitution require that every *person* (not just *citizen*) be afforded "due process of law." The INS may turn back persons at the border or even hold them in detention camps. The Coast Guard may intercept boats at sea and return persons to their country of origin.[8] Aliens have no constitutional right to come to the United States. However, *once in the United States, whether legally or illegally, every person is entitled to due process of law and equal protection of the laws.* People are entitled to a fair hearing prior to any government attempt to deport them. Aliens are entitled to apply for asylum and present evidence at a hearing of their "well-founded fear of persecution" if returned to their country.

NATIVE AMERICANS: AN HISTORICAL OVERVIEW

Christopher Columbus, having erred in his estimate of the circumference of the globe, believed he had arrived in the Indian Ocean when he first came to the Caribbean. He mistook the Arawaks for people of the East Indies, calling them "Indios," and this Spanish word passed into English as *Indians*—a word that came to refer to all Native-American peoples. But at the time of the first European contacts, these peoples had no common ethnic identity; there were hundreds of separate cultures and languages thriving in the Americas. Although estimates vary, most historians believe that seven to twelve million people lived in the land that is now the United States and Canada; twenty-five million more lived in Mexico; and as many as sixty to seventy million in all lived in the western hemisphere, a number comparable to Europe's population at the time.

In the centuries that followed, the native population of the Americas was devastated by warfare, famine, and, most of all, by epidemic diseases brought from Europe. Overall, the native population fell by 90 percent, the greatest human disaster in world history. Smallpox was the Europeans' most effective weapon, followed by measles, bubonic plague, influenza, typhus, diphtheria, and scarlet fever. Superior military technology, together with skill in exploiting hostilities between tribes, gradually overcame native resistance. By 1910, there were only 210,000 Native Americans in the United States. Their population has slowly recovered to the current 1.8 million.[9]

THE TRAIL OF BROKEN TREATIES

Intercourse Act of 1790
recognized Indian nations

land concessions by treaty with U.S. government

In the Northwest Ordinance of 1787, Congress, in organizing the western territories of the new nation, declared that: "The utmost good faith shall always be observed toward the Indians. Their lands and property shall never be taken from them without their consent." And later in the Intercourse Act of 1790, Congress declared that public treaties between the United States government and the independent Indian "nations" would be the only legal means of obtaining Indian land. As president, George Washington forged a treaty with the Creeks: In exchange for land concessions, the United States pledged to protect the boundaries of the "Creek Nation" and allow the Creeks themselves to punish all violators of their laws within these boundaries. This semblance of legality was reflected in hundreds of treaties to follow. (And, indeed, in recent years some Indian tribes have successfully sued in federal court for reparations and return of lands obtained in violation of the Intercourse Act of 1790 and subsequent treaties.) Yet Indian lands were constantly invaded by whites. Indian resistance would typically lead to wars that would ultimately result in great loss of life among warriors and their families and the further loss of tribal land. The cycle of invasion, resistance, military defeat, and further land concessions continued for a hundred years.

"INDIAN TERRITORIES"

Following the purchase of the vast Louisiana Territory in 1801, President Thomas Jefferson sought to "civilize" the Indians by promoting farming in "reservations" offered to eastern tribes west of the Mississippi River. But soon Indians who had been forced to move from Ohio to Missouri were forced to move again to survive the relentless white expansion. In 1815 President James Monroe designated as "Indian Territory" most of the Great Plains west of the Missouri River. Indians increasingly faced three unattractive choices: assimilation, removal, and extinction.

In 1814 the Creeks, encouraged by the British during the War of 1812 to attack American settlements, faced an army of Tennessee volunteer militia led by Andrew Jackson. At the Battle of Horseshoe Bend, Jackson's cannon fire decimated the Creek warriors. In the uneven Treaty of Fort Jackson, the Creeks, Choctaws, and Cherokees were forced to concede millions of acres of land.

forced land concessions

By 1830 the "Five Civilized Tribes" of the southeastern United States (Choctaws, Cherokees, Creeks, Chickasaws, and Seminoles) had ceded most but not all of their lands. When gold was discovered on Cherokee land in northern Georgia in 1829, whites invaded their territory. Congress, at the heeding of the old Indian fighter Andrew Jackson, passed a Removal Act, ordering the forcible relocation of the tribes to "Indian Territory" (now Oklahoma). The Cherokees tried to use the white man's law to defend their land, taking their case, *Cherokee Nation v. Georgia* (1831), to the U.S. Supreme Court. When Chief Justice John Marshall held that the tribe was a "domestic dependent nation" that could not be forced to give up its land, President Jackson replied scornfully, "John Marshall has made his decision. Now let him enforce it." A seven-thousand-man army pursued Seminoles into the huge Florida Everglades swamp and forced sixteen-thousand Seminoles, Cherokees, and other Indians on the infamous **"Trail of Tears"** march to Oklahoma in 1838.

Cherokee Nation v. Georgia **(1831)**

Encroachment upon the "Indian Territory" of the Great Plains was not long in coming. First, the territory was crossed by the Santa Fe and Oregon trails and a series of military forts built to protect travelers. In 1854, under pressure from railroad interests, the U.S. government abolished much of the original Indian Territory to create the Kansas and Nebraska territories that were immediately opened to white settlers. The tribes in the land—including Potawatomis, Kickapoos, Delawares, Shawnees, Miamis, Omahas, and Missouris—were forced to sign treaties accepting vastly reduced land reservations. But large buffalo-hunting tribes remained in the northern Dakotas and western Great Plains: the Sioux,

"Trail of Tears"
forced march to Oklahoma

Gambling casinos and bingo halls have provided a source of new income in many areas.

Cheyennes, Arapahos, Comanches, and Kiowas. (Other smaller tribes inhabited the Rockies to California and the Pacific Northwest; and sedentary tribes—Pueblos, Hopis, and Pimas—and migrating tribes—Apaches and Navajos—occupied the Southwest.) The Plains Indians took pride in their warrior status, often fighting among themselves.

INDIAN WARS

The "Indian Wars" were fought between the Plains Indian tribes and the U.S. Army between 1864 and 1890. Following the Civil War, the federal government began to assign boundaries to each tribe and created a Bureau of Indian Affairs (BIA) to "assist and protect" Indian peoples on their "reservations." But the reservations were repeatedly reduced in size until subsistence by hunting became impossible. Malnutrition and demoralization of the native peoples were aided by the mass slaughter of the buffalo; vast herds, numbering perhaps as many as seventy million, were exterminated over the years. The most storied engagement of the long war occurred at the Little Big Horn River in South Dakota on June 25, 1876, where Civil War hero General George Armstrong Custer led elements of the U.S. Seventh Cavalry to destruction at the hands of Sioux and Cheyenne warriors led by Chief Crazy Horse, Chief Sitting Bull, and Chief Gall. But Custer's Last Stand inspired renewed army campaigns against the Plains tribes; the following year Crazy Horse was forced to surrender. In 1881 destitute Sioux under Sitting Bull returned from exile in Canada to surrender themselves to reservation life. Among the last tribes to hold out were the Apaches, whose famous warrior Geronimo finally surrendered in 1886. Sporadic fighting continued to 1890 when a small malnourished band of Lakota Sioux was wiped out at Wounded Knee Creek.

THE ATTEMPTED DESTRUCTION OF TRIBAL LIFE

The **Dawes Act of 1887** governed federal Indian policy for decades. The thrust of the policy was to break up tribal lands, allotting acreage for individual homesteads in order to assimilate Indians into the white agricultural society. Farming was to replace hunting, and tribal life and traditional customs were to be shed for English language and schooling. But this effort to destroy Indian culture never really succeeded. While Indian peoples lost over half of their 1877 reservation land, they neither lost their communal ties nor accumulated much private property. The Dawes Act remained federal policy until 1934 when Congress finally reversed itself and reaffirmed tribal ownership of land.

Dawes Act of 1887
attempted forced assimilation

Life on the reservations was often desperate. Indians suffered the worst poverty of any group in the nation, with high rates of infant mortality, alcoholism, and other diseases. The BIA, notoriously corrupt and mismanaged, encouraged dependency, and regularly interfered with Indian religious affairs and tribal customs.

THE NEW DEAL

The New Deal under President Franklin D. Roosevelt came to Native Americans in the form of the **Indian Reorganization Act of 1934.** This act sought to restore tribal structures by recognizing tribes as instruments of the federal government. Tribal land ownership was restored and elected tribal councils were recognized as legal governments. Efforts to force assimilation were largely abandoned. The BIA became more sensitive to Indian culture and began employing Indians in larger numbers.

Indian Reorganization Act of 1934
recognized tribes as legal governments

Yet the BIA remained "paternalistic," frequently interfering in tribal "sovereignty." Moreover, in the 1950s Congress initiated a policy of "termination" of sovereignty rights for specific tribes that consented to relinquish their lands in exchange for cash payments. Only a few tribes chose this course, but the results were often calamitous: After the one-time cash payments were spent, Indian peoples became dependent upon state social welfare services and often slipped further into poverty and alcoholism.

THE AMERICAN INDIAN MOVEMENT

The civil rights movement of the 1960s inspired a new activism among Native-American groups. The American Indian Movement (AIM) was founded in 1968 and attracted national headlines by occupying Alcatraz Island in San Francisco Bay. Violence flared in 1972 when AIM activists took over the site of the Wounded Knee battle and fought with FBI agents. Several tribes succeeded in federal courts and the Congress to win back lands and/or compensation for lands taken in treaty violations. Indian culture was revitalized, and Vine Deloria's *Custer Died for Your Sins* and Dee Brown's *Bury My Heart at Wounded Knee* became national bestsellers.

In the 1990 census, about 1.8 million people—less than 1 percent of the nation's population—identified themselves as American Indians. About 800,000 of these people lived on tribal reservation and trust land, the largest of which is the Navajo and Hopi enclave in the southwestern United States (see Figure 10-4). Yet these peoples remain the poorest and least healthy in America, with high incidences of infant mortality, suicide, and alcoholism. Approximately half of all Indians live below the poverty line.

FIGURE 10-4

NATIVE AMERICANS' SETTLEMENTS

POWER AND GENDER

Gender roles involve power relationships. The traditional American family was patriarchal, and many cultural practices continue to reflect male dominance (see Chapter 3). Men still hold most of the major positions in industry, finance, academia, the military, politics, and government. Authority in many families still rests with the man. Today more than half of all married women work; more than half of women with children under six years of age work. Nonetheless, stereotyped gender roles continue to assign domestic service and child care to women, whether they work or not, and human achievement, interest, and ambition to men.

Despite increases in the number and proportion of working women, the nation's occupational fields are still divided between traditionally male and female jobs. Women continue to dominate the traditional "pink-collar" jobs (see Table 10-3). Women have made important inroads in traditionally male

TABLE 10-3

WOMEN'S WORK

	Percentage Female		
	1960	1983	1998
"White Collar"			
Women are increasingly entering white-collar occupational fields traditionally dominated by men:			
Architects	3	13	18
Computer analysts	11	28	29
College and university teachers	28	36	43
Engineers	1	6	11
Lawyers and judges	4	16	29
Physicians	10	16	27
"Pink Collar"			
Women continue to be concentrated in occupational fields traditionally dominated by women:			
Secretaries	98	99	98
Waitresses/Waiters	91	88	78
Nurses	97	96	93
Office clerks	75	82	89
"Blue Collar"			
Women continue to be largely shut out of blue-collar occupational fields traditionally dominated by men:			
Truck drivers	1	2	5
Carpenters	1	1	1
Laborers	17	19	22
Auto mechanics	1	1	1
Bartenders	21	44	55

SOURCE: U.S. Department of Labor, *Employment in Perspective: Working Women* (Washington, D.C.: U.S. Government Printing Office, 1983); National Research Council, National Academy of Sciences, *Women's Work, Men's Work* (Washington, D.C.: National Academy Press, 1985); *Statistical Abstract of the United States 1999* (Washington, D.C.: U.S. Government Printing Office, 1999): 425–426.

FIGURE 10-5

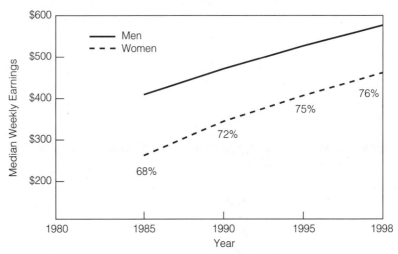

THE EARNINGS GAP: MEDIAN WEEKLY EARNINGS
OF MEN AND WOMEN

Note: Percentages indicate the ratio of women's to men's median weekly earnings.
SOURCE: *Statistical Abstract of the United States 1999* (Washington, D.C.: U.S. Government Printing Office, 1999): 44.

white-collar occupations—doctors, lawyers, and engineers, for example—although men still remain in the majority in these professions. However, women have only begun to break into the "blue-collar" occupations traditionally dominated by men. Blue-collar jobs usually pay more than pink-collar jobs. This circumstance accounts for much of the earnings gap between men and women (see Figure 10-5, "The Earnings Gap").

GENDER INEQUALITY: CULTURE OR BIOLOGY?

inequality as a product of cultural conditioning

How much of male dominance can be attributed to *biology* and how much to *culture*? Many scholars deny that biological differences necessitate any distinctions between male and female in domestic service or child-care responsibilities, authority in the family, economic roles in society, or political or legal rights. They contend that *existing gender differences are culturally imposed on women from earliest childhood*. The very first item in personality formation is the assignment of gender roles (you are a boy, you are a girl) and the encouragement of "masculine" and "feminine" traits. Aggression, curiosity, intelligence, initiative, and force are encouraged in the boy; passivity, refinement, shyness, and virtue are encouraged in the girl. Girls are supposed to think in terms of domestic and child-care roles, whereas boys are urged to think of careers in industry and the professions. Deeply ingrained symbols, attitudes, and practices are culturally designated as masculine or feminine. ("What a big boy!" "Isn't she pretty!") There are masculine and feminine subjects in school: Science, technology, and business are male; teaching, nursing, and secretarial studies are female. Boys are portrayed in roles in which they master their environment; girls, in roles in which they admire the accomplishments of men. It is this *cultural* conditioning that leads a woman to accept a family- and child-centered life and an inferior economic and political role in society—not her *physiology*.

Many writers have deplored the *sociopsychological barriers* to a woman's full human development.[10] There is a double standard of sexual guilt in which women are subject to greater shame for any sexual liaison, whatever the circumstances. Yet, while denied sexual freedom herself, the woman is usually obliged to seek advancement through the approval of men. She may try to overcome her powerlessness by using her own sexuality, perhaps at the cost of her dignity and self-respect. The prevailing male attitude is to value women for their sexual traits rather than for their qualities as human beings. Women are frequently portrayed as "sex objects" in advertising, magazines, and literature. They are supposed to entertain, please, gratify, and flatter men with their sexuality; it is seldom the other way around. There is even evidence of self-rejection among women: Female children are more likely to wish they had been born boys than male children are to wish they had been born girls.[11] The power aspects of gender roles are also ingrained in male psychology. Young men are deemed feminine (inferior) if they are not sufficiently aggressive, physical, or violent.

> **inequality as a product of sociopsychological barriers**

In contrast to these arguments about *culturally* imposed gender roles, other observers have contended that *physiological differences* between men and women account for differential gender roles.[12] The woman's role in the reproduction and care of the young is biologically determined. To the extent that she seeks to protect her young, she also seeks family arrangements that will provide maximum security and support for them. Men acquire dominant positions in industry, finance, government, and so forth, largely because women are preoccupied with family and child-care tasks. Men are physically stronger than women, and their role as economic providers is rooted in this biological difference. Whether there are any biologically determined mental or emotional differences between men and women is a disputed point, but the possibility of such differences exists. Thus, differential gender roles may be partly physical in origin.

> **inequality as a product of physiological differences**

THE LONG HISTORY OF WOMEN'S PROTESTS

The movement for women's rights in America is nearly as old as the nation itself. In 1776, Abigail Adams wrote to her husband John Adams at the Second Continental Congress while it was debating whether to declare American independence:

> *If particular care and attention is not paid to the ladies, we are determined to foment a rebellion and will not hold ourselves bound by any laws in which we have no voice or representation.*[13]

The political movement forecast by Abigail Adams did not really emerge until a generation later, however. The origins of the women's rights movement lie in the pre-Civil War antislavery crusade in which women played the major role (see Focus, "A Declaration of Women's Rights, 1848"). The first generation of feminists, including Lucretia Mott, Elizabeth Cady Stanton, Lucy Stone, and Susan B. Anthony, learned to organize, to hold public meetings, and to conduct petition campaigns as abolitionists. After the Civil War, the feminist movement concentrated on winning civil rights and the franchise for women. The suffragettes employed mass demonstrations, parades, picketing, and occasional disruptions and civil disobedience—tactics similar to those of the civil rights movement of the 1960s. The more moderate wing of the American suffrage movement became the League of Women Voters; in addition to the women's vote, they sought protection of women in industry, child-welfare laws, honest election practices, and the elimination of laws discriminating against the rights of women.

political equality
Nineteenth Amendment (1920)

The culmination of the early feminist movement was the passage in 1920 of the Nineteenth Amendment to the Constitution:

> *The right of citizens of the United States to vote shall not be denied or abridged by the United States or by any State on account of sex.*

The movement was also successful in changing many state laws that abridged the property rights of the married woman and otherwise treated her as the "chattel" (property) of her husband. But active feminist politics declined after the goal of women's voting rights had been achieved.

equality in employment
Civil Rights Act of 1964

Renewed interest and progress in women's rights came with the civil rights movement of the 1960s.[14] The Civil Rights Act of 1964 prevents discrimination on the basis of gender, as well as of race, in employment, salary, promotion, and other conditions of work. The Equal Employment Opportunity Commission (EEOC), the federal agency charged with eliminating discrimination in employment, has established guidelines barring stereotyped classifications of "men's jobs" and "women's jobs." State laws and employer practices that differentiate between men and women in terms of hours, pay, retirement age, and so on have been struck down. Under active lobbying from feminist organizations, federal agencies, including the U.S. Office of Education and the Office of Federal Contract Compliance, have established affirmative-action guidelines for government agencies, universities, and private businesses doing work for the government. These guidelines set goals and timetables for employers to alter their workforce to achieve higher percentages of women at all levels.

ERA
Equal Rights Amendment; a proposed amendment to the U.S. Constitution guaranteeing equality of rights of the sexes

For many years, feminist activity focused on the **Equal Rights Amendment (ERA)** to the Constitution, which would have struck down *all* existing legal inequalities in state and federal laws between men and women. The proposed amendment stated simply:

> *Equality of rights under the law shall not be denied or abridged by the United States or by any State on account of sex.*

The ERA passed the Congress easily in 1972 and was sent to the states, but it fell three states short of the three-fourths (thirty-eight) needed for ratification.

FOCUS

A Declaration of Women's Rights, 1848

When a delegation of American women was excluded from the World Anti-Slavery Convention in London in 1840, they realized that the cause of emancipation affected them as well as slaves. On July 19, 1848, they met in Seneca Falls, across the New York border in Canada, to draw up "The Seneca Falls Declaration of Sentiments and Resolutions." The Resolution parallels the Declaration of Independence and reads in part:

We hold these truths to be self-evident: that all men and women are created equal; that they are endowed by their Creator with certain inalienable rights; that among these are life, liberty, and the pursuit of happiness. . . .

The history of mankind is a history of repeated injuries and usurpations, on the part of man toward woman, having in direct object the establishment of an absolute tyranny over her. To prove this, let facts be submitted to a candid world.

He has never permitted her to exercise her inalienable right to the elective franchise.

He has compelled her to submit to laws, in the formation of which she had no voice. . . .

Having deprived her of this first right of a citizen, the elective franchise, thereby leaving her without representation in the halls of legislation, he has oppressed her on all sides.

He has made her, if married, in the eye of the law, civilly dead.

He has taken from her all rights in property, even to the wages she earns. . . .

He has monopolized nearly all the profitable employments, and from those she is permitted to follow, she receives but a scanty remuneration. He closes against her all the avenues to wealth and distinction which he considers most honorable to himself. As a teacher of theology, medicine, or law, she is not known.

He has denied her the facilities for obtaining a thorough education, all colleges being closed against her.

He allows her in Church, as well as State, but a subordinate position, claiming

Apostolic authority for her exclusion from the ministry, and, with some exceptions, from any public participation in the affairs of the Church.

He has created a false public sentiment by giving to a world a different code of morals for men and women, by which moral delinquencies which exclude women from society, are not only tolerated, but deemed of little account in man. . . .

He has endeavored, in every way that he could, to destroy her confidence in her own powers, to lessen her self-respect and to make her willing to lead a dependent and abject life.

Now, in view of this entire disfranchisement of one-half the people of this country, their social and religious degradation—in view of the unjust laws above mentioned, and because women do feel themselves aggrieved, oppressed, and fraudulently deprived of their most sacred rights, we insist that they have immediate admission to all the rights and privileges which belong to them as citizens of the United States.

Women are also acquiring greater power over their own lives through a series of *social and medical developments*. Advances in birth-control techniques, including "the pill," have freed women's sexuality from the reproductive function. Abortions are now a recognized constitutional right. Women can determine for themselves whether and when they will undertake childbirth and child rearing.

changing mores and medical advances

SEXUAL HARASSMENT AND THE LAW

The women's movement has succeeded in placing the issue of sexual harassment on the national agenda. Title VII of the Civil Rights Act of 1964 protects employees from sexual discrimination "with respect to compensation, terms, conditions, or privileges of employment." The Supreme Court held in 1986 that sexual harassment of employees could be "sufficiently severe" to alter the "conditions" of employment and therefore violate Title VII.

Sexual harassment may take various forms. There seems to be little doubt that it includes (1) conditioning employment or promotion or privileges of employment on the granting of sexual favors by an employee and (2) "tangible" acts of touching, fondling, or forced sexual relations. But sexual harassment has also been defined to include (3) a "hostile working environment." This phrase may include offensive utterances, sexual innuendoes, dirty jokes, the display of pornographic material, and unwanted proposals for dates. Several problems arise with this definition. First, it would appear to include speech and hence raise First Amendment questions regarding how far speech may be curtailed by law in the workplace. Second, the definition depends more on the subjective feelings of the individual employee about what is "offensive" and "unwanted" rather than on an objective standard of behavior that is easily understood by all. The Supreme Court wrestled with the definition of a "hostile work environment" in *Harris v. Forklift* in 1993. It held that a plaintiff need not show that the utterances caused psychological injury but only that a "reasonable person" would perceive the work environment to be hostile or abusive. Presumably a single incident would not constitute harassment; rather, courts should consider "the frequency of the discriminatory conduct," "its severity," and whether it "unreasonably interferes with an employee's work performance."

ABORTION AND THE LAW

Abortion is not an issue that can be easily compromised. The arguments touch on fundamental moral and religious principles. Proponents of abortion, who generally refer to themselves as "pro-choice," argue that a woman should be permitted to control her own body and should not be forced by law to have unwanted children. They cite the heavy toll in lives lost because of criminal abortions and the psychological and emotional pain of an unwanted pregnancy. Opponents of abortion, who often refer to themselves as "pro-life," base their belief on the sanctity of life, including the life of the unborn child, which they insist deserves the protection of law—"the right to life." Many believe that the killing of an unborn child for any reason other than the preservation of the life or health of the mother is murder.

One of the most controversial decisions in the Supreme Court's history was its ruling in ***Roe v. Wade*** (1973), which recognized abortion as a *constitutional* right of women. In this historic decision, the Court determined that

Roe v. Wade
abortion as a constitutional right

a fetus is not a "person" within the meaning of the Constitution, and therefore a fetus's right to life is not guaranteed by law. Moreover, the Court held that the "liberty" guaranteed by the Fifth and Fourteenth Amendments encompassed the privacy right of a woman to decide whether or not to terminate her pregnancy.

The Supreme Court's decision did not end the controversy over abortion. Congress banned the use of federal funds under Medicaid (medical care for the poor) for abortions except to protect the life of a woman (and later in cases of rape and incest as well). The Supreme Court upheld the constitutionality of federal and state *laws denying tax funds for abortions*. Although women retained the right to an abortion, the Court held that there was no constitutional obligation for government to pay for abortions:[15] the decision about whether to pay for abortion from tax revenues was left to Congress and the states.

no constitutional right to tax-funded abortion

About 1.5 million abortions are performed each year in the United States. This is about 43 percent of the number of live births. Most of these abortions are performed in the first three months; about 10 percent are performed after the third month.

incidence of abortion

The Supreme Court has upheld *some* restrictions on abortion—those which do not impose an "undue burden" on the exercise of a woman's privacy right to choose abortion. In *Planned Parenthood v. Casey* (1992), the Supreme Court reaffirmed *Roe v. Wade* but upheld Pennsylvania requirements for physician counseling prior to an abortion, a twenty-four-hour waiting period, and parental notification when minors seek an abortion. Justice Sandra Day O'Connor wrote the Court's opinion, establishing a new standard for constitutionally evaluating state restrictions on abortion: They must not impose an "undue burden" on women seeking abortion. Despite outcries from both pro-choice and pro-life forces, the *Casey* decision appears to place the Supreme Court's position on abortion almost exactly where public opinion polls suggest most Americans are: generally supporting a woman's right to choose an abortion but also supporting reasonable restrictions on the exercise of that right.

constitutionally allowable restrictions on abortion

reaffirming constitutional right to abortion; no undue burdens on women's right

Violence at abortion clinics inspired Congress to pass federal legislation in 1994 restricting demonstrations at these sites. Federal laws now supplement state and local laws prohibiting interference in access to abortion clinics.

ON THE WEB

EXPLORING POWER, RACE, AND GENDER

A great deal of information and a wide variety of points of view on race, ethnicity, gender issues, and civil rights are available on the Internet.

U.S. Commission on Civil Rights. The U.S. Commission on Civil Rights is the federal government's official clearinghouse for information regarding discrimination or the denial of equal protection of the laws. Its Web site (www.usccr.gov) includes a wide variety of public reports and studies on civil rights matters; all are available to the public free of charge.

U.S. Equal Employment Opportunity Commission. The U.S. Equal Employment Opportunity Commission also maintains a Web site with facts about employment discrimination as well as instructions on how to file a charge under Title VII of the Civil Rights Act of 1964, the Americans with Disabilities Act, and the Equal Pay Act.

NAACP. Many civil rights organizations also maintain their own Web sites. The National Association for the Advancement of Colored People (NAACP) is the nation's oldest civil rights organization. Its Web site (www.naacp.org) includes information on the organization's history, leadership, and current concerns.

NOW. The Web site, of the National Organization for Women (NOW) (www.now.org) includes studies on key gender issues, including violence against women, abortion and reproductive rights, and sexual harassment.

Center for Individual Rights. The Center for Individual Rights is a think tank that advocates and defends *individual* over *group* rights. Its Web site (www.cir-usa.org) provides information about efforts to eliminate racial or gender quotas or preferences. The center frequently engages in litigation on behalf of individuals who have been denied employment or admission to universities based on their majority group status.

ABOUT THIS CHAPTER

The United States has a long history of protest. The nation was in fact born as a protest against the injustices of colonialism—against powerlessness and the lack of a "voice" in controlling its own affairs. Despite that heritage, America's women and racial minorities have had a long and continuing fight against the inequalities imposed on them by their nation's laws and customs.

In 1776 Abigail Adams wrote to her husband John, who was then a delegate to the Continental Congress, cautioning him and his fellow delegates that when framing the new nation's laws they should "Remember the Ladies. . . . Do not put such unlimited power into the hands of the Husbands."* The "Ladies" did not find their voice until 1920, when the Nineteenth Amendment finally guaranteed women the right to vote. And the struggle for sexual equality continues today.

In this chapter, we explored the struggles and triumphs of African Americans, Hispanics, Native Americans, and women in the United States, as well as some of

the continuing inequalities these groups suffer. Now that you have read it, you should be able to

- discuss the civil rights movement of the 1950s and 1960s and the changes that it brought about in the Constitution and laws of the United States
- describe the philosophy of nonviolent direct action advocated by Martin Luther King, Jr.
- discuss the constitutional controversy over "affirmative action"
- describe the separate Hispanic groups in America
- describe the history of U.S. governmental policies toward Native Americans
- describe economic inequality between the sexes and various theories purporting to explain sexual inequality
- describe the various forms of sexual harassment and their status under civil rights law
- describe the Supreme Court's reasoning in *Roe v. Wade* regarding the constitutionality of abortion, as well as the Court's current approach toward abortion laws in the states

DISCUSSION QUESTIONS

1. Identify the initial goal of the civil rights movement. Discuss the Supreme Court case that marked the first step in attaining that goal and the constitutional amendment upon which the civil rights movement based its arguments. Why was the Supreme Court unable to implement its decision by itself?
2. Identify the key provisions of the Civil Rights Act of 1964.
3. Describe *nonviolent direct action* as advocated by Martin Luther King, Jr., its political purpose, and factors important to its success.
4. Describe how King and his followers were instrumental in the passage of the Voting Rights Act of 1965 and the Civil Rights Act of 1968. Briefly describe the content of each act.
5. Describe the purpose of affirmative-action programs. How does affirmative action differ from "color-blind" standards? What is the constitutional status of affirmative-action programs?
6. Describe the separate experiences of various Hispanic groups in American society.
7. Describe the cycle of broken treaties with Native-American tribes. Describe the historical occurrences

* L. H. Butterfield, Marc Friedlander, and Mary-Jo Kline, eds., *The Book of Abigail and John* (Cambridge, MA.: Harvard University Press, 1975): 121.

of the Trail of Tears march, the battle at the Little Big Horn River, and the massacre at Wounded Knee Creek.

8. Discuss the "cultural" and "biological" explanations of male dominance in society. Describe some of the important landmarks for women's protest movements.

9. Define various forms of sexual harassment. What federal law has been interpreted to ban sexual harassment?

10. What did the U.S. Supreme Court decide in *Roe v. Wade?* What restrictions on abortion has the Court allowed?

Chapter 11

Poverty and Powerlessness

POVERTY AS POWERLESSNESS

Powerlessness is the inability to control the events that shape one's life. The poor lack economic resources and are hence largely dependent on others for the things they need. Their lack of power derives from their dependency. But powerlessness is also an attitude, a feeling that no matter what one does it will have little effect on one's life. An attitude of powerlessness reinforces the condition of powerlessness. Persistent poverty generates a lack of motivation and feelings of meaninglessness, hopelessness, distrust, and cynicism. Constant defeat causes many of the poor to retreat into a self-protective attitude characterized by indifference and a pervasive sense of futility.

The poor often feel **alienated**—separated from society—because of their lack of success in obtaining important life goals. Persons who are blocked consistently in their efforts to achieve life goals are most likely to express powerlessness and alienation. These attitudes in turn become barriers to effective self-help, independence, and self-respect.[1]

To be *both* black and poor in a predominantly white, affluent society often magnifies feelings of powerlessness and alienation. Social psychologists are not always certain about the processes by which social inequalities are perceived or how these perceptions influence attitudes and behaviors. But African-American psychologist Kenneth B. Clark has provided some interesting insights into "the psychology of the ghetto."[2]

Clark argues that human beings who live apart from the rest of society, who do not share in society's affluence, and who are not respected or granted the ordinary dignities and courtesy accorded to others will eventually begin to doubt their own worth. All human beings depend on their experiences with others for clues to how they should view and value themselves. Black children who consistently see whites in a superior position begin to question whether they, or their family, or blacks in general really deserve any more respect from the larger society than they receive. These doubts, Clark maintains, become the seeds of "a pernicious self- and group-hatred."[3]

self-hatred and self-doubt
victims of poverty begin to blame themselves and see themselves as inferior

But all human beings search for self-esteem. According to Clark, teenage inner-city males often pretend to have knowledge about illicit activities and to sexual experiences that they have not really had. Many use as their role models the petty criminals of the ghetto, with their colorful, swaggering style of cool bravado.

Clark believes that the explanation for violence and crime in the inner city lies in the conscious or unconscious belief of many young African Americans that they cannot win meaningful self-esteem through the avenues available to middle-class whites, so they turn to "hustling"—pimping, prostitution, gambling, or drug dealing. They are frequently scornful of what they consider the hypocrisy and dishonesty of the larger society. They point to corruption among respected middle-class whites, including the police force.

POVERTY IN THE UNITED STATES

How much poverty really exists in America? According to the U.S. Bureau of the Census, in 2000 there were about thirty-five million poor people (those below the official poverty level) in the United States, or approximately 12.5 percent of the population (see Figure 11-1). The official poverty level is derived by calculating the minimum cash income required to maintain families of different sizes. The dollar amounts change each year to take into account the effect of inflation.

official definition of poverty
government estimates each year of the minimum cash income required for families of various sizes to subsist

This official definition of poverty emphasizes *subsistence levels;* it seeks to describe poverty objectively as the lack of enough income to acquire the minimum necessities of life. Liberals frequently view the subsistence definition of poverty as insensitive to a variety of needs, including entertainment, recreation, and the relief of monotony. Items that were "luxuries" a generation ago are now considered "necessities." Liberals also note that the official definition *includes* cash income from welfare and Social Security. Without this government assistance, the number of poor would be higher.

liberal objections to official definition of poverty

Conservatives also challenge the official definition of poverty: It does not include the value of family assets. People (usually older people) who own their own houses and automobiles may have incomes below the poverty line yet not suffer any real hardship. (More than 50 percent of the official "poor" own their own homes, and more than 65 percent own automobiles.) Many persons who are ranked as poor do not think of themselves as

conservative objections to official definition of poverty

FIGURE 11-1

POVERTY IN THE UNITED STATES

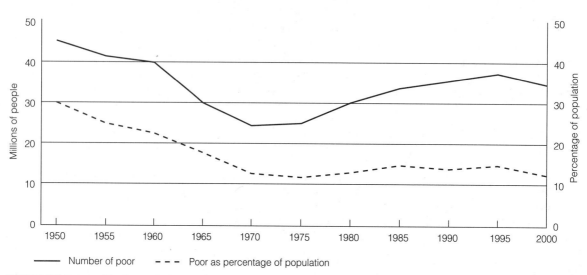

SOURCE: U.S. Bureau of the Census, *Current Population Reports* (Washington, D.C.: U.S. Government Printing Office).

"poor people"—students, for example. More important, the official definition of poverty *excludes* "in-kind" (noncash) benefits provided by government, benefits that include, for example, free medical care under Medicaid and Medicare, food stamps, public housing, and school lunches. If these benefits were "costed out" (that is, calculated as cash income), there might be fewer persons classified as poor.

IS THERE A CULTURE OF POVERTY?

the culture-of-poverty thesis
the idea that a lifestyle of poverty, alienation, and apathy is passed on from one generation to another

It is sometimes argued that the poor have a characteristic lifestyle or **culture of poverty** that assists them in adjusting to their world (see Focus, "Who Are the Poor?"). Like other aspects of culture, it is passed on to future generations, setting in motion a self-perpetuating cycle of poverty. The theory of the poverty cycle is as follows: Deprivation in one generation leads, through cultural impoverishment, indifference, apathy, or misunderstanding of their children's educational needs, to deprivation in the next generation. Lacking the self-respect that comes from earning an adequate living, some young men cannot sustain responsibilities of marriage, and so they hand down to their children the same burden of family instability and female-headed households that they themselves carried. Children born into a culture of alienation, apathy, and lack of motivation learn these attitudes themselves. Thus, the poor are prevented from exploiting any opportunities that are available to them.

Who Are the Poor?

Poverty occurs in many kinds of families and in all races and ethnic groups. However, some groups experience poverty in proportions that are greater than the national average. The following statistics indicate the percentage of Americans in various groups who were living below the poverty level in 1998 (see table).

Total population	12.7%
Husband-wife families	5.3
Families with female heads	29.9
White	10.5
African American	26.1
Hispanic	25.6
Over age 65	10.5
Under age 18	18.9

Poverty is most common among female-headed families. In 1998 the incidence of poverty among these families was 30 percent, compared with only 5 percent for married cou-ples. These women and their children constitute over two-thirds of all of the persons living in poverty in the United States. These figures describe the "fem-inization of poverty" in Amer-ica. Clearly, poverty is closely related to family structure. Today the disintegration of the traditional husband-wife family is the single most influential factor contributing to poverty.

Blacks experience poverty in much greater proportions than whites. Over the years, the poverty rate among blacks in the United States has been well over twice as high as the poverty rate among whites. Poverty among Hispanics is also significantly greater than among whites.

The aged in America experi-ence *less* poverty than younger people. The aged are not poor, despite the popularity of the phrase "the poor and the aged." The poverty rate for persons over sixty-five years of age is *below* the national aver-age. Moreover, the aged are much wealthier than younger age groups. They are more likely than younger people to own homes with paid-up mortgages. Medicare pays a large portion of their medical expenses. With fewer expenses, the aged, even with relatively smaller cash incomes, experi-ence poverty in a different fashion than a younger mother with children. Continuing in-creases in Social Security bene-fits over the years are largely responsible for this singular "victory" in the war against poverty.

Finally, we should note that about one of every five children in the United States lives in poverty.

POVERTY AS SUBCULTURE

It is probably more accurate to talk about a *subculture* of poverty. The prefix *sub* is used because most of the poor subscribe to the "middle-class American way of life," at least as a cultural ideal and even as a personal fantasy. Most poor people do not reject American culture but strive to adapt its values to the realities of economic deprivation and social disorganization in their own lives.

Another view of the culture of poverty emphasizes the **present-orientedness** of many poor people.[4] It is argued that the culture of poverty is produced pri-marily by present-orientedness rather than a lack of income or wealth. Individ-uals caught up in the culture of poverty are unable to plan for the future, to sacrifice immediate gratifications in favor of future ones, or to exercise the dis-cipline that is required to get ahead. It is true that some people experience poverty because of involuntary unemployment, prolonged illness, death of the

the culture of poverty as present-orientedness
the inability to plan or sacrifice for the future

breadwinner, or some other misfortune. But even when severe, this kind of poverty is not self-perpetuating. It ends once the external cause no longer exists. Other people will be poor no matter what their "external" circumstances are. They live in a culture of poverty that continues for generations because they are psychologically unable to provide for the future. Increased income is unlikely to change their way of life; the additional money will be spent quickly on nonessential or frivolous items. This culture of poverty may involve no more than a small portion of all families who live below the poverty line, but it generally continues regardless of what is done in the way of remedial action.[5]

POVERTY AS ECONOMIC DEPRIVATION

poverty
a result of current social and economic conditions, or parental transmission of values and beliefs

Opponents of the idea of a culture of **poverty** argue that this notion diverts attention from the *conditions* of poverty that foster family instability and present-orientedness. The question is really whether the conditions of poverty create a culture of poverty or vice versa. Reformers are likely to focus on the economic deprivation as the fundamental cause of the social pathologies that afflict the poor. They note that the idea of a culture of poverty can be applied only to groups who have lived in poverty for several generations. It is

Extreme poverty can also be found in rural America.

not relevant to those who have become poor during their lifetime because of sickness, accident, or old age. The cultural explanation basically involves *parental transmission of values and beliefs,* which in turn determines behavior of future generations. In contrast, the situational explanation of poverty involves social conditions—differences in financial resources—that operate directly to determine behavior. Perhaps the greatest danger in the idea of a culture of poverty is that poverty in this light can be seen as an unbreakable, puncture-proof cycle, which may lead to a relaxation of efforts to ameliorate the conditions of poverty. In other words, it is feared that the "culture of poverty" idea may become an excuse for inaction.

GOVERNMENT AND SOCIAL WELFARE

Public welfare has been a recognized responsibility of government in English-speaking countries for many centuries. As far back as the Poor Relief Act of 1601, the English Parliament provided workhouses for the "able-bodied poor" (the unemployed) and poorhouses for widows and orphans, the aged, and the handicapped. Today nearly one-third of the U.S. population receives some form of government benefit: Social Security, Medicare or Medicaid, disability insurance, unemployment compensation, government employee retirement, veterans' benefits, food stamps, school lunches, job training, public housing, and cash public assistance payments (see Table 11-1). Thus, the "welfare state" now encompasses a very large part of our society.[6]

SOCIAL INSURANCE

In the Social Security Act of 1935, the federal government undertook to establish a basic framework for social welfare policies at the federal, state, and local levels in America. The **social insurance** concept was designed to *prevent* poverty resulting from individual misfortune—unemployment, old age, death of the family breadwinner, or physical disability. Social insurance was based on the same notion as private insurance: the sharing of risks, the setting aside of money for a rainy day, and legal entitlement to benefits on reaching retirement or on occurrence of specific misfortunes. Social insurance was *not* to be charity or public assistance. Instead, it relied on people's (compulsory) financial contribution through payroll deductions to their own protection.

social insurance
compulsory savings for all with legal entitlement to benefits

The key feature of the Social Security Act is the Old-Age, Survivors, Disability Insurance program; this is a compulsory social insurance program financed by regular deductions from earnings, which gives individuals the legal right to benefit in the event that their income is reduced by old age, death of the head of the household, or permanent disability. It is not public charity but a way of compelling people to provide insurance against loss of income. Another feature of the Social Security Act was that it induced states to enact unemployment compensation programs. Unemployment compensation is also an *insurance* program, only in this case the costs are borne solely by the

major social insurance programs
Social Security

unemployment compensation

Medicare

TABLE 11-1

MAJOR GOVERNMENT SOCIAL INSURANCE AND PUBLIC ASSISTANCE PROGRAMS

Social Insurance Programs

Social Security	**Beneficiaries (millions)**
Retirement	30.6
Survivors	7.2
Disabled	6.1
Total	43.9
Unemployment Compensation	
Total	7.3

Public Assistance Programs

Cash Aid	**Beneficiaries (millions)**
Family assistance	12.6
SSI	6.9
General assistance	0.3
Medical Care	
Medicaid	41.3
Veterans	1.6
Maternal and child health services	13.0
Food Benefits	
Food stamps	26.8
School lunches	14.6
Women, infants, children	7.2
Nutrition for elderly	1.3
Housing Benefits	
Total	3.1
Education Aid	
Stafford Loans	3.7
Pell Grants	3.6
Head Start	0.7
Job Training	
Total	1.5

SOURCE: U.S. Bureau of the Census, *Statistical Abstract of the United States 1999* (Washington, D.C.: U.S. Government Printing Office, 1999): 121, 124, 389, 392.

employer. In 1965 Congress amended Social Security to add comprehensive health insurance for persons over sixty-five—Medicare. Medicare provided for prepaid hospital insurance for the aged under Social Security and for low-cost voluntary medical insurance for the same group under federal administration. Medicare, too, is based upon the insurance principle: Individuals pay for their medical insurance during their working years and enjoy its benefits after age sixty-five. Thus, the program resembles private medical hospital insurance, except that it is compulsory.

CROSS-NATIONAL PERSPECTIVE
Income of the Poor in Advanced Democracies

How does the United States compare to other nations in its distribution of income to its lowest income families? It is important to realize that *all* advanced industrialized democracies distribute income more equally than less-developed agricultural societies. As nations modernize and industrialize, the conditions of the poor improve and extremes of inequality are lessened.

But there is some evidence that the United States lags behind other advanced democracies in income equality. The figures in the table report the percentage of each nation's total income going to the lowest 20 percent of families. In the United States, in 1997, 4.7 percent of total income went to the lowest income group. Most other advanced democracies

managed to distribute larger shares of national income to their lowest income group. In

Japan, for example, the lowest income group received 8.7 percent of national income.

Percentage of total income received by lowest 20% of families	
Japan	8.7
Netherlands	8.2
Sweden	8.0
Belgium	7.9
Germany	7.0
Italy	6.8
Norway	6.2
Israel	6.0
United Kingdom	5.8
Canada	5.7
France	5.6
Denmark	5.4
Switzerland	5.2
United States	4.7

SOURCE: Data derived from the World Bank, *World Development Report 1997* (New York: Published for the World Bank by Oxford University Press, 1997).

PUBLIC ASSISTANCE

The distinction between the *social insurance* program and a *public assistance* (welfare) program is an important one that has on occasion become a major political issue. If the beneficiaries of a government program are required to have made contributions to it before claiming any of its benefits, and if they are entitled to the benefits regardless of their personal wealth, the program is said to be financed on the *social insurance* principle. If the program is financed out of general tax revenues, and if the recipients are required to show that they are poor before claiming its benefits, the program is said to be financed on the *public assistance* principle.

The purpose of public assistance is clearly *alleviative;* the idea is simply to provide a minimal level of subsistence to certain categories of needy persons. The federal government, under its Supplemental Security Income (SSI) program, directly aids three categories of recipients: the aged, the

social insurance versus public assistance

social insurance
contributions required

all are entitled to benefits

public assistance
financed out of tax revenues

benefits paid only to persons who are poor

major public assistance cash programs
SSI

TANF

general assistance

CASE STUDY

Senior Power

Senior citizens are the most politically powerful age group in the population. They constitute 28 percent of the voting-age population, but more important, because of their high voter turnout rates, they constitute over one-third of the voters on election day. Persons over sixty-five average a 68-percent turnout rate in presidential elections; this compares, for example, with a turnout rate of 34 percent for persons eighteen to twenty-one years old. In short, the voting power of senior citizens is twice that of young people. The American Association of Retired People (AARP) is the largest organized interest group in American politics and one of the most powerful in Washington. No elected officials can afford to offend the seniors, and seniors strongly support generous Social Security benefits.[a]

The Graying of America

The "baby boom" from 1945 to 1960 produced a large generation of people who crowded schools and colleges in the 1960s and 1970s and encountered stiff competition for jobs in the 1970s and 1980s. This baby-boom generation will be retiring beginning in 2010, and by 2030 they will constitute nearly 20 percent of the population (see the figure). Changes in lifestyle—less smoking, more exercise, better weight control—and medical advances may increase the aged population even more by extending life expectancies.

A Generational Compact?

Today's generation of workers is paying for the benefits of the last generation, and it is hoped that this generation's benefits will be financed by the next generation of workers. Taxing current workers to pay benefits to current retirees may be viewed as a *compact between generations*. Each generation of workers in effect agrees to pay benefits to an earlier generation of retirees, in the hope that the next generation will pay for their own retirement. But low birthrates (reducing the number of workers), longer life spans (increasing the number of retirees), and very generous benefits are straining workers' ability to pay. The generation compact is likely to break before today's younger workers reach retirement. Many of them, for good reason, have lost their confidence and trust in the system to support them in their old age.

The "Dependency Ratio"

Because current workers must pay for the benefits of current retirees and other beneficiaries, the *dependency ratio* becomes an important component of evaluating the future of Social Security. The dependency ratio for Social Security is the number of recipients in relation to the number of contributing workers. Americans are living longer, thereby increasing the dependency ratio. In the early years of Social Security, there were ten workers supporting each retiree—a dependency ratio of 10 to 1. But today, as the U.S. population grows older—because of lower birthrates and longer life spans—there are only three workers for each retiree, and by 2020 the dependency ratio will be two workers for each retiree. Virtually every family with two wage earners will be compelled to support one retiree!

Wealthy Retirees

Social Security benefits are paid to all eligible retirees, regardless of whatever other income they receive. There is no means test for benefits. The result is that large numbers of affluent Americans receive government checks each month. Of course, they paid into Social Security during their working years, and they can claim these checks as a legal "entitlement" under the insurance principle. But currently their benefits far exceed

[a]Susan MacManus, *Young versus Old* (Boulder, CO: Westview Press, 1996).

The Graying of America

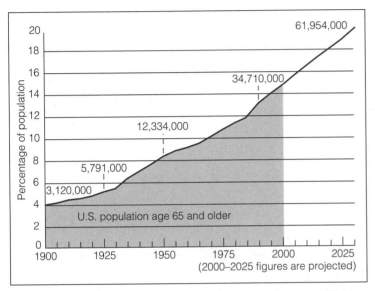

SOURCE: U.S. Bureau of the Census, *Statistical Abstract of the United States 1999* (Washington, D.C.: U.S. Government Printing Office, 1999): 25.

their previous payments. However, because the aged experience *less* poverty than today's workers (see Focus, "Who Are the Poor?") and possess considerably more wealth, Social Security benefits constitute a "negative" redistribution of income; that is, a transfer of income from poorer to richer people. The elderly are generally better off than the people supporting them!

"Saving" Social Security

The Social Security system appears to be adequately fi-nanced for the next several decades. (In 1983 a National Commission on Social Security Reform, appointed by President Reagan, recommended an increase in Social Security taxes and a gradual increase in the full retirement age from sixty-five to sixty-seven beginning in 2000. Congress adopted these recommendations.) But with the aging of the population and the resulting increases in the dependency ratio expected in the twenty-first century, Social Security will become a heavy burden on working Americans.

"Saving" Social Security is a popular political slogan in Washington. But agreement on exactly how to reform the system continues to evade lawmakers. In theory, Congress could reform Social Security by limiting COLAs to the true increases in the cost of living for retirees, or it could introduce means tests to deny benefits to high-income retirees. But, politically, these reforms are very unlikely. Yet another approach to reform is to allow the Social Security trust fund to invest in the private stock market with the expectation that stock values will increase over time. But if stock market investment decisions were made by the government itself, presumably the Social Security Administration, controversies would likely arise over these decisions. And critics object to the idea of the government making private investment decisions for Americans. Another reform frequently recommended is to allow American workers to deposit all or part of their Social Security payroll tax into an individual retirement account to buy securities of their own choosing. But such a plan would expose those individuals to the risk of bad investment decisions.

blind, and the disabled. The federal government, under its Temporary Assistance to Needy Families (TANF; formerly Aid to Families with Dependent Children) program, gives money to the states to assist them in providing welfare payments to families with children under eighteen. Welfare aid to persons who do not fall into any of these categories but who, for one reason or another, are poor is referred to as *general assistance* and is paid for entirely from state funds.

IN-KIND WELFARE BENEFITS

major public assistance in-kind programs

food stamps

school lunches

Medicaid

public housing

The federal government also provides many *in-kind (noncash) welfare benefits.* The Food Stamp program was begun in 1965; originally the poor were allowed to purchase food stamps at large discounts and use the stamps to buy food at stores; after 1977 the stamps were distributed free. Free school lunches (and in some cities breakfasts as well) are made available to children of the poor by federal payments to school districts. In 1965 Congress also authorized federal funds to enable states to guarantee medical services to all public assistance recipients. This program is known as Medicaid. Unlike Medicare, Medicaid is a welfare program designed for needy persons; no prior contributions are required, but recipients of Medicaid must be eligible for welfare assistance. In other words, they must be poor. Finally, the federal government assists in providing job training and low-cost public housing for the poor and educational programs for needy students.

WELFARE REFORM

entitlement

a guarantee of benefits to anyone who meets eligibility requirements set by law

In 1996 Congress passed and President Clinton signed a welfare reform act that ended the sixty-one-year-old guarantee of federal cash assistance to needy families with children. (The Social Security Act of 1935 had established Aid to Families with Dependent Children, AFDC, as a federal **"entitlement,"** a guarantee of benefits to anyone who meets eligibility requirements set by law.) The Welfare Reform Act replaced AFDC with a block grant of federal money to the states to assist them in providing their own cash welfare aid—TANF. States were given wide discretion to determine eligibility for cash assistance. But the focus of welfare reform was on "welfare to work"—moving welfare recipients off public aid and into jobs. Among major provisions of welfare reform:

WORK REQUIREMENTS   Adults receiving welfare benefits are now required to begin working within two years of receiving aid. States can exempt from this work requirement a parent of a child twelve months of age or younger.

RESTRICTIONS ON AID   TANF grant funds cannot be used for adults who have *received welfare for more than five years,* although state and local funds can be used. States can exempt up to 20 percent of their caseload from this

Welfare reform, officially Temporary Assistance to Needy Families, was passed by Congress in 1996, and its provisions took effect in 1997. Shortly thereafter, the Clinton Administration as well as Republicans in Congress were declaring welfare reform a success.

Declining Welfare Rolls

Indeed, the number of welfare recipients in the nation has dropped by over half over the last several years (see figure). Today, only about three percent of Americans are receiving cash welfare benefits—the smallest proportion since 1970. Perhaps some of this decline is attributable to the strong growth of the economy in the late 1990s. Declines in welfare rolls actually began *before* enactment of welfare reform. Some states initiated their own reforms under "waivers" from the federal government even before Congress passed welfare reform.

Continuing Welfare Needs

Yet, nearly everyone agrees that getting people off welfare rolls and onto payrolls is the main goal of reform, there are major obstacles to the achievement of this goal. First of all, a substantial portion (perhaps 25 to 40

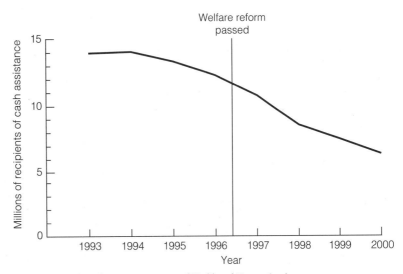

EVALUATING WELFARE REFORM

SOURCE: Data from the U.S. Department of Health and Human Services.

percent) of long-term welfare recipients have handicaps—physical disabilities, chronic illnesses, learning disabilities, alcohol or drug abuse problems—that prevent them from holding a full-time job. Many long-term recipients have no work experience (perhaps 40 percent), and two-thirds of them did not graduate from high school. Almost half have three or more children, making day-care arrangements a major

obstacle. It is unlikely that any counseling, education, job training, or job placement programs advocated by liberals could ever succeed in getting these people into productive employment. Policy makers argue whether or not there are five million jobs available to unskilled mothers, but even if there are such jobs available, they would be low-paying, minimum-wage jobs that would not lift them out of poverty.[a]

[a]Mary Jo Bain and David T. Ellwood, *Welfare Realities: From Rhetoric to Reform* (Cambridge, MA: Harvard University Press, 1994).

time limit. States can also opt to impose a shorter time limit on benefits. None of the funds can be used for adults who do not work *after receiving welfare for two years*. In addition, states will have the option to:

> Deny welfare assistance to children born to welfare recipients. Deny welfare to unwed parents under age eighteen unless they live with an adult and attend school.

MEDICAID   States will be required to continue to offer Medicaid coverage for one year to welfare recipients who lose ther welfare benefits because of increased earnings.

STATE FLEXIBILITY   States are permitted to align their food stamp program with other revamped welfare programs. They can establish a single set of eligibility and work requirements for food stamps, welfare checks, and other welfare programs.

HOMELESSNESS IN AMERICA

homeless
persons living in streets and public places

persons accepting housing in public shelters

The most visible social welfare problem in America is the nation's homeless "street people," suffering exposure, alcoholism, drug abuse, and chronic mental illness while wandering the streets of the nation's larger cities.

The term *homeless* is used to describe many different situations.[7] There are the street people who sleep in subways, bus stations, parks, or the streets. Some of them are temporarily traveling in search of work; some have left home for a few days or are youthful runaways; others have roamed the streets for months or years. There are the sheltered homeless who obtain housing in shelters operated by local governments or private charities. As the number of shelters has grown in recent years, the number of sheltered homeless has also grown. But most of the sheltered homeless come from other housing, not the streets. These are people who have been recently evicted from rental units or have previously lived with family or friends. These sheltered homeless often include families with children; the street homeless are virtually all single persons.

STREET PEOPLE

The ranks of the street homeless expand and contract with the seasons.[8] These homeless are difficult subjects for systematic interviewing; many do not wish to admit to alcoholism, drug dependency, or mental illness. (The television networks often sensationalize the topic, exaggerate the number of homeless, and incorrectly portray the homeless as middle-class white families victimized by economic misfortune and the high cost of housing.) Serious studies indicate that close to half of the street homeless are chronic alcohol and drug abusers, and an additional one-fourth to one-third are mentally ill.[9] The alcohol and drug abusers, especially "crack" cocaine users, are the fastest-growing groups among the homeless. Moreover, the alcohol and drug abusers and mentally ill among the homeless are likely to remain on the streets for long periods of time. Among the 15 to 25 percent of the homeless who are neither mentally ill nor dependent on alcohol or drugs, homelessness is more likely to be temporary.

Deinstitutionalization

Deinstitutionalization was a reform advanced by mental health care professionals and social welfare activists in the 1960s and 1970s to release chronic mental patients from state-run mental hospitals. It was widely recognized that aside from drugs, no psychiatric therapies have much success among the long-term mentally ill. Drug therapies can be administered on an outpatient basis; they usually do not require hospitalization. So it was argued that no one could be rightfully kept in a mental institution against his or her will; people who had committed no crimes and who posed no danger to others should be released. The nation's mental hospitals were emptied of all but the most dangerous mental patients. The population of mental hospitals declined from about 500,000 in 1960 to about 100,000 in 1990.

deinstitutionalization
release of mental patients who pose no threat to others

Homeless families seek temporary shelter, and sometimes live in their cars; others sleep in the streets.

DECRIMINALIZATION

decriminalization
abolishing confinement for vagrancy or public intoxication of persons who pose no danger to others

Vagrancy (homelessness) and public intoxication have been **decriminalized**. Involuntary confinement has been abolished for the mentally ill and for the substance abuser unless such a person is adjudged in court to be "a danger to himself or others." This means a person must commit a serious act of violence before the courts will intervene. For many homeless this means the freedom to "die with their rights on." The homeless are victimized by cold, exposure, hunger, the availability of alcohol and illegal drugs, and violent street crimes perpetrated against them, in addition to the ravages of illness itself.

OUTSIDE THE SOCIAL WELFARE SYSTEM

Social welfare programs are frequently irrelevant to the plight of the chronic mentally ill persons and alcohol and drug abusers in the streets. Most are "uncooperative"; they are isolated from society; they have no family members, doctors, or counselors to turn to for help. The nation's vast social welfare system provides them little help. They may lose their Social Security, welfare, and disability checks because they have no permanent address. They cannot handle forms, appointments, or interviews; the welfare bureaucracy is intimidating. Welfare workers seldom provide the "aggressive care management" and mental health care these people need.

ON THE WEB

EXPLORING POVERTY AND POWERLESSNESS

Many government agencies as well as private organizations maintain Web sites devoted to poverty and social welfare issues.

U.S. Department of Health and Human Services. The U.S. Department of Health and Human Services Web site (www.dhhs.gov) contains a wide variety of information on federal social welfare programs. The HHS site also includes a "health finder" gateway to health and human services information. In addition, the federal government's search engine for statistics on the Internet, "Fedstats" (www.fedstats.gov), provides an alphabetical index that includes many social welfare topics, including poverty, children, health care, HIV/AIDS, etc.

Social Security Administration. The Social Security Administration maintains a sophisticated Web site,

"Social Security Online" (www.ssa.gov), that assists users in estimating their own future Social Security benefits. It also explains the Social Security, Supplemental Security Income, and Medicare programs and their benefits.

Children's Defense Fund. The Children's Defense Fund is one of the more active interest groups lobbying in Washington on behalf of "the needs of the poor, minorities, children, and those with disabilities." Its Web site (www.childrensdefense.org) describes current issues and legislation pending in Congress affecting children and the poor.

American Medical Association. The American Medical Association is the leading organization representing the nation's physicians. Its Web site (www.ama-assn.org) includes press releases, policy statements, legislative positions, information for medical consumers, and access to the prestigious *Journal of the American Medical Association.*

Institute for Research on Poverty. The Institute for Research on Poverty at the University of Wisconsin is one of the nation's leading research centers focusing on the causes of poverty. Its Web site (www.ssc.wisc.edu/irp) provides up-to-date information on the characteristics of the nation's poverty population and changes over time in the poverty status of individuals and families.

American Association of Retired Persons. The American Association of Retired Persons (AARP) is the nation's largest interest group, with nearly forty million members. Its Web site (www.aarp.org) presents its strongly held views about the continuation and expansion of benefits for the elderly under Social Security and Medicare.

ABOUT THIS CHAPTER

Captain John Smith's ultimatum to his starving band of settlers in Jamestown in 1609 that "he who would not work must not eat" is probably the first recorded American welfare policy statement. It was not until the western frontier had finally closed and the Great Depression of the 1930s had reduced many of the prosperous to the ranks of the paupers that there was any discernible change in the American attitude toward poverty. When poverty exists in the midst of plenty, it is more difficult for the poor to bear.

In this chapter, we have explored various definitions of poverty, as well as some recent efforts to lift the poor from their position of powerlessness. Now that you have read it, you should be able to

- discuss various definitions of poverty and describe the characteristics of the poor
- discuss the theory of a subculture of poverty
- describe the relationship between poverty and powerlessness
- discuss how government policies might contribute to poverty
- identify major social insurance and public assistance programs and distinguish between the two types of programs

- describe the changing age composition of the American population and how this will affect Social Security in the future
- discuss the causes of homelessness

DISCUSSION QUESTIONS

1. Discuss the criteria used by the U.S. Social Security Administration to define the poverty line. Describe the emphasis of this official definition of poverty on subsistence levels. What are the criticisms of this definition of poverty?
2. Identify the groups of people who experience poverty in greater proportions than the national average.
3. Discuss the relationship between poverty and feelings of powerlessness. What are the feelings of the poor about themselves? What are their attitudes toward the larger society? Describe some of the forms of personal adjustment to poverty and the effect of poverty and discrimination on family life.
4. What is meant by the expression *culture of poverty?* Comment on the view of the culture of poverty as "present-orientedness." What are the policy implications of a culture of poverty? Discuss the arguments of those who oppose the idea of a culture of poverty.
5. Differentiate between social insurance programs and public assistance programs in terms of who pays, who benefits, and when they benefit. Give examples of each type of program and specify the type of strategy each expresses.
6. Why might government programs designed to remedy poverty actually contribute to continuing poverty? Discuss the criticisms of current public assistance programs.
7. What changes are occurring in the age composition of the nation's population? What do these changes mean for Social Security? How can the Social Security program be preserved?
8. What "reforms" may have contributed to homelessness in America?

Chapter 12

Power, Crime, and Violence

POWER AND INDIVIDUAL FREEDOM

For centuries people have wrestled with the question of balancing social power against individual freedom. How far can individual freedom be extended without undermining the stability of a society, threatening the safety of others, and risking anarchy? The early English political philosopher **Thomas Hobbes** (1588–1679) believed that society must establish a powerful "Leviathan"—the state—in order to curb the savage instincts of human beings. A powerful authority in society was needed to prevent people from attacking each other for personal gain—"war of every man against every man" in which "notions of right and wrong, justice and injustice, have no place." According to Hobbes, without law and order there is no real freedom. The fear of death and destruction permeates every act of life: "Every man is enemy to every man"; "Force and fraud are the two cardinal virtues"; and "The life of man [is] solitary, poor, nasty, brutish, and short." Freedom, then, is not the absence of law and order. On the contrary, law and order are required if there is to be any freedom in society at all.[1]

Thomas Hobbes
Freedom is not the absence of law; law is required to protect individual freedom. Governments are formed for collective self-protection.

THE PROBLEM OF CRIME

Crime rates are the subject of a great deal of popular discussion. Very often they are employed to express the degree of social disorganization or even the

crime rates
reported serious crimes per 100,000 people

effectiveness of law enforcement agencies. Crime rates are based on the Federal Bureau of Investigation's *Uniform Crime Reports,* but the FBI reports themselves are based on figures supplied by state and local police agencies. The FBI has established a uniform classification of the number of serious crimes per 100,000 people that are known to the police—murder and non-negligent manslaughter, forcible rape, robbery, aggravated assault, burglary, larceny, and theft, including auto theft. These serious crimes are totaled and divided by the population in order to ascertain crime rates. But these crimes are only a small portion of all crimes (see Focus, "It's a Real Crime!").

We should be cautious in interpreting official crime rates. They are really a function of several factors: the willingness of victims to report crime to the police, the adequacy of the system for reporting and tabulating crime, and the amount of crime itself.

FBI classification, serious crimes

criminal homicide

forcible rape

robbery

aggravated assault

burglary

larceny

auto theft

CHANGES IN CRIME RATES

The official FBI crime rate rose dramatically in the United States between 1960 and 1990. Increases occurred in both violent crime—murder, rape, robbery, and assault (see Table 12-1)—and property crime—burglary, larceny, and theft. Certainly some of the increase was a result of improved reporting. As more people insured their property, they filed more police reports in order to make insurance claims. The introduction of the 911 emergency phone number across the United States may also have increased reported crimes. The introduction of computers and sophisticated police data collection systems may also have contributed to the increases. But unquestionably crime itself also rose.

Since peaking in the early 1990s, however, crime rates have actually declined (see Figure 12-1). Law enforcement officials attribute recent successes in crime fighting to police "crackdowns," more aggressive "community policing," and longer prison sentences for repeat offenders, including "three strikes you're out" laws. (All are discussed later in this chapter.) In support of

TABLE 12-1

CRIME RATES
Offenses Reported to Police per 100,000 Population

	1960	1970	1980	1985	1990	1999
Violent Crimes	160	360	581	557	732	524
Murder	5	8	10	8	9	6
Forcible Rape	9	18	36	37	41	33
Robbery	60	172	244	209	257	150
Assault	85	162	291	303	424	336
Property Crimes	1,716	3,599	5,319	4,651	4,903	3,742

SOURCE: Federal Bureau of Investigation, *Uniform Crime Reports* (annual).

FOCUS

It's a Real Crime!

Crimes are often divided into two categories: felonies—crimes punishable by more than one year in prison—and misdemeanors—crimes punishable by less than one year. Most people who are convicted and incarcerated for a felony are sent to state prisons (or federal prison for federal felonies), while most people jailed for misdemeanors serve their sentences in city or county jails, which also hold people awaiting trial. All of the FBI uniform classified serious crimes are felonies; most other nonserious crimes are misdemeanors, although federal and most state laws define the sale and manufacturing of illegal drugs as felonies.

SERIOUS CRIMES
(crimes used to calculate crime rates)

Violent

Criminal Homicide: (a) murder and nonnegligent manslaughter (the willful killing of one human being by another); deaths caused by negligence, attempts to kill, assaults to kill, suicides, accidental deaths, and justifiable homicides are excluded; (b) manslaughter by negligence (the killing of another person through gross negligence; traffic fatalities are excluded)

Forcible Rape: the carnal knowledge of a female forcibly and against her will; includes rapes by force and attempts to rape, but excludes statutory offenses (no force used and victim under age of consent)

Robbery: the taking or attempting to take anything of value from the care, custody, or control of a person or persons by force or threat of force and/or by putting the victim in fear

Aggravated Assault: an unlawful attack by one person upon another to inflict severe bodily injury; usually involves use of a weapon or other means likely to produce death or great bodily harm (simple assaults are excluded)

Property

Burglary: unlawful entry, completed or attempted, of a structure to commit a felony or theft

Larceny-Theft: unlawful taking, completed or attempted, of property from another's possession that does not involve force, threat of force, or fraud; examples include thefts of bicycles or car accessories, shoplifting, pocket-picking

Motor Vehicle Theft: theft or attempted theft of self-propelled motor vehicle that runs on the surface and not on rails; excluded are thefts of boats, construction equipment, airplanes, and farming equipment

Arson: willful burning or attempt to burn a dwelling, public building, personal property, etc.

---

this claim, these officials observe that the greatest reductions in crime have occurred in the nation's largest cities, especially those such as New York City that have adopted tougher law enforcement practices. However, the booming economy of the 1990s with low unemployment may also have contributed to the decline in crime. It is by no means certain that crime rates will not rise again in future years.

VICTIMIZATION

How much crime is there in America today? We know that the FBI official crime rate understates the real amount of crime. Many crimes are not reported to the police and therefore cannot be counted in the official crime

Other Crimes

Simple Assaults: assaults and attempted assaults involving no weapon and not resulting in serious injury

Forgery and Counterfeiting: making, altering, uttering, or possessing, with intent to defraud, anything false in the semblance of that which is true

Fraud: fraudulent obtaining of money or property by false pretense; included are confidence games and bad checks

Embezzlement: misappropriation of money or property entrusted to one's care or control

Stolen Property: buying, receiving, and possessing stolen property, including attempts

Vandalism: willful destruction or defacement of public or private property without consent of the owner

Weapons: carrying, possessing, etc.; all violations of regulations or statutes controlling the carrying, using, possessing, furnishing, and manufacturing of deadly weapons or silencers (attempts are included)

Prostitution and Commercialized Vice: sex offenses such as prostitution and procuring

Sex Offenses: statutory rape and offenses against common decency, morals, etc.; excludes forcible rape and prostitution and commercial vice

Drug Abuse: unlawful possession, sale, use, growing, and manufacturing of drugs

Gambling

Offenses against the Family and Children: nonsupport, neglect, desertion, or abuse of family and children

Driving under the Influence

Liquor Laws: state/local liquor law violations, except drunkenness and driving under the influence

Drunkenness

Disorderly Conduct: breach of the peace

Vagrancy: vagabonding, begging, loitering, etc.

All Other Offenses: all violations of state/local laws, except as above and traffic offenses

Curfew and Loitering Laws: persons under age eighteen

Runaways: persons under age eighteen

SOURCE: Federal Bureau of Investigation, 1999.

rate. In an effort to learn the real amount of crime in the nation, the U.S. Justice Department regularly surveys a national sample of people, asking whether they have been a victim of a crime during the past year.[2] These surveys reveal that the **victimization rate** is many times greater than the official crime rate. The number of forcible rapes is three to five times greater than the number reported to police, the number of unreported burglaries is three times greater, and the number of robberies is over twice that of the reported rate. Only auto theft and murder statistics are reasonably accurate, indicating that most people call the police when their car is stolen or when someone is murdered (see Cross-National Perspective, "Murder and Homicide").

Why do people fail to report crime to the police? The most common reason interviewees give is the feeling that police cannot be effective in dealing with the crime. Other reasons include the feeling that the crime is "a private

victimization rates

national survey responses to the question of whether one has been the victim of a crime in the past year

FIGURE 12-1

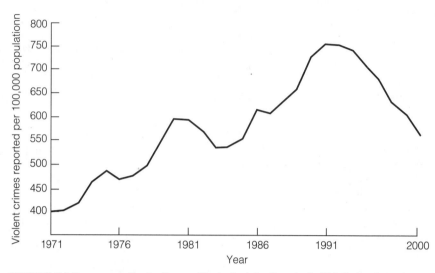

Violent Crime Rate

SOURCES: U.S. Department of Justice, Bureau of Justice Statistics, *Sourcebook of Criminal Justice Statistics*, 1997; Federal Bureau of Investigation, *Uniform Crime Reports*, 1999.

matter" or that the victim does not want to harm the offender. Fear of reprisal is mentioned much less frequently, usually in cases of assaults and family crimes.

THE CONSTITUTIONAL RIGHTS OF DEFENDANTS

Society needs the protection of police. But it is equally important in a free society to protect individuals *from* the police. Arbitrary searches and arrests, imprisonment without trial, forced confessions, beatings and torture, secret trials, excessive punishments, and other human rights violations are all too common throughout the world. The U.S. Constitution—especially the Fourth, Fifth, Sixth, and Eighth Amendments (see Table 12-2)—limits the powers of police and protects the rights of accused persons.[3]

GUARANTEE OF THE WRIT OF HABEAS CORPUS

habeas corpus
police may not hold a defendant without showing cause before a judge

An ancient right in English common law is the right to obtain a writ of **habeas corpus,** a court order directing police who are holding a person in custody to bring the prisoner into court to explain the reasons for the confinement. Police must bring held persons before a judge as soon as possible or release them upon their written pledge to appear in court. If a judge finds

TABLE 12-2

CONSTITUTIONAL LIMITS ON POLICE POWERS

Criminal Justice Process	Individual Rights
Investigation by law enforcement officers 　Expectation that police act lawfully	Fourth Amendment: Protection against unreasonable searches and seizures 　Warranted searches for sworn "probable cause"; exceptions: consent searches, safety searches, car searches, and searches incident to a valid arrest; evidence "in plain view" may be seized Fifth Amendment: Protection against self-incrimination 　Miranda rules
Arrest 　Arrests based on warrants issued by judges and magistrates 　Arrests based on crimes committed in the presence of a law enforcement official 　Arrests for "probable cause"	Habeas Corpus 　Police holding a person in custody must bring the person before a judge with cause to believe that a crime was committed and that the prisoner committed it
Hearing and bail 　Preliminary hearing where prosecutor presents testimony that a crime was committed and probable cause for charging the accused	Eighth Amendment: No excessive bail 　Defendant considered innocent until proven guilty; release on bail and amount of bail depends on seriousness of crime, trustworthiness of defendant, and safety of community
Indictment 　Prosecutor, or a grand jury in federal cases, issues formal document naming the accused and specifying the charges	Fifth Amendment: Grand jury (federal) 　Federal prosecutors (but not necessarily state prosecutors) must convince a grand jury that a reasonable basis exists to believe that the defendant committed a crime and that he or she should be brought to trial
Arraignment 　Judge reads indictment to the accused and ensures that the accused understands charges and rights and has counsel 　Judge asks defendant to choose a plea: guilty, *nolo contendere* (no contest), or not guilty; if defendant pleads guilty or no contest, a trial is not necessary and defendant proceeds to sentencing	Sixth Amendment: Right to counsel 　Begins in investigation stage, when officials become "accusatory," extends throughout criminal justice process 　Free counsel for indigent defendants
Trial 　Impartial judge presides as prosecuting and defense attorneys present witnesses and evidence relevant to guilt or innocence of defendant and make arguments to the jury; jury deliberates in secret and issues a verdict	Sixth Amendment: Right to a fair, speedy and public trial 　Impartial jury 　Right to confront witnesses 　Right to compel favorable witnesses to testify Fourth Amendment: Exclusionary rule 　Illegally obtained evidence cannot be used against defendant
Sentencing 　If the defendant is found not guilty, the process ends; defendants who plead guilty or no contest and defendants found guilty by jury are sentenced by fine, imprisonment, or both by the judge	Eighth Amendment: Protection against cruel or unusual punishment
Appeal 　Defendants found guilty may appeal to higher courts for reversal of verdict or a new trial based on errors made anywhere in the process	Fifth Amendment: Protection against double jeopardy 　Government cannot try a defendant again for the same offense

The U.S. Constitution limits the powers of police and protects the rights of accused persons. Here, a Los Angeles police officer frisks teenagers in a lineup along Hollywood Boulevard.

that the prisoner is being unlawfully detained, or that there is not sufficient evidence that a crime has been committed or that the prisoner committed it, the judge orders the prisoner's immediate release.

PROHIBITION OF BILLS OF ATTAINDER AND OF EX POST FACTO LAWS

bill of attainder
a legislative act that inflicts punishment without a trial

ex post facto law
making an act criminal after it is committed or retroactively increasing punishment

Protection against bills of attainder and against ex post facto laws was, like the guarantee of habeas corpus, considered so fundamental to individual liberty that it was included in the original text of the Constitution. A **bill of attainder** is a legislative act that inflicts punishment without a judicial trial. An **ex post facto law** is a retroactive criminal law that works to the detriment of the accused—for example, a law that makes an act a criminal one *after* the act is committed, or a law that increases the punishment for a crime and applies it *retroactively.*

PROHIBITION OF "UNREASONABLE" SEARCHES AND SEIZURES

unreasonable search
search without lawful warrant by judge, unless "incident to a lawful arrest"

The Fourth Amendment provides: "The right of the people to be secure in their persons, houses, papers, and effects, against unreasonable searches and seizures, shall not be violated, and no warrants shall issue, but upon probable

CROSS-NATIONAL PERSPECTIVE

Murder and Homicide

The United States is one of the more violent societies in the world. Crimes of violence—murder, homicide, rape, robbery, and assault—appear to be more common in the United States than in other advanced nations. Indeed, in acts of violence per capita, the United States resembles many troubled, less-developed nations.

The murder rate in the United States is about twice as high as that in most European nations and almost ten times higher than Japan's (see table). It is little wonder that many Japanese consider the United States a very dangerous place to visit. Victimization surveys, reporting the percent of respondents who say they have been victims of a crime in the last year, appear to confirm that the United States is the most crime-ridden of the advanced nations of the world. Over three times as many Americans as Japanese report that they have been victimized by crime. There are more people behind bars in the United States than in any other nation. With nearly one million prisoners, the nation's incarceration rate (prisoners in relation to the population) is over four times higher than other advanced nations.

	Victimization rate*		Murder rate†		Incarceration rate‡
United States	28.8	United States	9.4	United States	426
Canada	28.1	Sweden	7.2	United Kingdom	97
Australia	27.8	Canada	5.5	Germany	85
Netherlands	26.8	France	4.6	France	81
Spain	24.6	Australia	4.5	Spain	76
Germany	21.9	Germany	4.2	Finland	73
France	19.4	Belgium	2.8	Switzerland	73
United Kingdom	19.4	Spain	2.3	Australia	72
Belgium	17.7	Switzerland	2.3	Denmark	68
Norway	16.5	Italy	2.2	Belgium	65
Finland	15.9	Norway	2.0	Italy	60
Switzerland	15.6	United Kingdom	2.0	Norway	48
Japan	9.3	Japan	1.2	Japan	45

*Percentage of population who say they have been victims of a crime in the last year.
†Murders reported to the police per 100,000 population.
‡Prisoners per 100,000 population.
SOURCES: Data from Jan J. M. van Dijk, *Experience of Crime Across the World,* 2nd ed. (Netherlands: Klower, 1991); and Andrew J. Shapiro, *We're Number One* (New York: Vintage Books, 1992).

cause, supported by oath or affirmation, and particularly describing the place to be searched, and the persons or things to be seized." The requirement that the things to be seized must be described in the warrant is meant to prevent "fishing expeditions" into an individual's home and personal effects on the possibility that some evidence of unknown illegal activity might crop up. Exceptions to the requirement for a warrant are made if the search is: "incident to a lawful arrest," for the safety of police officers, for the preservation of evidence in danger of being immediately destroyed, or with the consent of the suspect. Indeed, most police searches today take place without a warrant under one or another of these exceptions. A "lawful arrest" can be made by the police if they have "probable cause" to believe a person has committed a crime; "probable cause" has been very loosely defined by the courts.

FREEDOM FROM SELF-INCRIMINATION

freedom from self-incrimination
no physical or psychological force can be used to obtain a confession or incriminating evidence from a defendant

Although the Fifth Amendment establishes a number of procedural guarantees, perhaps the most widely quoted clause of that amendment guarantees that no person "shall be compelled in any criminal case to be a witness against himself." The sentence "I refuse to answer that question on the ground that it might tend to incriminate me" is, today, a household expression. Freedom from self-incrimination has its origins in English resistance against torture and confession. It now embodies the ideas that individuals should not be forced to contribute to their own prosecution and that the burden of proof of guilt is on the state. The constitutional protection against self-incrimination applies not only to accused persons in their own trials but also to witnesses testifying in any public proceedings, including criminal trials of other persons, civil suits, congressional hearings, or other investigations. The silence of an accused person cannot be interpreted as guilt; the burden of proving guilt rests with the prosecution.

GUARANTEE OF A FAIR JURY TRIAL

fair jury trial
speedy

public

impartial

Trial by jury is guaranteed in both the original text of the Constitution and the Sixth Amendment: "In all criminal prosecutions, the accused shall enjoy the right to a speedy and public trial, by an impartial jury . . . and to be informed of the nature and cause of the accusation; to be confronted with the witnesses against him; to have compulsory process for obtaining witnesses in his favor. . . ." The requirement of a *speedy* trial protects the accused from long pretrial waits; but the accused may ask for postponements in order to prepare a defense. A *public* trial prevents secret proceedings, and *impartial* means that each juror must be able to judge the case objectively. Discrimination in the selection of the jury is forbidden. The guarantee of a fair trial can be violated if sensational pretrial publicity or an unruly courtroom hinders the jury from making an unbiased verdict. By tradition, a jury consisted of twelve persons, and the vote of the jurors had to be unanimous. This is still the requirement in most cases (and in all cases where the death penalty is possible), but recently the Supreme Court indicated that unanimity might not be required in some cases and six-person juries are also acceptable.

twelve-person unanimous jury not required in all cases

burden of proof on prosecution
"beyond reasonable doubt"

*The **burden of proof** rests with the prosecution.* It is up to the prosecution to convince a jury "beyond reasonable doubt" that the accused is guilty. Witnesses must appear in person against the accused. The accused or the counsel for the accused has the right to cross-examine those witnesses and may present witnesses on behalf of his or her own case. The accused may even obtain a "summons" to compel people to testify at the trial. If a guilty verdict is rendered, the defendant may appeal any errors in the trial to a higher court.

Protection against Double Jeopardy

The Fifth Amendment states: "Nor shall any person be subject for the same offense to be twice put in jeopardy of life or limb. . . ." Once a person has been tried for a particular crime and the trial has ended in a decision of not guilty, that person cannot be tried again for the same crime. However, this right does not prevent a new trial if the jury cannot agree on a verdict (a "hung jury") or if the verdict is reversed by an appeal to a higher court because of a procedural error. Moreover, an individual may be tried by federal and state courts on charges stemming from the same act. For example, in the well-publicized case involving Rodney King in 1992, in which police officers were videotaped beating King, a California jury found the officers *not* guilty of assault, but later the U.S. Justice Department won convictions against the officers in a federal court for violating King's civil rights. Moreover, a verdict of guilt or innocence in a *criminal* trail does not prevent victims (plaintiffs) from suing the accused (defendants) for damages in a *civil* trial. For example, O. J. Simpson was found not guilty of murder in a criminal trial but later found to be responsible for the deaths of two people in a civil trial. Civil courts, of course, can only assess monetary damages; they cannot impose criminal penalties.

no double jeopardy
if found not guilty, a person cannot be tried again for the same crime

Protection against Excessive Bail and Cruel and Unusual Punishments

Arrested persons are considered innocent until tried and found guilty. They are entitled to go free prior to trial unless their freedom would unreasonably endanger society or unless there is reason to believe that they would not appear for trial. **Bail** is supposed to ensure that the accused will appear. Bail may be denied for major crimes, but most accused persons are entitled to be released on bail pending their trial. The Eighth Amendment states that bail must not be "excessive," although there are no fixed standards for determining what "excessive" is. It also prohibits "cruel and unusual punishments," but it does not define this phrase.

bail
money held by court to ensure that defendant will appear for trial

The Right to Counsel

The Sixth Amendment states: "In all criminal prosecutions, the accused shall enjoy . . . the assistance of counsel for his defense." In a series of cases in the 1960s, the Supreme Court, under the leadership of Chief Justice Earl Warren, greatly strengthened the Sixth Amendment's guarantee of the right to counsel:

right to counsel
the right to an attorney in all criminal cases

right to free counsel for indigent defendants

counsel provided at beginning of investigation

defendants must be informed of rights upon arrest

- *Gideon v. Wainwright* (1963)—Ruling that equal protection under the Fourteenth Amendment requires that free legal counsel be appointed for all indigent defendants in all criminal cases.

- *Escobedo v. Illinois* (1964)—Ruling that a suspect is entitled to confer with counsel as soon as police investigation focuses on him or her, or once "the process shifts from investigatory to accusatory."
- *Miranda v. Arizona* (1966)—Ruling that police, before questioning a suspect, must inform the suspect of all his or her constitutional rights, including the right to counsel, appointed free if necessary, and the right to remain silent (see Figure 12-2). Although the suspect may knowingly waive these rights, the police cannot question anyone who at any point asks for a lawyer or indicates "in any manner" that he or she does not wish to be questioned. If the police commit an error in these procedures, the accused goes free, regardless of the evidence of guilt.

THE EXCLUSIONARY RULE

The exclusionary rule prevents illegally obtained evidence from being used in a criminal case. The rule, unique to the courts in the United States, was adopted by the U.S. Supreme Court in *Mapp v. Ohio* in 1961. Although illegally seized evidence may prove the guilt of the accused, it cannot be used in court, and the accused may go free because the police committed a procedural error.

Many trial proceedings today are not concerned with the guilt or innocence of the accused, but instead center on possible procedural errors by police or prosecutors. If the defendant's attorney can show that an error was committed, the defendant goes free, regardless of his or her guilt or innocence. Supreme Court Justice Felix Frankfurter wrote many years ago: "The

FIGURE 12-2

THE "MIRANDA CARD"

Used by San Francisco police to inform suspects of their rights at the time of arrest.

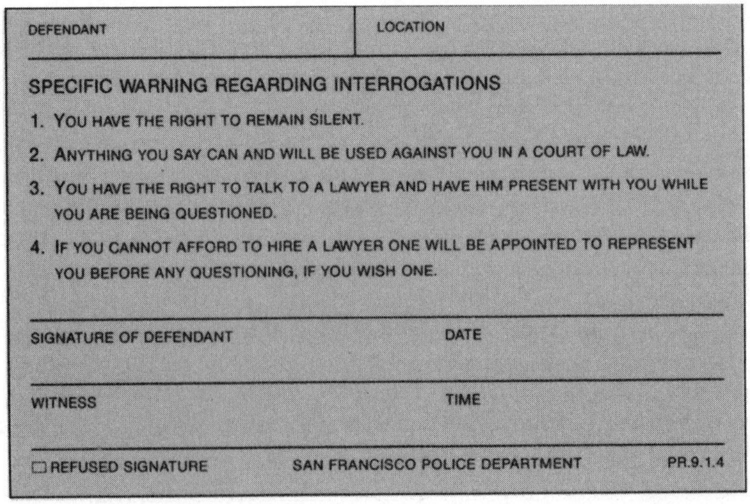

DEFENDANT	LOCATION

SPECIFIC WARNING REGARDING INTERROGATIONS

1. YOU HAVE THE RIGHT TO REMAIN SILENT.
2. ANYTHING YOU SAY CAN AND WILL BE USED AGAINST YOU IN A COURT OF LAW.
3. YOU HAVE THE RIGHT TO TALK TO A LAWYER AND HAVE HIM PRESENT WITH YOU WHILE YOU ARE BEING QUESTIONED.
4. IF YOU CANNOT AFFORD TO HIRE A LAWYER ONE WILL BE APPOINTED TO REPRESENT YOU BEFORE ANY QUESTIONING, IF YOU WISH ONE.

SIGNATURE OF DEFENDANT	DATE
WITNESS	TIME

☐ REFUSED SIGNATURE   SAN FRANCISCO POLICE DEPARTMENT   PR.9.1.4

history of liberty has largely been the history of procedural safeguards." These safeguards protect us all from the abuse of police powers. But Chief Justice Warren Burger attacked the exclusionary rule for "the high price it extracts from society—the release of countless guilty criminals."[4] Why should criminals go free because of police misconduct?

PLEA BARGAINING

Most convictions are obtained by guilty pleas. Indeed, about 90 percent of the criminal cases brought to trial are disposed of by guilty pleas before a judge, not trial by jury. **"Plea bargaining,"** in which the prosecution reduces the seriousness of the charges, drops some but not all charges, or agrees to recommend lighter penalties in exchange for a guilty plea by the defendant, is very common. Some critics of plea bargaining view it as another form of leniency in the criminal justice system that reduces its deterrent effects. Other critics view plea bargaining as a violation of the Constitution's protection against self-incrimination and guarantee of a fair jury trial. Prosecutors, they say, threaten defendants with serious charges and stiff penalties in order to force a guilty plea. The decision to plead guilty or go to jury trial rests with the defendant. A defendant may plead guilty and accept the certainty of conviction with whatever reduced charges the prosecutor offers, or accept the prosecutor's pledge to recommend a lighter penalty, or both. Or the defendant may go to trial, confronting serious charges with stiffer penalties with the hope of being found innocent. However, the possibility of an innocent verdict in a jury trial is only one in six. This apparently strong record of conviction comes about because prosecutors have already dismissed charges in cases where the evidence is weak or illegally obtained. Thus, most defendants confronting strong cases against them decide to "cop a plea."

plea bargaining
criminal defendants agree to plead guilty and forgo a jury trial in exchange for reduced charges or lighter penalties

THE DEATH PENALTY

The death penalty has been a continuing controversy in America. Opponents of the death penalty argue that it is "cruel and unusual punishment" in violation of the Eighth Amendment of the Constitution. They argue that it does not deter people from committing murder and that as an irrevolcable punishment, it does not allow for correction of injustice after an innocent person is put to death. In contrast, there is a strong sense of justice among many Americans that demands retribution for heinous crimes. Today, thirty-eight states and the federal government authorize the use of the death penalty.

The Supreme Court has held that "the punishment of death does not invariably violate the Constitution." In 1976, the Court upheld the death penalty, recognizing that the writers of the Bill of Rights accepted death as a common sanction of crime.[5] The Court also recognized that more than half of the nation's state legislatures had reenacted the death penalty since 1972. (In 1972, the Supreme Court had held that the death penalty when unfairly imposed, with some individuals receiving the death penalty for crimes for

which many others were receiving lighter sentences, was unconstitutional.[6])
Moreover, said the Court, the social purposes of retribution and deterrence
justify the use of the death penalty. This ultimate sanction is "an expression
of society's moral outrage at particularly offensive conduct." The Court upheld the death penalty in states where the trial was a two-part proceeding, the
second part of which provided the judge or jury with relevant information
and standards for deciding whether to impose the death penalty. The Court
approved the consideration of "aggravating and mitigating circumstances."
The Court also required automatic review of all death sentences by state
supreme courts to ensure that the sentences were not imposed under the influence of passion or prejudice, that aggravating factors were supported by
the evidence, and that the sentences were not disproportionate to the crimes.

Today, there are over three thousand prisoners nationwide on "death
row," that is, persons convicted and sentenced to death. But only ten to
twenty-five executions are actually carried out each year. Concerns about the
possibility of executing innocent persons has led to moratoriums on executions in some states.

CRIME AND DRUGS

It is difficult to estimate the various forms of drug use. According to the U.S.
National Institute on Drug Abuse (NIDA), there are twelve to fourteen million "problem drinkers," or about 6 percent of the population. There are an
estimated forty-five million cigarette smokers, or about 24 percent of the adult
population (significantly less than the 45 percent of the population who

Illegal drugs continue to be a problem.

smoked cigarettes in the 1940s and 1950s). About thirteen million people, or about 6 percent of the population, currently use illegal drugs, ranging from marijuana to cocaine and heroin. An estimated eleven million, or about 5 percent of the population, are current users of marijuana, although many more have smoked it at least once.[7] The medical evidence on the health effects of marijuana is mixed; conflicting reports have been issued about whether or not it is more dangerous than alcohol.[8] Recent referenda votes in California and in some other states indicate that voters approve of the use of marijuana for therapeutic purposes, but the U.S. government still outlaws its sale.

It is difficult to estimate drug use, to measure whether it is rising or falling over time, or to assess the effectiveness of antidrug efforts. The NIDA annually surveys households in the United States, asking respondents whether they have used drugs in the past month, the past year, or ever in their lifetime. Past-month, or "current," use is the most widely cited NIDA statistic. Based on this survey evidence, overall drug use has declined over the last decade (see Figure 12-3).

DRUG TRAFFICKING

Crime associated with drug trafficking is a serious national problem, whatever the health effects of various drugs. The world of drug trafficking is fraught with violence. Sellers rob and murder buyers and vice versa; neither can seek the protection of police or courts in their dealings with the other.

FIGURE 12-3

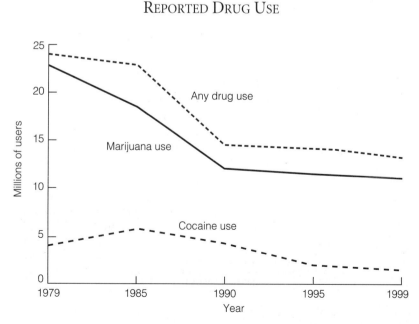

REPORTED DRUG USE

SOURCE: *National Household Survey on Drug Abuse* (annual); U.S. Substance Abuse and Mental Health Services Administration, Washington, D.C.

It is very difficult to estimate the total size of the drug market, but $20 to $25 billion per year is a common figure. This would suggest that the drug business is comparable in size to one of the ten largest U.S. industrial corporations. More important, perhaps, drugs produce huge profit margins: A kilo of cocaine sold in Colombia may cost only $3,600; when sold in the United States, that kilo may retail for $80,000 to $120,000.[9] The price of smuggling a single, easily concealable kilo may run to $15,000. These huge profits allow drug traffickers to corrupt police and government officials as well as private citizens in the United States and in other nations.

THE WAR ON DRUGS

antidrug policy

interdiction

enforcement

education

Federal antidrug efforts can be divided into three categories: interdiction, enforcement, and education. *Interdiction:* Efforts to seal U.S. borders against the importation of drugs have been frustrated by the sheer volume of smuggling. Each year increasingly larger drug shipments are intercepted by the U.S. Drug Enforcement Administration, the U.S. Customs Service, the Coast Guard, and state and local agencies. Yet each year the volume of drugs entering the country seems to increase. Drug "busts" are considered just another cost of business to the traffickers. It is not likely that the use of U.S. military forces to augment other federal agencies can succeed in sealing our borders. American pressure against Latin American governments to destroy coca crops and assist in interdiction has already resulted in strained relationships. Our neighboring countries wonder why the U.S. government directs its efforts at the suppliers, when the demand for drugs arises within the United States itself. *Enforcement:* The federal Drug Enforcement Administration (DEA), together with the FBI and state and local law enforcement agencies, already devote great effort to combating drugs; an estimated 40 percent of all arrests in the United States are drug-related. Federal and state prisons now hold a larger percentage of the nation's population than ever before. Sentences have lengthened for drug trafficking, and prisons are overcrowded as a direct result of drug-related convictions. Drug testing in government and private employment is increasing, but unless it is random, it is not very useful, and some courts have prevented random testing of individuals without their consent. *Education:* Efforts at educating the public about the dangers of drugs have inspired many public and private campaigns, from former First Lady Nancy Reagan's "Just say no" to Jesse Jackson's "Up with hope, down with dope," and police-community-school D.A.R.E. programs. But it is difficult to evaluate the effects of these efforts.

As a nation the United States is both wealthy and free, two conditions that make it a perfect market for illicit drugs. The costs of truly effective enforcement, both in terms of dollar expenditures and, more important, in terms of lost individual liberty, may be more than our society wishes to pay. (See Controversies in Social Science, "Should Drugs Be Legalized?")

Getting High

Drugs that affect behavior or consciousness or mood are referred to as *psychoactive drugs.* The table below lists the most commonly used and abused drugs and their intended and unintended effects.

Drug dependence, or "addiction," is said to occur when the user experiences (1) increased tolerance (user must take more and more to achieve the same effect), (2) withdrawal symptoms (when use is discontinued, the user experiences unpleasant physical or psychological reactions, or (3) compulsive use (the user cannot control use and expends unwanted time and resources in obtaining and using the drug).

Drug abuse does not necessarily imply dependence but means that the user impairs his or her functioning in life (repeated accidents, inability to work or concentrate, marital problems, etc.).

Drug	Intended Effects	Unintended Effects
Alcohol Sources: fermentation of grains and fruits	Lightheadedness ("buzz"); relaxation; release of inhibitions.	Slurred speech; poor coordination; anger and aggressiveness or moroseness; physical and psychological dependence; fetal alcohol syndrome in newborns.
Opiates codeine, morphine, heroin Source: poppy seeds	Pain relief; thrill ("rush"); experience of intense pleasure; euphoria; absence of anxiety and worry.	Death from overdose; serious physical discomforts with withdrawal (chills, sweating, vomiting, cramps, headaches); deterioration of social and personal life; infections including AIDS associated with sharing drug needles; abnormalities in fetus and newborn.
Stimulants Amphetamines: "speed," "uppers," "bennies"; Cocaine including "crack" (smoked), powdered (inhaled), solution (injected into vein) Source: coca leaf	Increased alertness; reduction in fatigue and boredom, enhanced endurance; increased energy and self-confidence.	Increase in tolerance; anguish and extreme depression following brief euphoria; hallucinations and moving flashes of light; crawling sensation under the skin ("coke bugs"); and abnormalities in fetus and newborn.
Hallucinogens (psychedelics) LSD ("acid") mescaline PCP ("angel dust") Sources: mescaline from cactus; mushrooms and laboratory processed	Changed perceptions, including dramatic sounds and colors; time perception altered; auditory and visual hallucinations; mystical, semi-religious experiences.	Extremely unpleasant reactions ("bad trip"); flashback hallucinations long after use; panic; irrational behavior (e.g., jumping from high places), disorientation; comatose condition.
Cannabis marijuana hashish Source: dried marijuana leaves; hashish from squeezed resin	Euphoria and sense of well-being; relaxation; improved tolerance of discomforting medical treatments.	Decreased alertness, coordination, and physical performance; sleepiness and lethargy; short-term memory loss; mild anxiety and irritability upon withdrawal.

CONTROVERSIES IN SOCIAL SCIENCE
Should Drugs Be Legalized?

Public opinion polls show that the vast majority of Americans support strong law enforcement efforts to halt illegal drug use in America. But the high costs of drug law enforcement, prisons overcrowded with drug law violators, the violence associated with drug trafficking, and the threats to civil liberties posed by antidrug wars all combine to inspire some observers to propose the legalization of drugs and government control of their production and sale.

"Prohibition" failed earlier in the century to end alcohol consumption, and the crime, official corruption, and enormous cost of futile efforts to stop drinking eventually forced the nation to end Prohibition. Similarly, it is argued that the legalization of drugs would end organized crime's profit monopoly over the drug trade, raise billions of dollars by legally taxing drugs, end the strain on relations with Latin American nations caused by efforts to eradicate drugs, and save additional billions in enforcement costs that could be used for education and treatment.[a] If drugs were legally obtainable under government supervision, it is argued that many of society's current problems would be alleviated: the crime and violence associated with the drug trade, the corruption of public officials, the spread of diseases associated with drug use, and the many infringements of personal liberty associated with antidrug wars.

But even the suggestion of drug legalization concerns Americans who believe that legalization would greatly expand drug use in the country. Cheap, available drugs would increase the numbers of addicted persons, creating a "society of zombies" that would destroy the social fabric of the nation. Cocaine and heroin are far more habit-forming than alcohol, and legalization would encourage the development of newer and even more potent and addictive synthetic drugs. Whatever the health costs of drug abuse today, it is argued that legalization would produce public health problems of enormous magnitude.[b] Cocaine is very cheap to produce; the current $5 to $10 cost of a "hit" is mostly drug-dealer profit; legalization even with taxation might produce a 50¢ "hit." Whatever the damages to society from drug-related crime and efforts to prohibit drugs, the damages to society from cheap, available drugs might be far greater.

[a]Ethan A. Nadelmann, "The Case for Legalization," *The Public Interest* (Summer 1988): 3–31.
[b]John Kaplan, "Taking Drugs Seriously," *The Public Interest* (Summer 1988): 32–50.

AN ECONOMIC PERSPECTIVE ON CRIME

Crime is not only a major concern of citizens, but also a topic of great interest to social scientists. Each of the social sciences brings a slightly different perspective to crime.

Economists tend to view crime as a product of people's rational calculations of the expected benefits and expected costs of criminal acts. They believe that the reason the United States has so much crime is that crime *pays*—that is, its benefits outweigh its costs. The economic approach to criminal justice emphasizes **deterrence**—that is, convincing potential lawbreakers that the certainty and severity of punishment will impose costs on them far in excess of any benefit they might derive from criminal acts.

deterrence
making the certainty and severity of punishment so great as to inhibit potential criminals from committing crimes

REQUIREMENTS FOR DETERRENCE

If law enforcement is to be a deterrent to crime, punishment must be *perceived* as: (1) fairly certain, (2) swift enough to establish a link between the crime and its consequences, and (3) severe enough to outweigh the benefits of the crime. These criteria for an effective deterrent policy are ranked in the order of their probable importance. It is most important that punishment for crime is certain in the minds of potential criminals. The severity of the punishment is probably less important than its certainty or swiftness.

deterring crime in theory
punishment must be certain, swift, and severe enough to outweigh benefits

QUESTIONS ABOUT DETERRENCE

All types of crimes declined in the 1990s (see Table 12-1). It is not clear whether this decline is a product of the deterrent effect of current criminal justice policies in America or economic expansion with low unemployment or the fact that more wrongdoers are behind bars and therefore prevented from committing crimes outside prison walls. (See Controversies in Social Science, "Do More Prisons Reduce Crime?")

The nation's **incarceration rate**—the number of people in prison per 100,000 population—has risen dramatically in the past decade. (Indeed, the incarceration rate nearly doubled from about four hundred to eight hundred

incarceration rate
the number of persons imprisoned per 100,000 population

FIGURE 12-4

LAW ENFORCEMENT IN RELATION TO REPORTED CRIME
(Actual crime is estimated to be two and a half times the reported offenses.)

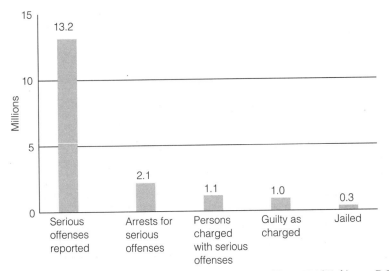

SOURCE: U.S. Bureau of the Census, *Statistical Abstract of the United States 1999* (Washington, D.C.: U.S. Government Printing Office, 1999).

CONTROVERSIES IN SOCIAL SCIENCE
Do More Prisons Reduce Crime?

In recent years, the average prison sentence has lengthened dramatically. Prison-building programs that began in the 1980s expanded the nation's prison capacity and resulted in fewer early releases of prisoners. Many state legislatures enacted mandatory minimum prison terms for repeat offenders (including popular "three strikes you're out" laws mandating life sentences for third violent felony offenders). And many states enacted determinant sentencing—legally prescribed specific jail terms for specific offenses—that limits judicial discretion in sentencing. The result of these changes has been a dramatic increase in the time served for violent offenses. The average time served for such offenses has doubled since 1990, and the average percent of total sentences served has risen from less than 50 percent to 80 percent.

At the same time, the nation's crime rate has declined dramatically. It is not clear, however, whether longer sentences and the resulting larger prison populations are responsible for these declining crime rates. It is possible that declining crime rates are primarily a result of the nation's booming economy of the 1990s with its low unemployment rates. And even if stricter criminal justice policies are partly or primarily responsible for declining crime rates, it is not clear whether these policies or the fact that there are more incapacitated wrongdoers, thereby preventing them from committing crimes outside prison walls, are creating a deterrent effect.

Nonetheless, there is a close correlation between rising incarceration rates (the number of prisoners serving at least one year per 100,000 population) and declining rates of violent crime (see figure).

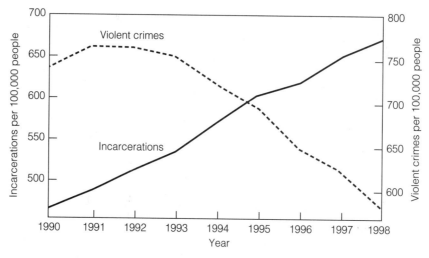

SOURCES: Incarcerations data from U.S. Department of Justice, Bureau of Justice Statistics, *Prisoners in 1998* and *Jail and Prison Inmates*, 1995. Crime data from U.S. Department of Justice, Bureau of Justice Statistics, *Sourcebook of Criminal Justice Statistics*, 1997; and Federal Bureau of Investigation, *Crime in the United States 1998: Uniform Crime Reports*, 1999.

between 1990 and 2000.) But does incarceration *deter* crime or simply *incapacitate* potential criminals?

If deterrence depends upon the *certainty* of punishment, then it is difficult to argue that deterrence is working. The likelihood of an individual's being jailed for a serious crime is less than one in a hundred (see Figure 12-4). Many crimes are not even reported by the victim. Police are successful in clearing fewer than one in five reported crimes by arresting the offender. The judicial system released almost half of the persons arrested and charged; others are not prosecuted, handled as juveniles, found not guilty, or permitted to plead guilty to a lesser charge and released. Only about one-third of convicted felons are given prison sentences. Thus, the certainty of punishment for a crime in America is very low.

Finally, a great deal of crime may be "irrational"—that is, criminals do not stop to weigh benefits against potential costs before committing the criminal acts. Violent criminal behavior, perhaps more than property crime, often shows little sign of rational calculation.

A PSYCHOLOGICAL PERSPECTIVE ON CRIME— THE ANTISOCIAL PERSONALITY

Some crimes are committed by individuals suffering various personality disorders. These people are not "insane" (see Case Study, "The Insanity Defense"), but they exhibit long-standing patterns of maladaptive behavior— inappropriate ways of coping with stress, solving problems, and relating to others. Personality disorders may have their origin in either genetic or environmental factors.

THE ANTISOCIAL PERSONALITY

Psychologists have identified an **antisocial personality** disorder that is often associated with criminal behavior. (Antisocial personalities are sometimes referred to as "psychopaths" or "sociopaths"; a "pathology" is a disease leading to death.) Individuals with antisocial personalities have little sense of responsibility for their action, little concern for others, and little or no sense of morality. It can be said that they lack a conscience. They behave impulsively, they seek immediate gratification, and they cannot tolerate frustration.

The behavioral characteristics used to identify the antisocial personality are (1) a lack of empathy and concern for others and (2) a lack of shame or guilt or remorse for their own actions however harmful they may be.

Antisocial personalities sometimes develop in children who first show signs of **attention deficit disorder (ADD),** which is diagnosed when children have significant problems in maintaining attention and consistently display impulsive uncontrolled behavior. Their disruptive behavior may lead to rejection by teachers, playmates, and even parents, thus leading to even more disruptive and aggressive behavior and eventually antisocial personality disorder.

antisocial personality
long-standing patterns of maladaptive behavior; lack of concern for others and no sense of guilt

attention deficit disorder (ADD)
difficulty maintaining attention; impulsive uncontrolled behavior

CASE STUDY

The Insanity Defense

How should society deal with a mentally ill person who commits a crime? Should the mentally ill be held responsible for their actions in the same fashion as everyone else? Or should criminal law recognize that the mentally ill may not be able to control their conduct?

In an historic nineteenth-century case, a mentally-ill Scotsman, M'Naghten, attempted to assassinate the English Prime Minister Robert Peel but instead shot his secretary. The trial judge was convinced by M'Naghten's senseless rambling and paranoid delusions that the defendant was insane, and he was sent to a mental hospital. But Queen Victoria was unsatisfied with the verdict; she asked the House of Lords to review the decision. The result was the *M'Naghten Rule*—that a defendant may be found not guilty by reason of insanity if he did not know at the time what he was doing or did not know

that what he was doing was wrong.

Later American courts expanded on the M'Naghten Rule, holding that people are not responsible for a crime if, as a result of a mental disease or defect, they lack the capacity to appreciate the wrongfulness of their conduct or the ability to conform their conduct to the law. The word *appreciate* is considered a looser term than "know" in the original M'Naghten Rule, implying that the defendant must have some understanding of the moral and legal consequences of his or her behavior.

Perhaps the most publicized successful insanity defense in American history was that of John Hinckley, Jr. Accused in a Washington, D.C., court of attempting to assassinate President Ronald Reagan in 1981, Hinckley was found not guilty by virtue of insanity. Many Americans were outraged by the verdict, and the insanity defense came

under attack in Congress. Congress responded by enacting the Insanity Defense Reform Act of 1984, designed to make it more difficult to successfully employ the insanity defense.

The act stipulates that the defendant's mental disease or defect must be "severe" in order to avoid guilt. The intent is to exclude nonpsychotic disorders such as antisocial personality. The act also shifted the burden of proof of insanity to the defendant; the prosecution need not prove that the person was sane beyond a reasonable doubt. And the defendant must prove insanity with "clear and convincing evidence."

Some states have adopted the use of the verdict "guilty but mentally ill." This verdict may be rendered when the jury decides that a mental disorder significantly impacted the judgment of the defendant at the time of the crime or his or her capacity to recognize real-

Genetic Explanations

A genetic cause of antisocial personality disorder is revealed in studies of criminal behavior across generations and among identical twins. For example, the criminal records of adopted sons have been found to be more similar to the record of their biological fathers than their adopted fathers. The criminal records of identical twins are much closer to each other than those of fraternal twins.

Theodore Kaczynski lived in a shack for some 20 years, rarely bathed, sent bombs to strangers, and was diagnosed by his state-appointed psychiatrist with paranoid schizophrenia. Should Kaczynski be jailed as a criminal or hospitalized as mentally ill? A jury convicted him of murder and sentenced him to death. His conviction is currently being appealed.

ity. The verdict allows a judge to impose a sentence that may be served either in a mental hospital or in prison or both. The intent is to keep a mentally-ill dangerous person off the streets.

Mental illness also intrudes into the criminal justice process early in the legal process when a judge declares that a defendant is not mentally competent to stand trial. After reviewing the psychological evidence, a judge may determine that a defendant is *not competent to stand trial* if

he or she is unable to understand the charges and unable to cooperate with a lawyer in preparing his or her defense. The judge's decision is based on the constitutional right to a fair trial; it is separate from the question of whether the defendant was insane *at the time the crime was committed.* The judge may drop criminal charges and commit the person to a psychiatric facility. Psychiatrists can later release the person after determining that he or she is no longer mentally incompetent.

Defendants have a better chance of convincing a judge that they are incompetent to stand trial than they have to convince a jury that they are not guilty by reason of insanity. Most juries hold individuals responsible for their criminal acts. Fewer than one percent of defendants charged with serious crimes are found not guilty by reason of insanity. Most defense attorneys consider the insanity defense a last resort.

Environmental Influences

Not all children with genetic predisposition to antisocial personality disorder or to criminal behavior develop these characteristics. Parental conduct is a better predictor of the emergence of antisocial personality than genetics. Disruptive children who are unsupervised or poorly supervised are much more likely to develop a pattern of delinquent behavior than children of parents who are involved in their everyday life. Parents who closely monitor ADD and intervene consistently to overcome it can help children avoid the development of antisocial and criminal behaviors.

Genetic and environmental factors often combine to cause antisocial personality disorder. Maternal drug use, maternal exposure to toxic agents, and low birth weight are associated with childhood problems of irritability, impulsiveness, inattention, and slow learning. These children are difficult to care for and they are at risk for abuse and neglect. Both genetic and adverse home factors tend to contribute to aggressive behaviors in children, especially hitting.

SOCIAL AND CULTURAL PERSPECTIVES ON CRIME

deviance
the failure to conform to social norms

criminology
the scientific study of crime, criminals, and punishment

Sociologists view crime as a form of **deviance**—the failure to conform to social norms. **Deviance** may range from the trivial (vulgar language) to the acute (serial murders). Not all deviance involves lawbreaking. While norms may differ from one society to another, all societies have norms and all societies impose some forms of punishment on those who violate norms. Not all sociologists who study deviance focus on crime (**criminology**), but those who do are generally referred to as criminologists.[10]

A sociological perspective on crime emphasizes its presumed "root causes"—poverty, unemployment, lack of opportunity, inequality, and discrimination. It shows how crime rates vary with gender, race, age, mobility, and other social characteristics of populations.

CRIME AND GENDER

Crime rates for women are much lower than those for men. Men account for about 86 percent of violent crime and 73 percent of property crime. Sociologists offer a variety of explanations for this differential: Males are socialized to be active, assertive, and dominant—traits conducive to criminal behavior—while females are socialized to be more gentle and nurturing. Parents often impose a "double standard" of morality, monitoring their daughters' behavior more closely than their sons', providing more opportunities for males to commit crimes. Some research indicates that girls feel more strongly attached to families than boys and are more likely to value their parents' norms. If men's crime rates were as low as women's, crime in the United States would not be a major social problem.

CRIME AND RACE

Crime disproportionately victimizes the poor and African Americans. A black male is almost eight times more likely to be murdered than a white male. And the poor and black are disproportionately represented among persons arrested and sentenced for crime. Blacks comprise 12.6 percent of the nation's population yet comprise 34.6 percent of all arrests for serious crimes, 46.9 percent of state prison inmates, and 41.6 percent of prisoners under sentence of death.

There are a variety of sociological explanations of racial differences on crime statistics, all of them controversial. (Indeed, some social scientists and some texts avoid mentioning these statistics or discussing possible explanations for them.) The higher rate of father-absent households among African-American families may result in less supervision and discipline of young males and fewer positive role models. Economic deprivation and conditions in inner-city neighborhoods where African Americans are concentrated are frequently cited as contributing to higher rates of crime.

Age and Crime

Crime is closely related to age. Crime is primarily a young man's activity. Men between the ages of sixteen and thirty-four commit most of the crimes in the nation. Indeed, overall arrests by age category show that about 9 percent involve persons under sixteen, 36 percent involve persons sixteen to twenty-five, and 30 percent involve persons twenty-six to thirty-four. In contrast, only 16 percent of arrests involve persons thirty-five to forty-four, only 7 percent involve persons forty-five to sixty-four, and only 1 percent involve persons over sixty-five.

Sociologists cite a variety of factors influencing the "crime-prone" age group: Peer influences and the urge to assert independence are greatest among adolescents. Young men who have not yet acquired full-time jobs or gotten married or fathered children are less likely to have acquired a stake in conformity to social norms. Maturity usually brings greater control over one's compulsions. Risk-taking behavior becomes less attractive. Sociologists note that all other things being equal, an increase or decrease in the proportion of the population in the most crime-prone age category of sixteen to twenty-five should result in increases and decreases in crime.

Subcultural Explanation

Crime is much more prevalent in urban areas. One explanation for the concentration of crime in the inner city centers on the subculture of the streets.[11] A disproportionate number of female-headed households among poor black families inspires young males to seek masculine identities through peer-group associations in gangs. The gangs develop a subculture of "toughness," exaggerated masculinity, demands for respect, and danger and thrill-seeking. These values lead young males to respond violently to remarks, gestures, and actions that most others would ignore. A reputation for violence brings respect, and symbols of violence, including guns, are marks of distinction. Arrest and imprisonment is sometimes regarded as a "coming of age." At the same time, these young males aspire to the wealth and material well-being of the larger culture. But economic opportunities are limited; drugs are a thriving business in the streets, and drug dealers provide role models. The gap between aspirations and opportunities creates the frustration that leads to crime.

But the problem with the criminal subculture thesis is that *most young males in the inner city do not turn to violence or crime.* While crime rates can be correlated with poverty, unemployment, age, and race, these conditions quite obviously do not cause crime, inasmuch as the majority of poor, unemployed, young, and black do *not* have criminal records. The overwhelming majority of children raised in single-parent households turn out to be law-abiding citizens. Sociological and cultural perspectives on crime, while helpful in identifying the factors associated with high crime rates and "deviant" behavior, fail to provide a policy remedy.[12]

VIOLENCE IN AMERICAN HISTORY

violence as a source of power and change

major instances of violence in American history
guerrilla warfare in the Revolution

Shays's Rebellion

violence of the Civil War era

the Indian Wars

vigilante violence

labor-management violence

racial violence

political violence—assassinations

Violence is not uncommon in American society. The nation itself was founded in armed revolution, and violence has been a *source of power* and a *stimulus to social change* ever since. Violence has been associated with most of the important movements in American history: the birth of the nation (revolutionary violence), the freeing of the slaves and the preservation of the Union (Civil War violence), the westward expansion of the nation (Indian Wars), the establishment of law and order in frontier society (vigilante violence), the organization of the labor movement (labor-management violence), the civil rights movement (racial violence), and attempts to deal with the problems of cities (urban violence). History reveals that the patriot, humanitarian, pioneer, lawman, laborer, African American, and urban dweller have all used violence as a source of power. Despite pious pronouncements against it, Americans have frequently employed violence even in their most idealistic endeavors.

THE REVOLUTIONARY WAR

Perhaps the most famous act of organized mob violence occurred in 1773 when a group of "agitators" in Boston, Massachusetts, illegally destroyed 342 chests of tea. The early Revolutionary War fighting in 1774 and 1775, including the battles of Lexington and Concord, was really a series of small guerrilla skirmishes designed more to intimidate Tories than to achieve national independence. The old American custom of tarring and feathering was a product of the early patriotic campaign to root out Tories. Aside from the regular clash of Continental and British armies, a great deal of violence and guerrilla strife occurred during the Revolution. Savage guerrilla forays along the eastern coast resulted in the killing of thousands of Tory families and the destruction of their property. The success of this violence enshrined it in our traditions.

SHAYS'S REBELLION

After the Revolutionary War, many armed farmers and debtors resorted to violence to assert their economic interests. If taxes owed to the British government and debts owed to British merchants could be denied, why not the taxes owed to state governments and the debts owed to American merchants? In several states, debtors had already engaged in open rebellion against tax collectors and sheriffs. The most serious rebellion broke out in the summer of 1786 in Massachusetts, when a band of insurgents, composed of farmers and laborers, captured courthouses in several western districts of that state and momentarily held the city of Springfield. Led by Daniel Shays, a veteran of Bunker Hill, the insurgent army posed a direct threat to the governing elite of the new nation. Shays's Rebellion, as it was called, was put down by a small mercenary army paid for by well-to-do citizens who feared that a wholesale attack on property rights was imminent. The growing domestic violence in the states contributed to the momentum leading to the Constitutional Convention of 1787, where propertied men established a new central government with the power to "ensure domestic tranquility," guarantee "the republican form of government," and protect "against domestic violence." Thus, the Constitution itself reflects a concern of the nation's Founders about domestic violence.

THE CIVIL WAR

The Civil War was the bloodiest war the United States ever fought. Total casualties of the northern and southern armies equaled American casualties in World War II; but when the Civil War occurred, the nation was only one-third as large as it was during the latter conflict. There were few families that did not suffer the loss of a loved one during the Civil War. In addition to military casualties, the toll in lives and property among civilians was enormous. A great deal of domestic violence also occurred both before and after the war. Beginning in 1856, proslavery and antislavery forces fought in "bleeding Kansas." In 1859 John Brown led a raid at Harper's Ferry, meant to start the freeing of the slaves in Virginia. Brown's capture, trial for treason, and execution made him a hero to many abolitionists, though Southerners believed that he had tried to incite slave uprisings. The guerrilla war that took place in the West during the Civil War has seldom been equaled for savagery; the fearsome Kansas Jayhawkers traded brutalities with Confederate guerrillas headed by William Quantrell. Later, western bandits, including Frank and Jesse James and the Younger brothers, who had fought as Confederate guerrillas, continued their forays against banks and railroads and enjoyed considerable popular prestige and support. Moreover, after the war, racial strife and Ku Klux Klan activity became routine in the old Confederate states. The Ku Klux Klan was first used to intimidate the Republicans of the Reconstruction era by violence and threats, and later used to force blacks to accept the renewed rule of whites.

THE INDIAN WARS

Unquestionably the longest and most brutal violence in American history was that between whites and Native Americans. It began in 1607 and continued with only temporary truces for nearly three hundred years, until the final battle at Wounded Knee, South Dakota, in 1890. The norms of Indian warfare were generally more barbaric than those in other types of warfare, if such a thing is possible. Women and children on both sides were deliberately and purposefully killed. Torture was accepted as a customary part of making war. Scalping was a frequent practice on both sides.

VIGILANTES

Vigilante violence (taking the law into one's own hands) arose as a response to a typically American problem: the absence of effective law and order in the frontier region. Practically every state and territory west of the Appalachians had at one time or another a well-organized vigilante movement. The first vigilante movement appeared in 1767–1769 in South Carolina, where the vigilantes were known as *regulators*—a term later used by San Francisco vigilantes in the 1850s. Vigilantes were frequently backed by prominent men; many later became senators, representatives, governors, judges, businessmen, and even clergy. Like Indian-fighters, vigilantes became great popular heroes. Antitheft and antirustling associations flourished in the West until World War I. Vigilantes often undertook to establish law and order and to regulate the morals of the citizens—punishing drunks, vagrants, ne'er-do-wells, and occasional strangers.

LABOR VIOLENCE

Violence was also a constant companion of the early labor movement in the United States. Both management and strikers resorted to violence in the struggles accompanying the Industrial Revolution. In 1887, in the bitter railroad strike in Pittsburgh, Pennsylvania, an estimated sixteen soldiers and fifty strikers were killed, and locomotives, freight cars, and other property were destroyed. The famous Homestead strike of 1892 turned Homestead, Pennsylvania, into an open battlefield. The Pullman strike of 1893 in Chicago resulted in twelve deaths and the destruction of a great deal of railroad property. In 1914, Ludlow, Colorado, was the scene of the famous Ludlow Massacre, in which company guards burned a miner tent city and killed nearly one hundred persons, including women and children. The Molly Maguires were a secret organization of Irish miners who fought their employers with assassination and mayhem. The last great spasm of violence in the history of American labor came in the 1930s with the strikes and plant takeovers ("sit-down strikes") that accompanied the successful drive to unionize the automobile, steel, and other mass-production industries.

RACIAL VIOLENCE

The long history of racial violence in the United States still continues to plague the nation. Slavery itself was accompanied by untold violence. It is estimated that one-third to one-half of those captured in African slave raids never survived the ordeal of forced marches to the sea, with thirst, brutalities, and near starvation the rule; the terrible two-month voyage in filthy holds packed with squirming and suffocating humanity; and the brutal "seasoning" whereby African blacks were turned into slaves. Nat Turner's slave insurrection in 1831 resulted in the deaths of fifty-seven white persons and the execution of Turner and his followers. Following the end of slavery, the white supremacy movement employed violence to reestablish the position of whites in the southern social system. Racial violence directed against blacks—whippings, torture, and lynching—was fairly common from the 1870s to the 1930s. During World War II, serious racial violence erupted in Detroit. Black and white mobs battled each other in June 1943, causing thirty-five deaths and hundreds of injuries, more than a thousand arrests, and finally the dispatching of federal troops to restore order.

ASSASSINATIONS

Political assassinations have not been uncommon. Four presidents (Lincoln, Garfield, McKinley, and Kennedy) have fallen to assassins' bullets, and others were the intended objects of assassination. Only Lincoln was the target of a proven assassination conspiracy; the other presidential victims were the prey of presumably freelance assassins in varying states of mental instability. In the 1930s, Senator Huey P. Long of Louisiana was murdered, and a bullet narrowly missed President Franklin Delano Roosevelt and killed Mayor Anton Cermak of Chicago, who was standing near the president. The wave of political assassinations and assassination attempts in more recent years, which cut down John F. Kennedy, Robert F. Kennedy, and Martin Luther King, Jr.; crippled George C. Wallace; and threatened the life of Ronald Reagan, may represent a "contagion phenomenon," unstable individuals being motivated to violence by highly publicized and dramatic acts of violence. But an even grimmer possibility is that political assassination may become a persistent feature of American society.

ON THE WEB

EXPLORING CRIME AND VIOLENCE

U.S. government agencies compile extensive material on crime, drugs, courts, and prisons. All major crime-fighting agencies have their own Web sites, including the U.S. Department of Justice; the Federal Bureau of Investigation; the Bureau of Alcohol, Tobacco and Firearms; and the Office of National Drug Control Policy.

U.S. Bureau of Justice Statistics. Perhaps the most informative criminal justice Web site is that maintained by the Bureau of Justice Statistics (www.ojp.usdoj.gov/bjs).

It includes data on criminal victimization compiled from annual surveys of the population that ask if they have been victims of crime in the past year. It also includes data on characteristics of victims, criminal sentencing by courts, prison populations, and persons on probation and parole. Much of the data on this Web site includes crime rates, prison populations, incarceration rates, and numbers of executions and is provided in colorful charts.

FBI. The Federal Bureau of Investigation's Web site (www.fbi.gov) is frequently accessed for information on current topics in national crime fighting. The FBI's "Ten Most Wanted" page includes names and photos of fugitives. But perhaps its most important data is the Uniform Crime Reports, which provides up-to-date police reporting of various types of violent and property crimes.

Sourcebook of Criminal Justice Statistics. The *Sourcebook of Criminal Justice Statistics,* published annually, brings together data on all aspects of the criminal justice system, including public attitudes toward crime and information such as the age, sex, and race of persons arrested and imprisoned in federal and state correctional institutions. This book can be accessed through its Web site (www.albany.edu/sourcebook).

Office of National Drug Control Policy. The Office of National Drug Control Policy is a coordinating agency in the "war on drugs." Its director is frequently referred to as the nation's "drug czar." Its Web site (www. whitehousedrugpolicy.gov) includes extensive information on reported drug use, as well as prevention, education, treatment, and enforcement efforts.

Drug Policy Foundation. The Drug Policy Foundation is a research organization that studies alternatives to the nation's current war on drugs. Its Web site (www.dpf. org) includes information on the legalization of drug use.

ABOUT THIS CHAPTER

More than two thousand years ago, Aristotle wrote of the problem of crime that "the generality of men are naturally apt to be swayed by fear rather than by reverence, and to refrain from evil rather because of the punishment that it brings, than because of its own

foulness." Power must be exercised by society for the very basic purposes of maintaining order and protecting the citizenry. A free democratic society must struggle with maintaining a balance between its exercise of police power and its safeguarding of individual freedom. In this chapter we have examined America's struggles with this problem. We have explored economic, psychological, and sociocultural perspectives on crime. And we have examined the violence that has been a part of most of the important social movements in American history.

Now that you have read Chapter 12, you should be able to

- describe the current status of crime in the United States as evidenced by crime and victimization rates

- describe the basic constitutional protections afforded to persons accused of crime

- discuss the constitutional issues arising from capital punishment

- describe the various potentially harmful substances—alcohol, tobacco, marijuana, cocaine, and heroin—and current antidrug policies

- describe the theory of deterrence, the requirements for deterrence, and why deterrence does not appear to be working well

- discuss the theory of the antisocial personality and whether insanity should excuse a defendant from criminal penalty

- discuss the subculture theory of street crime

- discuss the history of violence in the United States

DISCUSSION QUESTIONS

1. How did Thomas Hobbes justify the creation of a "Leviathan"? What dilemma is faced by a free society in protecting its citizens?
2. Discuss crime rates. How are they used, how are they determined, and what factors contribute to their inaccuracy? What is their current trend?
3. Suppose you have just been arrested by the police. Describe how the following constitutional rights of defendants would be of use to you: guarantee of the writ of habeas corpus; prohibition of bills of attainder and of ex post facto laws; prohibition of "unreasonable" searches and seizures; freedom from

self-incrimination; the right to counsel; guarantee of a fair jury trial; protection against double jeopardy; protection against excessive bail.

4. Choose two of the following cases that were decided by the Warren Court and discuss how each of them strengthened the rights of accused persons in criminal cases: *Mapp v. Ohio* (1961); *Gideon v. Wainwright* (1963); *Escobedo v. Illinois* (1964); *Miranda v. Arizona* (1966).

5. What are some of the difficulties that the police may encounter in their law enforcement function? What is the "exclusionary rule"?

6. Describe the major drug threats confronting the United States today. What is the legal status of various potentially harmful substances: alcohol, tobacco, marijuana, cocaine, and heroin?

7. What are the requirements for effective deterrence of crime?

8. Should the insanity defense protect defendants from criminal penalties?

9. Describe the subculture theory of street crime and the problem with the theory.

10. Discuss the arguments for and against capital punishment. Describe the 1972 Supreme Court decision regarding the constitutionality of capital punishment and the changes in state laws that followed it. Discuss the reasoning of the justices in the 1976 Court decision on capital punishment.

11. Discuss the history of violence in the United States. Using at least three specific eras or social movements as examples, describe the type of violence that was used and the kind of social change that was its goal.

Chapter 13

Power and Community

THE GLOBAL COMMUNITY

The world's population now tops six billion people. The last seventy years of the twentieth century saw a true population explosion, a tripling of the earth's inhabitants from about two billion people in 1930. But the rate of population growth is forecast to slow down in the twenty-first century. By 2050, the world's population is expected to stabilize around nine billion people.

demography
the study of the population and of population changes

Demography is the study of the population and of population changes—how births, death, and migration affect the number of people living in the countries of the world. Demographers theorize a three-stage model of world population growth (see Figure 13-1). For many centuries, the global population grew very slowly. The world's population reflected both a high **fertility rate** (the number of births per one thousand women of childbearing age) and a high **mortality rate** (the number of death per one thousand people). Life expectancy was short—less than forty years.

fertility rate
the number of births annually per one thousand women of childbearing age

mortality rate
the number of deaths annually per one thousand persons

The Industrial Revolution, however, which began first in England and western Europe and then extended to North America, drastically reduced the mortality rate, particularly the rate of infant deaths. For decades, even in the Western world, fertility rates remained high. The combination of high fertility rates and low mortality rates led, of course, to rapid population increases. Only in the last few decades has the fertility rate in the developed world declined, leading to a stabilization of the population.

FIGURE 13-1

Forecasting Model of Global Population Change

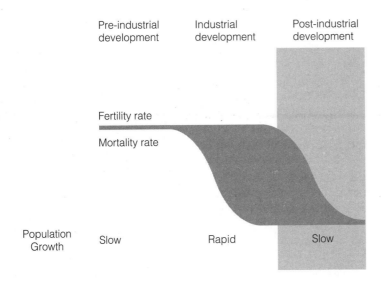

Today, in less-developed areas of Africa, Asia, and Latin America—areas that are currently in the process of industrialization—high fertility and low mortality account for continued world population growth. But with economic development, fertility in these areas of the world is expected to decline, and the world's population is expected to stabilize around nine billion people before the end of this century.[1]

As late as the 1970s, some commentators predicted that the world's population growth would soon exhaust the world's natural resources, leading to global starvation, malnutrition, and disease. Reflecting the views of Thomas Malthus, who predicted in 1798 that populations everywhere would grow faster than agriculture's ability to feed them, these "neo-Malthusians" forecast widespread human misery and death in the twenty-first century. (In 1971 biologist Paul Ehrlich called earth a "dying planet" suffering from "overpopulation"; his book *The Population Explosion* inspired Earth Day.) But just the opposite has occurred. Average life expectancy globally is now nearing seventy years. Infant death rates are declining everywhere, although they still remain unconscionably high in the less-developed countries of the world. And the world's natural resources, especially food, are actually *cheaper* today than a century ago. This is clear evidence that improved productivity is increasing the supply of food and resources faster than the demands of a growing world population.[2]

Around the world, women are having fewer children now than ever before. The United Nations estimates the current world fertility rate at 2.8 children per woman.[3] In developed regions, the fertility rate is estimated at 1.59, well below the replacement level fertility rate of 2.1 births per

TABLE 13-1

GLOBAL POPULATION FORECASTS

Millions of People

	1950	2000	2050
World	2,521	5,901	8,909
More-developed regions	813	1,182	1,155
Less-developed regions	1,709	4,719	7,754
Africa	221	749	1,766
Asia	1,402	3,585	5,268
Europe	547	729	628
Latin America and the Caribbean	167	504	809
North America	172	305	392
Oceania	13	30	46

SOURCE: U.N. Population Division, *World Population Prospects* (1998).

woman. (The fertility rate for the United States is 2.0; however, the U.S. population continues to grow through immigration.) The fertility rate in the less-developed regions of the world is dropping rapidly, from an estimated 5.25 in 1970 to 3.08 today. China, with the world's largest population, made the greatest fertility rate reductions from 1970 to 2000—from an estimated 6.0 to 1.8. Nonetheless, population growth in the less-developed areas of the world will add more than three billion people by 2050 (see Table 13-1).

THE SOCIOLOGY OF URBAN LIFE

About half of the world's population live in urban areas. Urbanization is greatest in the developed world, where about 80 percent of people live in or near cities. Only about 40 percent of people of the less-developed world live in urban areas. However, urban growth is proceeding more rapidly in Asia, Africa, and Latin America than in western Europe or the United States (see Cross-National Perspective, "Worldwide Urbanization"). What is the impact of urbanism on the way people interact? To deal with this question, sociologists first had to formulate a **sociological definition of urbanism**, one that would identify those characteristics most affecting social life. Sociologist Louis Wirth provided the classic definition of urbanism over fifty years ago: "For sociological purposes a city may be defined as a relatively large, dense, and permanent settlement of socially heterogeneous individuals."[4] Thus, according to Wirth, the distinguishing characteristics of urban life were *numbers, density,* and *heterogeneity*—large numbers of people, living closely together, who are different from one another.

sociological theory of urbanism

urbanism distinguished by numbers, density, and heterogeneity

Worldwide Urbanization

Urbanization is occurring worldwide. Cities throughout the world offer greater opportunities than rural areas. It is estimated that the world's urban areas are growing at twice the rate of the world's population generally. Millions of people migrate from the countryside in search of economic opportunity, health care, education, and higher standards of living in the world's largest cities. However poor and unpleasant life may be in many Third World cities, these cities hold the promise of a better life for rural migrants. Many residents of these cities have no running water and lack sewage facilities. Mountains of trash and garbage have become wretched shantytowns where the city's poor pick through waste to survive and build shacks from discarded materials. The problems of Third World cities make those of the largest U.S. cities seem minor by comparison.

Today, most of the largest cities in the world are found in less-developed societies (see table). Modernization brings urbanization, and as Third World nations move from agricultural to industrial economies, their cities grow exponentially. By 2015, only one of the world's largest cities will be in the United States—New York. In the past fifty years, Third World cities replaced Western cities in the list of the world's largest cities.

THE WORLD'S LARGEST CITIES
(in Millions of People)

1950		2015	
New York	12.3	Tokyo	28.7
London	8.7	Greater Bombay, India	27.4
Tokyo	6.9	Lagos, Nigeria	24.4
Moscow	5.4	Shanghai	23.4
Paris	5.4	Jakarta, Indonesia	21.2
Shanghai	5.3	São Paulo, Brazil	20.8
Buenos Aires	5.0	Karachi, Pakistan	20.6
Chicago	4.9	Beijing	19.4
Calcutta	4.4	Dhaka, Bangladesh	19.0
Osaka, Japan	4.1	Mexico City	18.8
Los Angeles	4.0	New York	17.6
Beijing	3.9	Calcutta	17.6
Mexico City	3.1	Delhi, India	17.6
Rio de Janeiro	2.9	Seoul	17.0
Greater Bombay, India	2.9	Manila	14.7

SOURCE: United Nations, *World Urbanization Prospects* (1995).

NUMBERS AND HETEROGENEITY

Large numbers of people involve a great range of individual variation. The modern economic system of the metropolis is based on a highly specialized and complex division of labor. We are told that in early farm communities a dozen occupations exhausted the job opportunities available to people. In a simple agricultural society, nearly everyone was a farmer or was closely connected to or dependent on farming. But in the modern metropolis, there are tens of thousands of different kinds of jobs. An industrial economy means

heterogeneity
diversity in occupation, income, education; ethnic and racial diversity

highly specialized jobs, hence the **heterogeneity** of urban populations. Different jobs result in different levels of income, dress, and styles of living. People's jobs shape the way they look at the world and their evaluations of social and political events. To acquire a job, one attains a certain level and type of education that also distinguishes one from those in other jobs with other educational requirements. Differences in educational level in turn produce a wide variety of differences in opinions, attitudes, and styles of living. Urban life concentrates people with all these different economic and occupational characteristics in a very few square miles.

Ethnic and Racial Diversity

Ethnic and racial diversities are also present. At the beginning of this century, opportunities for human betterment in American cities attracted immigrants from Ireland, Germany, Italy, Poland, and Russia; later the city attracted African Americans, Hispanics, and rural families. Newcomers bring with them different needs, attitudes, and ways of life. The "melting pot" tends to reduce some of the diversity over time, but the pot does not melt people immediately, and there always seem to be new arrivals.

Impersonal Relationships

segmental relationships
knowing many people, but only in their partial roles

Increasing the numbers of people in a community limits the possibility that each member of the community will know everyone else personally. Multiplying the number of persons with whom an individual comes into contact makes it impossible for that individual to know everyone very well. The result is a **segmentalization of human relationships,** in which an individual comes to know *many* people but only in highly *segmental, partial* roles. According to Wirth:

> The contacts of the city may indeed be face-to-face, but they are nevertheless impersonal, superficial, transitory, and segmental. The reserve, the indifference, and the blasé outlook that urbanites manifest in their relationships may thus be regarded as devices for immunizing themselves against the personal claims and expectations of others.[5]

Anomie

anomie
a sense of social isolation and loss of personal recognition and self-worth

Large numbers mean a certain degree of freedom for the individual from the control of family groups, neighbors, churches, and other community groups. But urbanism also contributes to a sense of **anomie**—a sense of social isolation and a loss of the personal recognition, self-worth, and feeling of participation that come with living in a small integrated society. The social contacts of urban dwellers are more anonymous than those of rural dwellers; they interact with persons who have little if any knowledge of their life histories.

SECONDARY GROUP MEMBERSHIPS

Rural life emphasized **primary group ties**—interactions within the extended family. Many sociologists believe that urban life emphasizes **secondary group ties**—interactions among members of age and interest groups rather than among families and neighbors. Urban life is said to center around voluntary associations and secondary group memberships—crowds, recreational groups, civic clubs, business groups, and professional and work groups. Sociologists believe that urban dwellers have a greater number of interpersonal contacts than rural dwellers and that urban dwellers are more likely to interact with people as occupants of specific social roles. In contrast, rural dwellers are more likely to interact with individuals as full personalities.

primary groups
family and neighborhood groups known personally

secondary groups
interest or voluntary groups

SOCIAL CONTROL MECHANISMS

Urban society also presents problems of social control. The anomie of urban life is believed to weaken social mores and social group controls. External controls through a series of formal institutions, such as laws, and organizations, such as the courts and the police, become more essential. Thus, **social control** in the cities depends in large degree on *formal mechanisms*. But laws generally express the minimum behavioral standard, and urban life involves a much wider range of behavior than rural life. Moreover, laws do not always succeed in establishing minimum standards of behavior; crime rates increase with increases in urbanism.

social control
urban society based more on formal institutions than on social groups

MOBILITY

Another characteristic of urban life is **mobility,** or ease of movement. Urban mobility is both **physical** (from one geographic area to another) and **social** (from one position of social status to another). Rural communities are more stable than urban communities in both respects. Traditionally rural dwellers were more likely to stay near the place of their birth. In contrast, urbanites frequently move from city to city or from one section of a city to another. Social mobility is also greater in the city because of the wider range of economic opportunities there. Moreover, urban dwellers are judged far less by their family backgrounds (which are unknown) than by their own appearances, occupational accomplishments, incomes, and lifestyles. Although mobility creates opportunities for individuals, it weakens the sense of community. City dwellers do not think of their city as a community to which they belong but rather as a place they happen to live—a geographical entity commanding little personal allegiance. Mobility also creates psychological stress (see Focus, "Urban Stress").

physical mobility
movement from one location to another

social mobility
movement from one social status to another

both kinds of mobility greater in urban than in rural societies

Urban Stress

Although no statistics directly measure the psychological health of a city, there are important measures of psychosocial pathology, such as rates of alcoholism, suicide, divorce, and crime. These measures reflect both the causes and effects of psychological stress. By comparing U.S. metropolitan areas on the basis of these measures, it is possible to derive overall rankings that reflect the areas' psychological well-being.[a] The ten highest- and ten lowest-stress metropolitan areas out of the 286 areas ranked are shown in the table.

It is interesting that higher stress ratings are *not* associated with unemployment or poverty levels of cities. On the contrary, higher stress levels were found in cities with milder climates and healthier economic conditions. Psychological well-being is not necessarily related to economic well-being.

However, cities with a large proportion of new residents (migrants from other areas) appear to have higher rates of divorce, suicide, alcoholism, and crime. Thus, southern and western cities with higher rates of new arrivals display higher rates of these pathologies.

Moving to a new area may attract people who are having trouble in life and who think a fresh start will help turn their lives around. For many the move fails, and their residence in new areas drives up the stress ratings. Or the move itself, even for relatively stable individuals and families, may produce stress. New arrivals face new social strains and the pressures of adjustment. They have distanced themselves from their old friends and relations and do not have the psychological support that helped them in the past.

HIGHEST- AND LOWEST-STRESS METROPOLITAN AREAS

Ranking

	Lowest stress	Alcoholism	Crime	Suicide	Divorce
1	State College, Penn.	1	33	8	20
2	Grand Forks, N.D.	38	9	1	52
3	Saint Cloud, Minn.	44	3	16	15
4	Rochester, Minn.	6	17	19	65
5	McAllen, Texas	48	102	6	11
6	Altoona, Penn.	73	7	77	3
7	Bloomington, Ind.	4	61	3	182
8	Provo, Utah	8	24	40	30
9	Utica, N.Y.	29	8	26	34
10	Akron, Ohio	11	114	53	7
	Highest stress				
277	Los Angeles, Calif.	275	284	235	112
278	San Francisco, Calif.	267	276	268	174
279	Jacksonville, Fla.	262	227	262	274
280	Odessa, Texas	178	279	217	280
281	Little Rock, Ark.	167	242	264	284
282	Lakeland, Fla.	280	250	219	282
283	Miami, Fla.	248	285	274	205
284	Las Vegas, Nev.	285	283	285	285
285	Reno, Nev.	286	201	286	286
286	Panama City, Fla.	260	246	250	278

[a]See Robert Levine, "City Stress Index," *Psychology Today* (November 1988): 53–58.

POLITICAL CONFLICT

Urban life presents a serious problem in **conflict** management. Persons with different occupations, incomes, and educational levels are known to have different views on public issues. People at the bottom of the social ladder look at police—indeed, governmental authority in general—differently from the way those on higher rungs do. Persons who own their homes and those who do not own their homes regard taxation in a different light. Families with children and those without children have different ideas about school systems. And so it goes. Differences in the way people make their living, in their income and educational levels; in the color of their skin; in the way they worship; in their style of living—all are at the roots of political life in the metropolis.

political conflict
heterogeneity of urban life presents greater potential for conflict among diverse peoples

SUMMARY OF SOCIOLOGICAL THEORY OF URBANIZATION

Thus, sociological theory provides us with a series of characteristics to look for in urban life:

- large numbers of people
- population density
- social and economic heterogeneity
- ethnic and racial diversity
- numerous but superficial, segmental, utilitarian relationships
- impersonality and anonymity
- greater interaction in secondary groups
- reliance on formal mechanisms of social control
- physical and social mobility
- greater potential for conflict

Not all these characteristics of urban life have been documented. Indeed, in a highly industrialized and urbanized society such as the United States, it is sometimes difficult to discern any differences between rural and urban dwellers. Furthermore, urban dwellers display a great range and variation in lifestyle; some reflect the "typical" style described by sociological theory, and others do not. Many retain their commitment to the extended family, and many city neighborhoods are stable and socially cohesive communities. Despite the plausibility of the hypothesis that urban life leads to anonymity, impersonality, and segmentalization in social relationships, it is hard to prove systematically that urban dwellers are becoming more impersonal or anonymous than are rural dwellers. Finally, sociologists can no longer focus on central-city lifestyles in describing urban living. We must now take account of suburban lifestyles because more people live in suburbs than in central cities. And the suburban way of life is in many ways quite different from the way of life described in sociological theory.

weaknesses of theory

WHERE DO AMERICANS LIVE?

Three out of four Americans live in population clusters called *metropolitan areas.* Most of the nation's population increase is occurring in the suburbs of these areas. Approximately 44 percent of all Americans live in these suburbs, 32 percent live in central cities, and 24 percent live outside metropolitan areas.

What is a metropolitan area? Briefly, it consist of a central city of fifty thousand or more persons and the surrounding suburbs, which are socially and economically tired to the city (see Figure 13-2). The U.S. Census Bureau refers to metropolitan areas as **Metropolitan Statistical Areas (MSAs)** or, in the case of large metropolitan complexes with connecting metropolitan areas, **Consolidated Metropolitan Statistical Areas (CMSAs).** The nation's largest metropolitan areas are listed in Table 13-2.

CENTRAL CITY VERSUS SUBURBAN GROWTH

Very few large *central cities* are growing. Metropolitan areas are growing because their *suburbs* are growing. In the nineteenth century, industrial workers had to live within walking distance of their places of employment. Hence, the nineteenth-century American city crowded large masses of people into relatively small central areas, often in tenement houses and other high-density neighborhoods. But new modes of transportation—the streetcar, the private automobile, and, finally, the expressway—eliminated the necessity for workers to live close to their jobs. Now an individual can work in a central busi-

MSA

metropolitan statistical area, a city of 50,000 or more, plus surrounding urban population

CMSA

consolidated metropolitan statistical area, a metropolitan complex of connecting MSAs

TABLE 13-2

METRO-AMERICA: METROPOLITAN AREAS WITH ONE MILLION OR MORE RESIDENTS

New York	19.9	Pittsburgh	2.7	New Orleans	1.4
Los Angeles	15.5	Phoenix	2.7	Orlando	1.4
Chicago	8.6	San Diego	2.7	Charlotte (NC)	1.3
Washington/Baltimore	7.2	St. Louis	2.5	Buffalo (NY)	1.2
San Francisco	6.6	Denver	2.3	Greensboro	1.1
Philadelphia	6.0	Tampa	2.2	Hartford (CT)	1.1
Boston	5.6	Portland (OR)	2.0	Nashville	1.1
Detroit	5.3	Cincinnati	1.9	Providence (RI)	1.1
Dallas/Ft. Worth	4.6	Kansas City	1.6	Rochester	1.1
Houston	4.3	Milwaukee	1.6	Salt Lake City	1.1
Atlanta	3.5	Sacramento	1.6	Bakersfield (CA)	1.0
Miami/Ft. Lauderdale	3.5	Norfolk (VA)	1.5	Jacksonville	1.0
Seattle/Tacoma	3.3	San Antonio	1.5	Oklahoma City	1.0
Cleveland	2.9	Columbus (OH)	1.4	Raleigh-Durham	1.0
Minneapolis	2.8	Indianapolis	1.4		

SOURCE: U.S. Bureau of the Census, 1999.

ness district office or industrial plant and spend his or her evening in a residential suburb miles away. The same technology that led to the suburbanization of residences has also influenced commercial and industrial location. Originally industry was tied to waterways or railroads for access to supplies and markets. This dependence was reduced by the development of motor truck transportation, the highway system, and the greater mobility of the labor force. Today, many industries locate in the suburbs, particularly light industries, which do not require extremely heavy bulk shipment that can be handled only by rail or water. When industry and people moved to the suburbs, commerce followed. Giant suburban shopping centers sprang up to compete with downtown stores. Thus, metropolitan areas became decentralized as people, business, and industry spread over the suburban landscape.

GOVERNING URBAN COMMUNITIES

Local government is not mentioned in the U.S. Constitution. Although we regard the American federal system as a mixture of federal, state, and *local* governments, from a constitutional point of view, local governments are really a part of state governments. Communities have no constitutional right to self-government; all their governmental powers legally flow from state governments. Local governments—cities, townships, counties, special districts, and school districts—are *creatures of the states,* subject to the obligations, privileges, powers, and restrictions that state governments impose on them. The state, either through its constitution or its laws, may create or destroy any or all units of local government. To the extent that local governments can collect taxes, regulate their citizens, and provide services, they are actually exercising *state* powers delegated to them by the state in either its constitution or its laws.

> **local governments are creatures of state governments; all their powers legally flow from state governments**

The fifty states have created over 87,000 local governments (see Table 13-3). What do they all do? Different units of government are assigned different responsibilities by each of the states, so it is difficult to generalize about what each of these types of local government is supposed to do. Indeed, even in the same state there may be overlapping functions and responsibilities assigned to cities, counties, school districts, and special districts.[6]

TABLE 13-3

LOCAL GOVERNMENTS IN THE UNITED STATES

Counties	3,043
Municipalities	19,372
Townships	16,629
School districts	13,726
Special districts	34,683
Total (including states and national government)	87,504

SOURCE: U.S. Bureau of the Census, *Census of Government,* 1997.

FIGURE 13-2

METROPOLITAN STATISTICAL AREAS

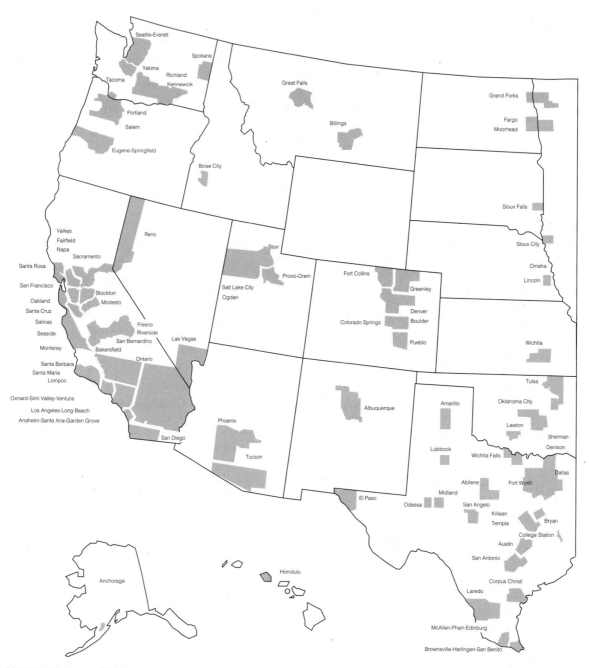

SOURCE: U.S. Bureau of the Census.

Duluth-Superior
St. Cloud
Minneapolis-St. Paul
Eau Claire
Appleton
Oshkosh
La Crosse
Rochester
Madison
Milwaukee
Racine
Kenosha
Rockford
Chicago
Kankakee
Waterloo
Cedar Falls
Dubuque
Cedar Rapids
Davenport
Rock Island
Moline
Des Moines
Peoria
St. Joseph
Topeka
Columbia
Lawrence
Kansas City
Springfield
Decatur
Champaign
Urbana
Rantoul
Fayetteville
Springdale
Little Rock
North Little Rock
Fort Smith
Pine Bluff
Texarkana
Longview
Shreveport
Monroe
Tyler
Alexandria
Houston
Baton Rouge
Lake Charles
Lafayette
New Orleans
Beaumont-Port Arthur-Orange
Galveston-Texas City

Green Bay
Muskegon
Norton Shores
Muskegon Heights
Grand Rapids
Lansing
East Lansing
Bay City
Saginaw
Flint
Detroit
Gary
Hammond
Battle Creek
East Chicago
Kalamazoo
Jackson
Ann Arbor
Toledo
Portage
South Bend
Fort
Wayne
Lima
Mansfield
Akron
Canton
Steubenville
Lafayette
West Lafayette
Kokomo
Springfield
Weirton
Wheeling
Norma
Bloomington
Muncie
Dayton
Columbus
Anderson
Hamilton
Cincinnati
Indianapolis
Middletown
Huntington
Bloomington
Evansville
Ashland
Louisville
Lexington
Fayette
Owensboro
Clarksville
Hopkinsville
Nashville
Davidson
Knoxville
Chattanooga
Huntsville
Memphis
Florence
Birmingham
Gadsden
Annison
Tuscaloosa
Columbus
Macon
Montgomery
Jackson
Biloxi
Gulfport
Mobile
Pensacola
Pascagoula
Moss Point
Panama City
Tallahassee
Albany

Cleveland
Lorain
Elyria
Youngstown
Warren
Williamsport
Pittsburgh
Altoona
Johnstown
York
Parkersburg
Marietta
Charleston
Washington
Richmond
Lynchburg
Johnson City
Roanoke
Petersburg
Kingsport-Bristol
Colonial Heights-Hopewell
Burlington
Raleigh
Greensboro
Winston-Salem
High Point
Charlotte
Gastonia
Fayetteville
Wilmington
Durham
Asheville
Greenville
Spartanburg
Columbia
Augusta
Charleston
North Charleston
Savannah
Jacksonville
Daytona Beach
Gainesville
Orlando
Melbourne-Titusville-Cocoa
Tampa-St. Petersburg
Bradenton
Sarasota
Fort Myers
West Palm Beach-Boca Raton
Fort Lauderdale-Hollywood
Miami

Rochester
Buffalo
Erie
Paterson-Clifton
Passaic
Binghamton
Elmira
Northeast
Pennsylvania
Reading
Harrisburg

Utica-Rome
Syracuse
Albany
Schenectady
Troy
Pittsfield
Fitchburg
Lepminster
Worcester
Poughkeepsie
Danbury
Newark
Lewiston
Auburn
Portland
Manchester
Nashua
Lowell
Lawrence-Haverhill
Springfield-Chicopee-Holyoke
Boston
Brockton
Hartford
New Bedford
Fall River
Providence-Warwick-Pawtucket
New London-Norwich
Bristol
New Britain
New Haven-West Haven
Meriden
Nassau-Suffolk
Waterbury
Bridgeport
Norwalk
Stamford
New York
Jersey City
Long Branch-Asbury Park
New Brunswick-Perth Amboy-Sayreville
Paterson-Clifton-Passaic
Trenton
Atlantic City
Allentown-Bethlehem-Easton
Vineland-Millville-Bridgeton
Philadelphia
Wilmington
Lancaster
Baltimore
Newport News-Hampton
Norfolk-Virginia Beach-Portsmouth

TYPES OF LOCAL GOVERNMENTS AND THEIR FUNCTIONS

Nevertheless, let us try to make some generalizations about what each of these types of government does, realizing, of course, that in any specific location the pattern of governmental activity may be slightly different:

functions of

rural counties

urban counties

cities

school districts

townships

special districts

- *Counties: rural*—keep records of deeds, mortgages, births, marriages; assess and levy property taxes; maintain local roads; administer elections and certify election results to state; provide law enforcement through sheriff; maintain criminal court; maintain a local jail; administer state welfare programs.

- *Counties: urban*—most of the same functions as the rural counties (except police and court systems, which often become city functions), together with planning and control of new subdivisions; mental health; public health maintenance and public hospitals; care of the aged; recreation, including parks, stadiums, and convention centers; and perhaps some city functions.

- *Cities*—provide the "common functions" of police, fire, streets, sewage, sanitation, and parks; over half of the nation's large cities also provide welfare services and public education. (In other cities, welfare is handled by county governments or directly by state agencies, and education is handled by separate school districts.)

- *School districts*—organized specifically to provide public elementary and secondary education; community colleges may be operated by county governments or by special districts with or without state support.

- *Townships*—generally subdivisions of counties with the same responsibilities as their county.

- *Special districts*—may be as large as the Port Authority of New York with more than $1 billion in diversified assets. However, special districts are usually established for mass transit, soil conservation, libraries, water and irrigation, mosquito control, sewage disposal, airports, and so on.

FORMS OF CITY GOVERNMENT

forms of city government

mayor-council

commission

council-manager

American city government comes in three structural packages. There are some adaptations and variations from city to city, but generally one can classify the form of city government as *mayor-council, commission,* or *council-manager.* Approximately 51 percent of American cities have the mayor-council form of government; 6 percent have the commission form; and 43 percent have the council-manager form. Figure 13-3 shows the general organization of these three forms of government.

FIGURE 13-3

Forms of City Government

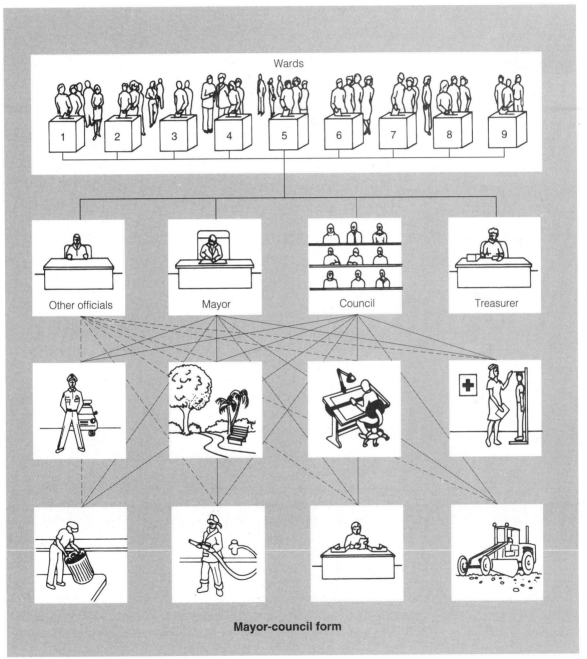

Mayor-council form

Continued

FIGURE 13-3

FORMS OF CITY GOVERNMENT (*Continued*)

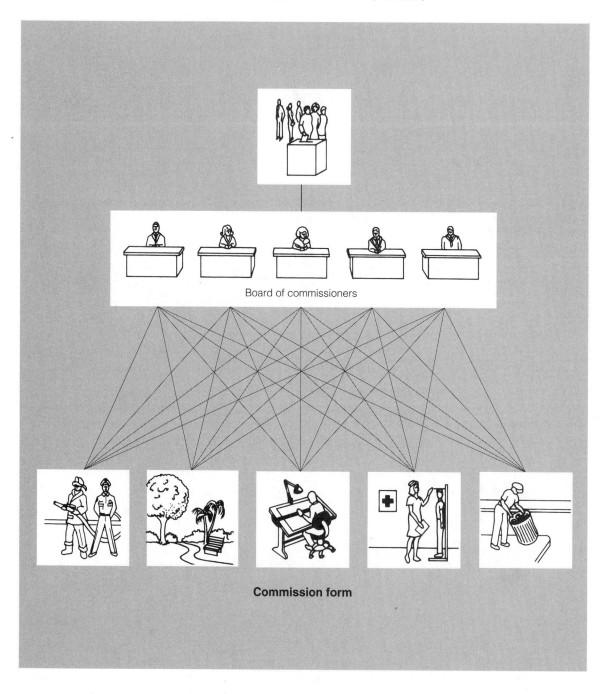

Board of commissioners

Commission form

FIGURE 13-3

FORMS OF CITY GOVERNMENT (*Continued*)

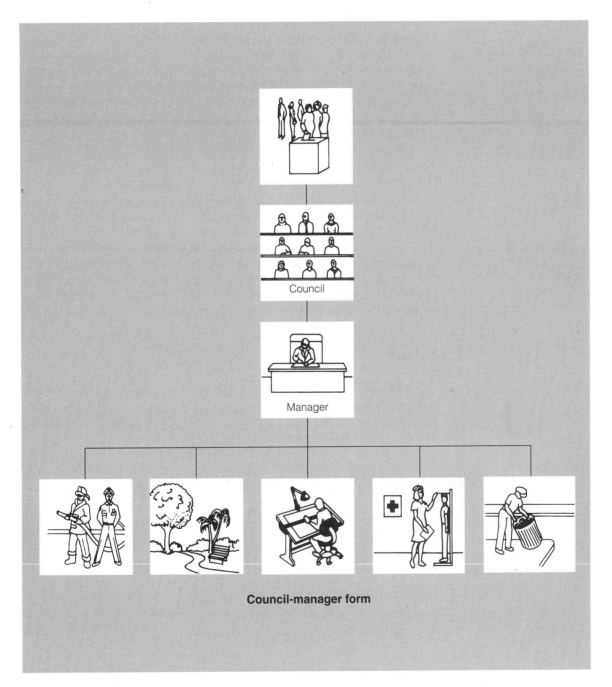

Council-manager form

Mayor-Council

The nation's largest cities tend to function under the *mayor-council* plan. This is the oldest form of American city government and is designed in the American tradition of separation of powers between legislature and executive. One may also establish subcategories of strong- or weak-mayor forms of mayor-council government. A strong mayor is the undisputed master of the executive agencies of city government and has substantial legislative powers in the form of budget making, vetoes, and opportunity to propose legislation. Only a few cities make the mayor the sole elected official among city executive officers; it is common for the mayor to share powers with other elected officials—city attorney, treasurer, tax assessor, auditor, clerk, and so on. Yet many mayors, by virtue of their prestige, persuasive abilities, or role as party leader, have been able to overcome most of the weaknesses of their formal office.

In recent years, large cities have been adding to the formal powers of their chief executives. Cities have augmented the mayors' roles by providing them with direction over budgeting, purchasing, and personnel controls. Independent boards, commissions, and individual council members have relinquished administrative control over city departments in many cities. Moreover, many cities have strengthened their mayors' position by providing them with a chief administrative officer (CAO) to handle important staff and administrative duties of supervising city departments and providing central management services.

Commission

The *commission* form of city government gives both legislative and executive powers to a small body, usually consisting of five members. The commission form originated at the beginning of the century as a reform movement designed to end a system of divided responsibility between mayor and council. One of the commission members is nominally the mayor, but he or she has no more formal powers than the other commissioners. The board of commissioners is directly responsible for the operation of city departments and agencies. In practice, one commission member will become responsible for the management of a specific department, such as finance, public works, or public safety. As long as the council members are in agreement over policy, there are few problems; but when commissioners differ among themselves and develop separate spheres of influence in city government, city government becomes a multiheaded monster, totally lacking in coordination. The results of the commission form of government were generally so disastrous that the reform movement abandoned its early support of this form of government in favor of the council-manager plan.

Council-Manager

The *council-manager* form of government revived the distinction between legislative "policy making" and executive "administration" in city government. Policy-making responsibility is vested in an elected council, and administration is assigned to an appointed professional administrator known as a manager, chosen by the council and responsible to it. All departments of the city government operate under the direction of the manager, who has the power to hire and fire personnel within the limits set by the merit system. The council's role in administration is limited to selecting and dismissing the city manager. The plan is based on the ideas that policy making and administration are separate functions and that the principal task of city government is to provide the highest level of services at the lowest possible costs—utilities, streets, fire and police protection, health, welfare, recreation, and so on. Hence, a professionally trained, career-oriented administrator is given direct control over city departments. (See Focus, "Who Really Runs This Town?")

THE CITY IN HISTORY

The United States developed an anticity bias in its rural beginnings and retained that bias long after it became a nation of city dwellers. When the first census was taken in 1790, a mere 5 percent of the nation's four million people lived in cities; there were only twenty-four towns with populations of twenty-five hundred or more. A strong anticity bias was already ingrained in the national character. In an age when technological progress was giving rise to the first industrial centers in Europe, the American social and economic outlook was decidedly agrarian. Most politicians and citizens distrusted cities, which Thomas Jefferson believed were not conducive to the exercise of virtue. Jefferson's warning notwithstanding, American cities steadily increased in population. The lure of urban life is reflected in the following Census Bureau figures showing the country's five most populous cities in 1820, 1870, 1950, 1980, 1990, and 2000.

from a rural to an urban America

1820		1870	
New York	152,000	New York	1,478,000
Philadelphia	65,000	Philadelphia	674,000
Baltimore	63,000	St. Louis	311,000
Boston	43,000	Chicago	299,000
New Orleans	27,000	Baltimore	267,000

1950		1980	
New York	7,896,957	New York	7,071,000
Chicago	3,620,962	Chicago	3,005,000
Philadelphia	2,071,605	Los Angeles	2,966,800
Los Angeles	1,970,338	Philadelphia	1,688,200
Detroit	1,849,568	Houston	1,594,100

1990		2000	
New York	7,323,000	New York	7,420,000
Los Angeles	3,485,000	Los Angeles	3,598,000
Chicago	2,784,000	Chicago	2,802,000
Houston	1,631,000	Houston	1,787,000
Philadelphia	1,586,000	Philadelphia	1,436,000

Who runs this town? Do the elected public officials actually make the important decisions? Or is there a "power structure" in this community that really runs things? Is city government of the people, by the people, and for the people? Or is it a government run by a small elite, with the masses of people largely apathetic and uninfluential in public affairs?

Social scientists have differed in their answers to these questions. Some social scientists (we shall call them *elitists*) believe that power in American communities is concentrated in the hands of relatively few people, usually top business and financial leaders. Elitists believe that this elite is subject to relatively little influence from the masses of people. Other social scientists (we shall call them *pluralists*) believe that power is widely shared in American communities among many leadership groups who represent segments of the community and who are held responsible by the people through elections and group participation.

Early Sociological Studies: "Middletown" and "Regional City"

One of the earliest studies of American communities, the classic study of Middletown (actually Muncie, Indiana), conducted by Robert and Helen Lynd in the mid-1920s and again in the mid-1930s, tended to confirm a great deal of elitist thinking about community power.[a] The Lynds found in Muncie a monolithic power structure dominated by the owners of the town's largest industry. Community power was firmly entrenched in the hands of the business class, centering on but not limited to the "X family."[b] This group's power was based on its control over the economic life in the city.

One of the most influential *elitist* studies of community politics was sociologist Floyd Hunter's *Community Power Structure,* a study of Atlanta, Georgia.[c] According to Hunter, no one person or family or business dominated "Regional City" (a pseudonym for Atlanta), as might be true in a smaller town. Instead, Hunter described several tiers of influentials, with the most important community decisions reserved for a top layer of the business community. Admission to the innermost circle was based primarily on one's position in the business world. These top decision makers were not formally organized but conferred informally and passed down decisions to government leaders, professional personnel, civic organizations, and other "front men." Hunter explained that the top power structure concerned itself only with major policy decisions; there were other substructures—economic, governmental, religious, educational, professional, civic, and cultural—that communicated and implemented the policies at the top levels.

Early Political Studies: New Haven

Perhaps the most influential of the *pluralist* community studies was Robert A. Dahl's *Who Gov-* *erns?,* a detailed analysis of decision making in New Haven, Connecticut.[d] Dahl chose to examine sixteen major decisions on redevelopment and public education in New Haven and on nominations for mayor in both political parties for seven elections. Dahl found a polycentric and dispersed system of community power in New Haven, in contrast to Hunter's highly monolithic and centralized power structure. Influence was wielded from time to time by many individuals, each exercising power over some issues but not over others. When the issue was one of urban renewal, one set of individuals was influential; in public education, a different group of leaders was involved. The business elite, said by Hunter to control Atlanta, was only one of many different influential groups in New Haven.

The mayor of New Haven was the only decision maker who was influential in most of the issue areas studied, and his degree of influence varied from issue to issue.

For many years, scholars studying community power argued over methods of research and interpretation of findings. Sociologists tended to study whole community social structures and interpret their findings in an elitist fashion. Political scientists tended to focus on local governmental decision making and interpret their findings as confirmation of the pluralist model. Yet even as research continued, American communities were undergoing changes in their power structures.

The Old Community Economic Elites

Traditionally, community power structures were composed primarily of economic elites whose goals were to maximize land values, real estate commissions, builders' profits, rent payments, and mortgage interest and to increase revenues to commercial enterprises serving the community. Communities were traditionally dominated by mortgage-lending banks, real estate developers, builders, and landowners. They were joined by owners or managers of local utilities, department stores, attorneys and title companies, and others whose wealth was affected by land use. Local bankers who financed the real estate developers and builders were often at the center of the elite structure.

These traditional community elites strove for consensus. They believed that community economic growth—increased capital investment, more jobs, and improved business conditions—benefited the entire community. Local government officials were expected to share in the elite consensus. Economic prosperity was necessary for protecting the tax base of local government. Moreover, economic growth was usually good politics. Growth-oriented candidates for public office usually had larger campaign treasuries than anti-growth candidates.[e]

The New Community Political Elites

Today, in many American communities the old economic elites are being replaced by new political elites. Many of the old economic elites sold their businesses to national corporations and vacated their positions of community leadership. Locally owned stores and factories became manager-directed plants and chain stores. The result was a weakening of community loyalties in the business sector. Local banks were merged into national banking corporations, and local bankers were replaced by banking executives with few community ties. City newspapers that were once independently owned by families who lived in the communities were bought up by giant newspaper and publication chains.

The nationalization of the American economy and the resulting demise of locally owned enterprises created a vacuum of leadership in community affairs. Professional politicians moved into this vacuum in city after city, largely replacing the local bankers, real estate developers, chambers of commerce, and old-style newspaper editors who had dominated community politics for generations. The new professional political elites work full-time at local politics. They are drawn primarily by personal ambition—not so much for wealth as for the power and celebrity that accompany running for and winning public office.[f]

The new political elites seldom have a large financial stake in the community, aside from their homes. They do not necessarily seek community consensus on behalf of prosperity. On the contrary, it's fashionable among new political elites to complain loudly about the problems created by growth—congestion, pollution, noise, unsightly development, or the replacement of green spaces with concrete slabs. No-growth movements appeal to people who already own their houses as well as to owners of already-developed commercial property. Curtailing growth freezes out competition for new homes, apartment complexes, and commercial centers. It allows owners of existing homes and properties to raise prices and rents to new residents. It is no surprise that "neighborhood associations," led by upper- and upper-middle-class homeowners, are at the forefront of no-growth politics.

[a]Robert S. Lynd and Helen M. Lynd, *Middletown* (New York: Harcourt, Brace & World, 1929), and *Middletown in Transition* (New York: Harcourt, Brace & World, 1937).

[b]The "X family," never identified in the Lynds's books, was actually the Ball family, glass manufacturers. Ball State University in Muncie, Indiana, is named for the family.

[c]Floyd Hunter, *Community Power Structure* (Chapel Hill: University of North Carolina Press, 1953).

[d]Robert Dahl, *Who Governs?* (New Haven, CT.: Yale University Press, 1961).

[e]Paul Peterson, *City Limits* (Chicago: University of Chicago Press, 1981): 20.

[f]Alan Ehrenhalt, *The United States of Ambition* (New York: Random House, 1991): 22.

ECONOMIC GROWTH

economic needs fuel growth

First as seaports, then as trading and manufacturing centers, cities in the United States grew in response to economic needs. "Villages expanded into towns; towns became metropolises," historian Lewis Mumford wrote in *The City in History.*

> Between 1820 and 1900, the destruction and disorder within cities was like that of a battlefield. . . . Industrialism, the main creative force of the nineteenth century, produced the most degraded urban environment the world had yet seen. . . . Men built in haste, and had hardly time to repent of their mistakes before they tore down their original structures and built again, just as heedlessly. The newcomers, babies, or immigrants, could not wait for new quarters: they crowded into whatever was offered. It was a period of vast urban improvisation: makeshift hastily piled upon makeshift.[7]

SOCIAL STRATIFICATION

social stratification in cities

By the late nineteenth century most large American cities had become socially and economically stratified. The affluent lived in their posh neighborhoods, comfortably isolated from the poor in their ethnic ghettos, whereas the middle classes tended to move to the less-expensive outlying areas. As populations spread, many central cities simply annexed those areas to which the middle class had gravitated. New York, for example, added more than 250 square miles in 1891, and in 1941 Boston doubled its area. Some states established automatic annexation procedures. By 1920, however, political opposition to the absorption of fringe areas mounted, and large cities, especially in the congested Northeast, found themselves unable to keep pace, through annexation or consolidation, with suburban migration.

SUBURBANIZATION

automobiles encourage suburban growth

During the 1920s, general prosperity and the increasing number of automobiles gave new impetus to the growth of the suburbs. In that decade, the suburban populations around the seventeen largest U.S. cities rose by nearly 40 percent, while the rate of growth for most cities fell sharply. But until the 1940s, the central city remained the focal point of business and industry; the surrounding suburbs were primarily commuter villages.

THE PROBLEMS OF THE INNER CITY

The nation's largest cities have become the principal location of virtually all of the social problems confronting our society—poverty, homelessness, racial tension, family instability, drug abuse, delinquency, and crime. Some of these problems were discussed in previous chapters (especially in Chapter 11, "Poverty and Powerlessness," and in Chapter 12, "Power, Crime, and Violence"), but it is important to note here that these problems are all made worse by their concentration in large cities. The concentration of social ills in the nation's cities is a relatively recent occurrence; as late as 1970 there were higher rates of poverty in rural America than in the cities.

SOCIAL AND ECONOMIC PROBLEMS

Why has the inner city become the locus of social problems? It has been argued that changes in the labor market from industrial goods-producing jobs to professional, financial, and technical service-producing jobs are increasingly polarizing the labor market into low-wage and high-wage sectors.[8] The decline in manufacturing jobs, together with a shift in remaining manufacturing jobs and commercial (sales) jobs to the suburbs, has left inner-city residents with fewer job opportunities. The rise in joblessness in the inner cities has in turn increased the concentration of poor people, added to the number of poor single-parent families, and increased welfare dependency.

social problems
joblessness

poverty

family disintegration

welfare dependency

economic problems
fewer high-paying manufacturing jobs

migrating of jobs to suburbs

OUT-MIGRATION

At the same time, inner-city neighborhoods have experienced an out-migration of working-class and middle-class families. The number of inner-city neighborhoods in which the poverty rate exceeds 40 percent has risen sharply.[9] The loss of working- and middle-class families creates further social instability. In earlier decades most inner-city adults were employed, and they invested their income and time in their neighborhoods, patronizing churches, stores, schools, and community organizations. Their presence in the community provided role models for youth. But their out-migration has decreased contact between the classes, leaving the poorest isolated and "truly disadvantaged." Inner-city residents now lack not only nearby jobs, but also access to job information, social learning through working role models, and (for some young women) suitable (that is, employed) marriage partners.

out-migration of working and middle class from inner city

CONCENTRATION EFFECTS

It is argued that joblessness and poverty are much more demoralizing when concentrated in the inner city. Neighborhoods that have few legitimate employment opportunities, inadequate job information networks, and poor schools not only weaken the work ethic, but also give rise to illegal income-producing activities in the streets—drugs, crime, prostitution. A jobless family living in a neighborhood where these ills are concentrated is influenced by the behaviors, beliefs, and perceptions of the people around them. These *concentration effects* make things worse. Moreover, the deterioration of inner-city neighborhoods saps the vitality of local businesses and public services, leading

concentration effects
absence of working role models

loss of job information

weakened work ethic

street-crime environment

deteriorating business and public services

Children often are left to play alone in poverty-stricken neighborhoods.

to fewer and shabbier movie theaters, restaurants, markets, parks, and play-grounds. Inner-city schools are particularly disadvantaged; as educational requirements for good jobs are rising, the quality of education available in the inner city is eroded by the concentration of children from poverty-impacted and disintegrating families. The fiscal burden on city governments increases: The cost of services to the inner city increases at the same time that the tax base is eroded by out-migrating businesses and working residents. In short, the problems of the inner city are the problems of the nation in concentrated form.

ON THE WEB

EXPLORING COMMUNITIES

United Nations. The best sources of information on the global community can be accessed through the official Web site of the United Nations (UN). The UN

home page (www.un.org) contains links to "United Nations Member States," an alphabetical listing of all UN member nations with links to official national Web sites of most nations. The UN's Economics and Social Department provides access to extensive information pertaining to such things as global environment, human settlement, population demographics, social development, human rights, and international trade.

Official City Sites. Virtually all large- and medium-sized American cities maintain Web sites, sponsored either by the city government itself, the city's chamber of commerce, or convention and visitors' bureaus. An independent service, Official City Sites, provides links to the Web sites of hundreds of U.S. cities (www.officialcitysites.org).

Local Government Organizations. Other sites of interest, especially to students of government, are those maintained by the following: National League of Cities (www.nlc.org), National Association of Counties (www.naco.org), and National Association of Towns and Townships (www.natat.org). These are organizations of local governments that provide extensive information on issues affecting communities.

International City-County Managers Association. Yet another major source of information on U.S. cities and counties is the International City/County Management Association (www.icma.org). This is the official organization of professional city and county managers. Among other things, its Web site advises students on the education and training requirements for city management.

ABOUT THIS CHAPTER

It has always been fashionable in the United States to deplore life in big cities. Thomas Jefferson believed cities were the source of human vice and that only a rural and small-town America could maintain democracy. When the first census of the United States was taken in 1790, only 5 percent of the American people lived in cities, whereas today three-quarters of our population live in large urban clusters known as metropolitan areas. We have changed from a rural society to an urban society. We are trying to cope with the social, psychological, economic, and political problems of urban life. We are particularly concerned with the deterioration of older central cities, the creation of African-American ghettos in large cities, "white flight" to the suburbs, and financial and governmental problems posed by growth and decline in metropolitan areas.

In this chapter, we have described where Americans live and the impact of urban life on social relations, psychological states of mind, government, and power relations. Now that you have read it, you should be able to

- describe changes over the past decade in central cities and suburbs of metropolitan areas and in nonmetropolitan areas
- identify the social characteristics associated with urban life
- discuss suburbanization and increasing separation of African-American central cities from white suburbs in large metropolitan areas
- discuss the social psychology of urban life
- describe various structures of government found in American cities
- describe "community power structures" and how they are changing over time
- describe the "concentration effects" of social problems in the inner city

DISCUSSION QUESTIONS

1. Describe overall growth and decline in central cities, suburbs, and nonmetropolitan areas of the United States. What is a CMSA?
2. According to sociologist Louis Wirth, what are the distinguishing characteristics of urban life?
3. Why do people choose to live in suburbs? What is meant by the statement "American life is becoming more, not less, segregated"?
4. How can we test the hypothesis that urban life is more impersonal than rural or small-town life?
5. What are the governmental functions of counties (rural and urban), cities, school districts, townships, and special districts?
6. What are the most common forms of city government?
7. What factors might account for the concentration of social problems in the inner city?
8. What is meant by *elitist* and *pluralist* descriptions of community power structures? What differences can be identified between older and newer community elites?

Chapter 14

Power among Nations

INTERNATIONAL POLITICS

The distinguished political scientist Hans Morgenthau wrote:

international politics
the worldwide struggle for power

> *International politics, like all politics, is a struggle for power. Whatever the ultimate aims of international politics, power is always the immediate aim. Statesmen and peoples may ultimately seek freedom, security, prosperity, or power itself. They may define their goals in terms of a religious, philosophic, economic, or social ideal. . . . But whenever they strive to realize their goal by means of international politics, they are striving for power.[1]*

In brief, we are reminded that the struggle for power is global—it involves all the nations and peoples of the world, whatever their goals or ideals, (see Cross-National Perspective, "Patriotism).

NATIONAL SOVEREIGNTY

sovereignty
legal power over internal affairs, freedom from external intervention, and legal recognition by other nations

There are about 200 independent nations in the world today. Of these nations 188 (as of 2000) are members of the United Nations. Yet all the nations of the world—whatever their size, location, culture, politics, economic system, or level of technological development—claim **sovereignty.** Sovereignty

CROSS-NATIONAL PERSPECTIVE

Patriotism

Americans express more pride in their own country and in the way their democracy works than the people of virtually any other country in the world. Only Canadians appear to be as proud of their country as Americans.

Question: How proud are you of [own country] and the way its democracy works?

	Proud	Not Proud
Canada	84%	16%
United States	83	17
Great Britain	68	32
Germany	68	32
Japan	66	34
Spain	54	46
Poland	25	75
Russia	21	79

If patriotism is defined as a preference for citizenship in one's own country, Americans are the most patriotic people in the world.

Question: How much do you agree or disagree with the following statement: I would rather be a citizen of [own country] than any other country in the world?

	Agree
United States	91%
Japan	89
Poland	88
Hungary	87
Philippines	87
Canada	81
Norway	78
Russia	75
Germany	74
Spain	73
Great Britain	72
Italy	63
Netherlands	50

SOURCE: International Social Survey Program, as reported in *Public Perspective,* June/July 1999.

means formal, legal power over internal affairs; freedom from external intervention; and political and legal recognition by other nations. Sovereignty is a legal fiction, of course: Many nations have difficulty controlling their internal affairs; they are constantly meddling in each other's internal affairs and even trampling on each other's political and legal authority. Nonetheless, the *struggle* to achieve sovereignty is an important force in world politics.

Although sovereignty is highly valued by all nations, it creates an international system in which no authority—not even the United Nations—is given the power to make or enforce rules binding on all nations. There is *no world government.* Nations cooperate with each other only when it is in their own interests to do so. Nations can make treaties with each other, but there is no court to enforce the treaties, and they can be (and are) disregarded when it becomes advantageous for a nation to do so.

INTERNATIONAL LAW

There is a series of customs and principles among nations—known as **international law**—that helps to guide relations among nations. But international

international law
a legal fiction that guides relations among nations

"law" is also a fiction: There is no international "police force" to enforce the law, and it is frequently broken or ignored. An International Court (at The Hague, the Netherlands) exists to decide conflicts according to international law, but nations do not have to submit to the authority of this court and can, if they wish, ignore its decisions. The United Nations has no real power to enforce its resolutions, unless one or more nations (acting in their own self-interest) decide to try to enforce a UN resolution with their own troops, or contribute troops to a joint "UN force." But UN forces are really the forces of sovereign nations that have voluntarily decided to contribute troops to enforce a particular resolution.

BRINGING ORDER TO INTERNATIONAL RELATIONS

The instability and insecurity of "the global game of power" have led to many attempts over the centuries to bring order to the international system.[2] Indeed, wars among nations have averaged one every two years, and if "civil wars" and "indirect aggressions" are counted, the rate of armed conflict is even greater.

THE BALANCE-OF-POWER SYSTEM—NINETEENTH CENTURY

the balance-of-power system, 1815–1914

One method of trying to bring order to international relations is the *balance-of-power system*. The nineteenth century saw a deliberate attempt to stabilize

International relations are important to every country.

international relations by creating a system of alliances among nations that was designed to balance the power of one group of nations against the power of another and thus to discourage war. If the balance worked, war would be avoided and peace would be assured. For almost an entire century, from the end of the Napoleonic Wars (1815) to World War I (1914), the balance-of-power system appeared to be at least partially effective in Europe. But an important defect in the balance-of-power system is that a small conflict between two nations that are members of separate alliances can draw all the member nations of each alliance into the conflict.

This defect can result in the rapid expansion of a small conflict into a major war between separate alliances of nations. Essentially this is what happened in **World War I,** when a minor conflict in the Balkan nations resulted in a very destructive war between the *Allies* (England, France, Russia, and eventually the United States) and the *Central Powers* (Germany, Austria–Hungary, and Turkey).

World War I
the Allies versus the Central Powers

Indeed, World War I proved so destructive (ten million men were killed on the battlefields between 1914 and 1918) that there was a worldwide demand to replace the balance-of-power system with a new arrangement— "collective security."

COLLECTIVE SECURITY—THE UNITED NATIONS

Collective security originally meant that *all* nations would join together to guarantee each other's "territorial integrity and existing political independence" against "external aggression" by any nation.[3] This concept resulted in the formation of *the League of Nations* in 1919. However, opposition to international involvement was so great in the United States after World War I that after a lengthy debate in the Senate, the United States refused to join the League of Nations. More important, the League of Nations failed completely to deal with rising militarism in Germany, Japan, and Italy in the 1930s. During that decade, Japan invaded Manchuria, Italy invaded Ethiopia, and Germany invaded Czechoslovakia; and the League of Nations failed to prevent any of these aggressions. Fascism in Germany and Italy and militarism in Japan went unchecked. **World War II** between the *Allies* (the United States, England, France, China, and the Soviet Union) and the *Axis Powers* (Germany, Italy, and Japan) was even more devastating than World War I: World War II cost more than forty million lives, both civilian and military.

efforts at collective security

the League of Nations

World War II
the Allies versus the Axis Powers

the United Nations
General Assembly

Security Council

secretary-general

specialized bodies

veto powers

Yet even after World War II, the notion of collective security remained an ideal of the victorious Allied powers, especially the United States, Great Britain, the Soviet Union, France, and China. The Charter of *the United Nations* was signed in 1945. The new organization originally included fifty-one members. The UN provided for (1) a Security Council with eleven members, five of them being permanent members (the United States, the USSR, Britain, France, and China) and having the power to veto any action by the Security Council; (2) a General Assembly composed of

USSR
Union of Soviet Socialist Republics (Soviet Union). Fifteen "republics" including Russia; under communist rule 1917–1991; upon dissolution of USSR in 1991, UN seat assumed by Russia

The United Nations General Assembly has authority over "any matter affecting the peace of the world."

all the member nations, each with a single vote; (3) a secretariat headed by a secretary-general with a staff at UN headquarters in New York; and (4) several special bodies to handle specialized affairs—for example, the Economic and Social Council, the Trusteeship Council, and the International Court at The Hague.

The Security Council has the "primary responsibility" for maintaining "international peace and security." For this reason the world's most powerful nations—the United States, Russia, Great Britain, France, and China—have permanent seats on the council and veto powers over all but procedural matters. (Germany and Japan, originally denied Security Council membership as defeated powers in World War II, are currently leading candidates for permanent Security Council seats.)

The General Assembly has authority over "any matter affecting the peace of the world," although it is supposed to defer to the Security Council if the council has already taken up a particular matter. No nation has a veto in the General Assembly; all UN member nations have one vote, regardless of their size or power. Most resolutions can be passed by a majority vote.

The United Nations proved largely ineffective during the long **Cold War** confrontation between the communist nations, led by the USSR, and the western democracies, led by the United States. Many of the new nations admitted to the UN were headed by authoritarian regimes of one kind or another. The western democracies were outnumbered in the General Assembly, and the USSR frequently used its veto to prevent action by the Security Council. Antiwestern and antidemocratic speeches became common in the General Assembly. The UN was overshadowed by the confrontation of the world's two **superpowers:** the United States and the USSR (the Soviet Union). Indeed, international conflicts throughout the world—in the Middle East, Africa, Latin America, southeast Asia, and elsewhere—were usually influenced by some aspect of the superpower struggle.

Cold War
political, military, and ideological conflict between communist nations, led by the USSR, and the western democracies, led by the United States, from 1945 to 1990

superpowers
Cold War term referring to the United States and the Soviet Union as the dominant world powers

REGIONAL SECURITY—NATO

The general disappointment with the United Nations as a form of collective security gave rise as early as 1949 to a different approach: **regional security.** In response to aggressive Soviet moves in Europe, the United States and the democracies of western Europe created the **North Atlantic Treaty Organization (NATO).** In the NATO treaty, fifteen western nations agreed to collective regional security: They agreed that "an armed attack against one or more NATO nations . . . shall be considered an attack against them all." The United States made a specific commitment to defend western Europe in the event of a Soviet attack. A joint NATO military command was established (with Dwight D. Eisenhower as its first commander) to coordinate the defense of western Europe. After the formation of NATO, the Soviets made no further advances into western Europe. The Soviets themselves, in response to NATO, drew up a comparable treaty among their own eastern European satellite nations: the *Warsaw Pact.* Note that these regional security agreements—NATO and the Warsaw Pact—were more like the nineteenth-century balance-of-power alliances than like the true concept of *collective security.* The original notion of collective security envisioned agreement among *all* nations, whereas NATO and the Warsaw Pact were similar to the older systems of separate alliances.

regional security
an attempt to bring order to international relations during the Cold War by creating regional alliances between a superpower and nations of a particular region

NATO
regional alliance of western democracies to protect themselves against Soviet aggression

The Warsaw Pact disintegrated following the dramatic collapse of the communist governments of eastern Europe in 1989. Former Warsaw Pact nations—Poland, Hungary, Romania, Bulgaria, and East Germany—threw out their ruling communist regimes and began negotiations leading to the withdrawal of Soviet troops from their territory. The Berlin Wall was smashed in 1989, and Germany was formally reunified in 1990, bringing together sixty-one million prosperous people of West Germany with seventeen million less affluent people of East Germany. United Germany continues as a member of NATO.

collapse of communist governments and Warsaw Pact

THE FUTURE OF NATO

The reduced threat of attack on western Europe has raised several questions regarding the future of NATO.[4] Should NATO expand its security protection to the newly democratic nations of eastern Europe? Three nations—Poland, Hungary, and Czech Republic—successfully appealed for membership in NATO in 1998. The peoples of these nations had previously attempted to resist Soviet (Russian) military intervention in their countries during the Cold War, and all exhibited a strong commitment to democracy. Russia strongly objected to this expansion of NATO and promises to oppose any further expansion of NATO to other eastern European Nations (especially Latvia, Estonia, and Lithuania, all previously incorporated into the old Soviet Union).

Another question confronting NATO is whether or not ethnic conflicts in eastern Europe, especially in the former Yugoslavia, threaten the security of western Europe. Should NATO forces be deployed outside the national boundaries of NATO nations? The combination of security and humanitarian concerns drew NATO into the former Yugoslavian province of Bosnia in 1995 to assist in resolving conflict among Serbs, Croats, and Muslims. The United States provided about one-third of the NATO military forces deployed in Bosnia. NATO again acted militarily to halt ethnic conflict in Kosovo in 1999. NATO forces, including U.S. aircraft, bombed targets in both Kosovo and Serbia Itself. (Even the Chinese Embassy in the Serbian capital of Belgrade was bombed, apparently by mistake.) Eventually, Serbian troops were withdrawn from Kosovo and replaced by NATO troops.

A REVITALIZED UN

The end of the Cold War has injected new vitality into the United Nations. Russia inherited the UN Security Council seat of the former USSR, and the Russian government has generally cooperated in UN efforts to bring stability to various regional conflicts. No longer are these conflicts "proxy" wars between the superpowers. Cooperation between the permanent members of the Security Council (the United States, Great Britain, France, and Russia, together with the acquiescence of China) has brought "a new world order" to international politics. But the United Nations and its Security Council must rely on "the last remaining superpower," the United States, to take the lead in enforcing its resolutions.[5]

A BRIEF HISTORY OF THE COLD WAR

For forty-five years following the end of World War II, the United States and the Soviet Union confronted each other in a protracted political, military, and ideological struggle known as the Cold War.

ORIGINS

During World War II, the United States and the Soviet Union joined forces to eliminate the Nazi threat to the world. The United States dismantled its military forces at the end of the war in 1945, but the USSR, under the brutal dictatorship of Joseph Stalin, used the powerful Red Army to install communist governments in the nations of eastern Europe in violation of wartime agreements to allow free elections. Stalin also ignored pledges to cooperate in a unified allied occupation of Germany; Germany was divided, and in 1948 Stalin unsuccessfully tried to oust the United States, Britain, and France from Berlin in a year-long "Berlin Blockade." Former British Prime Minister Winston Churchill warned America in a 1946 speech that the Soviets were dividing Europe with an "Iron Curtain." When Soviet-backed communist guerrilla forces threatened Greece and Turkey in 1948, President Harry S Truman responded with a pledge to "support free people who are resisting attempted subjugation by armed minorities or by outside pressures," a policy that became known as the Truman Doctrine.

CONTAINMENT

The threat of Soviet expansionism and communist world revolution caused the American government to assume world leadership on behalf of the preservation of democracy. The U.S. State Department's Russian expert, George F. Kennan, called for a policy of **containment:** "It is clear that the main element of any United States policy toward the Soviet Union must be that of a long-term, vigilant containment of Russian expansive tendencies."[6] To implement the containment policy, the United States first initiated the **Marshall Plan,** named for Secretary of State George C. Marshall, to rebuild the economies of the western European nations. Marshall reasoned that *economically* weak nations were more susceptible to communist subversion and Soviet intimidation. The subsequent formation of NATO provided *military* support to contain the USSR.

containment
a policy of preventing the enemy from expanding its boundaries and/or influence; describes U.S. foreign policy vis-à-vis the USSR during the Cold War

Marshall Plan
a U.S. program to rebuild the nations of western Europe in the aftermath of World War II in order to render them less susceptible to communist influence and/or takeover

THE KOREAN WAR

The first military test of the containment policy came in June 1950, when communist North Korean armies invaded South Korea. President Truman believed (correctly) that the North Koreans were acting on behalf of their sponsor, the Soviet Union. The Soviets had already aided Chinese communists under the leadership of Mao Zedong in capturing control of mainland China in 1949. The United States quickly brought the Korean invasion issue to the Security Council. With the USSR boycotting this meeting because the Council had refused to seat the new communist delegation from China, the Council passed a resolution calling on member nations to send troops to repel the invasion.

the Korean War
1950–1953

America's conventional (nonnuclear) military forces had been largely dismantled after World War II. Moreover, President Truman insisted on keeping most of the nation's forces in Europe, fearing that the Korean invasion was a diversion to be followed by a Soviet invasion of western Europe. But General Douglas MacArthur, in a brilliant amphibious landing at Inchon behind North Korean lines, destroyed a much larger enemy army, captured the North Korean capital, and moved northward toward the Chinese border. Then in December of 1950, disaster struck American forces as a million-man Chinese army entered the conflict. Chinese troops surprised American forces, inflicting heavy casualties, trapping entire units, and forcing U.S. troops to beat a hasty retreat. General MacArthur urged retaliation against China, but Truman sought to keep the war "limited." When MacArthur publicly protested against political limits to military operations, Truman dismissed the popular general. The Korean War became a bloody stalemate.

Dwight Eisenhower was elected president in 1952 after he had promised to "go to Korea" to end the increasingly unpopular war. He also threatened to use nuclear weapons in the conflict, but eventually agreed to a settlement along the original border between North and South Korea. Communist expansion in Korea was "contained" but at a high price: The United States lost over thirty-eight-thousand men in the war.

CUBAN MISSILE CRISIS

The United States initially welcomed Fidel Castro's overthrow of the repressive Batista regime in Cuba in 1959, but when Castro allied his government with Moscow and invited Soviet military intervention into the western hemisphere, Washington sought his ouster. Under President Eisenhower, the CIA had planned a large "covert" operation—an *invasion of Cuba* by a brigade of Cuban exiles. Newly installed president John F. Kennedy approved the Bay of Pigs operation in early 1961, but when Castro's air force destroyed the makeshift invasion fleet offshore, Kennedy refused to provide U.S. Air Force support. The surviving Cubans were forced to surrender.

thwarted Bay of Pigs invasion of Cuba
1961

The young president was tested again in 1961, when the Russians erected the *Berlin Wall,* physically dividing that city. Despite heated rhetoric, Kennedy did nothing. Eventually the Wall would become a symbol of Soviet repression.

Berlin Wall built
1961

The most serious threat of nuclear holocaust during the entire Cold War, however, was the Cuban missile crisis.[7] In 1962, Soviet Premier Nikita Khrushchev sought to secretly install medium-range nuclear missiles in Cuba in an effort to give the USSR immediate nuclear capability against U.S. cities. In October 1962, intelligence photos showing Soviet missiles at Cuban bases touched off the thirteen-day *Cuban missile crisis.* President Kennedy publicly announced a naval blockade of Cuba, threatening to halt Soviet vessels at sea by force if necessary. The prospect of war

Cuban missile crisis
1962

appeared imminent; U.S. nuclear forces went on alert. Secretly, Kennedy proposed to withdraw U.S. nuclear missiles from Turkey in exchange for Soviet withdrawal of nuclear missiles from Cuba. Khrushchev's agreement to the deal appeared to the world as a backing down; Secretary of State Dean Rusk would boast: "We were eyeball to eyeball, and they blinked." Kennedy would be hailed for his statesmanship in the crisis; Khrushchev soon lost his job.

THE VIETNAM WAR

The United States's involvement in Vietnam also grew out of the policy of "containment."[8] President Eisenhower had declined to intervene in the former French colony in 1956 when communist forces led by Ho Chi Minh defeated French forces at the battle of Dien Bien Phu. The resulting Treaty of Paris divided that country into North Vietnam, with a communist government, and South Vietnam, with a U.S.-backed government. When South Vietnamese communist (Vietcong) guerrilla forces threatened the South Vietnamese government in the early 1960s, President Kennedy sent a large force of advisers and counterinsurgency forces to assist in every aspect of training and support for the Army of the Republic of Vietnam (ARVN). By 1964 units of the North Vietnamese Army (NVA) had begun to supplement the Vietcong guerrilla forces in the South. President Lyndon B. Johnson ordered U.S. combat troops into South Vietnam in February 1965 and authorized a gradual increase in air strikes against North Vietnam. Eventually over 500,000 American troops were committed to Vietnam; over 2.8 million served there before the **Paris Peace Agreement** was signed in 1973; 47,366 were killed in action. A short history of the Vietnam War is presented in Chapter 8, "Vietnam: A Political History."

Paris Peace Agreement ending U.S. participation in Vietnam War, 1973

THE VIETNAM SYNDROME OF THE 1970S

A new isolationism permeated American foreign policy following defeat in Vietnam. The slogan "No more Vietnams" was used to oppose any U.S. military intervention, whether or not U.S. vital interests were at stake. Disillusionment replaced idealism. American leaders had exaggerated the importance of Vietnam; now Americans were unwilling to believe their leaders when they warned of other dangers. The USSR rapidly expanded its political and military presence in Asia, Africa, the Middle East, Central America, and the Caribbean in the late 1970s. The United States did little to respond to this wave of Soviet expansionism until the *Soviet invasion of Afghanistan* in 1979, when President Carter authorized the largest covert action in CIA history—the military support of the Afghan guerrilla forces fighting Soviet occupation. The Soviets suffered a heavy drain of human and economic resources in their nine-year war in Afghanistan, which some dubbed "Russia's Vietnam."

Afghanistan "Russia's Vietnam"

Rebuilding America's Defenses in the 1980s

A decision to rebuild America's military forces and reassert international leadership on behalf of democratic values gained widespread endorsement. In 1979 President Jimmy Carter presented Congress with the first request for an increase in defense spending in over a decade. The NATO nations jointly pledged to increase their defense efforts. British Prime Minister Margaret Thatcher, French President François Mitterand, and German Chancellor Helmut Kohl all held fast against a "nuclear freeze" movement that would have locked in Soviet superiority in European-based nuclear weapons. When the Reagan administration arrived in Washington in 1981, the defense buildup had already begun.

U.S. defense buildup
1979–1985

The Reagan defense buildup extended through 1985—with increases in defense spending, improvements in strategic nuclear weapons, and, perhaps more importantly, the rebuilding and reequipping of U.S. conventional forces. President Reagan also announced a new **strategic defense initiative (SDI)**, a research program to develop a defense against a ballistic missile attack, promptly labeled "Star Wars" by the media.

"Star Wars"
the strategic defense initiative (SDI) to develop a defense against ballistic missile attack

The American and NATO defense buildup of the 1980s, together with the promise of a new, expensive, and technologically sophisticated race for ballistic missile defense, forecast heavy additional strains on the weak economy of the Soviet Union. Thus in 1985, when new Soviet President Mikhail Gorbachev came to power, the stage was set for an end to the Cold War.

Gorbachev and Reform

Gorbachev believed that economic progress in the Soviet Union required a reduction in that nation's heavy military expenditures and improved relations with the United States. He announced reductions in the size of the Soviet military and reached agreements with the United States on the reduction of nuclear forces. More importantly, in 1988 he announced that the Soviet Union would no longer use its military forces to keep communist governments in power in eastern European nations. This stunning announcement (for which Gorbachev received the Nobel Peace Prize in 1990) encouraged opposition democratic forces in Poland (the Solidarity movement), Czechoslovakia, Hungary, Bulgaria, Romania, and East Germany to overthrow their communist governments in 1989. Gorbachev refused to intervene to halt the destruction of the Berlin Wall that same year, despite the pleas by the East German hard-line communist leader Eric Honnecker.

The Disintegration of the Soviet Union

Strong independence movements in the republics of the USSR emerged as the authority of the centralized Communist party in Moscow waned. Lithuania, Estonia, and Latvia—nations that had been forcibly incorporated into the Soviet Union in 1939—led the way to independence in 1991. Soon all of the fifteen republics of the USSR declared their independence, and the Union of Soviet Socialist Republics officially ceased to exist after December 31, 1991. The red flag with its hammer and sickle was replaced with the flag of the Russian Republic. Boris Yeltsin became the first elected president in the history of Russia.

RUSSIA AFTER COMMUNISM

The transition from a centralized state-run economy to free markets turned out to be more painful for Russians than expected. Living standards for most people declined, alcoholism and death rates increased, and even average lifespans shortened. President Boris Yeltsin was confronted by both extreme nationalists, who believed democracy weakened the power of Russia in the world, and the continuing efforts of Communists to regain their lost power. Ethnic conflict and political separatism, especially in the largely Muslim province of Chechnya, added to Russia's problems. (Only in 2000, after prolonged fighting, did Russian troops finally take control of most of the province.) Yet Yeltsin was able to overcome these political challenges and win reelection as president in 1996. But corruption, embezzlement, graft, and organized crime continue to undermine democratic reforms. Ill health eventually forced Yeltsin to turn over power to Vladimir Putin, who himself won election as president of Russia in 2000.

The United States has a vital continuing interest in promoting democracy and economic reform in Russia. Russia remains the only nuclear power capable of destroying the United States.[9]

THE CONTROL OF NUCLEAR ARMS

Nuclear weaponry made the Cold War infinitely more dangerous than any national confrontation in human history. The nuclear arsenals of the United States and the former USSR threatened a human holocaust. Yet, paradoxically, the very destructiveness of nuclear weapons caused leaders on both sides to exercise extreme caution in their relations with each other. Scores of wars, large and small, were fought by different nations during the Cold War years, yet American and Soviet troops never engaged in direct combat against each other.

In 1957 the USSR launched *Sputnik,* the first artificial satellite to orbit the earth. Americans were shocked to know that the Soviets led in the space race. By the early 1960s, a new and very dangerous balance of nuclear terror had emerged. Both the United States and the Soviet Union possessed large arsenals of nuclear weapons and intercontinental ballistic missiles (ICBMs), capable of carrying these weapons through space to targets in each other's homeland.

SALT I

Following the election of Richard Nixon as president in 1968, the United States, largely guided by former Harvard professor Henry Kissinger (national security adviser to the president and later secretary of state), began negotiations with the Soviet Union over nuclear arms. In 1972 the United States and the USSR concluded two and one-half years of Strategic Arms Limitation Talks (SALT) about limiting the nuclear arms race. The agreement, **SALT I,** consists of a treaty limiting antiballistic missiles (ABMs) and an agreement placing a numerical ceiling on offensive missiles. Under the offensive-arms agreement, each side was frozen at the total number of offensive missiles completed or under construction. Both sides could construct new missiles if they dismantled an equal number of older missiles. Each nation agreed not to interfere in the satellite intelligence-gathering activities of the other nation. Both nations pledged to continue efforts at further arms control—the SALT II talks.

SALT I: 1972
the ABM treaty agreement, and limits on the numbers of offensive missiles

SALT II

The United States and the Soviet Union signed the lengthy and complicated **SALT II** treaty in 1979. It set an overall limit on strategic nuclear launchers—ICBMs, SLBMs, bombers, and long-range cruise missiles—for each side. It also limited the number of missiles that could carry multiple nuclear warheads (MIRVs) and banned new types of ICBMs, with the exception of one new type of ICBM for each side. But the Soviets were allowed to keep 314 very heavy SS-18 missiles for which the United States had no equivalent. When the Soviet Union invaded Afghanistan, President Carter withdrew the SALT II treaty from Senate consideration. However, President Carter, and later President Reagan, announced that the United States would abide by the provisions of the unratified SALT II treaty as long as the Soviet Union did so.

SALT II: 1979
agreement limiting all types of nuclear launchers as well as number of warheads on launchers

START TALKS

In negotiations with the Soviets, the Reagan administration pushed for *reductions* in missiles and warheads, not merely for limitations on future numbers and types of weapons as in previous SALT talks. To symbolize this new direction, President Reagan renamed the negotiations the **Strategic Arms Reductions Talks,** or **START.** The president emphasized that any new treaty must result in reductions of strategic arms to levels equal for both sides. The Soviets objected strongly to President Reagan's research efforts in the field of ballistic missile defense (SDI). In 1983 the Soviets walked out of the START talks and out of talks seeking to limit European nuclear weapons. But by 1985, after President Reagan's reelection, the Soviets returned to the bargaining table at Geneva, Switzerland.

START talks
renamed arms control talks to emphasize reductions in strategic nuclear weapons

INF Treaty

The **Intermediate-Range Nuclear Forces (INF) Treaty** in 1987 was the first agreement between the superpowers that actually resulted in the destruction of nuclear weapons. It eliminated an entire class of nuclear weapons—missiles with an intermediate range, between three hundred and thirty-eight hundred miles. It was also the first treaty that resulted in equal levels (zero) of arms for the United States and the USSR. To reach an equal level, the Soviets were required to destroy more missiles and warheads than the United States. Finally, INF was the first treaty to provide for on-site inspection for verification. The proportion of each side's nuclear weapons covered by the INF Treaty was small, but this treaty set the pattern for future arms control agreements in its provisions for *reductions, equality,* and *verification.*

INF Treaty
eliminated intermediate-range ballistic missiles

U.S. principles in arms control
reductions

equality

verification

START I and II

The long-awaited agreement on long-range strategic nuclear weapons was finally signed in Moscow in 1991 by Presidents George Bush and Mikhail Gorbachev. The START I Treaty included a 30-percent reduction in the total number of deployed strategic nuclear delivery systems (ICBMs, SLBMs, and manned bombers); and a reduction of nearly 50 percent in the total number of strategic nuclear warheads to no more than six thousand.

START Treaties
reduction to three thousand warheads for each side

elimination of all land-based missiles with nuclear warheads

on-site verification

FIGURE 14-1

Strategic Nuclear Arms under START Treaties

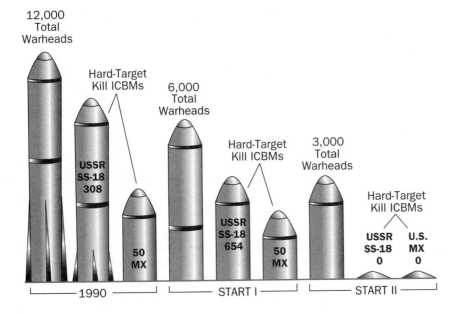

12,000 Total Warheads

Hard-Target Kill ICBMs

USSR SS-18 308

50 MX

6,000 Total Warheads

Hard-Target Kill ICBMs

USSR SS-18 654

50 MX

3,000 Total Warheads

Hard-Target Kill ICBMs

USSR SS-18 0

U.S. MX 0

— 1990 —   — START I —   — START II —

The ink had not yet dried on the new treaty when Russia's first democratically elected president, Boris Yeltsin, agreed to even deeper cuts in nuclear weapons and, more importantly, to the eventual elimination of all land-based missiles with multiple (MIRV) warheads. This historic agreement between Presidents Bush and Yeltsin in 1992, when fully implemented in 2003, will virtually eliminate the threat of a massive nuclear attack—a threat that had cast a menacing shadow over the world for decades. The START II Treaty includes a reduction to three thousand nuclear warheads for each side, together with the elimination of all "hard target kill" land-based missiles with multiple warheads, including Russia's huge SS-18 and the United States's MX, and a provision for on-site verification of these reductions by teams of observers from both nations (see Figure 14-1).

REGIONAL BALANCES OF POWER

end of Cold War focuses new attention on regional conflicts

The end of the Cold War does not ensure world peace. Iraq's invasion of Kuwait in 1990 and its threatened military takeover of Saudi Arabia and the Gulf states reminded the world that there are many other international conflicts and threats to peace (see Case Study, "American Military Power: 'Desert Storm'"). Regional struggles for power have their own roots. The easing of Cold War tensions focuses new attention on regional conflicts in Asia, Latin America, Africa, and especially the Middle East.

"new world order"
ending of Cold War provides opportunity for stable world peace

Regional powers can no longer drag the United States or Russia into their disputes by playing one power against the other. The western democracies, led by the United States, have been victorious in the Cold War, and now it is time to build a **"new world order"** of stability and peace. Yet questions remain about when, where, and how the United States should use its power to oppose aggression and maintain peace. The United States does not wish to become the world's policeman; yet today only the United States has the capability to project military force worldwide.

REGIONAL THREATS

Today, the principal threats to U.S. national security arise from regional powers. For nearly a half century, U.S. strategic defenses, force levels, and defense budgets were geared to the worldwide threat posed by the Soviet Union. Now U.S. military power is being redirected toward potential regional aggressors.

- *Iraq*   Saddam Hussein's army was reduced to about one-third of its former size in the Gulf War. The UN-sponsored economic blockade of Iraq has hampered that nation's efforts to rebuild these conventional forces. However, Iraq continues to harbor Scud missiles and continues in its efforts to acquire weapons of mass destruction—nuclear, chemical, and biological.

- *Iran*   Iran has been shopping for both conventional weapons and nuclear components in world arms markets. China and the former Soviet Union have supplied it with surface-to-surface missiles. Iran has also acquired a submarine force for operations in the Persian Gulf and a sizable air force. Iran supports terrorist groups throughout the Middle East and provides a beacon for violent Islamic fundamentalism. The Israelis consider Iran to be the principal threat to peace and stability in the Mideast.

- *Syria*   Syria's military forces are impressive. But with the collapse of the USSR, its key supplier, Syria must now pay for weapons in hard currency—an item in short supply in Syria. Syria's troops occupy most of Lebanon.

- *Libya*   Muammar Khadafy's military forces are not a major threat, yet Libya remains a major base for worldwide terrorist activity.

- *North Korea*   North Korea remains the most authoritarian and militarist regime in the world. It devotes a very large proportion of its economy and population to its military. It supports a one-million-man army with four thousand tanks, a large air force, and a large submarine force. North Korea's nuclear weapons program is very advanced. The death of its "Great Leader," Kim Il-Sung, has brought his son, "Dear Leader" Kim Jong Il, to power. Since the Korean War (1950–1953), the United States has maintained military forces in South Korea to deter invasion by North Korea. South Korea's army remains only about half as large as that of North Korea; in the event of war, the United States would need to provide immediate air combat support.

- *China*   The People's Republic of China now possesses the world's largest armed forces—over three million soldiers, nearly ten thousand tanks, and over four thousand combat aircraft. China has intercontinental ballistic missiles with multi-headed nuclear warheads capable of reaching the United States. China has always asserted that Taiwan is a province of China (as has the government of the Republic of China in Taiwan); Beijing continues to declare unification a goal. It has stated a preference for peaceful reunification, but the threat of force has always been present. The Beijing government's future policies in Hong Kong, the former British colony incorporated into the People's Republic of China in 1997, may signal China's future approach to Taiwan. Beijing continues to voice support for market reforms of its economy, but it acted with brutal force to suppress the democracy movement in Tiananmen Square in 1989.

CASE STUDY
American Military Power: "Desert Storm"

The U.S. military leadership had learned its lessons from Vietnam: define clear military objectives, use overwhelming and decisive military force, move swiftly and avoid protracted stalemate, minimize casualties, and be sensitive to the image of the war projected back home.

Saddam Hussein's invasion of Kuwait on August 2, 1990, was apparently designed to restore his military prestige following eight years of indecisive war against Iran, to secure additional oil revenues to finance the continued buildup of Iraqi military power, and to intimidate and perhaps invade Saudi Arabia and the Gulf states and thereby secure control over a major share of the world's oil reserves.

Early on, President George Bush described the U.S. military deployment as "defensive," but he soon became convinced that neither diplomacy nor an economic blockade would dislodge Hussein from Kuwait. The president ordered the military to prepare an "offensive" option.

The top U.S. military commanders—including the chairman of the Joint Chiefs of Staff, General Colin Powell, and the commander in the field, General Norman Schwarzkopf—had been field officers in Vietnam, and they were resolved not to repeat the mistakes of that war. They were reluctant to go into battle without the full support of the American people. If ordered to fight, they wanted to employ overwhelming and decisive military force; they wanted to avoid gradual escalation, protracted conflict, target limitations, and political inference in the conduct of the war. They presented the president with an "offensive" plan that called for a very large military buildup: elements of six Army divisions and two Marine divisions, with 1,900 tanks, 930 artillery pieces, and 500 attack helicopters; and over 1,000 combat aircraft. Coalition forces also included British and French heavy armored units, and Egyptian, Syrian, Saudi, and other Arab forces.

The president announced this buildup of forces on November 8 but immediately faced a barrage of criticism at home for abandoning his earlier defensive posture. Opponents urged the president to continue economic sanctions and avoid the heavy casualties that a land war was expected to produce. But the president was convinced that sanctions would not work, that Hussein would hold out for years and that he would become increasingly powerful on the world stage. He argued that Hussein would soon acquire nuclear weapons, that if unchecked he would soon dominate the Arab world and Mideast oil reserves. Secretary of State James Baker convinced the UN Security Council members, including the Soviet Union (with China abstaining), to support a resolution authorizing states to "use all necessary means" against Iraq unless it withdrew from Kuwait by January 15. Following an emotional debate in Congress, President Bush won a similar resolution by close margins in the House and Senate.

From Baghdad, CNN reporters Bernard Shaw and Peter Arnett were startled the night of January 16 when *Operation Desert Storm* began with an air attack on key installations in the city. Iraqi forces were also surprised, despite the prompt timing of the attack; Hussein had assured them that the United States lacked the resolve to fight, and that even if war broke out, U.S. public opinion would force a settlement as casualties rose. The air war accomplished three objectives: first, winning air supremacy by destroying radars, air defense control centers, and SAM launchers and airfields, as well as any Iraqi fighters that managed to get into the air; second, destroying strategic targets, including nuclear facilities, chemical warfare plants, command centers, and military communications; third, degrading Iraqi military forces by cutting off supplies, destroying tanks and artillery, and demoralizing troops with 'round-the-clock bombardment. Smart weapons performed superbly, and American television audiences saw videotapes of laser-guided smart bombs entering the doors and air shafts of enemy bunkers.

General Schwarzkopf's plan for the ground war emphasized deception and maneuver. He wanted to make the Iraqis believe that the main attack would come directly against Kuwait's southern border and would be supported by a Marine landing on the coast. While Iraqi forces prepared for attacks from the south and the east coast, General Schwarzkopf sent heavily armed columns in a "Hail Mary" play—a wide sweep to the west, outflanking and cutting off Iraqi forces in the battle area. The Iraqi forces, blinded by air attacks and obliged to stay in their bunkers, would not be able to know about or respond to the flanking attack. On the night of February 24, the ground attack began with Marines easily breaching berms, ditches, and mine fields and racing directly to the Kuwait city airport; helicopter air assaults lunged deep

into Iraq; armored columns raced northward across the desert to outflank Iraqi forces and then attack them from the west; and a surge in air attacks kept Iraqi forces holed up in their bunkers. Iraqi troops surrendered in droves, highways from Kuwait city were turned into massive junkyards of Iraqi vehicles, and Iraqi forces that tried to fight were quickly destroyed. After one hundred hours of ground fighting, President Bush declared a cease-fire.

The United States had achieved a decisive military victory quickly and with precious few casualties. Although the war left many political issues unresolved, it was the most decisive military outcome the United States had achieved since the end of World War II. President Bush chose to declare victory and celebrate the return of American troops.

The Gulf War taught the nation a number of lessons about the effective use of military power:

■ The rapid employment of overwhelming force is both politically and militarily superior to gradual escalation and employment of minimum force. The use of overwhelming force reduces total casualties and achieves an earlier and more decisive

victory. It reduces the opportunity for diplomatic interventions that may produce compromised, indecisive resolutions.

■ The nation's political leadership is vastly more effective when it concentrates on developing and maintaining foreign and domestic political support for war while leaving the planning and execution of military operations to the military leadership.

■ A rapid conclusion of hostilities ensures that public support will not erode over time and that protracted combat and a steady stream of casualties will not fuel antiwar sentiments.

■ Military forces can capture territory and destroy enemy forces but they cannot guarantee peace.

■ Only total military occupation of a country can ensure the removal of a hostile regime. Hussein continues to rule Iraq and to build chemical and biological weapons of mass destruction. Hussein remains a threat to stability in the region.

Perhaps the most important lesson is that the end of the Cold War does *not* mean that the United States no longer requires military power.

CONTROVERSIES IN SOCIAL SCIENCE
When Should the United States Use Military Force?

All modern presidents have acknowledged that the most agonizing decisions they have made were to send U.S. military forces into combat. These decisions cost lives. The American people are willing to send their sons and daughters into danger—and even to see some of them wounded or killed—but *only* if a president convinces them that the outcome "is worth dying for." A president must be able to explain why they lost their lives and to justify their sacrifice.

Only to Protect Vital Interests?

The U.S. military learned many bitter lessons in its long, bloody experience in Vietnam. Among those lessons:

- The United States should commit its military forces only in support of vital national interests.
- If military forces are committed, they must have clearly defined military objectives—the destruction of enemy forces and/or the capture of enemy-held territory.

- Any commitment of U.S. forces must be of sufficient strength to ensure overwhelming and decisive victory with the fewest possible casualties.
- Before committing U.S. military forces, there must be some reasonable assurances that the effort has the support of the American people and their representatives in Congress.
- The commitment of U.S. military forces should be a last resort, after political, economic, and diplomatic efforts have proven ineffective.

These guidelines for the use of military force are widely supported within the U.S. military itself. Contrary to Hollywood stereotypes, military leaders are extremely reluctant to go to war when no vital interest of the United States is at stake, where there are no clear-cut military objectives, without the support of Congress or the American people, or without sufficient force to achieve speedy and decisive victory with minimum casualties.

They are wary of seeing their troops placed in danger merely to advance diplomatic goals, or to engage in "peacekeeping," or to "stabilize governments," or to "show the flag." They are reluctant to undertake humanitarian missions while being shot at. They do not like to risk their soldiers' lives under "rules of engagement" that limit their ability to defend themselves.

To Support Important Political Objectives?

In contrast to military leaders, political leaders and diplomats often reflect the view that "war is a continuation of politics by other means"—a view commonly attributed to nineteenth-century German theorist of war Karl von Clausewitz. Military force may be used to protect interests that are important but not necessarily vital. Otherwise, the United States would be rendered largely impotent in world affairs. A diplomat's ability to achieve a satisfactory result often depends on the expressed or implied threat of military force. The distinguished international political theorist Hans Morgenthau wrote: "Since military strength is the obvious measure of a nation's power, its demonstration serves to impress others with that nation's power."

Currently American forces must be prepared to carry out a variety of missions in addition to the conduct of conventional war:

- Demonstrating U.S. resolve in crisis situations
- Demonstrating U.S. support for democratic governments
- Protecting U.S. citizens living abroad
- Striking at terrorist targets to deter or retaliate
- Peacemaking among warring factions or nations
- Peacekeeping where hostile factions or nations have accepted a peace agreement
- Providing humanitarian aid often under warlike conditions

In pursuit of such objectives, recent U.S. presidents have sent troops to Lebanon in 1982 to stabilize the government (Reagan), to Grenada in 1983 to rescue American medical students and restore democratic government (Reagan), to Panama in 1989 to oust drug-trafficking General Manuel Antonio Noriega from power and to protect U.S. citizens (Bush), to Somalia in 1992–1993 to provide emergency humanitarian aid (Bush and Clinton), to Haiti in 1994 to restore constitutional government (Clinton), and to Bosnia in 1995–1996 and Kosovo in 1999 for peacekeeping among warring ethnic factions (Clinton; see table).

MAJOR DEPLOYMENT OF U.S. MILITARY FORCES SINCE WORLD WAR II

Year	Area	President
1950–1953	Korea	Truman
1958	Lebanon	Eisenhower
1961–1964	Vietnam	Kennedy
1962	Cuban waters	Kennedy
1965–1973	Vietnam	Johnson, Nixon
1965	Dominican Republic	Johnson
1970	Laos	Nixon
1970	Cambodia	Nixon
1975	Cambodia	Ford
1980	Iran	Carter
1982–1983	Lebanon	Reagan
1983	Grenada	Reagan
1989	Panama	Bush
1990–1991	Persian Gulf	Bush
1992–1993	Somalia	Bush, Clinton
1994–1995	Haiti	Clinton
1995–1996	Bosnia	Clinton
1999–2000	Kosovo	Clinton

TERRORISM

The threat of terrorism creates two military requirements. The first is the ability to punish nations that sponsor terrorism and to dissuade other nations from continuing their support of terrorism. In 1986, the United States struck at Libya in a limited air attack in response to various Libyan-supported acts of terrorism around the world. In 1993 the United States struck Iraq's intelligence center in Baghdad in response to a foiled plot to assassinate former President George Bush. These types of operation are carried out by conventional military forces. A second requirement is the ability to take direct action against terrorists to capture or kill them or to free their hostages. These operations are carried out by highly trained, specially equipped special operations forces.

THE SPREAD OF MASS TERROR WEAPONS

The threat of mass terror weapons—nuclear, chemical, or biological weapons, especially those carried by medium- or long-range missiles—is likely to increase dramatically in the twenty-first century. Iraq, Iran, Libya, and North Korea, for example, are all likely to acquire mass terror weapons and long-range delivery systems, in the absence of any action by the United States to prevent them from doing so.

Unanticipated Threats

The United States anticipated very few of the dozens of crises that required the use of military force over the past decade. Few would have forecast that U.S. troops would be engaged in combat in Grenada in 1983, or Panama in 1989, or even the Persian Gulf in 1990–1991. General Colin Powell tried to convince the Congress that:

> The real threat is the unknown, the uncertain. In a very real sense, the primary threat to our security is instability and being unprepared to handle a crisis or war that no one expected or predicted. But it is difficult to convince taxpayers or their elected representatives to prepare for the unknown.[10]

MILITARY FORCE LEVELS

Overall military force levels in the United States are threat-driven, that is, determined by the size and nature of the perceived threats to national security. The end of the Cold War has brought about major reductions in U.S. military forces (for example, from 2.1 million active duty personnel in 1990 to

1.4 million today), as well as a restructuring of these forces to confront regional threats. Current U.S. defense policy envisions the need to respond simultaneously to two "Iraqi equivalent" threats—the military forces required by the United States to speedily and decisively defeat two opponents equal to Iraq in the Gulf War. (For example, if U.S. forces were involved again in the Persian Gulf region against Iraq or Iran, we would still want to be able to respond in Korea if North Korea decided to take advantage of our commitment in the Gulf and launch an invasion of South Korea.) But it is not clear whether today's forces could confront two such threats simultaneously. The United States benefited from a six-month buildup of forces in the Persian Gulf before "Operation Desert Storm," but it is unlikely that a new crisis would allow such a long lead time (see the Case Study, "American Military Power: 'Desert Storm'"). And the use of U.S. forces for humanitarian and peacekeeping purposes around the world places additional burdens on their war-fighting capabilities.

On the Web

EXPLORING POWER AMONG NATIONS

The Internet offers an almost limitless wealth of information on world affairs.

United Nations. The official Web site of the United Nations (www.un.org) includes a complete description of its organization, membership, and offices, as well as publications, statistics, documents, and treaties.

NATO. NATO forces are currently undertaking peacekeeping and crisis management missions in eastern Europe. NATO on the Internet (www.nato.int) provides researchers with information about the alliance's current activities and membership, the text of speeches by NATO officials, and the text of the original treaty signed in 1949.

U.S. Department of Defense. The U.S. Department of Defense maintains a "Defenselink" site (www.defenselink.mil) that provides extensive information on national security affairs. It contains the latest Pentagon (Defense Department) news releases; public statements by defense officials; the Secretary of Defense's *Annual Report to the President and Congress*; facts on U.S. military forces, weapons, and deployments; as well as direct links to the Web sites maintained by the Army, Navy, Air Force, and Marine Corps.

Central Intelligence Agency. The Central Intelligence Agency's official Web site (www.odci.gov) includes a history of the agency, the description of this organization, the statement of its mission, a "virtual tour" of its headquarters, as well as a link to the Center for the Study of Intelligence that provides previously classified documents to historians, political scientists, and interested citizens.

Council on Foreign Relations. The Council on Foreign Relations is an influential private policy-planning organization in the United States that focuses on issues relating to foreign policy. Its Web site (www.cfr.org) includes policy discussions and commentaries and summaries of articles appearing in the organization's journal, *Foreign Affairs*.

About this Chapter

"International politics, like all politics, is a struggle for power." Fighting among peoples and societies has been a common occurrence in the human experience throughout history. From time to time, nations have sought to provide greater order and stability to the international struggle for power. The advent of nuclear weapons made it imperative that nations seek a more stable world order, through direct negotiations as well as collective security arrangements. The collapse of communism in eastern Europe and the emergence of democracy in Russia reduced the threat of a nuclear holocaust. But regional conflicts continue to threaten world security.

In this chapter, we have explored some of the means, past and present, by which people have sought to avoid war. Now that you have read it, you should be able to

- discuss the meaning of *sovereignty* and describe the nature of international law
- discuss the concepts of a *balance of power, collective security,* and *regional security*
- describe the major events of the Cold War and the subsequent collapse of communism
- describe the major efforts to control nuclear weapons
- discuss major regional threats to security

Discussion Questions

1. Define *sovereignty* and discuss the role it plays in international politics. Describe the nature of international law.

2. Describe various systems of international order, giving specific examples of each type of system. Compare and evaluate the relative effectiveness of a balance-of-power system, collective security, and regional activity.

3. Discuss the SALT I ABM treaty. Why was the SALT II Treaty never ratified by the U.S. Senate? What kinds of weapons are eliminated by the INF Treaty?

4. Describe the superpower balance during the Cold War. List the major events of the Cold War.

5. Describe the principal threats to American security today.

6. Discuss the political and military "lessons" of the Gulf War.

7. Compare presidential leadership in the Gulf War with presidential leadership in the Vietnam War (see Chapter 8). How did U.S. military strategy differ in these wars?

NOTES

CHAPTER 1

1. Harold Lasswell and Abraham Kaplan, *Power and Society* (New Haven, Conn.: Yale University Press, 1950), p. 219.
2. C. Wright Mills, *The Power Elite* (New York: Oxford University Press, 1956), p. 9.
3. Ibid., p. 10.

CHAPTER 2

1. Chava Frankfort-Nachmias and David Nachmias, *Research Methods in the Social Sciences* (New York: St. Martin's, 1996).
2. Babbie Earl, *The Practice of Social Research*, 7th ed. (Belmont, CA: Wadsworth, 1995).
3. Barnard, H. Russell, *Research Methods in Cultural Anthropology,* 2nd ed. (Walnut Creek, CA: Alta Mira Press, 1994).
4. Laud Humphreys, *Tearoom Trade: Impersonal Sex in Public Places* (Chicago: Aldine, 1970).

CHAPTER 3

1. See Marvin Harris, *Cannibals and Kings: The Origins of Cultures* (New York: Random House, 1977).
2. Clyde Kluckhohn and William Kelly, "The Concept of Culture," in *The Science of Man in the World Crisis,* ed., Ralph Linton (New York: Columbia University Press, 1945), 97.
3. See Serena Nanda, *Cultural Anthropology,* 6th ed. (Belmont, Calif.: Wadsworth, 1997).
4. This approach was developed by Bronislaw Malinowski in *A Scientific Theory of Culture and Other Essays* (Chapel Hill: University of North Carolina Press, 1944).
5. Elvin Hatch, "The Good Side of Relativism," *Journal of Anthropological Research,* 53 (1997): 371–381.
6. See the argument presented by Thomas Sowell in "Cultural Diversity: A World View," *The American Enterprise* 2 (May/June 1991): 44–55.
7. Elizabeth M. Zechmeter, "In the Name of Culture: Cultural Relativism and the Abuse of the Individual," *Journal of Anthropological Research* 53 (1997): 319–347; see also Paul C. Rosenblatt, "Human Rights Violations across Cultures," in Carol R. Ember et al., *Research Frontiers in Anthropology* (Upper Saddle River, N.J.: Prentice-Hall, 1998).

8. William W. Stephens, *The Family in Cross-Cultural Perspective* (New York: Holt, Rinehart & Winston, 1963).
9. See William R. Jankowiak and Edward E. Fischer, "A Cross-Cultural Perspective on Romantic Love," *Ethnology* 31 (1992): 149–155.
10. U.S. Bureau of the Census, *Statistical Abstract of the United States 1999* (Washington, D.C.: U.S. Government Printing Office, 1999), 64.
11. U.S. Bureau of the Census *Statistical Abstract of the United States 1999,* 75.
12. Carol R. Ember and Melvin Ember, *Cultural Anthropology,* 9th ed. (Englewood Cliffs, N.J.: Prentice-Hall, 1999), ch. 16; George P. Murdock and Caterina Post, "Factors in the Division of Labor by Sex: A Cross-Cultural Analysis," *Ethnology* 12 (1973): 203–225.
13. Martin K. Whyte, "Cross-Cultural Codes Dealing with the Relative Status of Women," *Ethnology* 17 (1978): 217.
14. Martha G. Nussbaum and Jonathan Glover, *Women, Culture and Development* (Oxford: Clarendon Press, 1995), 2.
15. Beatrice B. Whiting and Carolyn P. Edwards, "A Cross-Cultural Analysis of Sex Differences in the Behavior of Children Aged Three Through Eleven," *Journal of Social Psychology* 91 (1973): 171–188; Eleanor E. Maccoby and Carol N. Jacklin, *The Psychology of Sex Differences* (Stanford, Calif.: Stanford University Press, 1974).
16. Marc H. Ross, "Female Political Participation: A Cross-Cultural Explanation," *American Anthropologist* 88 (1986): 841–858.
17. See Frank McGlynn and Arthur Tuden, *Anthropological Approaches in Political Behavior* (Pittsburgh: University of Pittsburgh Press, 1991).

CHAPTER 4

1. Melvin M. Tumin, *Social Stratification: The Forms and Functions of Social Inequality* (Englewood Cliffs, N.J.: Prentice-Hall, 1985); see also John Myles and Adnan Turegon, "Comparative Studies in Class Structure," *Annual Review of Sociology* (New York: McGraw-Hill, 1994).
2. Gerhard Lenski, *Power and Privilege* (New York: McGraw-Hill, 1966); Jack Roach, Llewellyn Gross, and Orville R. Gursslin, *Social Stratification in the United States* (Englewood Cliffs, N.J.: Prentice-Hall, 1969).

3. Richard Centers, *The Psychology of Social Classes* (Princeton, N.J.: Princeton University Press, 1949).

4. *The American Enterprise* (May/June 1993): 82.

5. Neil J. MacKinnon and Tom Langford, "The Meaning of Occupational Scores," *Sociological Quarterly* 35 (1994): 215–245.

6. See John J. Macionis, *Sociology,* 7th ed. (Upper Saddle River, N.J.: Prentice-Hall, 1999): ch. 9.

7. Kingsley Davis and Wilbert Moore, "Some Principles of Stratification," *American Sociological Review* 10 (April 1945): 243.

8. Edward N. Wolff, *Top Heavy: A Study of Increasing Inequality of Wealth in America* (New York: Twentieth Century Fund, 1995).

9. Herbert Gans, *The Urban Villagers* (New York: Free Press, 1962), 246; see also Edward C. Banfield, *The Unheavenly City* (Boston: Little, Brown, 1968): ch. 3.

10. Thomas R. Dye, *Who's Running America? The Clinton Years* (Englewood Cliffs, N.J.: Prentice-Hall, 1995).

CHAPTER 5

1. For a full discussion, see David C. Myers, *Psychology,* 6th ed. (New York: Worth, 2001), ch. 3.

2. J. C. Lochlin and R. C. Nichols, *Heredity Environment and Personality* (Austin: University of Texas Press, 1976); J. C. Lochlin and R. C. McCrae, "Heritabilities of Common Components of Personality," *Journal of Research in Personality* 32 (1998): 431–453.

3. W. Wright, *Born That Way: Genes Behavior Personality* (New York: Knopf, 1998).

4. H. Segall, *Human Behavior in Global Perspective* (New York: Pergamon, 1990), 244; also cited in Myers, *Psychology,* 89.

5. M. B. Oliver and J. S. Hyde, "Gender Differences in Sexuality," *Psychological Bulletin* 114 (1993): 29–51.

6. See Meyers, *Psychology,* ch. 11.

7. T. W. Adorno et al., *The Authoritarian Personality* (New York: Harper, 1950).

8. A. H. Maslow, *The Farther Reaches of Human Nature* (New York: Viking Press, 1971), 43.

9. Marvin E. Lickey and Barbara Gordon, *Medicine and Mental Illness* (New York: W. H. Freeman, 1991).

10. B. P. Dohrenwend, et al., "Socioeconomic Status and Psychiatric Disorders," *Science,* 255 (1992): 946–952.

11. Rollo May, *Power and Innocence* (New York: Norton, 1972).

12. Ibid., 21.

CHAPTER 6

1. See Daniel Yergen and Joseph Stanislaw, The Commanding Heights: The Battle between Government and the Marketplace That Is Remaking the Modern World (New York: Simon & Schuster, 1998).

2. However, see Robert Kuttner, *Everything for Sale: The Virtues and Limits of Markets* (New York: Knopf, 1997).

3. Karl E. Case and Ray C. Fair, *Principles of Economics,* 5th ed. (Upper Saddle River, N.J.: Prentice-Hall, 1999), ch. 6.

4. See U.S. Office of Management and Budget, *A Citizen's Guide to the Federal Budget,* Annual (Washington: Government Trading Office).

5. A. A. Berle, Jr., *Power Without Property* (New York: Harcourt Brace Jovanovich, 1959).

6. Margaret M. Blair, "Who's in Charge Here?" *Brookings Review* (Fall 1991): 8–13.

7. *Statistical Abstract of the United States 1999,* (Washington, D.C.: U.S. Government Printing Office, 1999), 790.

8. Michael Porter, *The Comparative Advantage of Nations* (New York: Free Press, 1991).

CHAPTER 7

1. Harold Lasswell, *Politics: Who Gets What, When and How* (New York: McGraw-Hill, 1936).

2. See Robert A. Dahl, *Democracy and Its Critics* (New Haven: Yale University Press, 1989).

3. See Charles Murray, *What It Means to Be a Libertarian* (New York: Broadway Books, 1997).

4. Alexis de Tocqueville, *Democracy in America,* originally published in 1835 (New York: Mentor Books, 1956).

5. See Forrest McDonald, *Novus Ordo Seclorum* (Lawrence, KS: University of Kansas Press, 1985).

6. Herbert J. Storing, ed., *The Anti-Federalist* (Chicago: University of Chicago Press, 1985).

7. *The Federalist* papers were a series of essays by James Madison, Alexander Hamilton, and John Jay, written in 1787 and 1788 to explain and defend the new Constitution during the struggle over its ratification. (*The Federalist,* Number 10, New York: Modern Library, 1937).

8. Samuel H. Beer, *To Make a Nation: The Rediscovery of American Federalism* (Cambridge, MA.: Harvard University Press, 1993).

9. James Madison, *The Federalist,* Number 10.

10. See Daniel J. Elazar, *American Federalism: A View from the States* (New York: Crowell, 1966); Thomas R. Dye, *American Federalism: Competition among Governments* (Lexington, MA.: Lexington Books, 1990); Paul Peterson, *The Price of Federalism* (Washington D.C.: Brookings Institution, 1995).

11. *Garcia v. San Antonio Metropolitan Transit Authority* 469 U.S. 528 (1985).

12. Theodore J. Lowi, *The Personal President* (Ithaca: Cornell University Press, 1987).

13. *The Federalist,* Number 45 (New York: Modern Library, 1937); *Printz v. U.S.*

14. *U.S. v. Morrison*

15. Alexander L. George and Julliette L. George, *Presidential Personality and Performance* (Boulder, CO: Westview Press, 1998).

16. See Louis Fisher, *Presidential War Power* (Lawrence, KS: University of Kansas Press, 1995).

17. Charles O. Jones, *The Presidency in a Separated System* (Washington, D.C.: Brookings Institution, 1994).

18. See Lawrence Baum, *The Supreme Court,* 6th ed. (Washington D.C.: CQ Press, 1997).

19. Bernard Schwartz, *A History of the Supreme Court* (New York: Oxford University Press, 1995).

20. *West Virginia State Board of Education v. Barrett* 319 U.S. 624 (1943).

21. *Planned Parenthood v. Casey* 505 U.S. 199 (1992).

22. See Margaret M. Conway, *Political Participation in the United States* (Washington, D.C.: CQ Press, 1991).

23. William H. Flanagan and Nancy H. Zingale, *Political Behavior of the American Electorate* (Washington, D.C.: CQ Press, 1998).

24. Paul Allen Beck, *Party Politics in America*, 8th ed. (New York: Longman, 1997).

25. Herbert J. McClosky et al., "Issue Conflict and Consensus Among Party Leaders and Followers," *American Political Science Review* 54 (June 1960): 595.

CHAPTER 8

1. Henry Steele Commager, *The Study of History* (Columbus, Ohio: Merrill, 1965): 79.

2. Richard Hofstadter, *The American Political Tradition and the Men Who Made It* (New York: Vintage Books, 1956): viii.

3. Frederick Jackson Turner, "The West and American Ideals," in *The Frontier in American History* (New York: Holt, 1921).

4. Hofstadter, *American Political Tradition,* 109.

5. Turner, "The West and American Ideals," 113.

6. Hofstadter, *American Political Tradition,* 323–324.

CHAPTER 9

1. Leon P. Baradat, *Political Ideologies: Their Origin and Impact,* 6th ed. (Upper Saddle River N.J.: Prentice-Hall, 1996).

2. Bernard Bailyn, *Ideological Origins of the American Revolution* (Cambridge, MA.: Harvard University Press, 1967); Clinton Rossiter, *1787 The Grand Convention* (New York: Macmillan, 1966).

3. Richard Hofstadter, *The American Political Tradition* (New York: Knopf, 1948).

4. Milton Friedman, *Capitalism and Freedom* (Chicago: University of Chicago Press, 1963).

5. For an entertaining expression of current liberal thought, see James Carville, *We're Right, They're Wrong* (New York: Random House, 1996); see also Jeffrey M. Berry, *The New Liberalism* (Washington, D.C.: Brookings Institution, 1999).

6. See William F. Buckley and Charles R. Kesler, *Keeping the Tablets: Modern American Conservative Thought* (New York: Harper & Row, 1988).

7. See William Ebenstein and Edwin Fogelman, *Today's Isms: Communism, Fascism, Capitalism, Socialism,* 10th ed. (Upper Saddle River N.J.: Prentice Hall, 1994).

CHAPTER 10

1. The classic essay on the impact of race on American Society is Gunnar Myrdal, *An American Dilemma* (New York: HarperCollins, 1944). See also Andrew Hacker, *Two Nations: Black and White, Separate, Hostile, Unequal* (New York: Charles Scribners, 1992).

2. *Brown v. Board of Education of Topeka, Kansas,* 347 U.S. 483 (1954).

3. Kenneth B. Clark, *Dark Ghetto: Dilemmas of Social Power* (New York: Harper & Row, 1965): 75.

4. For arguments in support of affirmative action, see Barbara R. Bergman, *In Defense of Affirmative Action* (New York: Basic Books, 1996); William G. Bowen and Derek Bok, *The Shape of the River* (Princeton, N.J.: Princeton University Press, 1998). For arguments in opposition to affirmative action, see Nathan Glazer, *Affirmative Discrimination* (Cambridge, MA.: Harvard University Press, 1987); Stephen Thernstrom and Abigail Thernstrom,

America in Black and White (New York: Simon & Schuster, 1997).

5. Rudolpho O. de la Garza et al., *Latino Voices: Mexican, Puerto Rican, and Cuban Perspectives on American Politics* (Boulder, CO: Westview Press, 1992).

6. See F. Chris Garcia, *Latinos in the Political System* (Notre Dame, IN: University of Notre Dame Press, 1988); Rodney Hero, *Latinos and the U.S. Political System* (Philadelphia, PA: Temple University Press, 1992).

7. American Security Council, *The Illegal Immigration Crisis* (Washington D.C.: ASC, 1994).

8. *Sale v. Haitian Centers Council* 125 L. Ed. 2nd 128 (1993).

9. Charles F. Wilkinson, *American Indians, Times and the Law* (New Haven, CT: Yale University Press, 1987).

10. See Carol R. Ember and Melvin Ember, *Anthropology,* 9th ed. (Upper Saddle River, N.J.: Prentice-Hall, 1999): ch. 16.

11. Martha C. Nussbaum and Jonathan Glover, *Women, Culture, and Development* (Oxford: Clarendon Press, 1995).

12. Lila Leibowitz, *Females, Males, Families: A Biological Approach* (Duxbury, MA: Duxbury Press, 1978).

13. Quoted in Jay M. Shafritz, *The HarperCollins Dictionary of American Politics* (New York: HarperCollins, 1992): 620.

14. Nancy E. McGlen and Karen O'Conner, *Women, Politics and American Society* (Upper Saddle River, N.J.: Prentice-Hall, 1996).

15. *Harris* v. *McRae,* 448 U.S. 297 (1980).

CHAPTER 11

1. Christopher Jenks and Paul E. Peterson, *The Urban Underclass* (Washington, D.C.: Brookings Institution, 1991).

2. Kenneth B. Clark, *Dark Ghetto: Dilemmas of Social Power* (New York: Harper & Row, 1965).

3. Ibid., 67.

4. William A. Kelso, *Poverty and the Underclass* (New York: New York University Press, 1994).

5. Edward C. Banfield, *The Unheavenly City* (Boston: Little, Brown, 1968): ch. 6.

6. Theda Skocpol, *Social Policy in the United States* (Princeton: Princeton University Press, 1995).

7. Robert C. Ellickson, "The Homelessness Muddle," *The Public Interest* (Spring 1990): 45–60.

8. Peter H. Rossi, *Down and Out in America* (Chicago: University of Chicago Press, 1989).

9. As reported in a survey of twenty-seven cities conducted by the U.S. Conference of Mayors. See *U.S. News & World Report,* January 15, 1990, 27–29.

CHAPTER 12

1. Thomas Hobbes, *Leviathan,* ed. Michael Oakeshott (New York: Crowell-Collier, 1962).

2. U.S. Department of Justice, *Criminal Victimization in the United States* (Washington, D.C.: Bureau of Justice Statistics, published annually).

3. See Akil Amar, *The Constitution and Criminal Procedures* (New Haven, CT: Yale University Press, 1997).

4. Chief Justice Warren E. Burger, address on the State of the Federal Judiciary to the American Bar Association, August 10, 1970.

5. *Gregg v. Georgia* 428 U.S. 153 (1976).

6. *Furman v. Georgia* 408 U.S. 238 (1972).

7. Substance Abuse and Mental Health Administration, *National Household Survey on Drug Abuse 1998* (annual).

8. Lynn Zimmer and John P. Morgan, *Marijuana Myths, Marijuana Facts* (New York: Lindesmith Center, 1997).

9. Ethan A. Nadelmann, "U.S. Drug Policy," *Foreign Policy* 70 (Spring 1988): 83–108.

10. See Frank Smallenger, *Criminal Justice Today,* 6th ed. (Upper Saddle River, N.J.: Prentice-Hall, 2001).

11. See Allen Liska and Steven Messner, *Perspectives on Crime and Deviance,* 3rd ed. (Upper Saddle River, N.J.: Prentice-Hall, 1999).

12. See James Q. Wilson, *Thinking About Crime,* rev. ed. (New York: Basic Books, 1983); James Q. Wilson and Richard J. Herrnstein, *Crime and Human Nature* (New York: Simon & Schuster, 1995).

CHAPTER 13

1. Population Reference Bureau, *World Population Data Sheet 1999* (Washington D.C.: Population Reference Bureau, 1999).

2. See Gregg Easterbrook, *A Moment on the Earth: The Coming Age of Environmental Optimism* (New York: Penguin Books, 1995).

3. United Nations, *The State of the World Population 2000* (New York: United Nations, 2000).

4. Louis Wirth, "Urbanism as a Way of Life," *American Journal of Sociology* 44 (July 1938).

5. Ibid., 24.

6. Thomas R. Dye, *Politics in States and Communities,* 10th ed. (Upper Saddle River, N.J.: Prentice-Hall, 2000).
7. Lewis Mumford, *The City in History* (London: Penguin Books, 1966): 11.
8. This thesis derives from sociologist William Julius Wilson, *The Truly Disadvantaged* (Chicago: University of Chicago Press, 1987).
9. See Christopher Jencks and Paul E. Peterson, eds., *The Urban Underclass* (Washington, D.C.: Brookings Institution, 1991).

CHAPTER 14

1. Hans Morgenthau, *Politics Among Nations* (New York: Knopf, 1960): 27.
2. See Glenn P. Hastedt, *American Foreign Policy: Past, Present, Future* (Upper Saddle River, N.J.: Prentice Hall, 2000).
3. Terms used in Article X of the Covenant of the League of Nations.
4. Michael Mandelbaum, *The Dawn of Peace in Europe* (New York: Twentieth Century Fund, 1996).
5. James N. Rosenau, *The United Nations in a Turbulent World* (New York: Lynne Rienner, 1992).
6. George F. Kennan, writing under the pseudonym "X," "Sources of Soviet Conduct," *Foreign Affairs* (July 1947): 25.
7. Grahn T. Allison, *Essence of Decision* (Boston: Little Brown, 1971).
8. Robert S. McNamara, *In Retrospect: The Tragedy and Lessons of Vietnam* (New York: Time Books, 1995).
9. See Robert Service, *A History of Twentieth Century Russia* (Cambridge, MA: Harvard University Press, 1998).
10. Testimony of General Colin Powell, Committee on the Budget, U.S. Senate, February 3, 1992.

PHOTO CREDITS

Index